More of Knight's Timely Illustrations

Walter B. Knight

Sword of the Lord Publishers
Murfreesboro, Tennessee

Printed in the United States of America

INTRODUCTION

Rev. Walter B. Knight wrote his first book, *3,000 Illustrations for Christian Service*, when he was 50 years old; and each subsequent book has become a best seller in its field. His book, *Master Book of New Illustrations*, can be found in the White House Library. It was one of 50 books selected by the Christian Booksellers' Association to be presented to the late President Lyndon B. Johnson. Knight's books of illustrations, including *Knight's Treasury of Illustrations* and *Knight's Up-to-the-Minute Illustrations*, are among the most valuable books in my library. They contain effective, useful illustrations on nearly every topic of interest to preachers and Christians.

This book, *More of Knight's Timely Illustrations*, the first printed by Sword of the Lord Publishers, is unsurpassed. Preachers and Christian workers everywhere will find it a valuable addition to their libraries. Every word was typed by Walter B. Knight himself. Throughout the manuscript, the reader will find touches of humor which are greatly needed in this day with ever-increasing problems and perplexities which, humanly speaking, defy a solution.

A feature of this book which differentiates it from other books of illustrations is the clinching of many of the illustrations with a Bible verse, a poetic gem and a brief application.

I became acquainted with the author when I purchased his book, *Knight's Master Book of New Illustrations*. I may have purchased every book written by Walter B. Knight. My first contact with Mr. Knight was a letter I received from him complimenting me on the use of illustrations in a sermon which appeared in THE SWORD OF THE LORD several years ago. I wrote back to say that I had used his illustration books with great profit, and since then we have become dear friends. We occasionally use his sermons in THE SWORD OF THE LORD, and people have written to tell of blessings received from reading them.

It is my prayer that preachers everywhere will purchase this latest book by our friend Walter B. Knight and use it to illustrate Bible truths that will result in the salvation of untold thousands and the building of stronger Christians.

Dr. Curtis Hutson
Sword of the Lord Publishers

DEDICATION

With quenchless love and fadeless memories of fifty-three years of happy married life, I dedicate this book, our latest, to my pricelessly precious wife:

Alice Marie Knight

On May 11, 1982, she entered death's portals to be forever with her Saviour whom she loved and faithfully served from childhood: "absent from the body. . .present with the Lord" (II Cor. 5:8).

We collaborated in all of our writings. She authored three fine books for children and teenagers. Many of her best illustrations appear in this book. For decades she wrote Sunday school quarterlies for the Union Gospel Press, Cleveland, Ohio.

One of God's most endearing and precious gifts to any man is a true and faithful wife: "Who can find a virtuous woman? for her price is far above rubies" (Prov. 31:10).

I marvel that God made you mine,
For when He frowned, 'twas then you shined!

With keen anticipation loved ones look forward to the time when we shall see her sweet and beautiful face in Heaven, not changed but glorified and aglow with the love of God: "whom he justified, them he also glorified" (Rom. 8:30).

"Well done, thou good and faithful servant. . . enter thou into the joy of thy Lord" (Matt. 25:21).

TABLE OF CONTENTS

6

ACCOUNTABILITY

Used or Misused Talents

In his effort to keep his son from versifying, Isaac Watts' father threatened him with physical punishment. Poetry, however, was in the soul of the boy; and he could no more repress the God-given talent than he could refrain from breathing.

After the reading of the Scriptures one morning, the Watts family knelt for prayer. Just then Isaac pointed to a mouse running up the bell rope and exclaimed,

There was a mouse for want of stairs,
Ran up the rope to say his prayers!

The children began to snicker. Observing the grieved expression on his father's face and anticipating the threatened punishment, Isaac ran to him and pleaded:

O Father, Father, pity take,
And I will no more verses make!

While still a boy, Isaac became a Christian. Using his divinely given talent, he gave to the church some of its most soulful hymns which will bless and challenge God's children as long as time lasts! Among them are: "Alas! and Did My Saviour Bleed"; "Joy to the World"; "Am I a Soldier of the Cross?" and "Jesus Shall Reign."

To each one of His children, God has given some *special* talent. Each one will give account to God for how he uses or misuses it: "So every one of us shall give account of himself to God" (Rom. 14:12).

* * * *

New Alcoholics—Kids Aged 9 to 12

The newest problem drinkers causing concern among the nation's doctors and mental health workers are not pressured executives, bored housewives or skidrow stumblebums: *they are children!* Authorities declare that this fact is a most serious problem and is growing worse!

Dr. Morris Chafetz, director of the National Institute on Alcohol and Alcohol Abuse, said, "It is not uncommon to see severe alcoholism problems in kids 9, 10, 11, 12 years old. It is a far more serious problem than we ever imagined!"

Great will be the heartache and accountability of the parents who serve alcoholic beverages in their homes! Parental influence determines the way children go in life.

How revealing is the ancient prophet's pronouncement: "The fathers have eaten sour grapes, and the children's teeth are set on edge" (Ezek. 18:2).

* * * *

Tubs and Bottoms

A lady called R. E. Neighbour and

asked, "Brother Neighbour, where is the Bible verse that says every tub must stand on its own bottom?"

"There is no such verse in the Bible," replied Dr. Neighbour, "but the thought is expressed in this verse: 'For we must all appear before the judgment seat of Christ; that every one may receive the things done in his body. . .whether it be good or bad' " (II Cor. 5:10).

* * * *

Most Serious Thought

William Gladstone, the renowned statesman, was asked, "What is the most serious thought which enters your mind?"

His instant reply was, "My personal accountability to God." "Give an account of thy stewardship" (Luke 16:2).

* * * *

Void Without Music

Paderewski said to a friend, "It is not from choice that my life is music and nothing more. When one is an artist, what else can he be? When a whole lifetime is too short to attain the heights he wants to reach, how can he devote any of the little time he has to things outside his art?

"I am nothing," he said, shaking his head negatively. "If you could know the dream of what I would like to be, you would realize how little I have accomplished. Indeed my life would be quite void without music. I cannot imagine what I would do if I were compelled to deny myself its comforts."

To each one of His children God has given a special talent. For how we use or misuse it, we will give account to Him: "So then every one of us shall give account of himself to God" (Rom. 14:12).

* * * *

Mute and Out of Circulation

Max Lang, a retired farmer who lives in Raymore, Saskatchewan, owns one of the finest collections of rare and valuable violins. It includes violins made by Stradivari, Andrea, Nicolaus Amati, Techler, Guadagnini, Leopold, Stainer and Gaspara De Salo.

The regrettable fact about this collection of rare instruments is that they are mute and out of circulation. They give forth no inspirational music.

How like those violins are some of God's children who are not using their God-given talents to impart hope, cheer and encouragement to needy ones about them!

* * * *

ASSURANCE

"I KNOW"

What wondrous blessings overflow,
When we can truly say, "I know!"
I know in whom I have believed.

I know the One I have received;
I know His blood avails for me,
I know that I was blind, but see;
I know that my Redeemer lives,

I know the gift He freely gives;
I know He'll keep me to the end,
I know He is my faithful Friend;
I know He's coming in the sky,
I know the time is drawing nigh.

R. E. Neighbour.

* * * *

Heart-Transforming Knowledge

One asked George Beverly Shea, "What do you know about God?" Shea replied, "Not much, but what I know has changed my life!" "Whether he is a sinner. . .I know not: one thing I know, that, whereas I was blind, now I see" (John 9:25).

* * * *

"Is Christ Real to You?"

During a revival meeting, George W. Truett became greatly interested in the conversion of a brilliant Baylor University student. He arranged for a private meeting with the outstanding student.

After an earnest conversation about the Saviour, the student asked Dr. Truett, "Is Jesus Christ *real* to you? Please don't give me a theoretical or a theological answer."

Tears came to Dr. Truett's eyes as he replied, "Son, Jesus Christ is more real to me than the skin that covers my bones!"

* * * *

"That I May Know Him"

Early in his ministry, an elderly lady told Norman Vincent Peale at the conclusion of a sermon, "You are going to be a great preacher if you ever get to know the Lord!"

Knowledge of the Lord is experimentally and progressively attained as Christians grow in Christlikeness and in the knowledge of God's Word.

Their undeviating purpose should be: "That I may know him, and the power of his resurrection, and the fellowship of his sufferings, being made conformable unto his death" (Phil. 3:10).

Ev'ry day He comes to me with new assurance,
More and more I understand His words of love;
But I'll never know just why He came to save me,
Till someday I see His blessed face above!

Told by Ralph M. Smith.

* * * *

Quiet Minds

Robert Louis Stevenson said, "Quiet minds cannot be perplexed or frightened, but go on in misfortune at their own private pace, like a clock during a thunderstorm."

God's children greatly cherish the promise: "And the work of righteousness shall be peace; and the effect of righteousness quietness and assurance for ever" (Isa. 32:17).

* * * *

"I ONLY KNOW"

I know not how that Calvary's cross
A world of sin could free,
I only know its matchless love
Has brought God's love to me!

I know not how that Joseph's tomb
Could solve death's mystery,

I only know a living Christ,
Our immortality!

* * * *

ATHEISM

More Brains in Stomach Than in Head

An atheist became angry with Len G. Broughton, who weighed less than a hundred pounds: "I'm going to beat you up and swallow you!"

Dr. Broughton smiled and said, "If you do, you'll have more brains in your *stomach* than in your *head!*"

Dwight D. Eisenhower said, "It takes no brains to be an atheist. Any stupid person can deny the existence of God—a supernatural power, but cannot ignore the marvelous order in which the universe about us moves: 'The heavens declare the glory of God, and the firmament sheweth his handywork' " (Ps. 19:1).

* * * *

The Greatest Miracle

Edward Herbert Lord of Cherbury said, "I believe that whoever studies anatomy will never be an atheist. Man's body and the coherence of its parts, being so strange and paradoxical, is the greatest miracle of nature."

Dr. George Gallup, world-famed statistician, said, "I could prove God statistically. Take the human body alone. The chance that all its individual functions would just happen is a statistical monstrosity!"

The psalmist said, "I will praise thee; for I am fearfully made:. . .and

that my soul knoweth right well" (Ps. 139:14).

* * * *

It's Inconceivable

"The idea of an orderly universe without God is inconceivable," said Dr. Wernher von Braun. "The grandeur of the cosmos confirms the certainty of creation."

How sublime is the *factual* statement: "In the beginning God created the heaven and the earth" (Gen. 1:1).

* * * *

"A Blob of Ooze"

Jean Paul Sortre defined man as a "blob of ooze on a sea of nothingness!"

The Bible defines man as a creature made in the image of God and endowed with limitless potentials, either for good or evil: "Thou hast made him a little lower than the angels, and hast crowned him with glory and honour" (Ps. 8:5).

* * * *

The Living Dead

Dr. Carl Jung, the famous psychiatrist, said, "Those psychiatrists who are not superficial have come to the conclusion that the vast neurotic miseries of the world could be termed a neurosis of emptiness. Men cut themselves off from the root of their being—from God—and their life turns empty, inane, meaningless without purpose. When God goes out, value goes, and life turns dead on our hands."

Jesus said, "I am come that they might have life, and that they might have it more abundantly" (John 10:10).

Oh that the world might hear Him speak,
The word of comfort that men seek;
To all the lowly and to the meek,
Jesus whispers peace.

* * * *

Vacuum in Head

A Sunday school teacher asked a class of boys, "Who can tell me what vacuum is?"

A boy raised his hand: "I've got it in my head, but I can't explain it!"

How like that boy are those of whom the Bible says, "Ever learning, and never able to come to the knowledge of the truth" (II Tim. 3:7).

* * * *

"God? Who's That?"

The following letter from a grief-stricken mother appeared in the Warsaw (Indiana) *Times-Union*:

"As I sat in a courtroom and heard the judge say, 'Twenty years,' my heart almost stopped! The sentence was punishment of my son for drinking, gambling and committing robbery which ended in the almost fatal shooting of a man. The sentence might have been less but for my son's sneering, defiant attitude.

"Before passing sentence, the judge asked, 'Young man, don't you believe in God?' My son laughed loudly and answered, 'God? Who's that?' I think every one in the courtroom turned to look at me.

"I went to church and Sunday school when I was young, but after I married I attended only on special days. Regretfully I say, 'If only I had those years to live over, it would be different. I would go to God's house faithfully and take my children with me. So many say they do not believe in making a child go to church if he doesn't want to, but how many children would go to school if they weren't made to go?"

The saddest words of tongue or pen,
The saddest are these: It might have been!

* * * *

"God is Dead"

Sometime ago there appeared two scribblings on the wall of a New York City railway station. The first read, "God is dead," and was signed: *Nietzsche.* The second, below it, read, "Nietzsche is dead," and was signed: *God!*

* * * *

Fool!

One Sunday morning, a note was brought to Dwight L. Moody just before he preached. On the note was written one word—*Fool.*

Moody announced to the audience, "I have a most unusual note this morning. Many times I have received letters from people who forgot to sign their names. But this is the first time a man ever signed his name and forgot to write the note!"

"The fool hath said in his heart, There is no God" (Ps. 14:1).

* * * *

When God Is Abandoned

Will Durant, famed historian, said, "The greatest question of our time is not communism versus individualism, not Europe versus America, not even the East versus the West. It is whether men can bear to live without God. Can civilization hold together if man abandons his faith in God?"

History answers with a resounding *NO.*

After France had officially abolished God and Sunday worship, Robespierre, in addressing the States-General, said, "Gentlemen, it is extremely necessary that we restore God to France!"

"Blessed is the nation whose God is the Lord; and the people whom he hath chosen for his own inheritance" (Ps. 33:12).

* * * *

BIBLE

Dismal Ignorance Exposed

A pastor, wanting to test the Bible knowledge of the pupils in his Sunday school, asked a 10-year-old boy, "Who broke down the walls of Jericho?"

The boy replied, "I didn't do it, and I don't know who did it!"

The teacher said, "The boy is telling the truth. He didn't do it!"

Visiting other classes, when the pastor continued to ask, "Who broke down the walls of Jericho?" he failed to receive a correct answer to the question.

Finally a teacher said, "Pastor, let's not bother further about who broke down the walls of Jericho. Let's join hands and rebuild the walls!"

This *fictitious* story vividly reveals the dismal ignorance of the Bible, even among teachers of our Sunday schools.

The teaching of the Bible in our Sunday schools must take precedence over everything else. Prime time must be given to this important task. Failure to do this, with resultant ignorance of the Bible, is inexcusable.

Told by Ralph M. Smith.

* * * *

The Bible Is a Mirror

Years ago in Philadelphia it was the custom of the Chief of Police to line up the drunks before a large mirror before locking them in cells and say, "Look at yourselves in the mirror!"

They saw themselves as they were: filthy, unkempt and bedraggled. Then the officer took a picture of each one.

The following morning, when the stumblebums had sobered up, he would show each his picture as he had looked the night before.

Some of them were whelmed with a

sense of shame, disgrace and self-loathing.

God's Word is a mirror: "For if any be a hearer of the word, and not a doer, he is like unto a man beholding his natural face in a glass: For he beholdeth himself, and. . .forgetteth what manner of man he was" (James 1:23,24).

The Bible is the only Book which accurately mirrors the true condition of the unregenerated heart of man: "Deceitful above all things, and desperately wicked" (Jer. 17:9). When we look "into the perfect law of liberty"—God's Word—and see ourselves as God sees us, we confess: "Woe is me! for I am undone. . .I am a man of unclean lips" (Isa. 6:5).

Years ago a missionary in Africa gave some pocket-size mirrors to the natives who had never seen their faces except as they were mirrored in streams or lakes.

A native princess was told that she was a most beautiful woman. Procuring a mirror, she went into her room to take a good look at her face. What the mirror revealed was her ugliness! She became so angry that she dashed the mirror to the floor and made a law that no mirrors were ever to be brought into her tribe.

* * * *

It Never Cloys

Dr. James M. Gray, former president of Moody Bible Institute, wrote of the influence of the Bible:

It fills the world with fragrance,
  Whose sweetness never cloys,
It lifts our eyes to Heaven,

It heightens human joys.

How blessed are those who can exclaim with the psalmist, "O how love I thy law! it is my meditation all the day" (Ps. 119:97).

* * * *

"If We Stray"

Dr. Joseph Parker said, "If we stray, it is not for want of light. If we persist in obeying our own perverted instincts and impulses, we must not be surprised if we end in the bog of despair or in the wilderness of destitution.

"Do nothing without consulting the divine Oracle—God's Word. Let this be our motto: 'To the law and to the testimony: if they speak not according to this word, it is because there is no light in them' (Isa. 8:20). Anything that cannot be confirmed by God's Word is unworthy to be admitted into our life as a directing force."

* * * *

A Wise Computer

A make-believe story with an irrefutable, factual conclusion is told of a meeting of the world's leading scientists who had assembled to construct the ultimate computer, a master brain that would answer all questions and solve all of life's mysteries.

When the computer was ready, the chief scientist fed into it the inquiry, "How did the world begin?"

Lights flashed, wheels whirred, tumblers clicked and the printout began. Then came the computer's unexpected answer: SEE GENESIS 1:1: "IN THE BEGINNING GOD CREATED THE HEAVEN AND THE EARTH!"

* * * *

Personal Perusal

Harry A. Ironside said, "What we get out of our Bible for ourselves, in the presence of God is worth far more than all that another person passes on to us: 'Search the scriptures' " (John 5:39).

Of the ancient Bereans it is written, "These were more noble than those in Thessalonica, in that they received the word with all readiness of mind, and searched the scriptures daily, whether those things were so" (Acts 17:11).

* * * *

God-Breathed

As a flutist blows his breath into his instrument, out comes melodious music.

God breathed into the Scriptures of the Old and New Testament, and from them flow sublime melodies and transforming power: "All scripture is given by inspiration of God [God-breathed]" (II Tim. 3:16).

* * * *

Imagination Run Wild

Carl C. Riedesel said, "Life, we are told, came into existence because atoms and molecules in a primordial slime bumped into each other often enough to produce a 'simple' protein. There is nothing simple about protein, of course, but that first one just had to be simple. Somehow, and quite accidentally, this primordial protein began to acquire the attributes essential to life and reproduction.

"Time went on; and one day, from slime, a creature crawled out onto the dry ground, took a sun bath, and decided to remain. More time passed. Time was cheap, so why worry about a few million years?"

How different is the Bible's *factual* account of the creation of man: "So God created man in his own image, in the image of God created he him" (Gen. 1:27).

* * * *

Unchanging Principles

Let us adjust ourselves to changing times as we adhere tenaciously to unchanging principles and the changeless Word of God: "For ever, O Lord, thy word is settled in heaven" (Ps. 119:89).

* * * *

Invaluable

William Lyon Phelps of Yale, one of America's highly esteemed professors, said, "I thoroughly believe in a university education for both men and women, but I believe a knowledge of the Bible without a college education is more valuable than a college course without the Bible."

* * * *

The Greatest Blessing

Immanuel Kant, a German philosopher, said, "The Bible is an inexhaustible fountain of all truths. The Bible is the greatest blessing ever given to humanity."

* * * *

Historical Research Confirms

George W. Cornell, an AP religious writer, said, "A swelling tide of discoveries through archeological and historical research has confirmed more and more of that ancient book—the Bible."

Dr. Baruch Ben-Yehudah, an Israeli mathematician and Bible scholar, affirmed, "A great deal of it [the Bible] has been thoroughly authenticated. Every day we're finding new things." "For ever, O Lord, thy word is settled in heaven" (Ps. 119:89).

* * * *

Straight From God

John Ruskin wrote in *Crown of Wild Olive:*

"The English people are in possession of a Book which tells them, straight from the lips of God, all they ought to do and need to know. For forty years I have read that Book with as much care as most of them and am thankful that on those that trust it I can press its pleadings. My endeavor has been to make them trust it more deeply than they do; trust it, not in their favorite verses only, but in the sum of it all; trust it, not as a fetish or

talisman, but as a captain's order, to be heard and obeyed."

How blessed are those who can say with the psalmist, "O how love I thy law! it is my meditation all the day" (Ps. 119:97).

* * * *

Our Weapon

When the British were encamped at Georgetown, General Washington held a council with his officers to plan strategy.

Most of the officers advocated delay. Then Washington asked Brigadier General Anthony Wayne, "What would you say, General?"

Wayne stood, glared at his fellow officers and barked, "I'd say nothing, Sir! I'd fight!"

God's children are engaged in a spiritual warfare. The "weapons of [their] warfare are not carnal, but mighty through God" (II Cor. 10:4a). Victory comes as they wield "the sword of the Spirit, which is the word of God" (Eph. 6:17).

* * * *

"Quick and Powerful"

A pastor became deeply burdened for the conversion of a prominent lawyer. He called at the lawyer's office and gave him a special invitation to attend the church service on the following Sunday evening.

The lawyer said, "I'll be there."

Then the pastor prepared a message especially for the lawyer.

At the close of the sermon, when the invitation was given for unsaved ones to publicly confess Christ, the lawyer was the first one to go forward. How elated the pastor was!

Later he asked the lawyer, "What was it in my sermon that caused you to confess the Saviour and seek His forgiveness?"

The lawyer replied, "Ah, pastor, it wasn't your sermon! It was your text from the Bible!"

God's Word is powerful to quicken slumbering souls into spiritual life: "For the word of God is quick, and powerful, and sharper than any twoedged sword" (Heb. 4:12).

* * * *

Transmuted Into Life

"There is nothing in the Bible that benefits you unless it is transmuted into life," said Henry G. Weston. "It must become a part of yourself, just like your food. Unless you assimilate it and it becomes body, bone and muscle, it does you no good."

Jeremiah wrote, "Thy words were found, and I did eat them; and thy word was unto me the joy and rejoicing of mine heart" (Jer. 15:16).

Of the incarnate Word, the Saviour, one has said, "Though Christ a thousand times in Bethlehem be born, it will avail you nothing unless He is born in you." "And the Word was made flesh, and dwelt among us" (John 1:14).

* * * *

Leap Year

In 1288 Queen Margaret of Scotland decreed that if a girl proposed matrimony during Leap Year, the one proposed to had to marry her, or prove that he was already engaged, or pay a fine of 100 pounds. Historians regard the queen's decree as the origin of Leap Year.

The queen's decree is a dead letter now. God's decrees, given in His Word, are eternal: "For ever, O Lord, thy word is settled in heaven" (Ps. 119:89).

* * * *

Life Is in Seed—Not Sower

How encouraging to the weakest of God's children who faithfully sow God's Word is the fact that spiritual life inheres not in the *sower* but in the Seed, the living Word of God: "So shall my word be that goeth forth out of my mouth: it shall not return unto me void, but it shall accomplish that which I please, and it shall prosper in the thing whereto I sent it" (Isa. 55:11).

* * * *

God Did It

Dr. Duane Gish, a biochemist and Associate Director of the Institute for Creation Research in San Diego, California, said, "A lot of scientific law tends to support the creation theory better than the theory of evolution. For example, fossil records show a remarkable absence of transitional forms. Their forms are demanded by the theory, but are absent everywhere."

The factual statement of the Bible has never been disproved:

"So God created man in his own image, in the image of God created he him; male and female created he them" (Gen. 1:27).

* * * *

The Most Valuable Thing

"It is my confident hope," said King George V, "that my subjects never cease to cherish their noble inheritance in the English Bible, which is the first of national treasures. Its spiritual significance is the most valuable thing the world affords."

Can we say with the psalmist, "The law of thy mouth is better unto me than thousands of gold and silver" (Ps. 119:72)?

* * * *

Nothing Else Needed

"I have made a covenant with my God that He send me neither visions, dreams, nor even angels. I am well satisfied with the gift of the Holy Scriptures, which give me abundant instruction and all that I need to know both for this life and for the life which is to come," said Martin Luther.

In His imperishable Word, God has spoken with finality. From what He has spoken in His Word, there is no court of appeals: "For ever, O Lord, thy word is settled in heaven" (Ps. 119:89).

* * * *

Settled at Last

I entered the world's great library doors,

I crossed their acres of polished floors,
I searched and searched their stacks and nooks,
But I settled at last on the Book of books—

The Bible

* * * *

Gets Sweeter

One asked George Mueller, "How many times have you read the Bible through?"

Mueller replied, "I have read it through sixty-six times, and I am now going through it for the sixty-seventh time. It gets more interesting and sweeter every time I read it!"

* * * *

Stops Bullet

During World War II, a small New Testament in his shirt pocket saved the life of Felix Rosser, an Abilene, Texas, businessman.

Rosser was shot in the chest while trailing a company of tanks from the 20th Armored Infantry Division through a typical German town. Without warning, a rapid-firing "burp" gun hit Rosser, penetrated the New Testament, and lodged between his ribs. The thickness of the Book slowed the speed of the bullet, preventing it from reaching Rosser's heart. It was removed by minor surgery.

The New Testament, a gift from a girl friend to him when he left the United States to go overseas, was an inexpensive but popular gift to a combat serviceman during World War II. Over its paper cover was a thick gold-plated steel cover engraved: "May This Keep You Safe From Harm."

"The Bible with a hole in it" has been on display in seminaries throughout the United States and has been used as a sermon topic by ministers throughout the country.

The Pentagon photographed it, printed it 4 x 6 feet, and placed it in the Washington, D.C., building for public display.

When we hide God's Word in our heart, it protects us from sin's destructiveness: "Thy word have I hid in mine heart, that I might not sin against thee" (Ps. 119:11).

* * * *

A Single Sentence

The German philosopher Immanuel Kant said, "A single sentence in the Bible has consoled me more than all the books I ever read besides."

Rivers of tears have been stanched by the comforting, sorrow-assuaging words of the Saviour, "Let not your heart be troubled: ye believe in God, believe also in me" (John 14:1).

* * * *

"Ever Learning. . .Never Able"

In a message, a pastor spoke of the fact that so many intellectuals are ignorant about what the Bible teaches.

He said, "One day I chanced to meet a psychiatric professor to whom I read from the Phillips Translation of the New Testament. The professor nodded agreement *until* he realized that the Book I read from was the Bible.

"The Bible is the Book upon which our civilizaton is built. Yet it seems if some supernatural power keeps intellectuals from reading it. Its contents could change the world!"

How powerless to discern spiritual realities are the spiritually blind intelligentsia: "But the natural man receiveth not the things of the Spirit of God: for they are foolishness unto him: neither can he know them, because they are spiritually discerned" (I Cor. 2:14).

How wise are all who sincerely pray: "Open thou mine eyes, that I may behold wondrous things out of thy law" (Ps. 119:18).

* * * *

Add Not, Delete Not

Robert Morrison was a pioneer missionary to China. As he translated the Bible into Chinese, he came to the passage: "We shall be like him; for we shall see him as he is" (I John 3:2).

His Chinese translator said, "Our people will never believe that they shall see their Saviour and their God face to face. I suggest that you change that translation."

Morrison replied, "Give them the Word of God as it is!"

It is hazardous to add unto or delete anything from the imperishable Word of God: "If any man shall add unto these things, God shall add unto him the plagues that are written in this book" (Rev. 22:18); "For ever, O Lord, thy word is settled in heaven" (Ps. 119:89).

* * * *

God's Mirror—His Word

An Australian ornithologist told reporters in Melbourne, "I had to give a budgerigar (a small parrot) tranquilizers because it was so frightened when it saw itself in the mirror in its cage. Because of inbreeding, it had a profuse growth of feathers. It began to behave oddly, screeching at night, fighting imaginary enemies and retreating to the corner of its cage."

How frightful is the reflected image of unregenerated man as he sees himself in God's mirror, the Bible! The Bible is the only Book extant which depicts accurately the true condition of mankind in his lostness: "The whole head is sick, and the whole heart faint. . . .there is no soundness in it; but wounds, and bruises, and putrifying sores" (Isa. 1:5,6).

* * * *

The Bible in Our Heart

Night watchman Robert Hanson always carries a small New Testament in his shirt pocket. "It gives me strength," he says. Policemen said it saved his life.

As Hansen was making his final rounds in the basement of a department store building, an intruder shot him in the chest. A 22-caliber bullet struck the New Testament and penetrated all but the back leather cover. "The shot struck like a sledge hammer," Hanson said. He was knocked down, but suffered only a bruised chest. The bruise was directly over his heart.

God's Word IN our hearts will save us from sin and spiritual death: "Thy word have I hid in mine heart, that I might not sin against thee" (Ps. 119:11).

* * * *

The Enduring Word

Sometime ago *Time* editorialized: "Archeological digging in Israel continues to turn up new evidence that the Bible is surprisingly accurate in historical particulars, more so than earlier generations of scholars ever suspected. After more than two centuries of facing the heaviest scientific guns that could be brought to bear against it, the Bible has survived and is perhaps the better for the siege. Even on the critics' own terms— historical facts—the Scriptures seem more acceptable now than they did when rationalists began to attack!"

* * * *

What Brings Victory

William Culbertson said, "Used effectively, the Word of God brings victory to the child of God. Lodged in the heart of the believer, it becomes a power for holiness."

Jesus said, "Now ye are clean through the word which I have spoken unto you" (John 15:3).

* * * *

How Short-Lived

Professor Benjamin Frankel of the Hebrew University in Jerusalem said, "The average lifetime of cosmological theory is very short. How do you account for creation out of nothing?

There is one theory that everything could have been created out of light in fifteen minutes. We can only say that we don't know more about genesis than is written in the Book of Genesis. There are so many theories that one doesn't know what to say—nothing proved.

"The Book of books (the Bible) and the Book of nature were written by the same great Author."

* * * *

Stopped Short of Heart

A bandit recently lunged at Louie D. Hairrston of Washington, D. C., with a foot-long butcher knife. Hairrston carries in his breast pocket a New Testament, which he reads at spare times. He said, "The bandit would have killed me had not the hard cover of my New Testament stopped the knife short of my heart!"

God's Word is a mighty defensive weapon: "And take the helmet of salvation, and the sword of the Spirit, which is the word of God" (Eph. 6:17). It is "quick and powerful, and sharper than any twoedged sword" (Heb. 4:12).

* * * *

The Mail-Order Catalog

The new minister called at the home of one of his members. Wanting to make a favorable impression on him, the housewife said to her little three-year-old daughter, "Darling, go and bring to Mother the Book which she loves best."

The little girl dashed away. Shortly she returned with her arms wrapped around a large mail-order catalog!

We are spiritually dwarfed when we neglect God's Word: "As newborn babes, desire the sincere milk of the word, that ye may grow thereby" (I Pet. 2:2).

Alice Marie Knight.

* * * *

When Bible Becomes God's Word?

"Neo-orthodox theology has long suggested that the Bible is not the word of God while it lies on a table unread. This heresy asserts that the Bible becomes the Word of God only when it is read," said Palmer Robertson.

Whether read or unread, the Bible is God's changeless Word: "For ever, O Lord, thy word is settled in heaven" (Ps. 119:89).

It is true that many of God's children are spiritually impoverished through failure to daily read and meditate upon God's Word. How blessed are those who exclaim: "O how love I thy law! it is my meditation all the day" (Ps. 119:97).

* * * *

Love Made the Difference

A friend gave a book to a beautiful young lady. When she began to read it, she thought: *How dry and uninteresting is this book,* and cast it aside.

Sometime later, at a social event, she was introduced to a charming, handsome young man whose name was Wood. In conversation with him,

21

she remarked, "I just began reading a book whose author is Wood, and whose initials are identical with yours! Isn't that a coincidence?"

"Not at all," was the reply. "I'm the author!"

After going home, the young lady didn't put the book down until she had finished reading it—long past the midnight hour. Later she became Mrs. H. W. Wood!

What made the difference? She had fallen in love with the author!

When we love God with all our heart, soul, mind and strength, we deeply love His Word and exclaim, "I have esteemed the words of his mouth more than my necessary food" (Job 23:12).

Told by R. E. Neighbour.

* * * *

Sweeter Than Sweet

There is a substance which exudes from the red serendipity berry of Nigeria which is said to be 1,500 times sweeter than sucrose.

The psalmist said of the statutes of the Lord, "More are they to be desired than gold: . . .sweeter also than honey in the honeycomb" (Ps. 19:10). He also exclaimed, "O how love I thy law! it is my meditaiton all the day" (Ps. 119:97).

* * * *

Warts and All

An artist did a painting of Oliver Cromwell, England's Puritan Protector, minus the unsightly warts on Cromwell's face. Upon completion of the painting, the artist showed it to Cromwell.

"Take it away," he demanded, "Paint another picture—*warts and all!*"

The Bible is the only Book extant which portrays mankind as it is: "The whole head is sick, and the whole heart faint. From the sole of the foot even unto the head there is no soundness in it; but wounds, and bruises, and putrifying sores" (Isa. 1:5,6).

For the fruitage of man's deceitful and desperately wicked heart, read your daily newspaper.

* * * *

Revealing and Satisfying

The explorers of space have affirmed that one principal reason for putting men on the moon was "to learn more about how the moon was formed and the earth evolved." Man's quest for knowledge is inborn and commendable.

How revealing and satisfying are these factual statements of God's Word: "And God said, Let there be lights in the firmament of the heaven. . . .And God made two great lights; the greater light to rule the day and the lesser light to rule the night: he made the stars also" (Gen. 1:14,16).

* * * *

The Enduring Word

God's Word is indestructible: "The word of the Lord endureth for ever" (I Pet. 1:25).

Of it, Will Houghton said: "The empire of Caesar is gone, the legions of Rome are mouldering in the dust, the avalanches that Napoleon hurled upon Europe have melted away, the pride of the pharaohs is fallen, the pyramids they raised to be their tombs are sinking every day into the desert sands. Tyre is a rock for bleaching fishermen's nets. Sidon has scarcely left a rock behind; but the Word of God still survives!

"All things threatening to extinguish it have only aided it. It proves every day how transient is the noblest monument that men could build, how enduring is the least Word that God has spoken. Tradition has dug for it a grave. Intolerance has lighted for it many a fagot. Many a Judas has betrayed it with a kiss. Many a Peter has denied it with an oath. Many a Demas has forsaken it; but the Word of God endures!"

* * * *

A University for Countless Men

Many great writers and orators, including Sir Winston Churchill, have owed the elegance of their style and grace of language to the King James Version. It has been in the past a university for countless men.

"Must everything in our age be predigested? Does the Bible have to be reduced to pablum? I refuse to believe that modern man, who split the atom and is exploring space, is unable to cope with the grandeur and the glory of the King James Version."

From a syndicated column by Inez Robb in *The Chicago Daily News.*

* * * *

The Spring Itself

Will H. Houghton, former president of Moody Bible Institute, wrote in his book, *Let's Get Back to the Bible:* "How well I remember the day when, sitting in my office with my Bible open before me, I looked up at the books surrounding me on the wall . . .and said something like this:

"*Books, some of you have been my companions for many years. . .I value you for what you are and for what you have meant to me. As I look at you, ranged on the shelves, I think of each one of you as a bottle of pure spring water. Thirsty, I reach up to drink from your pages. . . .*

"And then, taking in my hand my open Bible, I continued, *But, books, this is more than a bottle of spring water! This is the spring itself, and if you have anything of truth in your pages, that truth was first in embryo here!*"

* * * *

Bible Become Alive?

In plugging for people to go with him to the Holy Land, a pastor wrote in a circular letter, "Your Bible will become alive and vital. One's faith is greatly strengthened, which makes the whole trip worthwhile!"

How grateful we are that God's imperishable Word becomes alive and vital to myriads who will never have the privilege of visiting the Holy Land—humble ones who believe and cherish it. They glowingly testify with the psalmist, "O how love I thy law! it is my meditation all the day" (Ps. 119:97).

* * * *

How Casals Practiced the Cello

Ninety-six year old Pablo Casals, who was one of the world's greatest cello players, was interviewed by Martin Bernheimer of *The Los Angeles Times*. "How do you spend your day?" asked Bernheimer.

Casals replied, "First, I take a walk. Then I practice the piano. Then I play the cello. I do the same exercise I did when I was eighteen—scales, thirds, octaves, everything for more than an hour. Then I am ready for the Bach suites. On Mondays I play the first. On Tuesdays the second, and so on. On the seventh day I repeat the sixth suite. It is the most difficult."

"Do you feel that you know the Bach suites yet?" asked Bernheimer.

"Though I have played them for seventy-eight years," Casals said, "I do not know them. I find something new every day. Then I wonder why I never had discovered that detail sooner!"

God's Word is imperishable and its truth inexhaustible.

* * * *

GOD'S CARE

The Shortest Letter Ever Written

Victor Hugo wrote *Les Miserables*, the greatest epic drama ever written—majestically impressive. He submitted the manuscript to a publisher and expectantly waited.

Becoming restive, Hugo wrote to the publishers what was possibly the shortest "letter" ever written— only a large question mark:

(?)

The publisher's reply was also brief and ingenious—only a large exclamation point:

(!)

God is often working mightily for His children when they see little or no visible results from their faithful service. This is certain: "For God is not unrighteous to forget your work and labour of love" (Heb. 6:10).

* * * *

A Personalized Concern

During my chapel services, when I was chaplain of the U.S. Northeastern Penitentiary, Lewisburg, Pennsylvania, a guard often passed to me a slip of paper on which was written a number. I would announce, "Call for number____." The prisoner whose number was called would quietly withdraw from chapel.

Sin often degrades and depersonalizes its victims, making them mere numbers.

How different it is with those in God's great family: "He [the Saviour] calleth his own sheep by name" (John 10:3). Each one is personally precious to the Good Shepherd.

* * * *

"God Knows My Size"

Once I was dinner guest in the home of a friend whose husband, a prominent lawyer, had recently died.

During the meal my host looked intently at me, as if "sizing me up." At the conclusion of the meal, she said, "I believe the suits of my deceased husband would fit you. The Lord has told me to give them to you."

I replied, "If the Lord has told you to give them to me, they will fit perfectly, for He knows my size!"

For years I wore those elegant suits. How varied are God's methods to supply the needs of His children!

* * * *

Learn to Sit Loose

One of God's gracious saints was asked, "What is the secret of your poise and composure?" She replied, "I have learned to *sit loose!*"

Taut nerves are snapping and overwrought minds are breaking. Only those who have learned to *sit loose* and cast corroding care upon the ever-present Caretaker—the Saviour—will outride the storms and stresses of our distraught and fear-craven world.

* * * *

"Not One Thing Hath Failed!"

Charles S. Tindley, a black pastor, stood at Desperation Corner. He was serving a small, struggling church in Cape May, New Jersey, when a blizzard swept down, paralyzing the town. Dawn broke with no sign of relief. Nothing but stale bread was in the house. But Tindley said to his wife, "Set the table as we always do." Then he thanked God for his salvation, his health and his children. The

family listened in wonder. There was another One who also listened—the mighty God.

Just then there was a knock at the door. A Christian brother entered with his arms encircling large bags of groceries!

There is *one thing* God can't do. He cannot fail to fulfill His promise to His children. With God's ancient servant Joshua, they can say, "Not one thing hath failed of all the good things which the Lord your God spake concening you. . .and not one thing hath failed" (Josh. 23:14).

Adapted from *Moody Monthly.*

* * * *

OUR SLEEPLESS CARETAKER

Careless seems the great Avenger,
 For history's pages but record,
One death grapple in the darkness,
 'Twixt old systems and the Word,
Truth forever on the scaffold,
 Wrong forever on the throne!
Yet that scaffold sways the future,
 And behind the dim unknown,
Standeth God within the shadows,
 Keeping watch above His own.

James Russell Lowell.

* * * *

Serendipity

The word "serendipity" means the faculty of happening upon fortunate discoveries when not in search for them. The word was coined by Horace Walpole in 1754.

God often showers blessings on His children when they are not expected. He often works wondrously for them when there is not outward evidence that He is "in the shadows, keeping watch above His own!"

The Bible says, "No good thing will he withhold from them that walk uprightly" (Ps. 84:11).

* * * *

WHEN SPARROWS FALL

When sparrows fall God always sees,
So tenderly He cares for these,
Not one brown fledgling rends the air,
Except He sees and marks it there.
That God who has flung His planets far,
And touched with splendor every star,
Should care for one small feathered bird,
Amazes me, but I am stirred,
And comforted that I can call
The One who cares when sparrows fall!

Sybil Leonard Armes,
in *Baptist Standard.*

* * * *

"You Can't Hurt Me!"

An elderly woman was returning home from a prayer meeting which closed with the song, *Under His Wings I Am Safely Abiding.* As a holdup man accosted her, she fearlessly said, "You can't hurt me. I am covered with His wings!"

The would-be robber was so impressed by the courage of his intended victim that he quickly retreated to find a more fearful prey.

Physical deliverance is not always given to God's children, but He never fails to deliver them *spiritually.*

"He shall cover thee with his feathers, and under his wings shalt thou trust. His truth shall be thy shield and buckler" (Ps. 91:4).

* * * *

Encircled

Each one of God's children is the object of the heavenly Father's tender care and unfailing protection. He is *above* them: "The eyes of the Lord are over the righteous" (I Pet. 3:12); He is *before* them: "When he putteth forth his own sheep, he goeth before them" (John 10:4); He is *behind* them: "They drank of that spiritual Rock that followed them: and that Rock was Christ" (I Cor. 10:4); He *encircles* them: "The angel of the Lord encampeth round about them that fear him, and delivereth them" (Ps. 34:7); He is *with* them: "Fear thou not; for I am with thee" (Isa. 41:10); in death He *accompanies* them: "Yea, though I walk through the valley of the shadow of death, I will fear no evil: for thou art with me" (Ps. 23:4).

With unshakable trust in God, we confidently exclaim:

I know not where His islands lift,
Their fronded palms in air;
I only know I cannot drift
Beyond His love and care!
Whittier.

* * * *

Entangling God

A Hindu doctor said to a missionary: "We must not entangle God in human relationships. If He were tangled in them, He would be involved, unhappy, imperfect and, therefore, not God."

Our heavenly Father *is* fully involved in everything that pertains to His children. He enters feelingly and sharingly into their cares, heartaches and heartbreaks: "In all their affliction he was afflicted" (Isa. 63:9).

Does Jesus care when my heart is pained
Too deeply for mirth or song,
As the burdens press, and the cares distress,
And the way grows weary and long?

O yes, He cares, I know He cares,
His heart is touched with my grief;
When the days are weary, the long nights dreary,
I know my Saviour cares!

Frank E. Graeff.

* * * *

One Who Never Sleeps

While submitting evidence for his client who was accused of murder, the defense lawyer observed that the presiding judge closed his eyes and nodded several times. So when the judge announced a guilty verdict, he immediately appealed the verdict to the chief justice of England.

After reviewing the case, Chief Justice Lord Widgery dismissed the appeal, believing that Justice Robertson Chichton was not asleep during the trial, since his summation of the case to the jury contained evidence submitted during the twilight period in which the defense lawyer alleged he was not awake. Said the chief justice, "Whether he appeared to be asleep is a matter which the court finds very difficult to determine, but there is not sufficient ground for me to say that justice was not done."

How grateful we are that our heavenly Father, the righteous Judge, is ever awake and watchful. The Bible says, "He that keepeth thee will not slumber" (Ps. 121:3). His "eyes . . .are over the righteous" (I Pet. 3:12).

* * * *

Not Tomorrow's Bread

The Lord taught His disciples to pray, "Give us this day our daily bread" (Matt. 6:11).

The petition asks for today's bread only. It does not complain about yesterday's bread. It does not worry about the bread for next week or next month. The request focuses on bread for "this day."

Today's bread is the only bread we can now eat. Therefore, "Take. . . no thought for the morrow. . . .Sufficient unto the day is the evil thereof" (Matt. 6:34).

George Sweeting.

* * * *

God's Algebra

A dejected freshman sat across the desk from me. So cast down was he that he had no words to speak. He merely pushed across the desk a slip of blue paper, and looked appealingly at me.

I recognized the slip of paper. It was a notice from the college business office that the next payment was due. The young man had not come to ask financial help from me. Rather he had come in bewilderment of spirit to know what he should do. I knew that he was working long hours to meet his expenses and that he was careful with his expenditures. But the day of reckoning had come!

I noted on the account that he owed $29.75, due that very day. The notice had come five days earlier, but the time had passed without his having received any provision to meet the impending obligation.

I inquired, "In order to understand the problem and to pray more intelligently, would you care to tell me how much you have toward the bill?"

He spoke for the first time, quietly, "Seventy-five cents."

I pushed the blue slip back to him with the request, "Turn the statement over and write down an equation on the other side." Obediently he took out a pencil and wrote as I dictated: "Seventy-five cents is to $29.75 as . . ."

Faithfully he began writing the equation, having no idea how it was going to end: "Seventy-five cents is to $29.75 as five loaves and two fishes are to 5,000 men plus women plus children."

By the time I got to speaking of women and children, he had ceased writing. He dropped the pencil on the desk and bowed his head to pray. He asked forgiveness of the Lord for his little faith. He prayed for obedience and for the lowliness of heart that would trust God whatever the circumstances of the moment might be.

After praying with him, I reminded him of the basic principle of faith revealed to us in the Scriptures. Our problem is never to know *how* prayer is answered, only to be sure that we are acquainted with the One *who* answers prayer. The how is God's part. To know Him is our part.

Did God take care of him? He did! The student came into my office the next day to tell me with a smile that God had answered prayer; unexpected money had come, and the installment was paid.

In the years that followed his graduation, whenever we met at homecoming or at an alumni dinner, he would invariably repeat to me: "Seventy-five cents is to $29.75 as five loaves and two fishes are to 5,000 men plus women plus children!"

Always—not *how*, but *who*!

V. Raymond Edman, in
Not Somehow. . .But Triumphantly
(Zondervan Publishing House).

* * * *

The Kangaroo Rat

How unfailing is God's care of His creatures: "He giveth to the beast his food, and to the young ravens which cry" (Ps. 147:9).

The kangaroo rat is a desert creature which never drinks a drop of water. It eats small, juicy tubers that grow in the desert and are found an inch or two below the surface of the desert sands.

God has also provided thirst-slaking, living water for mankind; but myriads spurn the Saviour's offer: "If any man thirst, let him come unto me and drink" (John 7:37).

I heard the voice of Jesus say,
"Behold I freely give
The living water, thirsty one,
Stoop down, and drink, and
live."

* * * *

What Is Man?

"The surgeon peers inside a man and marvels at his symmetry and complex working mechanism," said Ralph S. Bell.

"The psychologist seeks to analyze a man's behavior and to follow the varied paths that his emotions travel.

"The psalmist lifted his eyes in wonder that an infinite God would show concern for finite man: 'When I consider thy heavens, the work of thy fingers, the moon and the stars, which thou hast ordained; What is man, that thou art mindful of him?' " (Ps. 8:3,4).

Each one of God's children is the object of His tender care and solicitous concern: "He careth for you" (I Pet. 5:7).

Be not dismayed whate'er betide,
God will take care of you;
Beneath His wings of love abide,
God will take care of you!

* * * *

CHARACTER

A Sure Indication

You can tell a man's character by how he treats those who can do nothing for him.

* * * *

SELF-REVEALING

You tell on yourself by the friends you seek,
By the very manner in which you speak,
By the way you employ your time,
By the use you make of dollars and dimes.
You tell what you are by the way you walk,
By the things of which you delight to talk,
By the manner in which you bear defeat,
By so simple a thing as how you eat.
By books you choose from the well-filled shelf,
In these ways and more, you tell on yourself,

So there's really no particle of sense,
In an effort to keep up false pretense.

From a church bulletin.

* * * *

How Revealed

Goethe said, "Men show their character in nothing more clearly than by what they think laughable."

Quintilian, a Latin rhetorician, said, "Laughter costs too much which is purchased by sacrifice of decency."

The Bible says, "For as the crackling of thorns under a pot, so is the laughter of the fool: this also is vanity" (Eccles. 7:6).

* * * *

Building Men

Cecil Rhodes, who established the Rhodes Scholarships, said to General William Booth, founder of the Salvation Army, "I am trying to build up new countries. You are trying to build up new men. You have chosen the better part!"

We are all blind until we see,
That in the human plan,
Nothing is worth the building,
If it does not build the man!

Why build these cities glorious,
If man unbuilded goes?
In vain we build the world,
Unless the builder grows!

* * * *

The Most Important Thing

When General William Dean was captured by the North Koreans, he was permitted to write one letter home. That letter, addressed to his son, said, "Bill, remember that integrity is the most important thing of all. Let it always be your aim."

* * * *

CHILDREN
(See also Parental Responsibility)

Little Feet and the Future

Doing big things shows others *who* we are. Doing small things shows others *what* we are.

A question: "For who hath despised the day of small things?" (Zech. 4:10).

So few of us are big enough to become little enough to be used of God. Said Samuel to disobedient Saul, "When thou wast little in thine own sight, wast thou not made the head of the tribes of Israel?" (I Sam. 15:17).

The future goes forward on the feet of *little* children!

Jesus said, "Take heed that ye despise not one of these little ones" (Matt. 18:10).

* * * *

BABY DEAR

Where did you come from, baby dear?
Out of everywhere into the here.
Where did you get those eyes so blue?
Out of the sky as I passed through.

What makes the light of them sparkle
  and spin?
Some of the starry spokes left in.
Where did you get that little tear?
I found it waiting when I got here.
What makes your forehead so smooth
  and high?
A soft hand stroked it as I went by.
What makes your cheek like a warm
  white rose?
Something better than anyone
  knows.
Whence that three-cornered smile of
  bliss?
Three angels gave me at once a kiss.
Where did you get that pearly ear?
God spoke, and it came out here.
Where did you get those arms and
  hands?
Love made itself into hooks and
  bands.
Feet, whence did you come, you dar-
  ling things?
From the same box as the cherubs'
  wings.
How did they all just come to you?
God thought about me, and so I grew.
But how did you come to us, you

dear?
God thought of you, and so I am here!

George McDaniel.

* * * *

Each One Is a V. I. P.

It was the children's first day in school. How excited they were! The teacher asked, "Children, what is here now which was not here fifteen years ago?"

A boy leaped to his feet and said proudly, "Me!"

The boy deemed himself unique and of great importance. He was right! Each one of us is precious and important to God. Each one is precious to and personally known to the Saviour: "He calleth his sheep by name" (John 10:3).

Before we were conceived in our mother's womb, God knew us: "Before I formed thee. . .I knew thee. . .I sanctified thee, and I ordained thee" (Jer. 1:5). Each one of God's children is elect "according to the foreknowledge of God" (I Pet. 1:2).

Throughout God's creation, diversity is His mode of operation. There is infinite variation in snowflakes. Each one is a perfect geometric design and dazzlingly beautiful!

No two of God's children are identical. When God made you and me, he threw away the mold.

In contemplation of God's presence or foreknowledge, we exclaim, "O the depth of the riches both of the wisdom and knowledge of God! how unsearchable are his . . .ways past finding out!" (Rom. 11:33).

* * * *

Latent Potentials

Only God knows about the latent potentials resident in the most unpromising of children.

As a child, Winston Churchill was a dullard. His father thought he could never earn a living in England.

Gilbert Keith Chesterton, an English writer, could not read until he was 8 years of age. One of his teachers said to him, "If we could open your head, we would not find any brain, only a lump of white fat!"

Thomas Edison's first teacher described him as "addlebrained." His father almost convinced him that he was a "dunce."

The parents of Albert Einstein feared that he was dull. He did so badly in high school courses, except mathematics, that a teacher asked him to drop out, saying, "You will never amount to anything, Einstein."

Will Rogers spent three years in the fourth grade. Then he said, "I left the entire school business for life."

Abraham Lincoln's formal education totaled less than two years.

* * * *

No Time to Lose

Horace Bushnell said, "Every Christian father and mother should understand that when their child is three years old, they have done more than half of all they will ever do for his character."

* * * *

INVALUABLE

Measures there are for silver and
gold,
By carats the worth of diamonds are
told;
But there is no measure in all the
earth,
To tell what a boy or girl is worth!

* * * *

Pricelessly Precious Gifts

A baby is a small member of the
animal kingdom that makes love
stronger, days shorter, nights longer,
the bankroll smaller, the home happier, clothes shabbier, the past forgotten, and the future worth living
for!

* * * *

Adversely Affected

Dr. Richard E. Palmer, president of
the American Medical Association,
said, "TV violence is a mental health
problem and an environmental issue.
If the programming a child is exposed
to consists largely of violent content,
then his perceptions of the real world
may be significantly distorted and his
psychological development adversely
affected."

* * * *

Television Violence

"Violent television programming is
unquestionably increasing the aggressive attitudes and behavior of children viewing them," declared Dr.
Robert M. Liebert, professor of psychology and psychiatry at the State
University of New York, in the
Chicago Tribune.

"There is a positive relationship
between the amount of violence a
child watches and the amount of aggression seen in his daily attitudes
and behavior. The single best predic-
tion of how aggressive a young male
will be at age 19 is the amount of television violence he has been exposed
to," said Dr. Liebert.

* * * *

"The National Scandal"

The American Medical Association
is deeply concerned about TV violence, and its board has decided that
it is bad for the mental health of
American children. The association's
concern was sparked by an article by
Dr. Michael B. Rothenberg of the
University of Washington which
urged doctors to protest "the national
scandal" of violence on TV, and it has
authorized the publication of a booklet telling parents what kind of TV
programs are suitable for their
children.

Dr. Rothenberg said, "There is an
average of six times more violence
during one hour of children's television than there is in one hour of adult
television. All this adds up to an increase in aggressive behavior among
American children. One hundred and
forty-six articles in behavioral science journals, representing fifty studies involving 10,000 children and ad-
olescents from different backgrounds
showed that violence viewing
produces increased aggressive
behavior in the young."

* * * *

PLIABLE CLAY

Each little child God sends our way,
Is like a piece of pliable clay;
'Tis ours to mold and shape and trim,
To make the precious one pleasing to
Him.

* * * *

Quick Learners

How quick to learn are infants and children!

Arnold Toynbee, possibly the greatest historian of all times, said, "When I was four years old, my mother began telling me bedtime stories from history. She made me a historian in embryo." His monumental work on the rise and fall of civilizations brought him world renown and an enduring place in the annals of mankind.

The Bible says, "Whom shall he [God] teach knowledge? and whom shall he make to understand doctrine? them that are weaned from the milk, and drawn from the breast" (Isa. 28:9).

* * * *

God and Mud Puddles

As I glanced out the window, I saw both my boys doing *exactly* what I'd told them not to do—playing in a mud puddle, shoes and all. I began to scold!

"But, Mommy," 4-year-old Joe-Joe interrupted, "if God didn't send the rain and make mud puddles, we wouldn't have to play in the mud!"

I had to laugh. As I returned to my work, I mused about what Joe-Joe had said: "If God wouldn't...then I wouldn't...."

It was funny for a 4-year-old boy to say, but how many times do we as Christians reason the same way?

"If the children wouldn't disobey, I wouldn't have to scream at them."

"If only my husband would understand, I wouldn't have to nag."

"If God wouldn't...I wouldn't have to...."

Lord, I know I can't do anything in myself, but You can do it in me. Help me not to play in mud puddles!

Told by Ardeen B. Zearfaus.

* * * *

Read and Weep!

Dr. Morris Chafetz, director of the National Institute on Alcohol and Alcohol Abuse, warned, "It is not uncommon to see severe alcoholic problems in children 9, 10, 11 and 12 years of age. It is a far more serious problem than we ever imagined!"

* * * *

"Mommy, What Is God Like?"

Tommy asked, "Mommy, what is God like?"

Mother replied, "How I wish I could answer your question. But God is so powerful, wise and loving that one cannot tell all that God is like, Tommy."

A look of disappointment came upon Tommy's face. Stating his question differently, he later asked Daddy, "Have you ever seen God?"

Daddy replied, "No, Tommy. The Bible tells us that God is a Spirit, and we cannot see a Spirit. It also tells us that no man has seen God at any time; but Jesus, God's Son, has declared or shown Him to us. When Jesus healed the sick, fed the hungry, comforted sorrowing ones, and raised the dead, He showed us what God is like. Jesus said, 'He that hath seen me hath seen the Father' " (John 14:9).

Sometime later, when Tommy was sitting beside an old retired sea captain on a bench by the sea, he asked him also, "Have you ever seen God?"

As the old captain pointed to the setting sun and the shafts of golden light shining on the incoming tide, tears welled in his eyes and trickled down his weather-beaten face. Then he replied, "My boy, it is getting to the place where I can't see anything else!"

How blind are those who cannot see God throughout His creation: "The heavens declare the glory of God; and the firmament sheweth his handy-work" (Ps. 19:1).

Alice M. Knight.

* * * *

What Do You Think?

A Sunday school teacher asked her class, "Is there anything God can't do?" A boy quickly replied, "Yes, ma'am. God can't please everybody!"

Paul said, "For if I yet pleased men, I should not be the servant of Christ" (Gal. 1:10).

* * * *

BEAUTIFUL MEMORIES

God give me patience when little hands

Tug at me with ceaseless small demands,

Give me gentle words and smiling eyes,

And keep my lips from hasty, sharp replies!

Let me not in weariness, confusion or noise

Obscure my vision of life's fleeting joys,

That when in years to come my house is still

Beautiful memories its rooms may fill!

* * * *

"Out of the Mouth of Babes"

Harry A. Ironside said, "When I was talking to a group of boys and girls in San Francisco, I said: 'How sad it is to know that each time you say no to Jesus the heart gets harder and harder until by and by God calls it a heart of stone.' One little girl, only five years old, thought of her own dear father who never went to hear the Word of God. When she got to her home, she ran into her father's arms and said, 'Daddy, Daddy, feel your heart! Is it getting like stone?' "

* * * *

HEART OF A CHILD

In the breast of a bulb
Is the promise of spring;
In the little blue egg
Is a bird that will sing;
In the soul of a seed
Is the hope of the sod;
In the heart of a child

Is the Kingdom of God!

William L Stidger.

* * * *

"IT IS WORTHWHILE"

I found a seed, a tiny thing,
I handled it with care;
"I want for it the best," I said,
"Because it is so rare."
I found a nice smooth piece of ground,
I dug a hole just so;
Down into it I placed the seed,
And longed for it to grow.
The days and weeks lapsed into months,
Still had the seed not grown,
And then I learned to cultivate,
Before the seed is sown.

One day I met a little child,
A precious gift from God,
I thought about the little seed
In the neglected sod.
I lovingly prepared a heart,
God's Word I planted there;
I tilled it with the love of Christ,
And watered it with prayer.
Ere long into that little face
There stole a welcome smile,
A tiny hand slipped into mine;
I said, "It is worthwhile!"

* * * *

"Daddy, Do You Pray?"

Coming home from church, little Pamela ran to her father and asked, "Daddy, do you pray?"

"Who put you up to asking me that question, your mother or your aunt?" the father sternly asked.

"Neither, Daddy. The pastor said in church that Christians pray," was her answer.

After a moment's silence, the father said, "Pamela, you go your way and I'll go mine."

"But, Daddy, tell me, which way are you going?"

The question went like a dart to his heart and was repeatedly iterated there: "Which way are you going?"

Before long Pamela's father sought and found the One who said in the long ago, "I am the way...no man cometh unto the Father but by me" (John 14:6).

Alice Marie Knight.

* * * *

Take Heed

Spurgeon said, "A child of five, if properly instructed, can believe and become regenerated like an adult.

"I have usually found a clearer knowledge of the Gospel and a warmer love toward Christ in a converted child than in the adult convert. I have sometimes met with a deeper spiritual experience in a child of ten or twelve than in some persons fifty or sixty. I have known children who wept themselves to sleep under a crushing sense of sin."

Jesus warned, "Take heed that ye despise not one of these little ones" (Matt. 18:10).

* * * *

The Most Critical Period

"The time from prenatal growth to four years of age has been identified as the most critical period in a person's total development," said Jeanette Watson, director of the Office of Early Childhood Development.

"One researcher suggests that fifty per cent of a child's thinking patterns are determined before the age of four.

"A child needs a sense of security, a basic trust in others, and a self identity that tells him he is important to himself and to others. A child who has received loving care and gentle restraint is more likely to assume a responsibility for his own behavior as he grows older."

For a child's *spiritual* development, it is essential to bring him early to the One who dearly loves the little children and who said long ago, "Suffer little children, and forbid them not, to come unto me: for of such is the kingdom of heaven" (Matt. 19:14).

* * * *

Two and a Half Conversions

Dwight L. Moody reported the results of one of his meetings thus: "Two and a half conversions!"

One asked, "Two adults and a child?"

"Oh, no," said Moody, "two children and one adult. The children gave their whole lives to God. The adult had only half a life to give!"

The future goes forward on the feet of little children.

* * * *

The Hole in the Fence

A father took his little boy on his knee and told him the story of the lost sheep; how it found a hole in the fence and crawled through; how glad it was to get away; how it skipped and played in the sunshine until it wandered so far away it could not find its way back to the sheepcote. Then something happened: a wolf began to chase the sheep! Then the good shepherd came and rescued it and carried it back to the fold.

The boy listened with both ears. How astounded the father was when the boy asked, *"Did they nail up the hole in the fence?"*

The Circuit Rider.

* * * *

CHOOSING

Backbone or Wishbone, Which?

It is said that the lions could not eat Daniel because he was all backbone.

So many have only a wishbone where the backbone ought to be.

Daily we are making choices. The poet was wrong when he wrote:

Once to every man and nation,

Comes the moment to decide,
In the fight 'twixt truth and falsehood,
Between the good or evil side.

Not once but daily throughout life we are making choices. Our tomorrows are determined by the choices we make today. The continuous choices we make mold our characters and determine our destinies.

* * * *

Only One Thing Left

In his book, *Man's Search for Meaning,* Viktor Frankl wrote of his days in prison: "We who lived in concentration camps can remember the men who walked through the huts comforting others, giving away their last piece of bread. They may have been few in number, but they offer sufficient proof that everything can be taken from a man but one thing: freedom to choose one's attitude in any given set of circumstances."

The memory of some is excoriated. Of them it can be said: "[They] departed without being desired" (II Chron. 21:20).

The memory of others is enshrined in grateful hearts. Of them we can say, "[They] being dead yet speaketh" (Heb. 11:4).

* * * *

Not in the Stars

Shakespeare said, "The fault, dear Brutus, is not in our stars but in ourselves. Each one of us is free to chart our destiny in the exercise of choice."

* * * *

Gray Trousers, Blue Jacket

During the Civil War a man living in a borderline state was divided in his allegiance. He was sympathetic toward both the North and the South, as the story is told.

After troublesome thought, he decided upon a novel plan: "I'll wear the Confederate gray trousers and the blue Union jacket."

Soon a fierce battle spread in the region where he lived. Then the soldiers of the Union Army shot him in the trousers, and the Confederate soldiers shot him in the jacket.

The moral of the story is: It can be doubly disastrous to "halt between two opinions" (I Kings 18:21). Long ago the Saviour said, "No man can serve two masters" (Matt. 6:24).

"Choose you this day whom ye will serve" (Josh. 24:15).

* * * *

Homeless and Friendless

Years ago an old man died on Staten Island, homeless and friendless. He had once been one of America's most brilliant lawyers and Vice-President of the United States. In his youthful years, he decided against Christ. In the wake of that destiny-determining decision there followed a life of crime and treasonable acts, culminating in the murder of Alexander Hamilton.

You ask his name? Aaron Burr.

Each one must make a decision in reference to the destiny-determining question, "What shall I do then with Jesus?" (Matt. 27:22).

Told by R. E. Neighbour.

* * * *

Hell's Hottest Places

Dante said, "The hottest places in Hell are reserved for those who, in a period of moral crisis, maintain their neutrality."

We cannot be neutral about the destiny-determining question: "What shall I do then with Jesus which is called Christ?" (Matt. 27:22).

What will you do with Jesus?
Neutral you cannot be!
Someday your heart will be asking:
"What will He do with me?"

* * * *

Alone

One of the saddest and most touching scenes is the painting of Christ before Pilate—standing solitarily, though serenely. Ineffable tenderness, goodness and kindness radiate from His face. It is said that some, after gazing fixedly upon the painting, have exclaimed: "My Lord and my God!"

It was alone the Saviour stood
In Pilate's judgment hall;
Alone the crown of thorns He wore,
Forsaken thus by all!

Can you reject such matchless love?
Can you His claim disown?
Come, give your all in gratitude,
Nor leave Him thus alone.

* * * *

One Thing Can't Be Given

Patrick Henry said, "I have now disposed of all my property to my family. There is one thing more I wish I could give them—the Christian religion. If they had that, and I had not given them one shilling, they would be rich; and if they had not that, and I had given them all the world, they would be poor."

* * * *

Go Home. Decide Later

One Sunday night in Chicago, as Moody concluded a sermon on the text, "What shall I do then with Jesus?" (Matt. 27:22), he said to the audience, "Now I want you to go home. Come back next Sunday, and decide what you will do with Jesus."

That was the night of the great Chicago fire! Some of those who perished in the holocaust were in Moody's audience!

Later Moody said regretfully, "I learned one lesson from that night that I've never forgotten. Now when I witness, I press Christ upon people then and there. I try to bring them to a decision on the spot. I would rather have my right hand cut off than give an audience or a person a week to decide what they will do with Jesus."

Now is the only time we may have! The Bible warns, "Now is the accepted time; behold, now is the day of salvation" (II Cor. 6:2). Later may be too late! It was too late for the five foolish virgins: "Lord, Lord, open to us. But he answered and said...I know you not" (Matt. 25:11,12).

* * * *

CHRISTIAN LIVING

Victorious Living

Live as if Christ died yesterday, arose this morning, and is coming back today!

* * * *

Whose Memory Is a Benediction

One has said, "He has achieved success who has lived well, gained the respect of intelligent men, the love of little children, filled his niche and accomplished his task, left the world better than he found it, whether by an improved poppy, a perfect poem or a rescued soul; never lacked appreciation of earth's beauty or failed to express it; always looked for the best in others and given the best in service; whose life was an inspiration and memory a benediction."

The Bible says, "The memory of the just is blessed: but the name of the wicked shall rot" (Prov. 10:7).

* * * *

Converted in a Dream

An actress said to Roland Hill, "I was converted in a dream." Hill answered, "Now that you were converted in your sleep, others will observe how you walk when you are awake."

* * * *

Shame

Warren Wiersbe said, "There are some men who preach so well when in the pulpit that it is a shame they should ever come out of it. When they are out of it, they live so badly that it is a shame they would ever enter it."

"*Be ye clean, that bear the vessels of the Lord.*"—Isa. 52:11.

* * * *

Christlikeness Needed

A hard-working missionary in India said to a Hindu friend, "I've been in India for twenty years and in all that time I've won only a handful of converts. What is the trouble?"

The Hindu replied, "Live like Jesus Christ, and you'll have all India at your feet tomorrow!"

The Hindu's statement, though manifestly incorrect, should challenge all God's children to Christlikeness in word and deed.

Today many others are saying, often mutely, "We would see Jesus" (John 12:21).

* * * *

So to Live Is Heaven

Ah, may we join that choir invisible of those immortal dead who live again in minds made better by their presence; live in deeds of daring rectitude; in scorn of miserable aims which end in self; in thoughts sublime which pierce the night like stars and with their mild persistence urge man's search for vaster issues. So to live is Heaven!

George Eliot.

* * * *

"We Shall Be Changed" (I Cor. 15:52)

To live above with the saints we
    love,
Ah, that will be glory!
To live below with the saints we
    know,
Well, that's a different story.

* * * *

THE CHRIST INSTEAD

Not merely in the words you say,

Not merely in the deeds expressed,
But in the most unconscious way
   Is Christ confessed.

Was it a beatific smile?
   A holy light upon your brow?
Oh, no! I felt His presence, while
   You smiled just now.

To me 'twas not the truth you taught,
   To you so clear, to me still dim;
But when you came to me, you brought
   A sense of Him.

And from your eyes He beckoned me,
   And from your heart His love was shed,
Till I lost sight of you, and saw
   The Christ instead.

* * * *

"Easy to Be Entreated"

In a prayer in the U. S. Senate, Peter Marshall pled, "O God, when we are wrong, make us easy to change. When we are right, make us easy to live with!"

"But the wisdom...from above is . . .easy to be entreated."—Jas. 3:17.

* * * *

Beyond the Rat Race

Arthur G. Gish said in *Beyond the Rat Race,* "Exciting possibilities lie in dropping out of the consumer rat race and experimenting with new styles of living. The good life consists not of getting a larger piece of the rotten consumer pie, but in baking a new pie. Don't just *talk* about the way life should be. Begin to *live* that life *now* and demonstrate what can be done."

Nothing is to be rejected per se

because it is old: "Stand ye in the ways, and see, and ask for the old paths, where is the good way, and walk therein, and ye shall find rest for your souls" (Jer. 6:16).

Nothing is to be rejected per se because it is new: "Every scribe which is instructed unto the kingdom of heaven...bringeth forth out of his treasure things new and old" (Matt. 13:52).

"Prove all things; hold fast that which is good."—I Thess. 5:21.

* * * *

Good Advice—Bad Example

How confusing it is for someone to give good advice while setting a bad example!

I'd rather see a sermon
   Than hear one any day;
I'd rather one would walk with me,
   Than merely show the way.

The eye is a more ready pupil,
   And more willing than the ear;
Good advice is often confusing,
   But example is always clear.

* * * *

Spiritual Exercise

Writing in *Sport,* Dr. Wildor Hollman of Hamburg, West Germany, declared: "Males who do not practice any kind of sport have lost on an average one-third of their former performance capacity of heart and circulation by the time they reach the age of 55. On the other hand, physically trained persons between 50 and 60 years old are as fit as the average person between 20 and 30 who takes no physical exercise."

To maintain bodily health, physical exercise is a must. Spiritual exercise—prayer, the study of God's Word, church worship—is essential to maintain spiritual health: "Exercise thyself...unto godliness. For bodily exercise profiteth little: but godliness is profitable unto all things, having promise of the life that now is, and of that which is to come" (I Tim. 4:7,8).

* * * *

When Under Fire

A minister asked a big sergeant of a Highland regiment, "What led you to become a Christian?"

His reply was, "There was a private in our company who was converted in Malta before our regiment came to Egypt. We gave that fellow an awful time. One night he came in from sentry duty tired and wet. Before going to bed, he knelt to pray. I whammed him on the side of his head with my muddy boots! He kept on praying, however. Next morning I found my boots beautifully polished by the side of my bed. That was his reply to me. It broke my heart, and I was saved that day!"

How we react when under fire either furthers or fetters the Gospel. It is written of the Saviour: "Who, when he was reviled, reviled not again; when he suffered, he threatened not" (I Pet. 2:23).

* * * *

"I Want to Be Like Christ"

During a fierce battle in World War II, a shell exploded near a soldier, sending fragments of sharp, hot metal in every direction! The face of the soldier was horribly lacerated and burned. He was flown to a veteran's hospital in the United States.

There the soldier's wounds healed satisfactorily, but his facial features were badly distorted.

One day a plastic surgeon, a Christian, said, "I believe that I can restore your features to their former likeness. Do you have a photograph of yourself which I can follow in my effort?"

The soldier replied, "Sir, I was never handsome." Then he chanced to see on the wall of the surgeon's office Warner Sallman's picture of Christ. Said he, "Sir, I would like to look like that man."

The plastic surgeon did his best. After the soldier's "new" face was completely healed, he came to thank the skillful surgeon for what he had done. Looking at Sallman's picture of Christ hanging on the wall, he stated, "Sir, my face now looks so much like his. Who is the man?"

"That is a picture of Jesus Christ," replied the surgeon.

The soldier said, "I have heard good things about Him, but I do not know much about Him. I would like to be like Him."

Giving the soldier a New Testament, the medic said, "Read this little book. It will help you to get better acquainted with Him."

The soldier read the Book and was deeply impressed. Soon he received the Saviour into his heart.

Going to the one who had given him Christlike features in his face, he joyfully exclaimed, *"Now that I look like Christ, I will do my very best to live like Him!"*

Shouldn't this be the undeviating purpose of each one of us who has experienced Christ's transforming, saving power?

"But we all, with open face beholding as in a glass the glory of the Lord, are changed into the same image from glory to glory, even as by the Spirit of the Lord."—II Cor. 3:18.

Told by Ralph M. Smith.

* * * *

The World's Largest Room

An earnest young man from the University Extension Service called upon a nonprogressive farmer and did his best to interest him in a new book on soil conservation and new methods in agriculture. "Would you like to buy the book?" asked the young man, as he concluded his talk.

The farmer drawled, "Son, I don't farm half as good as I know how already!"

The largest room in the world is the room for improvement. Most of us *know* better than we *do*. It is better not to know than to know and not do: "For it had been better for them not to have known the way of righteousness, than, after they have known it, to turn from the holy commandment delivered unto them" (II Pet. 2:21).

* * * *

THE SUM OF HUMAN HAPPINESS

Not what we have, but what we use;
Not what we see, but what we choose;
Not what seems fair, but what is true;
Not what we dream, but what we do;
Not what we take, but what we give;

Not as we pray, but as we live—
These are the things that mar or bless,
The sum of human happiness.

Mrs. I. Whitson

* * * *

The Peg-Legged Confederate Veteran

In his earlier years, R. E. Neighbour frequently preached against the card, the theatre and the dance. At the conclusion of one such message, he gave an invitation for all who would renounce these three things to come forward and show their intention.

The first one to respond to the invitation was a peg-legged Confederate veteran who said he would give up dancing!

The Bible says, "And now also the axe is laid unto the root of the trees: every tree...which bringeth not forth good fruit is hewn down, and cast into the fire" (Luke 3:9).

When our heart is right with God, we will seek to do only those things which bring honor to Him "that in all things he [Christ] might have the preeminence" (Col. 1:18).

The Christian life doesn't consist of our lopping off a twig of evil here, and a branch there. It consists of Christ changing the heart—the source of evil. The Bible says, "For from within, out of the heart of men, proceed evil thoughts, adulteries, fornications, murders, Thefts, covetousness, wickedness, deceit. . .pride" (Mark 7:21,22).

* * * *

"Little Christs"

The early followers of Christ were called Christians—"little Christs."

The Apostle Paul said, "For to me to live is Christ" (Phil. 1:21). Exultingly he exclaimed, "Christ liveth in me" (Gal. 2:20).

Christians should be Christlike in word and deed.

There is a great difference between being a nominal Christian and a Christlike Christian.

Our undeviating desire should be to let others see the beauty of Jesus in us. When that happens, the words said of Peter and John may be said of us: "They took knowledge of them that they had been with Jesus" (Acts 4:13).

Let the beauty of Jesus be seen in me,
All His wonderful passion and purity;
O Thou Spirit divine, All my nature refine,
Till the beauty of Jesus be seen in me.

Albert Orsborn.

* * * *

CHRISTMAS

A Christmas Prayer

O Lord, help me to survive this holiday week! Keep me from nibbling on all the ingredients as I prepare this festive meal. Stop me from continuing to taste-test the stuffing long after I know it is seasoned correctly. Help me to remember that onion dip is only an appetizer and that soon I will be eating a full meal. Keep me from using bleu cheese dressing on my salad instead of diet French.

Let me remember that although mushrooms have little or no caloric value, the gravy they are floating in does. Guide my hand away from the butter that I would like to glob on the vegetables. Allow me to admit I know that an average yam has more calories than a medium-sized baked potato, and that a third of a cup of cranberry sauce is more fattening than both of them combined.

Prevent me from forcing down a piece of pumpkin pie when I am already filled beyond belief. And if I don't heed the message, don't let me put whipped cream on top. Guide my feet away from the refrigerator in the days that follow, that I may not repeat the sins of my weak will with the leftovers.

Ruth Rosenfeld in
The Austin-American Statesman.

* * * *

What Silenced the Guns?

A day was dawning on a battlefield in France during World War II. The fog was so dense no one could see but a short distance from the trenches. During the night the Germans had drawn back their lines a little and the French soldiers had gone forward a few yards. Between the two positions a lonely farmhouse was still standing.

As the sun came up, heavy guns began to boom. But suddenly both sides ceased firing, and a strange silence ensued. Here's why: On the intervening green meadow, a little baby was seen crawling on its hands and knees. He seemed perfectly happy as he clutched a dandelion!

Long ago a Baby came into our warring world to bring peace to men and nations. What a change His coming wrought! William Lecky, the astute Irish historian and essayist, said, "The three short years of the public ministry of Jesus have done more to soften and regenerate mankind than all the moralizing of all the moralists and all the philosophizing of all the philosophers since the world began!"

* * * *

CHRISTMAS WON'T BE GONE

Presents lie beneath our tree,
  Waiting for the dawn,
When they all have been unwrapped,
  Christmas won't be gone!

Still its joy will fill the air,
  Singing near and far,
Gentle as a flake of snow,
  Radiant as a star!

Lois Duncan
in Home Life.

* * * *

THE STAR ROAD

The star road is the fairest road
  That we may ever follow,
It winds as sweetly as a song
  Through desert and through hollow.
It leads us to high mountain peaks,
  And into promised lands,
And, at its end, a Baby sleeps
  With tiny, outflung hands.

The star road is the straightest road,
  Although it climbs and dips,

There always is a garden spot,
  A spring for dry, parched lips.
There is always a bit of shade
  When midday gilds the skies,
And, at the end, a mother stands
  With wonder in her eyes!

Oh, we who follow in the path,
  That starlight has made bright,
Need never fear the crash of storms,
  The tumult of the night.
For through the crowding centuries,
  The angel voices call,
And, at the end, the manger waits,
  A haven for us all.

Margaret E. Sangster.

* * * *

Reflective Joy

I feel the influence of the season beaming into my soul from the happy looks of those around me. Surely happiness is reflective, like the light of Heaven; and every countenance, bright with smiles and glowing with innocent enjoyment, is a mirror transmitting to others the rays of a supreme and everlasting benevolence.

Washington Irving.

* * * *

What He Wanted Most

During World War II, in a home where the father was away in the army, a mother asked her little boy, "What would you like to have more than anything for Christmas?"

The boy looked at a picture of his dad dressed in his military uniform and said, "I would like for Daddy to step out of that picture and be home with us for Christmas!"

That's exactly what the Saviour did some 2000 years ago. He stepped forth from the images and mental pictures men had of God, and showed the world what God is like: "And the Word was made flesh, and dwelt among us, (and we beheld his glory, the glory as of the only begotten of the Father,) full of grace and truth" (John 1:14).

Adapted from *Home Life*.

* * * *

UNSPEAKABLY PRECIOUS

No other gift can e'er compare,
Nor was there ever gift so fair;
Yet, here's a Gift we all may share:
"His unspeakably precious Gift!"

From Heaven afar this Gift was sent,
A sacrifice for sin 'twas meant;
It spoke to earth of God's intent:
"His unspeakably precious Gift!"

"Unspeakable—no tongue can tell,
So precious—without parallel;
'Tis Christ, the Lord Immanuel,
"God's unspeakably precious
Gift!"

Author unknown.

* * * *

No Mail Route to Heaven

Julianne Holland, age 13, wanted to do her part for Jesus at Christmas. She addressed her letter about Jesus to the local post office. It went to the desk of Donald L. Orner, director of customer services at the postal center in Harrisburg, Pennsylvania. Julianne's letter said:

"Every Christmas people think about getting presents, getting together with friends and having a good time because Jesus was born. By being born He let love into the world, let blind people see, let crippled people walk.

"So for this Christmas, don't think about your presents. Just think about Jesus and all He did and try to spread the real spirit of Christmas!"

Orner replied to the letter, saying, "My Dear Julianne: We have no mail route to Heaven, but I am sure that Jesus is aware of what you wrote. He knows our thoughts and our feelings, and your beautiful letter flowed out across all the miles that no mailman could ever travel and touched His heart.

"Perhaps, too, Julianne, some of those who ask for presents are really asking for love, but to know that they are loved they need some *physical object* to show it. You said that your letter wouldn't get anywhere; but it touched my heart. Merry Christmas, and may God bless you!"

The Associated Press relayed Julianne's beautiful letter around the world. The *Los Angeles Times* featured it on the front page.

How great is the chain reaction of a loving thought!

Adapted from *Christianity Today*.

* * * *

CHURCH

"The Same Old Crowd!"

M. R. DeHaan often told a fable about a tavern owner's parrot. It conveys a searching message for every Christian.

The owner of the old tavern, which had operated for many years, sold it to a church group. Enthusiastically the church removed the bar, put in new lights, installed pews and refurbished the whole place. Then the doors were opened for the first worship service.

A parrot, belonging to the former owner, had unintentionally been left behind. The wise old bird sat on a rafter and watched the proceedings from his lofty perch.

When the minister entered, the parrot squawked, "New proprietor!"

As the robed choir marched in, he quipped, "New floor show!"

Then, as the parrot looked over the congregation, he dolefully said, "Same old crowd!"

The fable may elicit a smile, but its message cannot be overlooked. When people are converted, they become new creatures. They seek new associates. They enjoy the fellowship of a new crowd whose lives have been transformed by grace divine.

Long ago the psalmist said, "I am companion of all them that fear thee" (Ps. 119:63).

* * * *

A Closer Walk

A Christian wife, who yearned to know God in a more vital way, left her husband in a parking lot after a morning worship service and went back into the church. When she returned, her husband asked, "Why did you go back into the church?"

She replied, "I was trying to find God." Then she explained: "I just couldn't seem to feel God's presence or get through to Him in the midst of 'pomp and circumstance' and ceremony. So I went back and knelt alone in the prevailing silence and prayed, *If you are really here, God, reveal Thyself to me and give me a plenitude of peace and power!*"

Just a closer walk with Thee,
Grant it, Jesus, is my plea;
Daily walking close to Thee,
Let it be, dear Lord, let it be.
                                    Anon.

* * * *

PROGRAMMED PRECISELY

I often get the feeling
    As I'm seated so concisely,
That I'm fed to a computer,
    Which is programmed quite precisely.

As I scan the printed program,
    My instructions are quite clear:
Please be seated, or stand only
    Where the asterisks appear.

Sing one stanza, and remain standing,
    When the Scripture text is read;
Please retain the sacred elements
    As we break communion bread.

After benediction I'm ejected,
    Then, I pause and sigh a prayer:

Lord, I'm programmed, punched, and slotted,
Please don't spindle, fold, or tear!
Wilfred Martens.

* * * *

"Face Without Works Is Dead"

"Daddy, I want a watch so I can tell the time," pleaded little Jimmy.

"Very well, son, I'll get you a watch."

Going to a toy store, Daddy bought the watch. Jimmy was especially delighted because its face was very pretty.

Before Jimmy retired that night, he set the watch at eight o'clock and put it under his pillow.

The next day was Sunday, and the family usually got up at eight to get ready for Sunday school and church. When Jimmy awoke, he looked at his watch. It was eight o'clock. He leaped from his bed and ran downstairs. Seeing Mommy and Daddy sound asleep, he shouted, "Get up, sleepyheads! It's eight o'clock!"

Daddy looked at his wrist watch. It was only five o'clock! "Go back to bed, Jimmy. Your watch doesn't keep good time."

In the morning church service, the minister's text was, "Faith without works is dead." "Why, Daddy," whispered Jimmy, "he's preaching about my watch!"

"Your watch?" asked Father in surprise.

"Yes, Daddy. *Face* without works is dead!"

How like Jimmy's watch are some people. They put on a good face or front before people at church, but within them there is only spiritual deadness.
Alice Marie Knight.

* * * *

A Profound Truth in Simple Language

Edgar A. Guest expressed profound truth in simple language. He wrote of the church: "The church stands as a symbol of the finest aims and aspirations of the human heart. It has outlived persecution from without and open disloyalty from within. It has withstood bitter and unrelenting attacks of atheists and cynics of every age. It has outlived changing times of peace and war, prosperity and depression, and many fads and fancies.

"A church to me is the symbol of faith in the life eternal. It typifies decency, kindliness and fair dealing. It offers comfort to the sorrowing. With the Golden Rule it would make neighbors of all of us!"
Herschel H. Hobbs, in
Adult Life and Work Lessons.

* * * *

Burning Churches and Hearts

The Los Angeles Religious News Service affirmed, "Every five hours some church, synagogue or other religious building in the United States is destroyed by fire."

The physical destruction of religious buildings is deplorable. Spiritual rekindling of churches, however, is urgent. Churches need members with burning hearts, aglow with the love of God. This would revolutionize churches: "Did not our hearts burn within us, while he talked with us by the way, and while he opened to us the scriptures?" (Luke 24:32).

Set us afire, Lord, still us, we pray.
While the world perishes, we go our way.
Purposeless, passionless, day after day.
Set us afire, Lord, still us, we pray.

* * * *

A Plant in Corner of Heart

Oliver Wendell Holmes said, "There is a plant in the corner of my heart called *reverence,* and it needs watering at least once a week."

That's what the church is for!

"I was glad when they said unto me, Let us go into the house of the Lord."—Ps. 122:1.

* * * *

Any "Tate" Members in Your Church?

Lincoln Eng, rector of St. Bartholomew's Episcopal Church, Beaverton, Oregon, said in the monthly magazine of the Episcopal Diocese of Chicago that every church has a "Tate family."

"There is old man Dic Tate who wants to run everything in the church.

"Uncle Ro Tate wants to change everything.

"Sister Agi Tate stirs up trouble whenever possible. Her brother Irri Tate helps, too.

"Brother Hesi Tate and Sister Vege Tate pour cold water on any new proposals.

"Sister Imi Tate tries to have the church mimic everybody else.

"When the church budget is announced, Brother Devas Tate stands in the meeting and objects.

"Brother Poten Tate wants to be a big shot.

"But not all members of the Tate family are bad, for Brother Facili Tate is quite helpful, and Miss Felici Tate is a delightful member.

"What a joy to the pastor is Brother Cogi Tate and his twin brother Medi Tate!"

What kind of a Tate are *you*?

* * * *

Sleeping Pills

Someone has given this definition of a hospital: A place where they wake you to give you a sleeping pill!

It can be said of some churches: They are places where the command must often be given to sleeping, indifferent Christians: "Awake thou that sleepest...and Christ shall give thee light" (Eph. 5:14).

* * * *

They That Wait...

Leonard Ravenhill, the English evangelist, said, "The sickness of the church, I believe, is due to this: we have taught people to witness and to work, but we have not taught them to worship."

Too much is made of church activities, and too little of church passivity—unhurried waiting before God: "Be still, and know that I am God" (Ps. 46:10).

Only those who wait quietly and

receptively before God "renew their strength...and [do] not faint" (Isa. 40:31).

* * * *

Needless Millions for Psychiatrists

In addressing an audience in Oklahoma City, a psychologist stated: "Emotionally disturbed people spend millions of dollars annually to receive from psychiatrists what they could find in church for nothing."

Long ago the fearful, distraught psalmist said, "But as for me, my feet were almost gone; my steps had well nigh slipped. Until I went into the sanctuary of God; then understood I their end" (Ps. 73:2,17).

* * * *

All-Pervasive Death

As Charles Spurgeon stood in his pulpit one Sunday, he asked, "Have you ever read the *Ancient Mariner?*" Continuing, he said, "I daresay you thought it one of the strangest imaginations ever put together, especially that part where the mariner represents the corpses of all dead men rising up to man the ship—dead men pulling the rope, dead men steering, dead men spreading the sails. I thought what a strange idea that was!

"But I have lived to see it done! I have gone into churches where I have seen a dead man in the pulpit, dead men as deacons, and dead men sitting to hear!"

Long ago the all-knowing Saviour gave this appraisal of a church: "I know thy works, that thou hast a name that thou livest, and art dead" (Rev. 3:1).

* * * *

It Worked!

"When the church preaches morality, morals often decline. When the church preaches Christ crucified and risen, morality prevails," said J. Sidlow Baxter.

As Paul began his ministry in morally corrupt Corinth long ago, he "determined not to know any thing among [them], save Jesus Christ, and him crucified" (I Cor. 2:2).

His decision worked wonders! Later Paul wrote in a letter to Corinth: "Know ye not that the unrighteous shall not inherit the kingdom of God? . . .[nor] fornicators, nor idolaters, nor adulterers, nor effeminate, nor abusers of themselves with mankind, Nor thieves, nor covetous, nor drunkards, nor revilers, nor extortioners...And such were some of you: but ye are washed . . .sanctified. . .justified in the name of the Lord Jesus, and by the Spirit of our God" (I Cor. 6:9-11).

* * * *

An Unrecognized Fact

Said Rev. George H. Slavin, "The need of the church is a need that we do not recognize: We've backslidden. We will accept it in generalization, but we don't say, 'Woe is me! I have sinned!' "

Not until God's children penitently plead, "Create in me a clean heart, O God; and renew a right spirit within me" (Ps. 51:10) will churches be revived and recapture their erstwhile zeal for perishing ones: "Oh that my head were waters, and mine eyes a fountain of tears, that I might weep day and night for the slain of the daughter of my people" (Jer. 9:1).

* * * *

Fiddlesticks

In his message to the Southern Baptist Convention, retiring president Carl E. Bates told this story:

"Colin Morris, a missionary to Zambia, told of a native who was found dead of starvation not a hundred yards from the missionary compound. An autopsy revealed that he had only a few leaves in his stomach and what appeared to be a ball of grass!

"Meanwhile, back home, the mission's sponsoring denomination was engaged in a bitter fight over what to do with the unused bread left after communion."

Human hunger, sorrow, and suffering must always be a primary concern of God's children if they would be like the Saviour whose loving heart was filled with compassion for the hungry, shepherdless multitudes: "I have compassion on the multitude, because they. . .have nothing to eat" (Mark 8:2).

"He was moved with compassion on them, because they fainted, and were scattered abroad, as sheep having no shepherd" (Matt. 9:36).

* * * *

"Be Still and Know"

In *Moody Monthly*, Bruce Shelley said, "If in the life of the church today we could call a halt to half our endeavors and devote the time to quietness, waiting (before God) and listening, we would gather again with hearts aflame with a burning enthusiasm. There would be a day of new activity and a new dynamic."

How spiritually impoverished, in our hurry, worry, bury day, are individuals and churches which fail to sustainedly obey the quieting, spirit-renewing directive, "Be still, and know that I am God" (Ps. 46:10).

* * * *

Religious Externals

A. W. Tozier said in *The Pursuit of God:*

"Every age has its own characteristics. Right now we are in the age of religious complexity. The simplicity which is in Christ is rarely found among us. In its stead are programs, methods, organizations, and a world of nervous activities which occupy time and attention but can never satisfy the longing of the heart. The shallowness of our inner experiences, the hollowness of our worship, and that servile imitation of the world which marks our promotional methods—all testify that we in this day know God only imperfectly, and the peace of God scarcely at all.

"If we would find God amid all the religious externals, we must first determine to find Him, and then proceed in the way of simplicity. Now as always God reveals Himself to 'babes' and hides Himself in thick darkness from the wise and prudent: 'I thank thee, O Father, Lord of heaven and earth, because thou hast hid these things from the wise and prudent, and hast revealed them unto babes. Even so, Father: for so it seemed good in thy sight' (Matt. 11:25,26). We must simplify our approach to God!"

With deep, solicitous concern for the Corinthian Christians, Paul warned, "But I fear, lest by any means, as the serpent beguiled Eve through his subtilty, so your minds should be corrupted from the simplicity that is in Christ Jesus" (II Cor. 11:3).

To do thy will is more than praise,
    As words are less than deeds;
The simplest trust can find Thy ways,
    We miss with chart of creeds.
                    Whittier.

* * * *

Change and Decay

After centuries of slow disintegration, the Colosseum, one of ancient Rome's most spectacular monuments, is succumbing to the assaults of auto fumes, heavy traffic vibrations and industrial pollution. The historic arena has been partially closed to protect sightseers from chunks of falling masonry.

A legend of the Middle Ages affirms that when the Colosseum falls, the world will fall!

The gnawing tooth of time inevitably reduces man-made structures to rubble. However, the passing centuries cannot erode Christ's

church, the spiritual structure which the Saviour founded upon Himself. It is composed not of stone and mortar, but of "living stones"—born-again men, women, boys and girls.

Jesus said, "Upon this rock I will build my church; and the gates of hell shall not prevail against it" (Matt. 16:18).

The church's one foundation
    Is Jesus Christ her Lord;
She is His new creation
    By Spirit and the Word:
From Heaven He came and sought her
    To be His holy bride;
With His own blood He bought her,
    And for her life He died.
                    Samuel J. Stone.

* * * *

Why Shortchange Yourself?

Martin Luther said, "To gather with God's people in united adoration of the Father is as necessary to the Christian life as prayer."

When a Christian habitually absents himself without cause from fellowship with Christians "of like precious faith," spiritual poverty ensues. He becomes cold, critical and unbelieving:

"But Thomas, one of the twelve... was not with them when Jesus came. The other disciples...said...We have seen the Lord. But he said...Except I shall see in his hands the print of the nails...I will not believe" (John 20:24,25).

* * * *

An Awesome Miscarriage

In an awesome miscarriage of

nature sometime ago in Tucuman, Argentina, a two-headed baby boy was born!

Dr. Paul J. Schwan said the heads acted independently, but that the torso had only one set of internal organs. Both heads were well-formed and the baby could be fed through either mouth!

There is only *one head* of the church which Jesus Christ founded: God "set him at his own right hand... Far above all principalities, and power, and might, and dominion... and gave him to be the head over all things to the church, Which is his body, the fulness of him that filleth all in all" (Eph. 1:20-23).

* * * *

Not Out but Up

"Recently a group of clergymen attended a denominational 'refresher course' in Kansas City," reported *Decision*. "They listened to a series of radical speakers, one of whom, after ridiculing what he considered the 'ineptness' of local congregations in dealing with social issues, told the ministers, 'If I were you, I would go home and burn down my church!' The Apostle Paul had a better idea. He wrote to Timothy, Build a fire under the gift of God that is within you (cf. II Tim. 1:6).

"The church on fire can work marvels! But if the fire is doused by unbelief, the church can hardly pay its bills. The spiritual flame that kindles the church does not flicker and die because of lack of fuel, but rather because it is smothered. Such fire,

given a chance, is like the burning bush that Moses saw in the desert—*arderet et non combureretur*—it burns without being consumed!"

Most ministers need to be fired—not *out* but *up!*

* * * *

The Personally Present Corpse

Robert McCracken of Riverside Church, New York, told a story about a minister who made this announcement one Sunday morning: "The funeral of John Doe will be held in this church tomorrow at 3 o'clock. Mr. Doe will be here for the first time in ten years!"

Christians shortchange themselves when they habitually absent themselves from God's house without cause.

"And let us consider one another to provoke unto love and to good works: Not forsaking the assembling of ourselves together, as the manner of some is; but exhorting one another: and so much the more as ye see the day approaching."—Heb. 10:24,25.

* * * *

Leprosy's Spawning Place

William Cowper wrote:

When nations are to perish in their sins, 'Tis in the church the leprosy begins.

God gave this command to His ancient people: "Be ye clean, that bear the vessels of the Lord" (Isa. 52:11).

* * * *

Bite and Devour

In *Music Man,* a song says that people in Iowa can "stand nose to nose for days and days and never see eye to eye!"

This is true of God's children in churches where the atmosphere is surcharged with "envy, strife and division."

The Bible warns, "But if ye bite and devour one another, take heed that ye be not consumed one of another" (Gal. 5:15). And, "Behold, how good and how pleasant it is for brethren to dwell together in unity" (Ps. 133:1).

* * * *

The New Song Church

An inmate of the federal penitentiary in Atlanta calls himself the bishop of the "Church of the New Song." He has won a court battle to allow himself and his congregation to practice their religion.

When anyone is transformed by the grace of God, he becomes a "new creature" in Christ Jesus, and he can joyously exclaim, "He brought me up also out of an horrible pit. . . . And he hath put a new song in my mouth,

even praise unto our God" (Ps. 40:2,3).

* * * *

Football: Our Nation's New Religion

Carl Rowan, columnist for *Field Enterprises,* described professional football as our nation's new Sunday religion. "It is, in truth, a microcosm of what the whole society could be like if only people were as devotedly religious about the rest of life as they are about football."

Hundreds of thousands make football their choice every Sunday from September into January. It gets the priority. A few ease their conscience by rushing from an early church service to the stadium.

But Sunday football is not alone in having pushed the church to the sidelines. Golf and a dozen other sports have their loyal following and it is "business as usual" for many grocery stores, novelty stores and others.

Point the finger of guilt in all directions. Be sure it comes back to stop at the line of customers. Recognize them?

The Baptist Standard.

* * * *

CIGARETTES
(See also Drugs)

"Why Will Ye Die?"

Said Dr. William Foege, director of the U. S. Center for Disease Control, "More than 1,000 premature deaths

per day are connected with cigarette smoking. We've accepted cigarette smoking, which is a cruel epidemic much worse than infectious disease!"

* * * *

No. 1 Cancer Killer

The American Cancer Society reports:

"Lung cancer has become the third major cancer killer of American women, underscoring the risk of smoking.

"Smoking habits are established in the teens, and in the great majority of cases, teenage girl-smokers will become adult women-smokers. Formerly, girls have never smoked to the extent teenage boys did, but now they have caught up with them.

"Lung cancer remains the leading cancer-killer among men, with a mortality range that has increased twenty times in forty years."

Adapted from
The Austin-American Statesman

* * * *

Disastrous Sidestream

Dr. Joseph B. Stocklen, President of the American Lung Association, said, "There is *four times* as much carbon monoxide in sidestream smoke from the burning end of a cigarette than in the mainstream smoke which is inhaled by the smoker."

* * * *

"Why Will Ye Die?"

Dr. Neil Soloman affirmed, "More than eighty percent of all lung cancer, as well as fifty percent of all bladder cancer, could be prevented if people simply stopped smoking."

The question is still pertinent: "Why will ye die?" (Ezek. 18:31).

* * * *

"Climbing at a Rapid Pace!"

Dr. Arthur Holleb, Senior Vice President for Medical Affairs of the American Cancer Society, said, "The rate of lung cancer among American women is climbing at such a rapid pace that it will soon overtake heart failure as the No. 1 cause of death!"

* * * *

When the Mountain Smoked

In "Back Talk" in *Christian Herald*, one wrote, "I used to attend church regularly. I suffered through smoke-filled board meetings, circle groups and church dinners without complaint. But when the air of the Bible study group became murky with cigarette smoke, I decided to give a rather strained, though serviceable, interpretation to Exodus 20:18, "And all the people saw the . . .mountain smoking: and when the people saw it, they removed, and stood afar off."

* * * *

Preventable Cause of Death

J. Dudley Youman, M.D., said, "Cancer of the lung is expected to be the number one cause of cancer death in women by 1985. Smoking related cancer of the lung is now the number one *preventable* cause of death in the United States. In a recent check of Austin, Texas, hospitals, there were twelve persons dying from smoking-related cancer! The hazards of smoking cigarettes include not only cancer but also risks to pregnancies, chronic lung disease, shorter life, bad breath, and, not the least, addiction to a powerful chemical—nicotine!"

* * * *

Needed: Gas Masks

Dr. Otto A. Olson, Jr., is president of the Central Canada Synod of the Lutheran Church and also a member of the Executive Council. One day, in attending a meeting of the Council, he donned a gas mask to emphasize his displeasure in inhaling cigarette smoke. Dr. Olson explained: "The gas mask was a Christmas gift from my son who heard me complain of the smoke at a recent meeting."

One characteristic of a lady or gentleman is a high regard for the likes and dislikes of others.

* * * *

Do You Know. . . .

That smoking is the chief cause of chronic bronchitis and lung cancer? That smoking speeds up your heartbeat?

The minute you stop smoking your body goes to work to repair the damage. Your cough will lessen or disappear, and you will breathe easier. Your circulation will improve, and so will your sense of taste and smell. Your heart and lungs will have a chance to defend themselves.

Kick the habit. It's a matter of life and breath!

* * * *

Put Out of Business

In addressing the Senate Juris-prudence Committee (Texas), Dr. Jim H. Calhoun, a surgeon, said, "Air pollution in a cigarette-smoke-filled office or conference room is higher than the levels at which industry in smog-troubled Los Angeles is shut down. Smoking is a main factor in most heart and lung diseases. If smoking were discontinued altogether, I would be put out of business!"

* * * *

"You Smoke, I Chew"

Bill Pinson told of a nonsmoker on an airplane who was greatly annoyed by the smoking passenger seated next to him who persisted in blowing large quantities of smoke in his direction. The nonsmoker pulled a card from his billfold and handed it to the smoker. Printed on the card were beautifully engraved words: "I see you smoke. I chew. Don't blow your smoke on me and I won't spit on you!"

Civil, courteous people show a high regard for the rights and feelings of others. "Be courteous" (I Pet. 3:8).

* * * *

Peril to Nonsmokers

Recent experiments at Texas A & M University indicate that thirty minutes in a smoke-filled room significantly increases the non-smoker's heart rate, blood pressure and the amount of carbon monoxide in his blood.

A team of researchers at the University of Cincinnati Medical Center reported that smoke drifting from the burning ends of cigarettes and cigars contains cadmium which definitely is harmful when inhaled by onlookers.

Another research team at Wayne State University in Detroit found that acute illness, mostly respiratory, was twice as prevalent among young children whose parents smoked at home than among children whose parents did not smoke at home.

* * * *

CONFESSION OF SIN

Make Amends

Grant Smith, a British detective, planted drugs and other evidence on four men in 1969 to enhance his promotion. All four were convicted. Later Smith confessed his sin and the convicted ones were cleared of all guilt.

Telling why he confessed his wrong, Smith said, "I want to be totally committed to Christ. I know I cannot do that until I have come to terms with my fellowmen."

We cannot be right with God if it is possible for us to make amends for wrongs we have done and to others and fail to do it. "First be reconciled to thy brother, and then come and offer thy gift" (Matt. 5:24).

* * * *

It's Much Easier

to say, "We have sinned" than to say, "I have sinned," and penitently confess, "Against thee, thee only, have I sinned, and done this evil in thy sight" (Ps. 51:4).

If we want our sins to be covered, we must uncover them before God: "He that covereth his sins shall not prosper: but whoso confesseth and forsaketh them shall have mercy" (Prov. 28:13).

* * * *

As God Sees Us

Tennyson said,

Oh, that a man may die in me,
That the man I am may cease to be.

When we see ourselves as God sees us, we say with the ancient prophet, "Woe is me! for I am undone; because I am a man of unclean lips. . .for mine eyes have seen the King" (Isa. 6:5).

* * * *

Americans Are Forgiving

A national leader tells of being invited into former President Nixon's office almost a year before his resignation. The President asked him and others gathered what they thought he should do about Watergate.

The man, a Christian, says that he told the President that the American people are very forgiving. "Even at this date, if you went to them and said, 'I did wrong. I'm very sorry. Please forgive me,' they would do it."

The President listened, then

turned to the next person for his suggestion.

How difficult it is for most of us to say, "I have sinned!"

* * * *

"It's Me! It's Me, O Lord!"

In a prayer in the U. S. Senate, Peter Marshall, a former chaplain, said, "Our Father, we are beginning to understand at last that the things that are wrong with our world are the sum total of all the things that are wrong with us as individuals!"

What would happen if even an appreciable number of us would penitently plead, "Create in me a clean heart, O God; and renew a right spirit within me" (Ps. 51:10)?

* * * *

Don't Underplay Wrongdoing

In commenting on the verse, "I will restore to you the years that the locust hath eaten" (Joel 2:25), Catherine Marshall said:

"Our part in this restoration is to look squarely at the place where we got off the track and have the courage not to minimize our sin or to blame it on anybody but ourselves. The reason we must not underplay wrongdoing is that the price of setting it right came high—even to God Himself. He knew that at a given point in history, Christ Jesus would die on a cross and, by the shedding of His blood, make possible the Father's forgiveness of you and me—past, present, and future."

Great spiritual blessings would come to our spiritually impoverished churches if more of us were confessing our sins and penitently pleading, "Create in me a clean heart, O God; and renew a right spirit within me" (Ps. 51:10).

* * * *

The Heaviest Burden

A deeply distressed Christian man entered a doctor's office and said, "I greatly need your help! I can't sleep! I can't eat!"

After thoroughly examining the man, the doctor stated, "I am unable to find anything physically wrong. Manifestly you are emotionally disturbed." The Christian doctor then asked, "Is there something you have done wrong that is hurting your conscience?"

The man replied heatedly, "I didn't come here for a sermon!" and stomped out of the office.

Later he returned and apologetically said, "Your question revealed my trouble. I defrauded a friend out of $100 and I can't forget it. What must I do?"

"Write a letter to your friend, confess the wrong and enclose a check for the $100."

After he had followed the doctor's instructions, peace came. In getting right with the defrauded one, he got right with God. "That was the heaviest burden I ever dropped!" he told the medic.

Long ago David had a similar experience. He sinned grievously and he was emotionally and physically distressed as long as his sin went unconfessed. "When I kept silence, my bones waxed old through my roaring all the day long. For day and night thy hand was heavy upon me . . .I acknowledged my sin unto thee . . .and thou forgavest. . .my sin" (Ps. 32:3-5).

* * * *

CONSCIENCE

To Feel No Pain

In his column on *Better Living,* Malcolm Nygren said, "To feel no pain would be very dangerous. You could cut off a finger or char your flesh without noticing it. It is just as dangerous to feel no pain in your conscience. That kind of pain is a warning, too. A tender conscience is as vital as a fire alarm, and you need it a lot more often."

How imperiled is the individual who has sinned so long against his conscience that it no longer disturbs him. And how wise are those who so live as "to have always a conscience void of offence toward God, and toward men" (Acts 24:16).

* * * *

Nagging Consequences of Bad Memories!

Clyde Narramore said:
"As a psychologist, having had the privilege of working with many people through the years, let me assure you that there is certainly a case for personal purity!

"First of all, it has to do with one's memory. Someone has said that life is a book of memories. This is true. And memory is the mirror that reflects the past. Who knows the nagging conse-quences of bad memories! A person may stand in the choir and even while he sings a beautiful anthem, memory will tune his mind to some vulgar moments in his life!

"How many parishioners sit in church hearing a tremendous challenge from the pulpit, then—all unbidden—their thoughts flash to sordid scenes in their past! Personal impurity soils the present, casts a shadow on the future, and brings remorse as you think about the past!"

The Bible tells of a lost soul, in the place of anguish, who pleaded for mercy too late and was adjured: "Son, remember" (Luke 16:25).

* * * *

Only Yapping of Puppy

After hearing a searching sermon on restitution by Duncan Campbell, an Irish farmer said to him, "When you preached, all I could hear was the yapping of a puppy!"

"Yapping of a puppy?" asked Campbell with a quizzical look.

"Yes," continued the farmer. "The yapping was in my memory. Years ago, when I was a lad, I stole a puppy from a farmer. I took it across the border and sold it for five pounds. The farmer is now dead, but I must go to the widow and pay her the five pounds with due interest!"

God requires us to make amends for past misdeeds, so far as we are able to do it: "God requireth that which is past" (Eccles. 3:15).

Alice Marie Knight.

* * * *

CONSECRATION
(See also Will of God)

"NONE OF SELF AND ALL OF THEE!"

O the bitter pain and sorrow,
  That the time could ever be,
When I proudly said to Jesus,
  "All of self and none of Thee!"

But He sought me, I beheld Him
Dying on the accursed tree,
And my divided heart said faintly,
  "Some of self and some of Thee!"

Higher than the highest mountain,
  Deeper than the deepest sea;
Lord, Thy love at last has conquered,
  "None of self and *all of thee!*"

Anonymous.

* * * *

Signing Carte Blanche

Consecration is our signing carte blanche a blank sheet of paper and submissively asking God to inscribe thereon His perfect plan for our life: "Lord, what wilt thou have me to do?" (Acts 9:6).

* * * *

"We Are Yours! Do With Us What You Will!"

Some years ago there was a madman in Germany, Adolf Hitler, whose satanic purpose was the extermination of Jews and conquest of Europe.

As he concluded one of his fiery harangues before 100,000 youths, they stood en masse and said with one voice: "We are yours! Do with us what you will!"

What wouldn't happen if even an appreciable number of God's children would say to Jesus, "We are yours! Do with us what you will!"?

* * * *

Have You Counted the Cost?

After years of self-giving service in Africa, David Livingstone returned to England and lectured in different universities. What a pathetic object he was. Emaciated by African fevers, he weighed less than eighty pounds. His arm, torn and fragmented by a lion, hung limp at his side.

At the conclusion of a challenging message, a student approached him and said, "Dr. Livingstone, I want what you have! I would give my life—everything—to have it!"

Dr. Livingstone replied, "That's what it cost me!"

Truly he could say with Paul, "Christ Jesus my Lord: for whom I have suffered the loss of all things" (Phil. 3:8).

* * * *

Willing to Be Made Willing

In the mind of God it was not primarily the sacrifice of Isaac as much as it was the sacrifice of Abraham—the total dedication of himself, his plans, his ambitions— that was expressed in Abraham's willingness to sacrifice his only son, his willingness to do what the heathen nations did for their gods in the sacrifice of their firstborn.

* * * *

What Consecration Isn't

Consecration is not our giving anything to God. It is our taking our hands off of what already belongs to God: ". . .ye are not your own. . .ye are bought with a price. . .glorify God in your body, and in your spirit, which are God's" (I Cor. 6:19,20).

* * * *

"LIVE AND LOVE THROUGH ME"

For compassion, Lord, I pray,
For zeal to do my best each day,
For strength to battle for the right,
For hope that shines through starless
  night,
For faith to always carry on
And keep within my heart a song;
For Christlike love for all I meet,
For power to lift those in defeat,
For a will committed unto Thee:
Lord, live and love and work through
  me.

Bernie Nether Milam.

* * * *

Total Dedication

Fritz Kreisler, the renowned violinist, played *Danny Boy* before a large audience. At its conclusion, the people stood en masse and applauded uproarously.

Kreisler disclosed the secret of his mastery of the violin. He said that over the years, other things—some good, some marginal—sought to distract him from the strait and narrow way of total dedication to his violin, but he undeviatingly forged ahead.

To obtain excellence in any field of human endeavor, the way is strait and narrow, entailing total dedication, sacrifice and self-discipline. Many miss the opportunity and satisfaction of praiseworthy achievement by their failure to give themselves fully to developing God-given talents.

The Saviour said, "Enter ye in at the strait [narrow] gate. . .strait is the gate, and narrow is the way, which leadeth unto life, and few there be that find it" (Matt. 7:13,14).

Our abundant entrance into God's kingdom entails dedication and self-discipline: "But I keep under my body, and bring it into subjection" (I Cor. 9:27); ". . .we must through much tribulation enter into the kingdom of God" (Acts 14:22).

Give of your best to the Master;
  Give of the strength of your youth;
Throw your soul's fresh, glowing ardor
  Into the battle for truth!

* * * *

Withholding Nothing

Mstislav Rostropovich is acclaimed the world's greatest cellist. His dedication to his chosen instrument is *total*. *Newsweek* commented:

"There is an evangelical passion about Rostropovich that makes his concerts revivalist meetings. He plays with missionary zeal, glorifying music, teaching the gospel of the cello as if it were the instrument of salvation, giving to every work—from the grace of Haydn and the dignity of Elgar to the exhortation of Shostakovitch— the intensity and devotion of prayer."

God wants His people to give Him *total* dedication. He entreats us, "I beseech you. . .[to] present your bodies a living sacrifice, holy, acceptable unto God, which is your reasonable service" (Rom. 12:1).

I knelt in tears at the feet of Christ,
  In the hush of the twilight dim;
And all that I was, or hoped, or sought,
  I surrendered unto Him!

* * * *

A Christian

Ralph M. Smith gave this definition of a Christian: "A Christian is eyes through which God sees; a voice through which God speaks; hands by which God helps; and feet used of God to go forth with the character-changing Gospel of His saving grace."

* * * *

No Sacrifice Too Great

The motto of the missionary C. T. Studd was: "If Jesus Christ be God and died for me, there is no sacrifice too great for me to make for Him."

Can any of us say with the Apostle Paul: "Christ Jesus my Lord: for whom I have suffered the loss of all things" (Phil. 3:8)?

* * * *

"I'll Try to Be That Man"

When Dwight L. Moody was visiting England, he heard Henry Varley say, "The world has yet to see what God will do with a man who is fully and wholly consecrated to the Holy Spirit!"

Moody thought, *He said, "a man." He did not say, "a great man," nor "a learned man," nor "a rich man," but simply "a man." I am a man, and it lies within a man himself whether he will or will not make the entire and full consecration. I will try my utmost to be that man!*

* * * *

Total Surrender

After his conversion, B. H. Carroll, renowned exegete and founder of the Southwestern Baptist Seminary, Ft. Worth, Texas, wrote on the flyleaf of his Bible:

"Take my mind and let it think for Thee. Take my tongue and let it speak for Thee. Take my eyes and let them see for Thee. Take my hands and let them work for Thee. Take my feet and let them go for Thee. Take my heart and let it love for Thee, for I belong altogether to Thee!"

* * * *

What Would Jesus Do?

Charles M. Sheldon, author of *In His Steps,* wrote:

"What would be the result in this city if every church member should be a true disciple of Jesus and do as Jesus would do? What is the test of Christian discipleship? The test would be the same today as long ago: 'If any man will come after me, let him deny himself, and take up his cross, and follow me' (Matt. 16:24).

"I believe that Jesus would demand as close a following, as much suffering, as great self-denial, as when He lived in person on the earth and said, 'Whosoever he be of you that forsaketh not all that he hath, he cannot be my disciple'" (Luke 14:33).

Jesus, I my cross have taken,
All to leave, and follow Thee;
Destitute, despised, forsaken,
Thou, from hence, my all shalt be:
Perish ev'ry fond ambition,
All I've sought, and hoped, and known;
Yet how rich is my condition,
God and heav'n are still my own!

Henry F. Lyte.

* * * *

COURAGE

Good Horse Sense

Good horse sense knows how to say, "Nay!"

Daniel said it did: He "purposed in his heart that he would not defile himself with the portion of the king's meat, nor with the wine which he drank" (Dan. 1:8).

* * * *

"Allons! Forward!"

As General Ferdinand Foch, commander in chief of the Allied Armies in World War I, neared death, he seemed to envision his mighty army charging the enemy and being hurled back with great loss. With all the strength he could muster, he commanded, *"Allons! Allons!* Forward! Forward!" Then he entered death's portals.

In our encounter with mighty forces of evil and implacable foes, God's command to His children is, "Forward! Forward!"

* * * *

Niemoeller's Failure

Martin Niemoeller said, "In Germany, the Nazis came for the communists, and I didn't speak up because I was not a communist. Then they came for the Jews, and I didn't speak up because I was not a Jew. Then they came for the Trade Unionists, and I didn't speak up because I was not a Trade Unionist. Then they came for the Catholics, and I, a Protestant, didn't speak up. *Then they came for me!* By that time there was no one to speak up for anyone."

Dante said, "The hottest place in Hell is reserved for those who, in time of crisis, preserve their neutrality."

Though love repine and reason chafe,
There comes a voice without reply;

'Tis man's perdition to be safe,
When for the truth he ought to die.

* * * *

He Died/Lived for His Faith!

One asked Dwight L. Moody, "Would you be willing to die for Jesus Christ?" Moody lapsed into deep and heart-searching thought, then tearfully said, "Yes! If the situation ever arose, I would be willing to die for Jesus Christ!" Then he added, "I want you to know that it is often easier to *die* for Christ than to daily and sacrificially *live* for Him!"

So he died for his faith. That's fine,
More than most of us do!
But say, can you add to that line
That he lived for it, too?

It is easy to die. Men have died
For a wish or a whim,
From bravado, or passion, or pride,
Was it harder for him?

But to live—every day to live out
All the truth that he dreamt,
While friends met his conduct with doubt
And the world with scorn and contempt.

Was it thus that he plodded ahead,
Never turning aside?
Then we'll talk of the life he led,
Never mind how he died!

* * * *

"GOD, GIVE US MEN!"

God give us men! A time like this demands
Strong minds, great hearts, true faith and ready hands;
Men whom the lust of office does not kill;
Men whom the spoils of office cannot buy;

Men who possess opinions and a will;
Men who have honor—men who will not lie;
Men who can stand before a demagogue
And spurn his treacherous flatteries without winking;
Tall men, sun-crowned, who live above the fog
In public duty and in private thinking;
For while the rabble, with their thumb-worn creeds
Their large professions and their little deeds,
Mingle in selfish strife, lo! Freedom weeps,
Wrong rules the land, and waiting Justice sleeps.

Josiah Gilbert Holland, 1819-1881

* * * *

Unprotesting Protestants

On Reformation Sunday, a faithful pastor spoke these timely words:

"If Martin Luther and Zwingli were to rise from their graves, they would drive us from our churches and say to us: 'You are not Protestants at all. You only commemorate our protests. Do you not see that what we said in our times to a decadent church must be said *today*—not in the same words but in the same spirit? What we said must be thunderously iterated to a decadent society, dedicated to lust and grasping greed. Repent and turn to God. Put off your lukewarmness. Protest again, not against ancient ghosts, but against the enemies who dominate our age!'"

"*Cry aloud, spare not, lift up thy*

voice like a trumpet, and shew my people their transgressions, and. . . their sins."—Isa. 58:1.

* * * *

Hyman Appelman's Choice

An army officer became greatly interested in a young Jewish man. Inviting him to attend the Temple Baptist Church, Washington, D. C., with him, the Jew accepted and listened in wonderment as the minister proclaimed the all-glorious Gospel of God's love and power, so fully exemplified in the life, death and resurrection of Jesus Christ.

The young man was convicted of sin and accepted Christ as the long-promised Messiah whose coming fulfilled many Old Testament Scriptures.

Going home, he confronted his parents and exclaimed, "I'm a Christian!"

Stunned and grieved, they tried to persuade him to foreswear his decision, but to no avail. He continued steadfast.

Later a rabbi pleaded with him to change his decision. He spoke of the strained relationship his new faith had created between his parents and himself, and the forfeiture of earthly riches. "Consider well what you will lose," he warned.

He replied, "If I am right, and I know I am, see what I will gain: eternal life and spiritual riches beyond compare!"

That courageous young man became Dr. Hyman Appelman, one of America's greatest evangelists and exegetes of the Scriptures. Like Moses of old, he esteemed "the reproach of Christ greater riches" than the ephemeral wealth of the passing world.

Told by Colonel W. J Rushing.

* * * *

Bravo!

Governor Reubin Askew, a former governor of Florida, did not serve liquor in the governor's mansion. He remarked recently, "It is surprising how *early* people go home when you don't serve them booze!"

"Woe unto him that giveth his neighbour drink, that puttest thy bottle to him."—Hab. 2:15.

* * * *

The Needful Quality

Sir Winston Churchill said, "Courage is the first of needful human qualities because it is the quality which guarantees all the others."

God's command to His children is, "Be strong and of a good courage" (Josh. 1:6).

* * * *

Europe's Greatest Scene

In commenting upon the courageous stand of Martin Luther at the Diet of Worms where he said, "Unless I can be shown by Scripture that I have spoken falsely, I will not recant," Thomas Carlyle said, "That moment was the greatest scene in modern European history, the point from which the whole subsequent history of civilization takes its rise!"

* * * *

"Lift Ye Up a Banner" (Isa. 13:2)

When President Franklin Delano Roosevelt died in 1945, the nation went into mourning and lowered the flag at half-mast. During that time, Charles Woodbridge, a Presbyterian minister, engaged a young man in earnest conversation about his need of the Saviour.

As he pressed home the claims of the Gospel, the young man insistently refused to accept them or the Saviour. When he stood to leave, he said, "Dr. Woodbridge, if you would lower your standards just a little bit, your church would be filled to overflowing."

Woodbridge walked silently to a window of his study and said, "Young man, do you see that flag flying at half-mast? Let me tell you that when that standard is lowered, it means somebody has died. As long as I live, the standard of the Gospel will never be lowered for any man alive!"

God's command to His servants has not been rescinded: "Preach the word. . .reprove, rebuke, exhort with all longsuffering and doctrine" (II Tim. 4:2).

* * * *

"If God Be for Us"

When the Apostle Paul stood firmly for Christ with a minority of faithful Christians, he exclaimed, "If God be for us, who can be against us?" (Rom. 8:31).

Napoleon was dead wrong when he said, "God is on the side of large battalions."

Jonathan said, "There is no restraint to the Lord to save by many or by few" (I Sam. 14:6).

* * * *

"You May Be Killing Your Dentist!"

Dr. Omar Reed, director of the American Society for Preventive Dentistry, claims that "dentists die young. . .because they are 'burned out' by the emotional trauma of dealing with fearful patients."

We are living in a fear-craven world, a world in which "Men's hearts [are] failing them for fear, and for looking after those things which are coming on the earth" (Luke 21:26).

What a challenge to God's children to impart cheer and courage to fearful ones! Long ago God's servant, Paul, said to his terrified fellow-voyagers, "There stood by me this night the angel of God. . .Saying, Fear not. . . Wherefore, sirs, be of good cheer: for I believe God" (Acts 27:23-25).

* * * *

A Story Worth Telling

What happened to the men who signed the Declaration of Independence? Their stories are worth telling.

Five of them were captured by the British, tried as traitors and tortured before they died. Twelve had their homes ransacked and burned. Two lost their sons in the Revolutionary War. Nine fought and died from wounds or hardships suffered in the war.

All the signatories of the Declaration knew that the penalty for signing it would be death if they were captured.

With great courage and complete dedication to the rightfulness of their cause, they "pledged their lives, their fortunes, and their sacred honor" to defend their freedom.

'Tis man's perdition to be safe,
When for the truth he ought to die.

* * * *

Sublime Words

Many people in our nation were deeply moved by the courage displayed in the heroic life-giving deed of Fireman Patrick J. Cleary of New York City. Cleary climbed a 24-foot ladder to the third floor of a burning building and brought down a trapped child! He went up again and reached the child's anguished mother, helping her to descend the ladder. Then he collapsed on the sidewalk and died of a massive heart attack! Just prior to his last heroic deed, he had been on duty at three other fires.

How challenging are the words: *Duty* and *courage!*

In a letter to his son, General Robert E. Lee said, "Do your duty in all things. You cannot do more. You should never wish to do less."

* * * *

God Is Still on the Throne

During the darksome days following the assassination of President Lin-coln, Maj. Gen. James A. Garfield calmed the frenzied mob with these reassuring words: "Fellow citizens, clouds of darkness are round about God. His pavilion is surrounded by dark waters and thick clouds. But justice and judgment are the habitation of His throne. Mercy and truth go before His face. Fellow citizens, God reigns, and the government in Washington still lives!"

However drear and dark outward conditions may be, God's children can triumphantly say, "God lives! He is still on the throne, ruling and over-ruling, arranging and rearranging, and causing all things to work together for the good of His children, in keeping with His eternal purpose."

This is my Father's world,
O let me ne'er forget
That though the wrong seems oft so strong,
God is the Ruler yet.

* * * *

Man's Inhumanity

Christians in Chad, Africa, were mercilessly persecuted for refusing to participate in old tribal initiation rites which are pagan. A number of pastors, evangelists and other church leaders who declined to commit acts counter to their faith, such as drinking chicken blood offered to idols and handling fetishes, have been buried alive with just part of a leg left above the ground, or, for a slower death, been buried with only the head exposed—a terrifying warning to others who resist.

According to *New York Times* correspondent Henry Kamm, flogging, burning with coals, scarring, sexual indignities, mock burials and other acts of humiliation are employed.

Adapted from *Christianity Today*
(Nov. 8, '74)

* * * *

A Plea for Fortitude

The English clergyman, Bishop Oliver Hart, said, "Lord, give us fortitude to endure the things which cannot be changed, and the courage to change the things which should be changed, and the wisdom to know one from the other."

* * * *

Must Trample Over Fallen Body

Years ago an unsaved young man, utterly devoid of any moral conviction, said to his Christian father, "Dad, I'm going to open a tavern. It's a lucrative business, you know."

A look of shame and sorrow pervaded the father's face. Weeping, he begged his son not to bring shame upon the family's name. But his pleading was in vain.

On the opening day the son waited in the dimly lighted interior of the tavern, looking for customers to enter. None came.

Going to the entrance of the taven, he was astonished to see his father standing there and pleading with those who would enter to desist.

Burning with anger, the son clinched his fist and struck his father in the face. He fell to the sidewalk. With blood trickling down his face, he said, "Son, if anyone enters this tavern, he will have to trample over my fallen body!"

* * * *

Faint Not

In *A Tale of Two Cities*, Charles Dickens depicted the era of the French Revolution: "It was the age of wisdom; it was the age of foolishness. It was the epoch of belief; it was the epoch of incredulity. It was the season of light; it was the season of darkness. It was the spring of hope; it was the winter of despair. We had everything before us; we had nothing before us. We were all going directly the other way. In short, *the period was like the present period!*"

Say not, "The days are evil. Who's to blame?"
And fold the hands and acquiesce, oh, shame!
Stand up, speak out, and bravely, in God's name!
It matters not how deep entrenched the wrong,
How hard the battle goes, the day how long,
Faint not, fight on! Tomorrow comes the song!

Maltbie Davenport Babcock.

* * * *

Don't Run Away

Sir Winston Churchill said, "If you meet danger promptly and without flinching, you will reduce it by half. Never run away from anything. Never!"

To God's children comes the command, "Be strong and of a good courage" (Josh 1:6).

Thro' days of toil when heart doth fail,

God will take care of you;
When dangers fierce your path assail,
God will take care of you.

C. D. Martin.

* * * *

"No Other Choice!"

Mrs. Janice C. Patterson, an elementary teacher in Fuller Elementary School, Raleigh, N. C., resigned her position after being told by public school officials that she must cease observing a minute of silent prayer daily with her first grade pupils. She said in reference to her decision: "My conscience leaves me no other choice."

In a letter to the parents of her pupils, Janice said, "God deserves at least a minute a day. We all need God's help to be more loving to one another."

* * * *

Not Golden But Yellow

In commenting on the Nazi havoc in his native Germany, Martin Niemoeller said, "I do not exclude myself from this guilt. On the contrary, I stress at every opportunity that I, too, have failed; for I, too, have been silent when I should have spoken!"

Silence is not always golden. Sometimes it is plain yellow.

"Nevertheless among the chief rulers also many believed on him; but ... did not confess him, lest they should be put out of the synagogue: For they loved the praise of men more than the praise of God."—John 12:42,43.

* * * *

THE CROSS

Mankind's Best Hope

In 1973, a violent earthquake erupted on Helmacy Island, off Iceland's southern coast, bringing death and destruction. Silhouetted by a pillar of fire was a cross on top of a nearby church, an enduring symbol of mankind's best hope for today and eternity.

"But God forbid that I should glory, save in the cross of our Lord Jesus Christ" (Gal. 6:14).

* * * *

Where the Flame Cannot Reach

In a forest fire there is one place of safety where the flames cannot reach—where the fire has already burned itself out.

That is what Calvary means. It is the place where the fire of God's judgment against sin burned itself out completely.

Tell the joyful story,
Sound it far and wide,
Christ has paid the ransom,
On the cross He died.

* * * *

Luther's Answer to Satan

At times Martin Luther was deeply depressed. 'Twas then that the accuser, Satan, mercilessly assailed him by enumerating sins Luther had committed, and asking: "Now Martin, what do you say about these foul sins?" Luther replied, "The blood of Jesus Christ. . .cleanseth us from all sin" (I John 1:7).

* * * *

'TWAS I

'Twas I that shed that precious blood,
   I nailed Him to the tree,
I crucified the Christ of God,
   I joined the mockery!

Of all the frenzied multitude,
   I feel that I am one,
And in the din of voices rude,
   I recognize my own!

Around the cross the throng I see
   Mocking the Sufferer's groan,
Yet still my voice, it seems to be
   As if I mocked alone.

Author Unknown.

* * * *

He Drew the Cross on the Ground

During his imprisonment in a Soviet Union labor camp, Aleksandr Solzhenitsyn, becoming so discouraged, reached the point where he didn't care whether or not the guards killed him.

One day during a labor break, when he was working with a labor detail outside, a stranger sat down beside him. Solzhenitsyn had never seen him before and never saw him again. The stranger took a stick and drew a cross on the ground. Solzhenitsyn stared fixedly at the cross, then said,

"I realize therein lies man's freedom."

The cross and its message bring freedom from sin and its enslaving power: "If the Son. . .shall make you free, ye shall be free indeed" (John 8:36).

* * * *

THE GREATEST RANSOM PAYMENT

No one can ever comprehend
   The mighty ransom price
The King of Glory paid—in full,
   By His great sacrifice.
In leaving all His riches and
   The splendor of His throne,
To come to this needy world, to live
   And die to save "His own."

Although He suffered torture, and
   Was slain by howling foes—
Thanks to His sovereign power, He
   Triumphantly arose,
To claim, again, His royal throne
   On Heaven's blissful shore,
Where He, the Victor over death,
   Now reigns forevermore!

Oh, what supernal love it took,
   To pay the awesome price,
To save His "bride";—then share with her,
   His home in Paradise!
May this triumphant King of kings
   Abide with you each day,
And keep you in His tender care,
   Each step along your way.

Florrie Estelle Hudson,
a blind poet.

* * * *

The Remedy Refused

According to an AP news item, a 26-year-old mother, who had given birth to a baby girl by Caesarean section, died because she refused a blood transfusion on the grounds that it would be contrary to her religious beliefs.

Dr. Richard Buchanan, staff pathologist at Elyria (Ohio) Memorial Hospital, said the woman died in the hospital shortly after she had given birth to the baby, who survived. The mother and her husband were members of Lorain's Spanish congregation of Jehovah's Witnesses.

Physical death could have been averted had the mother received the remedy so readily available. Spiritual death can be averted for all who receive the remedy for sin: "The blood of Jesus Christ. . .cleanseth us from all sin" (I John 1:7).

* * * *

Stigmata

According to *The Calgary Herald,* shortly before Easter, 1972, some doctors in Oakland, California, reported that ten-year-old Gloretta Robinson was "periodically bleeding from the hands, feet and side in a classic display of stigmata"—the wounds that Christ received during the Passion and Crucifixion. They diagnosed the condition as an "Easter bleeding syndrome."

The newspaper commented, "Stigmatization in a religious sense is the appearance on a living person of the final wounds of Jesus Christ on the cross—nails piercing His hands and feet and the spear wounding His side."

The alleged periodic bleeding of Gloretta is totally unrelated to the vicarious suffering of the Saviour for the sin of the world. When Paul said, "I bear in my body the marks of the Lord Jesus" (Gal. 6:17), he was referring to his own suffering, not to Christ's suffering.

Christ suffered once and finally. His Calvary suffering will never be repeated: "For Christ also hath once suffered for sins. . .that he might bring us to God" (I Pet. 3:18).

* * * *

Topped by the Cross

During World War II, Some of the cities of Germany were reduced to rubble by attacks from the air and ground artillery. Berlin suffered greatly. What ghastly sights of war's desolation and destruction were evinced! In the midst of crumbled buildings, one structure remained: the tower of the Kaiser Wilhelm Church, topped by the cross!

The cross of Christ and its message will ever be indestructible!

* * * *

One in Christ

"The hot Mexican sun beat down on Taxco's marketplace. Our group of American tourists disembarked from the buses like scavengers to invade the town's countless souvenir shops. Soon I became caught up in the frenzy of shopping and haggling, unsure of what I was buying.

"Suddenly from one of the nearby buildings came the sound of a man singing in Spanish. The melody seemed so familiar. I listened more closely. It was *The Old Rugged Cross*. I forgot my intended purchases and followed the sound to a small white building labeled *Iglesia Presbiteriana.*

"Slipping through the grilled iron doors and into a crude pew in the empty sanctuary, I found a singer, a sturdy Mexican in rough work clothes. A dark-eyed young woman accompanied him on an old piano. The man's uplifted face reflected the meaning of the words. I followed along with my own: 'And I love that old cross, where the dearest and best. . . .'

"The song ended; I moved to the front of the church and dropped some money in the collection plate there. The three of us smiled at one another. That had to be our communication— that and the wonderful hymn.

"I don't know why they were there—rehearsing perhaps for a service. But as I stepped outside *I knew* I was taking home from Taxco something more precious than souvenir trinkets. I had shared a moment of deep communion with two who were strangers, yet loved ones. And I had come away with a new awareness of the Saviour who makes us all brothers and sisters in Him!"

In speaking of the *spiritual unity* of believers, Jesus said, "That they all may be one; as thou, Father, art in me, and I in thee, that they may be one in us" (John 17:21).

Told by Tilde Merkert.

* * * *

A New Low Depth

Man's inhumanity to man plummeted to a new low depth of shame when crucifixion was devised as a mode of ending the life of a human being!

Apart from its seemingly interminable suffering, it was a shameful death. So ignominious was this method of execution that at first only slaves suffered it. It was inflicted for the most heinous crimes.

Cicero, a Roman statesman, orator and writer, said of crucifixion, "Let the very name of the cross be far away not only from the body of a Roman citizen, but even from his thoughts, his eyes and his ears."

To the Jews, the cross connoted something much more serious than public shame and ignominy. They believed that the curse of God was on those who died by crucifixion: "He that is hanged is accursed of God" (Deut. 21:23).

How dearly we should love the Son of God who died on the cross and redeemed us with His precious blood! He was made a curse for us: "Christ hath redeemed us from the curse of the law, being made a curse for us: for it is written, Cursed is every one that hangeth on a tree" (Gal. 3:13).

Oh, the love that drew salvation's plan!
Oh, the grace that bro't it down to man!
Oh, the mighty gulf which God did span
    At Calvary!

* * * *

Beyond Comprehension

As Martin Luther thought on the anguished, forlorn cry of the Saviour, "My God, my God, why hast thou forsaken me?" he exclaimed, "Who can understand this? God being forsaken by God!"

Alone upon the cross He hung
That others He might save,
Forsaken then by God and man,
Alone His life He gave!

* * * *

"Towering O'er the Wrecks of Time"

On the south coast of China, on a hill overlooking the harbor of Macao, Portuguese settlers once built a massive cathedral. During a typhoon, the building fell in ruins—all except the front wall.

Withstanding the elements through the years stood a great bronze cross high on the top of that wall.

In 1825 Sir John Bowring was shipwrecked nearby. Clinging to the wreckage of his ship, he caught sight of that great cross, and it showed him where he could reach shore and safety.

His dramatic rescue moved him to write the hymn, "In the Cross of Christ I Glory," a hymn which will inspire and challenge God's children to faithful service as long as time shall last.

In the cross of Christ I glory,
Towering o'er the wrecks of time;
All the light of sacred story

Gathers round its head sublime.
Sir John Bowring.
Told by Theodore Martin.

* * * *

The Cross, a Magnet

Through the centuries, the cross of Jesus has been a magnet. It continues to be a magnet, drawing the heart and mind of mankind to the One who suffered and died vicariously thereon: "And I, if I be lifted up from the earth, will draw all men unto me" (John 12:32).

* * * *

The Universal Virus

At a Kansas Air Force base, Staff Sgt. Tor Olsen contracted hepatitis, suffered complete failure of the liver, and fell into a coma which lasted for days. He was flown to a medical center in San Antonio. Doctors decided that there was only one last-ditch recourse left to save the 22-year-old man's life: a drastic procedure called "total body washout."

As surgeons drained virtually all of his diseased blood from his body, a machine pumped into his arteries a salt solution containing albumin and other agents. Then 12 pints of donor blood were pumped into his circulatory system. The entire operation took less than an hour.

Next day, Sgt. Olsen was singing hymns with his parents! Recovery was dramatic! Doctors informed him that he could expect to lead a normal and productive life.

Long ago when Adam sinned, the virus of sin entered the blood stream of mankind: "As by one man sin entered into the world, and death by sin. . .so death passed upon all men" (Rom. 5:12).

The sinless Son of God shed His blood, untainted by sin, to provide a sure way to eliminate the deadly virus of sin for all who will accept it: "Come now, and let us reason together, saith the Lord: though your sins be as scarlet, they shall be as white as snow; though they be red like crimson, they shall be as wool" (Isa. 1:18).

* * * *

The Universal Malady

A bold headline in a recent newspaper announced: *Autopsy of Ancient Mummy to Reveal Cause of Death.* The AP dispatch following it said:

"An electric saw cut into an ancient mummy at the University of Pennsylvania Museum lab, sending a cloud of rust-colored dust.

"Dr. Michael Zimmerman, a pathologist, spread open the mummy's chest, exposing brittle bones, calcified organs and the powdery residues of flesh, skin and linen wrappings. The procedure was aimed at learning of what the man died some 3,000 years ago. The procedure may take months of examination."

Sometimes we do not know the cause of *physical* death, but the Bible tells us the cause of *spiritual* death: "Wherefore, as by one man sin entered into the world, and death by

sin. . .for that all have sinned" (Rom. 5:12).

Sin is a universal malady, so it requires a universal remedy. God in mercy has provided that remedy: 'In that day a fountain shall be opened . . .for sin and uncleanness' (Zech. 13:1).

The dying thief rejoiced to see
That fountain in his day;
And there may I, though vile as he,
Wash all my sins away.

Wm. Cowper.

* * * *

THE CROSS WAS HIS OWN

They borrowed a bed to lay His head
When Christ the Lord came down,
They borrowed an ass in the mountain pass
For Him to ride to town,
But the crown that He wore, and the cross that He bore
Were His own—the cross was His own.

He borrowed the bread when the crowd He fed
On the grassy mountain side,
He borrowed the dish of broken fish
With which He satisfied,
But the crown that He wore, and the cross that He bore
Were His own—the cross was His own.

He borrowed a room on His way to the tomb
The Passover lamb to eat,
They borrowed a cave for Him a grave,
They borrowed a winding sheet.
But the crown that He wore, and the cross that He bore

Were His own—the cross was His own.

Author unknown.

* * * *

Trodden Under Foot

All who enter a lost hereafter must trample over the body of Jesus Christ who died a vicarious death to save men from going out into a lost hereafter. The Bible says of those who reject the Saviour's offer of eternal life, "Of how much sorer punishment, suppose ye, shall he be thought worthy, who hath trodden under foot the Son of God, and hath counted the blood of the covenant. . .an unholy thing, and hath done despite unto the Spirit of grace?" (Heb. 10:29).

* * * *

DEATH
(See also Resurrection)

Spiritual Death

William Winogrond, assistant chancellor of the University of Wisconsin, was believed dead for nearly twelve hours after a heart attack. Doctors had declared him clinically dead. Then a small, weak flutter of his eyelid caught someone's attention. He made a complete recovery and was in good health after the serious heart attack.

Physical death is a *certainty:* "And as it is appointed unto men once to die" (Heb. 9:27). Spiritual death is a *possibility* and may be averted by acceptance of the Saviour. Pleadingly God asks, "Make you a new heart and a new spirit: for why will ye die?" (Ezek. 18:31).

* * * *

"SHOULD YOU GO FIRST"

Should you go first and I remain
  To walk the road alone,
I'll live in memory's garden, dear,
  With happy days we've known!

In spring I'll wait for roses red,
  When fades the lilac blue,
In early fall when brown leaves fall
  I'll catch a glimpse of you!

Should you go first and I remain
  For battles to be fought
Each thing you've touched along the
    way,
  Will be a hallowed spot!
I'll hear your voice, I'll see your smile,
  Though blindly I may grope,
The memory of your helping hand,
  Will buoy me on with hope!

Should you go first and I remain
  To finish with the scroll,
No length'ning shadows shall creep
    in,
  To make this life seem droll!
We've known so much of happiness,
  We've had our cup of joy,
And memory is one gift of God,
  That death cannot destroy!

Should you go first and I remain
  One thing I'd have you do:
Walk slowly down the path of death,
  For soon I'll follow you!

I'll want to know each step you take,
That I may walk the same,
For some day down that lonely road,
You'll hear me call your name!

Albert Kennedy Rowswell
(Appeared in *Congressional Record*
June 9, 1941).

* * * *

Spiritually Dead

A premature infant boy was pronounced stillborn at a hospital in Dallas, Texas, and sent to a funeral home. The mortician placed the infant on an embalming table and delayed his embalming until later. But then. . .he heard the baby crying! Immediately he was sent to a hospital where an all-out but unsuccessful effort was made to save the baby.

Each one of us came into the world spiritually dead: "Behold, I was shapen in iniquity; and in sin did my mother conceive me" (Ps. 51:5); "They go astray as soon as they be born" (58:3).

How devoid of any hope this universal fact would be but for the Saviour's promise: "I am come that they might have life, and that they might have it more abundantly" (John 10:10).

* * * *

Lonely

Stanley Riddell, a 65-year-old man in London, took his life because of a parrot's constant repeating of sayings learned from Riddell's deceased wife.

In commenting upon his death, *The Calgary Herald* said, "Riddell was a lonely man following the death of his wife. The parrot's constant use of expressions the wife had taught it was too much for him to bear."

How crushing are life's sorrows without the help of the One who enters feelingly and sharingly into our heartaches and heartbreaks: "Jesus wept" (John 11:35).

He knows, He loves, He cares,
Nothing this truth can dim;
He does the very best for those,
Who leave the choice with Him.

* * * *

"At Home With the Lord"

"In death the Christian goes Home to be forever with the Lord," said Dr. Angel Martinez. "It is wrong to say of our friends and loved ones who die in the Lord that we have lost them. How can anything or anyone be lost when we know where they are?"

"Sustained and soothed by an unfaltering trust," the believer can know that saved loved ones are at rest and are infinitely blessed: 'Absent from the body. . .present with the Lord' " (II Cor. 5:8).

* * * *

Life's Greatest Purpose

Said William James, "The greatest purpose of life is to spend it for something that will outlast it."

* * * *

Calories and Coronaries

There is an indissoluble relationship between calories and coronaries. The longer the waistline, the shorter the lifeline: "Put a knife to thy throat, if thou be a man given to appetite" (Prov. 23:2).

* * * *

Help for Bereft Ones

One of life's greatest psychological and emotional jolts comes when dear friends and precious loved ones are taken away from us by death. Whelming grief and numbing loneliness are inescapable.

Euphemizing death by poetic gems often fails to stanch blinding tears of sorrow and remove doubt and confusion. Spoken words of comfort are *good*. Empathic help is *better*. Words of sympathy may not always fulfill their intended purpose. *Action* is needed.

The mother of Jane's little playmate died. The next morning Jane told her mother how sorry she was for her friend.

Mother, too, was grieved. She asked Jane, "What did you say to your little friend?"

Jane replied, "Mother, I didn't say anything. I just sat beside her, and put my arms around her while we both wept!"

How Christlike we are when we, who have known sorrow, enter sharingly and understandingly into the heartbreaks and heartaches of others. He made the sorrows of others His very own. He wept with the Bethany sisters, Mary and Martha, whose brother, Lazarus, had died: "Jesus wept" (John 11:35).

* * * *

Deducting the Sublime From the Bizarre

Said Edgar Bergen, the famed ventriloquist:

"A few years ago I was in a railway station in a tiny town. Along came two porters carrying a coffin. When they put it down, I rapped on the box and asked, 'Is everything all right in there?'

"The 'corpse' replied, 'Let me out! Let me out!'

"The porters took to their heels and ran like bolts of lightning. When last heard of, they were still running.

"When the train arrived at the station, the baggageman alighted and asked, 'Where are the guys to load this stuff?'

"I didn't mention why they left, but I did help get the coffin on the train. I almost got a hernia helping lift it."

Shakespeare said, "And this our life, exempt from public haunt, finds tongues in trees, books in the running brooks, sermons in stones, and good in everything."

Can the sublime be deduced from the bizarre Bergen incident? Let's see:

Only death's Conqueror, the Saviour, can extricate from death its victims. How fear-allaying and hope-bringing are His triumphant words: "He that believeth in me, though he were dead, yet shall he live" (John 11:25).

* * * *

THE INEVITABLE

The boast of heraldry, the pomp of

pow'r,
And all that beauty, all that wealth
e'er gave,
Await alike th' inevitable hour,
The paths of glory lead but to the
grave!

Sir Thomas Gray.

* * * *

Wanted: a Legal Definition of Death

An Associated Press dispatch said, "Hospitals spend thousands of dollars a day and waste specialized facilities on patients who may be dead. Doctors and lawyers want a new legal definition of death."

McCarthy DeMere, chairman of the American Bar Association's Law and Medicine Division, said, "Present definitions of death are inadequate." His committee proposed that a human body with irreversible cessation of brain function be adjudged dead, according to usual and customary standards of medical practice."

Only God knows when irreversible spiritual death occurs, but it does occur: Esau "found no place of repentance, though he sought it carefully with tears" (Heb. 12:17).

* * * *

Only a Heartbeat

When the disastrous flash flood swept down Big Thompson Canyon in Colorado in 1976, seven Campus Crusaders drowned in the turbulent water. Afterward, Mrs. Vonette Bright, wife of the Campus Crusade founder, said:

"It's still hard for me to talk about it. I glanced at my watch at about 9:45 p.m. Then I heard a siren sound like an air raid warning and a voice saying, 'Attention! Evacuate immediately!' Then the warning changed, 'Run, run to your cars! Don't take anything! Evacuate! Seek higher ground!'

"The last words of some staff members of Campus Crusade were, 'We're going to die, but we are ready. Lord Jesus, we love You.' This was their triumphant prayer as their car was washed down the Big Thompson Canyon."

There is only a heartbeat, or a step, between each one of us and death, so let us be momentarily ready to go into the presence of death's Conqueror, the Saviour.

* * * *

Fit to Live

After learning that his son Quentin, a World War I pilot, had been killed, Theodore Roosevelt wrote in tribute: "Only those who do not fear to die are fit to live!"

* * * *

Death—a Peaceful Transition

Dr. Elizabeth Kubler-Ross, noted Chicago psychiatrist, said in the *Chicago Daily News:*

"People who have been declared medically dead and have survived never again fear death. My research has convinced me that life continues beyond the grave. I used to regard death as a natural termination of individual existence. Now I am certain that it is not.

"For seven years I have interviewed people who experienced 'death' through accident or illness and who were resuscitated after periods as long as twelve hours. In some respects their reports were absolutely identical. They related fantastic feelings of peace and wholeness when they 'died.' The blind could see and missing limbs were restored, patients told me. At the moment of death, they could see their own bodies from above. Also common to the experience of several hundred persons was a greeting by loved ones who had previously died. You see what you most want to see. None of these are ever left alone. They are welcomed, greeted and helped in the transition.

"Death is the shedding of the physical body. It is an absolute and beautiful transition. I am one hundred percent sure of an after life. The psyche (soul) lives!" affirmed the psychiatrist.

When God's children come to the sunset gate of life, they can confidently say, "For we know that if our earthly house of this tabernacle were dissolved, we have a building of God, an house not made with hands, eternal in the heavens" (II Cor. 5:1).

* * * *

Death: a Moving Day for Christians

As his earthly life ebbed away, Dwight L. Moody caught a glimpse of the glory awaiting him and exclaimed, "Heaven opens before me! If this is death, it is sweet! There is no valley here!"

A son standing at his bedside said, "No, Father, you are dreaming."

"No, no," said Moody, "I am not dreaming. I have seen the children's faces! This is my triumph! This is my coronation day!"

For Christians, death is moving day, leaving the "vile body" or "body of humiliation" (Phil. 3:21). They are "absent from the body, and. . .present with the Lord" (II Cor. 5:8). Death is the Christian's "leaving thine out-grown shell by life's unresting sea."

A friend greeted John Quincy Adams by asking, "Well, how is John Quincy Adams today?"

"Thank you," replied the eighty-year-old Adams. "John Quincy Adams is quite well, but the house where he lives (his body) is becoming quite uninhabitable. *But I am not the house!* I shall have to move out soon, but John Quincy Adams is quite well, thank you!"

* * * *

"I Don't Want to Die!"

Recently the legs of a teenage boy were blown off by a land mine near the infamous wall which separates East from West Germany. "Help! Help!" he pled piteously. "I've done nothing wrong! I'm just 16 years old! I don't want to die!"

His cries were unavailing. Mercifully, death soon ended his agony.

Man's inhumanity to man
Makes countless thousands mourn!

* * * *

"It's All Downhill"

Years ago a terminally ill rich man called his coachman to his bedside and said, "Ah, Sykes, I am going on a long and rugged journey, worse than any you ever drove me on!"

Wanting to be helpful, the coachman ineptly said, "But, sir, there's one comfort—it's all downhill!"

To go down in death without God and without hope is the greatest of tragedies: "The rich man. . .died, and was buried; And in hell he lift up his eyes, being in torments" (Luke 16:22,23).

* * * *

America's "Ace of Aces"

In commenting upon death, Eddie Rickenbacker, America's "Ace of Aces," the most decorated pilot in World War I, said, "I have cheated the Grim Reaper more times than anyone I know. I'll fight like a wildcat until they nail the lid of my pine box down on me! It is the easiest thing in the world to die. The hardest is to live."

How blessed are those who die in Christ: "Blessed are the dead which die in the Lord. . .that they may rest from their labours; and their works do follow them" (Rev. 14:13).

* * * *

"I Have Played the Fool"

Before Saul, the first king of Israel, ignominiously terminated his life as a suicide, he exclaimed dejectedly and defeatedly, "I have played the fool, and have erred exceedingly" (I Sam. 26:21).

As Paul neared life's setting sun, he joyfully and triumphantly said, "I have kept the faith" (II Tim. 4:7).

* * * *

Hair Stands on End

Francoise Sagan, French authoress of bestselling novels, wrote in *Realities,* "At times I wake in the middle of the night, and my hair stands on end when I think that I am going to die one day!"

How rayless and starless is the night of death for those who do not have a living hope in the living Saviour! But how luminous is the Valley of Death for God's children! At life's terminus, "It shall be light" (Zech. 14:7).

* * * *

The Democracy of the Morgue

In death, the prince and the pauper are equal. The democracy of the morgue plays no favorites. The Roman poet Horace wrote, "Pale death, with impartial step, knocks at the poor man's cottage and at the palace of kings!"

"For as in Adam all die, even so in Christ shall all be made alive."—I Cor. 15:22.

* * * *

A Sorrow-Assuaging Reality

In a Sunday morning service W. A. Criswell told this interesting story:

"Sometime ago, I held a revival

meeting in eastern Tennessee. At the close of the meeting, a grief-stricken father said to me, 'Recently I received a telegram from the War Department which began with the ominous words, "We regret to inform you." My son had fallen in battle in Vietnam! Before leaving us, he had confessed his faith in Christ as his Saviour and had followed his Lord in baptism. Though our sorrow and loss are great, we are comforted in knowing that our dear son was ready to go and is now with the Saviour: "Absent from the body. . .present with the Lord" (II Cor. 5:8). I have a picture of my noble boy in the uniform of his country; and each time I look at it, I thank God that he was saved! '"

How sorrow-assuaging and hope-bringing are the triumphant words of the death-conquering Saviour: "I am he that liveth, and was dead; and, behold, I am alive for evermore" (Rev. 1:18).

* * * *

Have and Are

When we die, we leave behind all we *have*. We go with what we *are*. The Bible says, "For we brought nothing into this world, and it is certain we can carry nothing out" (I Tim. 6:7).

* * * *

Only a Heartbeat

The caption of a news dispatch from London said: *Air Disaster Due to Pilot Error.* Then followed an explanation of Britain's worst air disaster:

"Pilot's error caused Britain's worst disaster which killed 118 persons aboard in June, 1972. Attorney General Sir Peter Rawlinson told a public inquiry that the pilot of the British European Airways aircraft, which crashed seconds after takeoff from London's Heathrow Airport, may have suffered a mild heart attack."

Sudden death was probably remote from the minds of those aboard that ill-fated plane. Yet it came!

Since there is just a heartbeat between anyone and death, it is wise to be momentarily ready to meet God—at peace with Him and man: "Prepare to meet thy God" (Amos 4:12).

How blessed are those who can confidently say at death's portals, "I am now ready. . .the time of my departure is at hand. . . .I have finished my course" (II Tim. 4:6,7).

* * * *

"AT EVENING TIME IT SHALL BE LIGHT" (Zech. 14:7).

When the crimson sky and the setting sun
Proclaim to the world that thy work is done,
May you walk serenely through the twilight gray,
Go Home and rest at the end of the day.

* * * *

"A Wreck Must Mark the End"

Robert Ingersoll was a self-proclaimed atheist. How dark and dismal were his comments on death! "It may be best in the happier moments of the voyage, when eager winds are kissing every sail, to dash against the unseen rock, and in an instant hear the billows roar above the sunken ship! For whether in mid-sea or among the breakers of the farther shore, a wreck must mark the end of each and all. Every life will, at its close, become a tragedy as sad and deep and dark as can be woven of the warp and woof of mystery and death!"

For those who do not believe in death's Conqueror, the Saviour, death is a trapdoor into nothingness and impenetrable darkness.

For the Christian, death is a translation from earth to Heaven, to be forever with the Lord: "Absent from the body...present with the Lord" (II Cor. 5:8).

* * * *

"But a Step Between Me and Death" (I Sam. 20:3).

In the fall of 1972, a train wreck occurred in Saltillo, Mexico, in which more than 200 men, women and children were killed and 1,011 were injured. Some survivors underwent amputations in order to be freed from twisted steel in coaches which were piled on one another. Some entire families perished!

The passengers on the train were returning from Real de Catorce, where they had gone on an annual religious pilgrimage "to pray to St. Francis."

Leovigildo Ricera, one of the passengers who survived, told reporters, "The train was moving like a wild animal. I felt the danger and told my wife to hold to her seat tightly!"

Authorities said blood tests indicated that the engineer, Melchor Sanchez, had been drinking before the train derailed on a downhill curve, going about 75 miles per hour—twice the speed limit designated for that section of the track.

This is another horrendous example of the havoc and sorrow wrought by the merciless, deranging destroyer—alcoholic liquors!

How uncertain is life: "There is but a step between me and death" (I Sam. 20:3). Possibly any thought of death was remotely removed from those jovial pilgrims!

* * * *

A Stage

Shakespeare said:

All the world's a stage
And all the men and women merely players;
They have their exits and their entrances.

When we make our exit from the stage of life, will we dejectedly say, "I have played the fool" (I Sam. 26:21), or will we radiantly say, "I have kept the faith" (II Tim. 4:7)?

* * * *

Suicide Is Untenable

Charles Pinckney Luckey was the pastor of a Congregational church in Middlebury, Connecticut. He was apparently a fine physical specimen at fifty. With no prior warning, he began to lose his balance. After examination, the medical doctor could find nothing wrong with him and hoped that the condition would go away. It didn't.

Shortly thereafter Luckey began to lose his vision. In three weeks he was totally blind! Specialists surveyed his wilting frame. Their diagnosis was *Creutzfeld-Jakob*, a lethal disease.

The crisis came shortly after he entered Columbia Presbyterian Hospital, New York. To his secretary he dictated the following letter:

"What does a Christian do when he stands over the abyss of his own death, and the doctors have told him that his disease is ravaging his brain, and that his whole personality may be warped? Does the Christian have the right of self-destruction, especially when he knows that the changed personality may bring out the horrible beast in himself?

"Well, after 48 hours of self-searching study, it comes to me that ultimately and finally the Christian is to always view life as a gift from God, lovingly bestowed upon him by his Creator, and it is not his to smash. So I conclude that suicide is untenable, not because I lack the courage to take my life, but because of my deep abiding faith in the Creator who knew and loved me before I was fashioned in my mother's womb. But I do not think it wrong to pray for an early release from my disease-ravished body."

The letter concluded: "Lovingly given to my congregation and to my friends if it seems in good taste."

Luckey's prayer was answered. He sank into a coma, and soon entered

life eternal: "Absent from the body . . .present with the Lord" (II Cor. 5:8).

When our friends and loved ones die in the Lord, we can confidently say,"The Lord gave, and the Lord hath taken away" (Job 1:21).

* * * *

"The Field of Blood" (Matt. 27:8).

Sometime ago a burial crew in New York City buried Claude Solomon in Potter's Field. Potter's Field in New York is 45 acres of ground on the windy edge of Hart Island in the East River where, just as it happened to Judas years ago, society still buries unclaimed ones.

Solomon was eighty-two years old. His religion, family and past were unknown. He died a penniless pauper, from the ravages of time, in the crowded ward of a city hospital; and since there was nothing else to do with his body, it was put rudely to rest in Potter's Field.

Solomon's body arrived at the field in midmorning on the day of his interment, along with eight other dead ones, all in pine boxes.

"Man, it's cold out here, ain't it?" asked the truck driver. Nobody answered.

The burial crew removed the boxes from the truck and arranged them in a row. It had rained the night before and frozen. Now the ice was thin, and the coffins broke through the crust and sank into the mud and water.

Little beside Solomon's name was known, except he was detached from people and a drifter.

How like Claude Solomon are many today—human driftwood tossed on the bosom of a seething sea, abandoned by men but precious to God and not beyond His mercy and forgiveness: "Who is a God like unto thee, that pardoneth iniquity?" (Mic. 7:18).

* * * *

DESTRUCTION OF THE UNBORN—
FETICIDE, ABORTION

A Horrible Crime

"Abortion is the killing of human life—biologically, medically and scientifically. It is factual that life begins at fertilization," affirmed Steven Hotze, M.D., founder of Texas Doctors for Life, Inc.

"Over ninety-nine percent of all abortions have nothing to do with rape, incest or threat to the mother's life. At 18 to 25 days after conception, the heart begins to beat. At 45 days, brain waves can be detected. By 6 to 7 weeks, the fetus will respond to touch sensations. Even at this early stage, there is no reason to think that the unborn baby does not feel pain as his/her body is dismembered, poisoned, or otherwise destroyed by the various brutal techniques concealed under the bland euphemism 'termination of pregnancy!' "

* * * *

Never Again!

Although abortion is a ten-minute procedure, the memory of it stays continuously with some women. One lamented, "The mental pressure of what I was really doing, the guilt, has left me depressed and suicidal. I could never do this again, no matter what the circumstances might be!"

Lord Byron said of an accusing conscience:

No ear can hear nor tongue can tell,
The tortures of that inward hell!

* * * *

The Hallmark of Life

Dr. Eugene Diamond of Chicago's Stritch School of Medicine has stated: "To consider a fetus not to be a separate person but merely a part of the mother has not been tenable since the sixteenth century when Arantius showed that maternal and fetal circulations were separate. A fetus is certainly alive, since it possesses that hallmark of life—the ability to replace dying cells."

* * * *

Too Young to Live

Dr. Charles Rice of Notre Dame Law School has written: "If an innocent human being can be killed because he is too young, that is, he has not lived nine months from his conception, there is no reason in principle why he cannot be killed because he is too old, or too retarded, or too black, or too politically undesirable. The philosophy is Nazi Germany's."

****

In commenting upon abortion, President Ronald Reagan said, "There is one individual not being considered at all: the one who is being aborted. All advocates of abortion have already been born!"

****

Pope John Paul II said, "To destroy unborn children is an unspeakable crime!"

****

"Before Thou Camest Out of the Womb"

Miss Julie Turnquest, a registered nurse who works in surgery in Deaconness Hospital, Minneapolis, gave to her supervisor a statement in which she respectfully refused to assist in or prepare for the performance of an abortion. A dozen other nurses joined her in signing the statement.

A doctor who regularly performs abortions *on demand* in his office angrily confronted Nurse Turnquest, hinting that she might be asked to resign.

"I am not fearful of that," she said, "and I do not judge you, but I have strong convictions about this, based on Scripture which tells us that God planned our lives before we were formed in our mother's womb: 'Before I formed thee. . .and before thou camest out of the womb I sanctified thee' " (Jer. 1:5).

The Presbyterian Journal.

****

Herod Would Smile

Joel Hyde, a member of the U. S. House of Representatives, said in an address in the House, "Abortion is violence against the unborn. It is wholesale slaughter of innocents which would make Herod smile. We have had approximately one million abortions—twice as many deaths as in all our wars!"

****

Horrible to Nurses

"Most nurses find the destruction of life the very antithesis of what they believe," said Mrs. Cynthia Kinsella, dean of the School of Nursing at City Hospital, New York. "The concept of abortion is very difficult for them to accept. Nurses in delivery rooms have been accustomed to making every conceivable effort to save babies, even those of one to three pounds. They have found that sometimes they are 'salting out' bigger babies than those they have worked to save."

****

"You Can't Walk Away From That!"

A dispirited, conscience-stricken young woman who had undergone an abortion said, "I think this is going to affect me for the rest of my life. I don't feel anything right now except relief. But it is the kind of thing that hits you later, and you never quite forget it. You can walk away from the hospital, but you can't walk away from that—the abortion."

****

The Right of Life

New York's Senator James Buckley introduced a resolution in the Senate which said, "With respect to the right of life, the word 'person' applies to all human beings, including their unborn offspring at every stage of their biological development, irrespective of age, health, function, or condition of dependency."

* * * *

Twins Aborted

A pregnant girl who had an abortion, later learned that twins were aborted. Deep depression ensued. Suicide was contemplated. Whenever she saw a pregnant woman, she had a burning hatred toward her, though she was a stranger to her. When her sister-in-law became pregnant she hoped that she would lose her baby.

An ill-at-ease conscience and emotional distress are often the aftermath of the planned destruction of unborn infants.

* * * *

Had Beethoven Been Aborted

A. Dudley Dennison, M.D., says in *Give It to Me Straight, Doctor* (Zondervan Publishing House):

"I would approve of and sign for an abortion when rape or incest has occurred. I would approve and sign for an abortion when there is substantial risk that the child would be born with grave physical or mental defects. The tragedy of mongoloidism, the defects from German measles in the pregnant mother, the horror of Huntington's chorea appearing explosively when a man is in the prime of life. . .and the heartache of PKU Tay-Sach's disease of familial idiocy and other grave inheritable diseases move me to approve of the removal of a fetus. Yet I would do this knowing of a case where the mother was tubercular, the father syphilitic, and of their children, one was born blind, one was deaf and dumb, and one also tuberculous. If I had ended the one pregnancy, *I would have denied the world of Beethoven!*"

* * * *

An Unenviable Record

New York City has the unenviable record of being the largest abortion center in the western world!

Bernard N. Nathanson, M.D., once the director of the center for Reproduction and Sexual Health, said, "No longer is there a serious doubt in my mind that human life exists within the womb from the very onset of pregnancy."

* * * *

Simply Because a Mother Wills It

In the Christian Medical Society's *Journal*, Dr. Carl Henry wrote:

"Is the life of a helpless fetus forfeitable simply because the mother wills its death and the parents sense no Good Samaritan obligation to spare it? If so, do the mother and father in principle forfeit any rights of their own when they become senile and their children are disposed to put them out of the way? If the decision to preserve or destroy a living fetus lacking full human life rests upon a parent's personal convenience or upon a social consideration such as the population explosion, is not the case even stronger for a child to dispose of parents when senility overtakes them? If we are free to destroy human life and to deny its dignity at one stage, why not at another?"

* * * *

"I Can't Live With Contradictions"

Nancy E. Thompson, M.D., who works among the Navajo Indians, said:

"Some of my fellow staff members work themselves sick trying to help a child to be born and live, and then send a young pregnant Navajo elsewhere for an abortion because she has too many children or just wants an abortion.

"Well, I can't live with such contradiction, and I will not work in a place where such contradiction exists. Either I am for helping children and people have life, or I am not going to stay in medicine. I don't know whether the unborn children will get enough to eat; and though I care about this, I will still try to right obvious injustices. I will not kill an infant, whether in embryo or fully developed. The coming child is a person and anyone in medicine knows that!"

Malcontents

Professor James C. Koch of Austin, Texas, said:

"I have been a professor of economics at St. Edwards University for the past fifteen years. But unlike most academic liberals that I know, I have been unable to purge my mind of the notion that abortion is a grave wrong.

"Beside the ethical and philosophical reasons for my opposition, I get further reinforcement from the gibes I get from the groups that advocate abortion. For example, the militants of the Women's Lib Movement—a loose association of whimpering malcontents, unhappy at home, unhappy at work; miserable if married, miserable if not; depressed with children, depressed without them . . . . The father, who is equally responsible for the pregnancy, is not even considered by the court or the movement. Only the woman and her physician."

* * * *

"Raw Political Power"

Justices Rehnquist and White, in expressing their dissenting opinions to the Supreme Court's decision permitting abortion, accused the majority of the court of "using raw political power to impose a constitutional barrier to state efforts to protect human life by investing mother and doctors with a constitutionally protected right to exterminate it!"

* * * *

From Conception

Dr. Micheline Matthews-Roth of the Department of Microbiology and Molecular Genetics at Harvard said,

"Studies in embryology and genetics have conclusively proved that the embryo from conception is a living human being."

* * * *

Predetermined Gender

It is possible now to pre-select the gender of a baby-to-be, whether a boy or a girl. The procedure, called *Amniocentesis*, enables medics to determine by testing the amniotic fluid from the mother's uterus whether the nascent infant is male or female.

If the gender of the developing baby isn't the gender wanted by the mother, she can undergo an abortion, apart from any consideration of even therapeutic reasons!

The Bible says that children are an heritage of the Lord. He watches over them, determining what each one will be. How wrong it is for whimsical reasons to thwart His wondrous and eternal purposes.

"For this child I prayed; and the Lord hath given me my petition which I asked of Him."—I Sam. 1:27.

* * * *

"The Might-Have-Been Baby Waves at Me"

A mother of three children had a so-called "convenient" abortion during her fourth pregnancy. In describing the mixed reactions of herself and her husband, she said, "Our common denominator is one of shame! We were losing life that day, not giving life. I began to panic! I have only this ghost—a very little ghost—that ap-

pears only when I'm seeing something beautiful, like a full moon on the ocean; and the might-have-been baby waves at me. I wave back at the baby. It is not a memory I like to dwell on."

Adapted from
The Presbyterian Journal.

* * * *

Totally Dedicated to Saving Babies

"Infants born with serious heart or artery defects are being surgically cured by first being made to 'die,'" said Dr. William Mustard of the Hospital for Sick Children, Toronto. "The surgical procedure involves draining the babies of blood and then dropping their body temperature to about sixty degrees. This permits surgeons to perform complex repairs to such defects as malformed arteries or leaky heart chamber walls.

"You're really operating on an infant who's 'dead.' This creates a perfectly bloodless surgical field. You have about an hour to do this. After the surgical repair is completed, the patient is warmed and the blood is restored. It's astonishing!" exclaimed Dr. Mustard.

It is praiseworthy that there are medics who are totally dedicated to saving babies when so many unborn, unwanted babies are being "salted out"—wantonly destroyed for selfish reasons.

* * * *

Reminiscent of Hitler's Germany

Dr. Paul Mark, professor of sociology at St. John's University in Collegeville, Minnesota, believes that

"America's growing acceptance of abortions could lead to legislating 'mercy killings' for the sick, aged, mentally ill and hopeless alcoholics."

Dr. Mark said:

"Abortions remind me of Hitler's Germany where they viewed many human lives as not worth living and exterminated millions. That started with the chronically ill, then it took in alcoholics, retarded children and ended by killing six million Jews!

"Abortions are a $150 million-a-year business in New York state, where they are becoming flooded with quacks, untrained people and unsanitary conditions.

"I recently sat in on a three-day symposium of pro-abortionists in Los Angeles. Not once during the three days were the rights of the unborn child as a human being even mentioned. They called the babies 'protoplasm,' 'products of conception,' and then joked about the 'substantial killing' that could be made in the New York abortion market."

* * * *

A Tragic Error

Many believe the Supreme Court of the United States made a tragic error when a majority of its members decreed that the killing of an unborn child is a fundamental right, inherent in the Constitution, and decreed that abortion is allowable "up to seven months."

Abortion "up to seven months" is the destruction of human life. Life is precious. The defenseless, developing fetus in the mother's womb has the inalienable right to life. Our laws must safeguard this sacred, infrangible right.

* * * *

A DIRGE OF THE UNBORN

My little feet will never run
  On early morning lawn;
My feet were crushed before they had
  A chance to greet the dawn!

My growing height will never be
  Recorded on the wall;
My growth was stopped when still
  unborn,
  Unseen and very small!

My lips and tongue will never taste
  The good fruit of the earth;
For I myself was judged to be
  A fruit of little worth!

I'll never walk the shores of life
  Or know the tides of time;
For I was coming but unloved,
  And that was my only crime!

Fay Clayton, in
Voice of the Nazarene.

* * * *

DISCOURAGEMENT—
ENCOURAGEMENT

Only a Word

One day a woman met Dr. Robert W. Dale on a street and said, "God bless you, Dr. Dale."

"May I ask your name?" Dr. Dale said.

The woman replied, "Never mind my name. If you could only know how you have made me feel hundreds of times and what a happy home you have given me! God bless you!"

A dark thread of depression ran through Dr. Dale's life. He spoke of "the strange, morbid gloominess" he often battled with for weeks at a time. Later he said of the unknown woman, "She seemed to take the dark cloud with her! The mist broke; the sunlight came. I breathed the free air of the mountain of God!"

It takes little either to encourage or discourage us. The Saviour often said to discouraged ones, "Be of good cheer."

Many are waiting a kind, loving word,
Help somebody today!
Thou hast a message, O let it be heard,
Help somebody today!

Carrie E. Breck.

* * * *

A LETTER CAME TODAY

A letter came today—
Just a plain white homey letter came today,
From a long-time friend a continent away.
Strange, I thought, that such a simple thing
Could so neatly turn a winter day to spring!

Robert Caldwell.

* * * *

Sees Only Hole in Doughnut

Two farmers were neighbors. One was an incurable optimist; the other, a grumpy, repelling pessimist.

One day the optimist said to the pessimist, as the sun shone in its resplendent glory, "What a bright and glorious day!"

"Yes," said the pessimist, "but I fear that the sun will burn up my crop."

Meeting later, as refreshing rain fell upon the parched ground, the optimist said to his pessimistic neighbor, "How grateful I am for the Heaven-sent showers!"

The pessimist said, "But I am afraid the rain will drown my crop."

The optimist resolved to do his best to cure his neighbor of his dismal, defeatist outlook on life.

One day they went duck hunting. Each killed a duck. The optimist whistled for his dog to retrieve the kill. The dog appeared to walk on water! How proud was the optimist when his dog placed the duck at his feet!

"Now, what do you say?" asked the optimist of the pessimist.

He replied, "But the dog can't swim."

Told by Ralph M. Smith.

* * * *

Post-Mortem Praise

Said Christopher Morley, "If we discovered that we had only five minutes to say all we have wanted to say, every telephone would be occupied by those calling other people to say, 'I love you!'"

Do not wait to say, "I love you." Speak words of commendation and encouragement *now.* How worthless is post-mortem praise!

TELL HIM NOW

If with pleasure you are viewing
Any work a man is doing,
  If you like him or you love him, tell
  him now;
Don't withhold your approbation
Till the parson makes oration,
  And he lies with snowy lilies o'er his
  brow.

For, no matter how you shout it,
He won't really care about it,
  He won't know how many teardrops you
  have shed;
If you think some praise is due him,
Now's the time to slip it to him,
  For he cannot read the tombstone when
  he's dead.

More than fame and more than money
Is the comment kind and sunny,
  And the hearty, warm approval of a
  friend;
For it gives in life a savor,
It makes you stronger, braver
  And it gives you heart and courage to the
  end.

If he earns your praise, bestow it,
If you love him, let him know it,
  Let the words of true encouragement be
  said;
Do not wait 'til life is over,
And he's underneath the clover,
  For he cannot read the tombstone when
  he's dead!

F. W. Brazier.

Would-Be Escapists

"Historians tell us," said Dr. George Sweet, "that the real reason for the Children's Crusade in 1212 A. D., was that the young people were trying to escape from the realities of their world.

"Did they escape? Sadly, they did not. When they reached Genoa and Venice, they met every kind of evil. Slave traders carried some off to Egypt, many became ill and died, while others turned back, without a cross, without a song. All were disillusioned and discouraged."

Christians sometimes lament, "Oh that I had wings like a dove! for then would I fly away, and be at rest" (Ps. 55:6).

The Saviour prayed thus for God's children: "I pray not that thou shouldest take them out of the world, but that thou shouldest keep them from the evil" (John 17:15).

* * * *

"I'll Stay Where You Want Me to Stay, Dear Lord!"

A young minister, defeated and unhappy in his pastorate, prayed that God would lead him to some influential person at a forthcoming convention who would enter helpfully and understandingly in effecting a change in his situation.

He met that person as if by divine arrangement. After expressing a desire to help, the more mature and experienced pastor gave this sound and needed advice: "Young man, you'll never be happy anywhere until you get happy *where you are!*"

It was just the advice the unhappy young minister needed. Dedicating himself anew to the all-glorious service of Christ, he continued for some three years longer in the church where he was, and won the victory over discouragement. God crowned those three years with signal success!

The grass-is-greener-on-the-other-side-of-the-fence attitude brings discontentment and unhappiness. *Acres of Diamonds* beneath your doorstep was the truth which one of God's spiritual giants, Dr. Russell Conwell, emphasized in a lecture which he delivered more than 6,000 times.

If you are where God has placed you, let this be your resolve: "I'll *stay* where you want me to stay, dear Lord!"

Told by William Cook.

* * * *

How Little It Takes!

Three students at Southwestern Baptist Theological Seminary ganged up on a fellow student to see how he would react to their suggestions about imagined illness.

On Monday morning they stood at intervals along the walkway leading to a classroom building.

As the student approached, the first one said, "You don't look well this morning. Are you ill? Is anything wrong?"

The student replied, "I'm feeling fine!"

Then the second one said, "My, you look burdened and bothered. Maybe I can share your difficulties. At least, I can try."

"Thank you for your concern," the student said, "but everything is okay with me."

Before he entered the classroom, the third one said to him, "My, you look so ill and distressed. It is evident something is wrong. Can I help you?"

Suddenly the student succumbed to a feeling of illness and distress. He was excused from the class by the teacher and went dejectedly to his room—the victim of negative suggestions and discouraging words.

It takes little to discourage us: a frown or a cutting, critical word. Likewise, it takes little to encourage us: a kindly look, a warm handclasp, or a word of commendation.

How rewarding and ennobling it is to say to distraught discouraged ones, 'Be of good cheer' (Isa. 41:6).

Told by Ralph M. Smith.

* * * *

Where Rest Is Found

Some years ago a distraught man, filled with anxiety and exhausted from lack of sleep, sought the help of a psychiatrist in Florence, Italy.

The doctor learned that, despite the man's low mental state, he was in good physical condition. Then he said to the patient, "I'll tell you what you need. A circus is now performing in our city. The star performer is a clown named Grimaldi, acclaimed to be the world's funniest clown. Go and see him. He will make you laugh and cure your sadness."

The man said dejectedly, "He can't help me. *I am Grimaldi!*"

Long ago the psalmist pleaded, "Oh, that I had the wings like a dove! for then would I fly away, and be at rest" (Ps. 55:6).

How like God's children of old are many of His children today. Of them it was said, "They have forgotten their restingplace" (Jer. 50:6).

How gracious and fear-allaying is the Saviour's invitation to God's restless children: "Come unto me, all ye that labour and are heavy laden, and I will give you rest" (Matt. 11:28).

> I came to Jesus as I was,
> Weary and worn and sad;
> I found in Him a restingplace,
> And He hath made me glad!
>
> Horatius Bonar.

* * * *

"The Damp of Hell"

Do you ever get down in the mouth and feel that the world has caved in on you?

Elijah did: He "sat down under a juniper tree: and he requested for himself that he might die. . .O Lord, take away my life" (I Kings 19:4).

Paul did: "We were pressed out of measure, above strength, insomuch that we despaired even of life" (II Cor. 1:8).

Spurgeon did: "Personally I have often passed through the dark valley of despair!"

Alexander Whyte did: His biographer, G. F. Barbour, said of him, "Resolute as was Dr. Whyte's character, he had seasons of deep depression regarding the results of his work in the pulpit and among his people."

John Henry Jowett did: He wrote to a friend in 1920, "You seem to imagine that I have no ups and downs, but just a level and lofty stretch of spiritual attainment with unbroken joy and equanimity. By no means! I am often perfectly wretched and everything appears most murky."

Andrew Bonar did: He wrote in his journal, July 4, 1857: "I was very melancholy, I may say, on Saturday evening. The old scenes reminded me of my ministry, and this was accompanied with much regret for past failures. I see in retrospect so much that was altogether imperfect and so much that was left undone."

G. Campbell Morgan did: On the tenth anniversary of his marvelous ministry at London's Westminster Chapel, he astounded his congregation by saying, "During these ten years, I have known more of visions fading into mirages, or purposes failing of fulfillment, and of things of strength crumbling into weakness than ever before in my life."

John Donne considered discouragement "the damp of Hell!"

Often God's children dejectedly ask with the psalmist, "Why art thou cast down, O my soul. . .why art thou disquieted in me" (Ps. 42:5).

Through grace, we can be victorious over spiritual depression: "Now thanks be unto God, which always causeth us to triumph in Christ" (II Cor. 2:14).

* * * *

Always From Beneath

"I have noticed," said Amy Carmichael, "that when God has purposes of blessing some person, the devil of Discouragement, who is one of Satan's most useful servants, is sure to come and whisper all sorts of miserable, depressing thoughts. Do not forget that discouragement is always from *beneath*, while encouragement is always from *above*."

In the long ago "David was greatly distressed; for the people spake of stoning him. . .but [he] encouraged himself in the Lord his God" (I Sam. 30:6).

* * * *

"Down in the Mouth"

Are you ever discouraged and "down in the mouth?" If so, remember Jonah, who was "down in the mouth" but came out all right. "A great fish swallowed up Jonah. . . . And the Lord spake unto the fish, and it vomited out Jonah upon the dry land" (Jonah 1:17; 2:10).

> If you trust and never doubt,
> He will surely bring you out;
> Take your burden to the Lord
> and leave it there.
>
> C. Albert Tindley.

"The Mighty God"

Too many of God's children dejectedly and defeatedly say, "Look what the world has come to!"

God's radiant, triumphant children exclaim, "Look *Who* has come to the world: 'The mighty God' (Isa. 9:6); 'The Lord strong and mighty, the Lord mighty in battle' " (Ps. 24:8). He came to give "beauty for ashes, the oil of joy for mourning, the garment of praise for the spirit of heaviness" (Isa. 61:3).

Though whelming evil abounds, God's grace superabounds. God is still on the throne, "keeping watch above His own!"

> This is my Father's world,
> O let me ne'er forget,

> That though the wrong seems
> oft so strong,
> God is the ruler yet!
>
> Maltbie Babcock.

* * * *

A Mighty Stimulus

The American industrialist Charles Schwab said, "I have never seen a man who could do real work except under the stimulus of encouragement, enthusiasm and the approval of the people for whom he is working."

How little it takes to either discourage or encourage us!

> Only a word of anger,
> But it wounded one sensitive heart;
> Only a word of sharp reproach,
> But it made the teardrops start!
>
> Only a word of kindness,
> But it lightened one heart of its
> grief;
> Only a word of sympathy,
> But it brought one soul relief!
>
> Anon.

* * * *

UPHELD

> When the storm's a rumblin'
> And our strength's a crumblin'
> And Oh! so sore we're tried;
> When the wind's a blowin'
> And our spirit's lowerin,'
> O Lord, support us on the leanin'
> side!
>
> When the loved one's taken
> And the heart's a breakin'
> And sorrow's multiplied;
> When we're crushed and grievin'
> And our hope's a leavin,'
> O Lord, support us on the leanin'
> side!

When the thunder's roarin'
And the torrent's pourin'
And sweepin' in the tide;
When we're rowin,' rowin'
And our courage goin',
O Lord, support us on the leanin'
side!

When we're weak and fallin'
And we need recallin',
Be Thou our Stay, our Guide;
As we're heav'nward hiein'
When a livin' dyin',
O Lord, support us on the leanin'
side!

Edith L. Mapes.

* * * *

"The Spirit of Heaviness"
(Isa. 61:3).

At times Martin Luther succumbed to deep and darksome depression. His face became like a blown-out lamp—dark and cheerless.

His wife was a woman of great wisdom and spiritual understanding. Wanting to extricate her husband out of his despondency, she conjured up a novel idea: She dressed in black and covered her face with a black veil, formerly worn by women when loved ones were taken from them by death.

How startled Luther was when she came into his presence and exclaimed, "Martin, God is dead!"

"Foolish woman," he mused. "That's impossible! God cannot die!"

'Twas then she became God's messenger with a greatly needed message to her dejected husband.

"Martin, for days you have been the embodiment of despondency—sullen and cheerless, acting like God is dead!"

How repellent are God's children when they become dejected and discouraged and fail to triumph in the One who long ago entered history's stream "to give. . .beauty for ashes, the oil of joy for mourning, the garment of praise for the spirit of heaviness" (Isa. 61:3).

Told by Rev. Francis Dixon.

* * * *

DRUGS

A Dead-End Street to Emptiness

"When smoked, marijuana moves quickly into the blood stream and acts on the blood stream and the brain and nervous system. It affects the user's mood, memory, concentration; it retards speech and distorts hearing, vision, and sense of space and time. The user may have delusions and mild hallucinations on his 'trip' that can last from three to five hours. . . . Like alcohol, it lowers inhibitions and makes it easier for the users to forget their morals. It is a dead-end street to emptiness.

"Drugs are a cop-out on life, while Jesus is the introduction to life: 'I am come that they might have life, and that they might have it more abundantly' " (John 10:10).

A. Dudley Dennison in
Give It to Me Straight, Doctor
(Zondervan Publishing House).

* * * *

Hooked

A boy 15 years old regretfully confessed:

"I started to smoke pot about two years ago. It was fun, I thought, and I didn't see that it was doing me any harm. Some months later I realized that I was 'hooked' and couldn't stop, though some so-called experts say it isn't addictive. I became alarmed when I could not remember where I had put things and blanked out on telephone numbers and addresses that used to come easy. Then I resolved to shake the enslaving habit when it became apparent that I was in serious trouble at school. My grades were going down and I flunked three subjects.

"It has been three months since I quit the habit. My school work has improved but it's nowhere near what it was two years ago. I still have some very crazy dreams. The worst mistake I ever made in my life was experimenting with the lousy stuff! It messes up my life plenty. I hope to God that I get back to normal again!"

* * * *

How They Rate

The Drug Enforcement Administration affirms that tranquilizing tablets are now the cause of more sickness and death in the United States than any other drug. Alcohol is rated second, heroin third, marijuana fourth.

* * * *

Kids or Mice

In commenting upon the findings of a national research commission on marijuana, which advocated the lifting of the ban on marijuana, a high school teacher said:

"I don't know what kind of research the commission did that brought them to the conclusion that marijuana is harmless. I am a high school teacher and see these kids every day. I tell you it's a tragedy what is happening to hundreds of them. I've seen bright teenagers deteriorate into zombies, lose interest in school work, sports, friends and cleanliness. Their reactions to almost everything become distorted. They become lethargic, passive and depressed. On Mondays especially, they come to class stoned and fall asleep during the study period. The most frightening part of it all is that they cannot think straight. That teenagers should take such a chance with their precious mental machinery horrifies me!

"I wonder if those addlebrained commission members have children of their own. If not, I suggest that they go to any high school in the country and talk with the teachers. This is where the research should be done—not in the laboratories where they measure the effects of chemicals on mice. I really don't care much about mice. I love kids, and I hate to see what marijuana is doing to them!"

* * * *

Potent and Perilous

Dr. Samuel Irwin, professor of psychopharmacology at the University of Oregon Medical School, said, "The drug (nicotine) has a high psychotic dependence liability, moderate tolerance development, and a potential for physiologic dependence in some genetically prone individuals. With chronic use, the primary hazards are cancer of the lungs, larynx and mouth, irritation of the respiratory system, chronic bronchitis and pulmonary emphysema, damage to the heart, blood vessels and impaired vision. If taken orally, death may occur within a few minutes. Nicotine is one of the most poisonous drugs!"

* * * *

The Nation's Number One Drug

The nation's number one drug problem is alcoholism, according to a new government report. A total of 9.6 million Americans are alcoholics, according to the National Institute on Alcohol Abuse and Alcoholism.

* * * *

Number One Drug Problem

Editorialized *Baptist Standard:*
"Marijuana is a new problem for our time. We do not have the answer as to how it can be controlled. All the attention given to it pushes into the background the older problem of controlling alcohol, but alcohol costs industry billions of dollars annually in absenteeism and accidents, and takes the lives of thousands on the streets and highways.

"There is quite a contrast in our trying to deal with the two evils. We license outlets for alcoholic beverages and send police scurrying on raids for pot parties. Somebody may someday explain our variance when they write about our decline in civilization."
Alcoholic beverage is the medically acknowledged number one drug problem in America.
Many believe that the difference between a marijuana party and a cocktail party is the difference between six and a half dozen, however the latter can be more disastrous than the former.

* * * *

The Deadliest of Them All

For a nation to profess great interest in most of the ills that offer even a remote threat to human life, the indifference toward *the proven killer alcohol* is curious indeed. Let a deodorant be shown to contain some ingredient that appears to produce cancer in mice, and it is likely to be forced off the market by prompt government action.

After the Surgeon General's report that smoking is injurious to health, laws were passed requiring solemn warnings in cigarette advertising and on every package of cigarettes. Radio and TV spots, paid for by federal funds, encourage smokers to stop.

But let it be shown that approximately nine million Americans are excessive drinkers; that an alcoholic's lifespan is shortened by ten to twelve years; that at least half of the 55,500 automobile deaths per year are directly traceable to drinking; that three-fourths of all prison inmates committed their crimes after drinking; that alcohol is now in first place on the teenage drug abuse scene—let all these grim statistics be cited, and most people simply shrug their shoulders and turn their attention to something else.

The National Council on Alcoholism reports that alcoholic employees cost American business $4.3 billion a year in absenteeism, sloppy work, and eventual expense of training replacements, not to mention the more personal and social costs of their addiction. The National Institute on Alcohol Abuse and Alcoholism estimates that the total dollar cost of alcoholism may be as high as $15 billion a year.

Despite the damaging effects of even moderate drinking and the deadly effects of alcohol additions. . . most people simply refuse to take the problem of alcohol seriously.

Most curious of all is the increasing permissiveness toward drinking exhibited by the churches. One would think that Christians, of all people, would shun any indulgence responsible for as many assorted woes as this one. Apparently not.

G. Liken Taylor, Editor,
Presbyterian Journal in
Christianity Today.

* * * *

Born Hooked

An appalling report was given sometime ago in *Calgary Herald.* It affirmed in part: In any typical year, at least 1,300 babies were born in Calgary in a trap. Shortly after birth the infants, often born prematurely, showed signs of tremors, vomiting, diarrhea, fever, breathing difficulties, extreme irritability, sweating, and convulsions—essentially the same symptoms as those of a junkie (dope addict) in a prison cell going without heroin. The babies are, in fact, addicts, day-old junkies hooked in the womb by the heroin in their mother's blood. The signs are the outward manifestations of the horror of heroin withdrawal."

The terrible entail of sin involves even unborn generations: "Wherefore, as by one man sin entered into the world, and death by sin; and so death passed upon all men, for that all have sinned" (Rom. 5:12). Innocent babes often suffer physically as the consequence of paternal or maternal sins.

Lowell said, "They enslave their children's children who compromise with sin."

* * * *

Help! Help! Help!

The Baptist Standard editorialized:

"The American Medical Association has been asked by the Council on Mental Health to protect the public against a significant problem of alcoholism, drug dependence and other disorders existent among practicing physicians.

"This is another chapter in a deteriorating society. The report quoted one study as showing narcotic addiction among physicians varies from thirty to one hundred times that in the general population. Turn in any direction and the same general problem exists in varying degrees. The Christian ministry is not immune from its own embarrassment.

"Our permissive society has dropped one standard after another. The entertainment world has sunk below the gutter. The print media wallows in it.

"Standards have vanished. One who wants to advocate them is branded as a prude or something worse. Forgive us our sins and give us a label. We want it as a contrast to so many around us!"

* * * *

A Horrendous Sound

In a large hospital in Manhattan, one often hears a sudden, high, shrill wail that is unmistakable. Every nurse in pediatrics knows at once that the cry announces the birth of another heroin-addicted baby! "It's the most horrendous sound I ever heard!" said nurse Mary Jones. "You can't mistake it. Perspiring, sneezing, vomiting and in pain, the newborn infant of an addicted mother heads into life with every possible card stacked heartbreakingly against him!"

* * * *

DRUNKARDS

"Not a Disease"

Dr. Jules Masserman, professor of Psychology and Neurology at Northwestern University, says that generally alcoholism is *not* a disease, but rather a form of deviant behavior. He says, "On the basis of a third of a century of intensive interest, laboratory research and clinical experience in the field, I feel justified in maintaining that no one has demonstrated any consistent genetic, constitutional, dietary, infectious, or other purely physiological causes of alcoholism, although an excessive intake of any drug can injure body and brain tissue, impair resistance and thus escalate the advance effects."

* * * *

If a Disease. . .

If alcoholism is a disease, it is the only disease that is bottled and sold; the only disease that requires a license to be in business; a self-imposed disease by choice; the only disease that produces revenue for the government; the only disease which incites rape, murder and other crimes; the only disease which causes violent deaths on the highways; the only disease promoted by advertisement. Saddest of all, it robs children of a secure, happy home.

* * * *

Strange Silence

Drunkenness is the major drug problem of our society. It has killed more Americans than all the wars of our history!

The computers spell out the sad statistics. Seventy-nine percent of American men and 63 percent of the women spend 16.5 billion dollars each year—twice the amount spent on all religion and welfare—for our most addictive and damaging drug.

America reaps annually 25,000 alcohol-related deaths on the highways; 28,000 deaths from cirrhosis of the liver, which is due mainly to alcoholism; nine million alcoholics; and nine million problem drinkers.

Why hasn't there been a massive campaign against alcohol? Why doesn't the medical profession go after the drug that is working far more havoc than marijuana? The reason is that people don't like to campaign against their own vices.

Dr. A. J. Dennison, Jr.,
What's the Prescription, Doctor?

* * * *

A Plague

An article on alcoholism which appeared in *Time* stated, "The upsurge of problem drinking among the young is only part of a more disturbing nationwide problem. In the past few years alcoholism, among youths and adults alike, has at least been recognized as a plague.

"After heart disease and cancer, alcoholism is the country's biggest health problem. Most deaths attributed to alcoholism are caused by cirrhosis of the liver. An alcoholic's life span is shortened by ten to twelve years.

"In half of all murders in the United States, the killer or the victim, or both, have been drinking. A fourth of all suicides are found to

have significant amounts of alcohol in the blood stream."

* * * *

Drunkenness Among Women

Dr. David Smith, professor of pediatrics at the University of Washington in Seattle, said, "We now know clearly that alcohol is the most common teratogen agent that causes birth defects. I would advise women considering pregnancy or who are already pregnant to avoid alcohol altogether. The price of even moderate drinking may be *paid by the infant* in the form of growth deficiency, a small brain, facial distortion, poor coordination, skeletal and heart defects. Alcohol is more damaging to women than to men. If alcohol were a new agent coming on the market for the first time and we found these adverse effects, it would be banned immediately!"

* * * *

Women Pay Earlier

A recent University of Toronto study found that the average time of hazardous drinking before an illness occurs is 14.1 years shorter for women than for men and that alcoholic women have twice as much cirrhosis of the liver as men.

Alcoholism begins with the first drink! Touch not, taste not, handle not!

* * * *

A Feeble Half-Start

For thirty years Watson Spoelstra

was the sportswriter for the *Detroit News*. Until his conversion he freely imbibed alcoholic liquors. Here's how his turning to God occurred:

His eighteen-year-old daughter Ann was stricken with a brain hemorrhage. Her life hung in the balance. Going into the hospital chapel, Spoelstra knelt and entered into a silent agreement with God. He prayed, "I never paid much attention to You, God, but You must be in this room somewhere. Do something for Ann, and I'll let You do something for me!"

It was a feeble half-start, but God accepted his challenge. Ann recovered.

In commenting afterwards upon Ann's recovery, Spoelstra said, "That was God's easy part. It was tougher for Him to deal with a rogue like me. I can't explain how it works, but somehow the Lord just takes away the desire for alcohol. He did it in my case!"

* * * *

Traitors

General John J. Pershing, leader of the American Expeditionary Forces in World War I, said, "Banish the entire liquor industry from the United States, close every tavern, every brewery, suppress drinking by severe punishment to the drinker, and, if necessary, death to the seller, or maker, or both, *as traitors;* and the nation will suddenly find itself amazed at the efficiency, and startled at the increase in its labor supply. I know what is the greatest foe to my

men, greater even than the bullets of the enemy—alcohol!"

* * * *

Doctors Sick of It

Dr. P. A. Meehan, an Irish physician, said, "Most Irish doctors are getting heartily sick of alcoholics. They are sick of listening to the complaints of mothers and wives; sick of the nervous state of children whose health is being wrecked; sick of the road accidents and of the damage to hospital property by people being brought here in the middle of the night—intoxicated."

* * * *

Needed: a Hatchet Brigade

An AP dispatch said, "Trying to run a liquor store next door to a building that's being demolished is both hazardous and unprofitable," tavern owner P. L. Dulworth complained. His place adjoins the historic Hotel Dallas which is being razed to make way for downtown progress.

"First time that 6,000 pound ball hit the doomed structure, it cost me $1,500 worth of damage—the awning broke off wedging the front door open; a neon sign shattered and bottles of liquor toppled from shelves to the floor," fumed Dulworth.

We do not advocate lawlessness, but we have great admiration for Frances Willard and her praying "hatchet brigade" whose prayers and actions discomfited and put many saloons out of business years ago.

"Woe unto him that giveth his

neighbour drink, that puttest thy bottle to him, and makest him drunken also."—Hab. 2:15.

* * * *

Cocktails Can Eat Stomach!

Dr. Linda L. Shanbour, a University of Texas physiologist, and Larry L. Tague, a research associate, said:

"Consuming cocktails rapidly, as people do at parties or before dinner, causes the lining of the stomach to erode away and actually to start bleeding. Alcohol breaks down a complex transplantation system within cells which normally carries acid into the stomach. As a result, the acids start acting on the gastric mucosa, or stomach lining. Within thirty minutes after consumption of two or three martinis, part of the stomach lining is eroded away by the acid, and hemorrhaging occurs!"

Alcoholic beverages are industrially unsafe, physiologically unsafe, judgmentally unsafe and eternally unsafe: "Know ye not that the unrighteous shall not inherit the kingdom of God? . . . Nor thieves, nor covetous, nor drunkards" (I Cor. 6:9,10).

* * * *

Exit Brain

Shakespeare said, "O God, that men should put an enemy in their mouths to steal away their brains!"

* * * *

Drowned

Sir Walter Scott penned:

He bids the ruddy cup go round,
Till sense and sorrow both are drowned!

* * * *

As Masters Take Slaves

The Journal of the American Medical Association said: "Drink has taken five million men, women and youths in the United States—taken them as masters take slaves, and new acquisitions are going on at the rate of 200,000 a year!"

* * * *

Industrial Hangover

Dr. J. R. Drumwright, assistant medical director for Phillips Petroleum Company, said, "Alcoholism and problem drinking among employees is causing an industrial hangover for industry in the United States. The hidden cost of problem drinking amounts to about $15 billion every year in losses for industry. The losses come in decreased productivity, absenteeism, tardiness, accidents, cost of training new people and poor decisions."

How helpless the alcoholic is to overcome his addiction unless he has God's help and the help and encouragement of others who have been set free from the great destroyer—alcohol.

"If the Son. . .shall make you free, ye shall be free indeed."—John 8:36.

* * * *

A Chance to Live

In an article in *Parade* entitled "The Food Shortage," it was stated, "Over 3 million tons of malt, barley, corn and other grains were used annually in the United States to produce beer, whiskey and other alcoholic spirits."

If this needless waste of grain were eliminated, starving millions around the world would have a chance to live.

God's ancient prophet Isaiah asked, "Wherefore do ye spend money for that which is not bread? and your labour for that which satisfieth not?" (Isa. 55:2).

* * * *

Helpless Without God's Help

Harold E. Hughes, U. S. Senator, said:

"If I could, I would remove alcohol from the earth. No good comes from it. It is the most destructive thing I know of on the face of the earth.

"After working with alcoholics and their problems for twenty years, I know that alcohol destroys people, homes, families, children, and everything a person believes in. I don't think anybody can come back from alcohol without finding God.

"My family prayed for me. I had bargained with God a lot in the course of the war and in the post-war years, but one day I came to the point of surrender (to God). I had been thinking about self-destruction. Most alcoholics consider suicide at some point if they keep on drinking.

"I had hurt everyone I loved, and felt that if I didn't stop hurting them I didn't want to live. So I prayed. It was perhaps my first honest prayer in ten years. There was no eloquence in my prayer. I remember well what I

said, 'God, help me. I can't help myself. If there is any purpose in my life, You've got to direct it. I can't.'

"That was the end of it, and something happened! Deliverance came, grand and glorious! What I had been powerless to do, God did instantly. He broke the shackles of enslaving habit!"

"Therefore if any man be in Christ, he is a new creature: old things are passed away; behold, all things are become new."—II Cor. 5:17.

He is able to deliver thee,
He is able to deliver thee;
Tho' by sin opprest,
Go to Him for rest;
Our God is able to deliver thee.
W. A. Ogden.

* * * *

How Does One Become a Drunkard?

Declared the Alcoholism Council of San Fernando Valley, California:

"Alcoholics are more susceptible than non-drinkers to heart attack, high blood pressure, emphysema, diabetes and, of course, cirrhosis of the liver. Alcoholism ranks a close third to cancer and heart disease as man's greatest killer.

"A fourth of all who die from fire while smoking in bed are alcoholics. One out of every three who commit suicide are alcoholics. The suicide rate for problem drinkers is fifty-eight times greater than for non-heavy drinkers. The alcoholic employee who is still working averages a loss of twenty-two more working days a year and dies twelve years sooner than non-alcoholics who may be working at his side."

How does one become an alcoholic? Only by imbibing alcoholic beverages! Alcoholism begins with the first drink. Don't forget: Be wise! Touch not, taste not, handle not!

* * * *

Camouflaged

A. Dudley Dennison, M.D., spoke timely in *Give It to Me Straight, Doctor* (Zondervan Publishing House):

"We can make more varieties of this poison, alcohol, package and advertise it in more deceptive ways, and pretend better that it isn't *the major drug problem* in our society. We can even change the terminology to blend with the camouflage over the enemy—alcohol—that has killed more Americans than all the wars in our history! For example:

He drinks whiskey and rum,
Scotch on the rocks—what fun!
He drinks himself nigh to extinction!
In grandmother's day, they called him a souse,
Today, he's a man of distinction.

"We spend $27.2 billion each year—twice what is spent on all religion and welfare—for our most addictive and damaging drug—alcohol!"

* * * *

Cuts Twelve Years Off His Life

Dr. Stuart S. Nemir, psychiatrist, warned:

"A problem drinker can cut from ten to twelve years off his life. Today we are all under tremendous pressure. I frequently see executives who feel the daily increasing need for high productivity. We have a sense of failure if we don't excel. We have to excel, not just do a good job—this idea pervades our culture. Problem drinkers deal with pressure by blunting their feelings and find alcohol an easy way to relieve tension."

* * * *

Fearful of Everything

Dr. J. J. Rowan, assistant education director for the Texas Commission on Alcoholism, said:

"The guy who used to brag about his drinking, then defends it, then won't talk about it, is an alcoholic. He begins to hide. He's intolerant of his job and boss, and is suspicious of his fellow workers. He's fearful of everything."

"*Wine is a mocker, strong drink is raging: and whosoever is deceived thereby is not wise.*"—Prov. 20:1.

Don't forget: Alcoholism begins with the first drink! Play safe: "Touch not; taste not; handle not" (Col. 2:21).

* * * *

FAITH

WHAT IS FAITH?

It is trust beyond all doubting
In God who rules above,
It is obedience without question,
It is resting in His love.

It is smiling through the teardrops,
It is struggling through each test,
It is the firm belief our Father
Is a God who knoweth best.
It is knowledge He will give us,
Light for each step of the way,
Grace for problems we encounter,
And strength for each new day.

Lois Mae Cuhel.

* * * *

"I Believe God"

The following lines were written on a prison wall in a concentration camp during World War II: "I believe in the sun, even when it is not shining! I believe in love, even when I feel it not! I believe in God, even when He is silent!"

A faith which glorifies God exclaims in the midst of storm and stress, peril and perplexity, "I believe God" (Acts 27:25).

O for a faith that will not shrink,
Tho' pressed by every foe,
That will not tremble on the brink
Of any earthly woe.

Wm. H. Bathurst.

* * * *

The Not-Expecting-Much Attitude

An old lady asked a speaker before he began his address, "Do you ever get nervous before you speak?"

He replied, "Yes, I do!"

The old lady said, "Well, you need not get nervous tonight, for we are not expecting much!"

Does not the not-expecting-much attitude characterize many of God's children when they go to God seeking His blessings?

William Carey, a pioneer missionary, said, "Undertake great things *for* God. Expect great things *from* God!"

Thou art coming to a King,
Large petitions with thee bring,
For His grace and pow'r are such,
None can ever ask too much!"

* * * *

Scientists May Be Shocked

"If Viking I's laboratories fail to come up with any trace of life on Mars, past or present, scientists will have to go back to the drawing board and devise a new theory for the origin of life," said Dr. Harold Klein, Viking's head biologist.

"Scientists have based their quest for life on Mars on the assumption that the theory of life's origin on earth—the theory of chemical evolution—would have to apply in some way to Mars as well. It would be a shock to find the chemical evolution theory disproved," said Dr. Klein, "but it's just a theory."

God is the Giver of physical and spiritual life: "God that made the world and all things therein. . .giveth to all life, and breath, and all things" (Acts 17:24,25); "And the Lord God formed man. . .and breathed into his nostrils the breath of life; and man became a living soul" (Gen. 2:7).

The Bible says, "Through faith we understand that the worlds were framed [ages were planned] by the word of God" (Heb. 11:3).

* * * *

"NOT KNOWING"

So on I go, not knowing,
I would not, if I might;
I'd rather walk in the dark with God
Than go alone in the light;
I'd rather walk by faith with Him,
Than go alone by sight.

* * * *

Fortuitous Atoms

Jonathan Swift, English clergyman and satirist, said, "That the universe was formed by a fortuitous concourse of atoms, I will no more believe than that the accidental jumbling of the alphabet would fall into a most ingenious treatise of philosophy."

God's eternal Word says, "In the beginning God created the heaven and the earth" (Gen. 1:1); "For ever, O Lord, thy word is settled in heaven" (Ps. 119:89).

* * * *

Wrong-Way Jim

Jim Marshall of the Minnesota Vikings ran the wrong way for a touchdown against his own team in a National Football League game. He was sincerely trying, but he was sincerely wrong!

Many sincere, though deluded, ones say, "It doesn't matter what you believe, just so you are sincere in your belief."
A nurse in a Chicago hospital mistakenly gave a lethal dose of medicine to a patient. She was sincere in what she did, but sincerely wrong.

* * * *

Easy to Find God

In affirming his faith in God, Aleksandr Solzhenitsyn said while living under communism in the Soviet Union, "How easy it is for me to live with You, Lord. How easy it is for me to believe in You."

* * * *

An Admonition

Dr. V. Raymond Edman often admonished, "Don't doubt in the dark what God has revealed in the light."

* * * *

"Taste and See"

The daughter of Karl Marx said, "I was brought up without any religion. I do not believe in God. But I came across a prayer in an old German book which began, 'Our Father which art in heaven.' I thought, *If the God of that prayer existed, I think I could believe in Him.*"

"*O taste and see that the Lord is good: blessed is the man that trusteth in him.*"—Ps. 34:8.

* * * *

"Through Faith We Understand" (Heb. 11:3).

A man came to Moody, asking for an explanation of a difficult passage in the Bible. "How do you explain it?" he asked Moody.

"I don't," was his reply.
"Well, how do you understand it?"
"I don't understand it," Moody replied.

The interrogator said, "You don't believe it then."

"Oh, yes," said Moody. "I do believe it. I believe many things I don't understand and can't explain."

"Through faith we understand that the worlds [ages] *were framed by the word of God."*—Heb. 11:3.

* * * *

Don't Miss Personal Application

Vance Havner said, "If you cannot always get the right explanation for some Scripture, be sure you don't miss the *personal* application of it." God's trustful children can *experience* divine truths which they cannot *explain.*

* * * *

"My Faith Looks Up to Thee"

"When politicians speak of faith," said Harvey Cox in a Southern Baptist seminar, "voters should ask, 'Faith in what?' Faith in God through Jesus Christ is the most trustworthy faith. Nowadays when somebody says, 'I believe,' it's not easy to know whether he is talking about God or about a Chevrolet."

How radiant we are when we sing from our hearts:

My faith looks up to Thee,
Thou Lamb of Calvary,
Saviour divine!

* * * *

One Utterly Believing Person

It has been said that the history of the world might be changed if one utterly believing person should arise!

How challenging to God's children is the Saviour's sure promise: "If thou canst believe, all things are possible to him that believeth" (Mark 9:23).

* * * *

Not Certain

George Whitefield, the great evangelist, asked a coal miner in Cornwall, England, "What do you believe?"

"I believe what my church believes," he replied.

"And what does your church believe?"

"Well, my church believes what I believe."

"But what do you *both* believe?" the evangelist persisted.

The Bible says, "Be ready always to give an answer to every man that asketh you a reason of the hope that is in you with meekness and fear" (I Pet. 3:15).

* * * *

A Statistical Monstrosity

George Gallup, world-famed statistician, said, "I could prove God statistically. Take the human body alone. The chance that all the functions of the body would just happen is a statistical monstrosity."

* * * *

Get in the Wheelbarrow

Some years ago a daring aerialist pushed a wheelbarrow, with a grooved wheel, over a steel wire above Niagara Falls. At the conclusion of the daring exhibition, the aerialist observed a boy looking at him with wonder and admiration.

Said the aerialist, "My boy, do you believe that I could put you in the wheelbarrow and then push it back to the American side of the falls?"

Instantly the boy replied, "I surely do!"

"Then get in the wheelbarrow," said the daredevil.

Swiftly the boy dashed away. When last heard of, he was still running.

How like that unbelieving boy are many of us. We manifest our unbelief by our not "undertaking great things *for* God and expecting great things *from* God."

Alice Marie Knight.

* * * *

"They'll Stop Coming to the Bakery"

Louis Cassels, United Press International correspondent and religious columnist, told a convention of the Protestant Church-Owned Publishers Association:

"Modern men are sick and tired of being told what they can't believe. They want to know what, if anything, they can believe. They feel they've been cast long enough in the role of a captive audience for theologians engaged in a reckless competition to see who can administer the rudest shock to the faithful. . . . If they persist in handing out stones when people ask for bread, they'll finally quit coming to the bakery!"

"Preach the word."—II Tim. 4:2.

* * * *

Convinced

A Christian lawyer said to his non-Christian lawyer friend, "If I made up a brief just as I would present it to the Supreme Court of the United States, I can show you that there is a God, and Christ is the Son of God. I can show you that the Bible is the Word of God. Will you read it if I put in legal form such evidence as would be accepted in any court in the world?"

The friend agreed to read it.

The Christian lawyer got the evidence ready; and after the unbelieving lawyer read it, he said, "You have convinced me. There is a God, and Christ is His Son, and the Bible is God's Word. I believe it!"

To each one comes the Heaven-given challenge, "O taste and see that the Lord is good: blessed is the man that trusteth in him" (Ps. 34:8).

* * * *

What Faith Isn't

Joseph Addison said in *Religion and Society*, "We have been told so often that action is a necessary expression of the Christian faith that we have come to think that action *is* the Christian faith. If we lose the faith in our frenzy to be active, we become like chickens without heads. We run in a panic, not knowing where we are running, or why."

How desperately urgent is the need to obey God's stabilizing command, "Be still, and know that I am God" (Ps. 46:10).

* * * *

"What Ain't So"

The humorist Josh Billings said, "It is better to know nothing than to know what ain't so."

The Bible speaks of some who "received not the love of the truth, that they might be saved. And for this cause God shall send them strong delusion, that they should believe a lie" (II Thess. 2:10,11).

In the long ago, Adam and Eve believed what wasn't so, with resultant direful consequences to themselves and mankind: "Wherefore, as by one man sin entered into the world, and death by sin; and so death passed upon all men, for that all have sinned" (Rom. 5:12).

* * * *

"ALL'S WELL SO FAR"

The optimist fell ten stories,
    And at each window's bar,
He cried out to his friends:
    "All's well so far!"

* * * *

ONLY BELIEVE

Faint not nor fear, His arms are near,
He changes not and thou art dear;
Only believe and thou wilt see
That Christ is all in all to thee!

* * * *

Believing Is Seeing

Augustine said, "Understanding is the reward of faith. Therefore seek not to understand that you may believe, but rather believe that you may understand."

Many say, "Seeing is believing," but the Saviour taught, "Said I not unto thee, that, if thou wouldest believe, thou shouldest see the glory of God?" (John 11:40).

* * * *

Except Faith

In 1923 a disastrous earthquake occurred in Japan! More than 165,000 persons perished! Bishop McKim sent this message to friends in America: "All lost but faith in God!"

* * * *

The Greatest Unused Power

Roger Babson, world-famed statistician, said, "The greatest undeveloped resource of our country is faith, and the greatest unused power is prayer."

How challenging is the simple faith shown by a black man who prayed, "O Lord, help me to remember that nothin's goin' to happen to me today that You and me together can't handle!"

Even a little faith in the almighty God can change humanly impossible situtations: "Is any thing too hard for the Lord?" (Gen. 18:14).

Long ago, in the midst of storm and stress, Paul triumphantly exclaimed, "Sirs. . . I believe God" (Acts 27:25).

* * * *

FAITHFULNESS

KEEP A-GOIN'

If you strike a thorn or rose,
　Keep a-goin',
If it hails or if it snows,
　Keep a-goin',
Ain't no use to sit and whine,
When the fish ain't on your line;
Bait your hook and keep a-tryin';
　Keep a-goin'.

If the weather kills your crop,
　Keep a-goin',
Though it's work to reach the top,
　Keep a-goin',
Suppose you're out of every dime,
Getting broke ain't any crime;
Tell the world you're feelin' fine,
　Keep a-goin'.

* * * *

A Fight Well Fought

At a verdant site on the campus of Bob Jones University is the tomb of Dr. Bob Jones, Sr., founder of the university. An epitaph on his tomb is a paraphrase of the words of the Apostle Paul: "I have fought a good fight, I have finished my course, I have kept the faith: Henceforth there is laid up for me a crown of righteousness, which the Lord, the righteous judge, shall give me at that day" (II Tim. 4:7,8).

The epitaph says:

A FIGHT WELL FOUGHT
A RACE WELL RUN
A FAITH WELL KEPT
A CROWN WELL WON!

What more could be said of any of God's messengers when they come to life's setting sun!

* * * *

"Dad, I Kept My Vow!"

"I was thirteen years old when my father died," said Dr. Ed Brooks Bowles. "He had been a preacher for thirty years. My mother, brothers and I received the word of his passing as we waited outside the hospital room.

"I remember clearly as though it were yesterday. My response was that of any boy that age. I could not believe it. I would not believe it. I spoke to him with the expectation that he would awaken. Moments passed. Then the reality of it swept over me. I climbed upon the bed where his body lay, as I had often done in life. I placed my arms around his neck. Then words came to me. I said, 'Dad, I will follow in your steps!'

"The words were spoken with sincerity, but their full meaning would not be grasped until six years passed and God consummated His call to me to preach. Then the vow I had made to my father surfaced with singular significance, 'Dad, I will follow in your steps!' The memory of it is one of the treasured moments of my life. When I meet him again in Heaven, I want to be able to say, 'Dad, I kept my vow!' "

How great will be our joy when we come to life's setting sun if we can say to our heavenly Father, "I have kept the faith" (II Tim. 4:7); "I was not disobedient unto the heavenly vision" (Acts 26:19).

* * * *

"Well Done!"

Often God's children see little or no results of their "labour of love." They plead, "Let thy work appear unto thy servants" (Ps. 90:16), that is, "Show us some fruitage of our labor."

This is certain: "For God is not unrighteous to forget your work and labour of love" (Heb. 6:10). God rewards faithful service.

If you give the best of your service,
   Telling the world the Saviour is come;
Be not dismayed when men don't believe you,
   He understands, He'll say, "Well done!"

But if you try and fail in your trying,
   Hands sore and scarred from work you've begun;
Take up your cross, run quickly to meet Him,
   He'll understand, He'll say, "Well done!"

If when this life of labor is ended,
   And the reward of the race you run;
"Oh! take sweet rest prepared for the faithful,"
   Will be His blest, and final, "Well done!"

                           Lucy E. Campbell.

* * * *

"EVER SURE"

Let us with a gladsome mind
Praise the Lord, for He is kind:
   For His mercies aye endure,
   Ever faithful, ever sure.

All things living He doth feed,
His full hand supplies their need:

For His mercies aye endure,
Ever faithful, ever sure.

                           John Milton.

* * * *

BE STRONG

It matters not
   How deep entrenched the wrong,
How hard the battle goes, the day how long,
Faint not, fight on!
   Tomorrow comes the song!

* * * *

"What's the Matter With Mrs. Craig Anyway?"

Mrs. Lila Craig hasn't missed attending church in 1,040 Sundays. In telling this outstanding record, a Nashville (Tenn.) newspaper commented:

"It makes one wonder, what's the matter with Mrs. Craig. Doesn't she have unexpected company? How is it that she never goes anywhere on Saturday night so that she is too tired to attend the worship service the next morning? Doesn't she ever 'beg off ' to attend picnics or family reunions, or have headaches, colds, nervous spells, or tired feelings? Doesn't she ever oversleep or need time to read her Sunday newspaper? Hasn't she ever become angry at the minister or had her feelings hurt by someone and felt justified in staying home to hear a good sermon on the radio or TV? What's the matter with Mrs. Craig anyway?"

We shortchange ourselves when we habitually absent ourselves, without

FAITHFULNESS, FATHERS

110

a cause, from God's house: "And let us consider one another to provoke unto love and to good works: Not forsaking the assembling of ourselves together, as the manner of some is" (Heb. 10:24,25).

* * * *

"Love Never Faileth"—Try It!

"When I was nine years old, I was in a Sunday school class in the Second Baptist Church, Hot Springs, Arkansas," said Ralph M. Smith. "The superintendent had a difficult time in getting a teacher for the class. The teachers came and went because the boys were mischievous and hard to control.

"The pastor induced a layman to teach the class. He was not well educated and read with difficulty. In teaching the lesson, he would call upon each boy to read a verse of the Scripture lesson and then talk about it. However, the teacher had the main requisite for imparting the eternal truths of God's Word—love. He loved us and we loved him. He provided wholesome activities and social events for us. He saw beneath our

roughness the latent qualities which could make us useful in service for God and man.

"I was in his class for three years.

"How rewarding were his belief in us and his faithfulness to our class! Out of the class came a lawyer, a judge and three ministers of the Gospel!"

* * * *

Thrown Out of Church

George Fox of England, the founder of the Society of Friends, was once evicted from a church. His frenzied persecutors cried, "Let us heave him out of the church!"

In telling about it, Fox said, "When they got me out, they threw me over a hedge. Afterwards they dragged me into the street, stoning and beating me exceedingly. Yet when I got upon my legs again, I declared unto them the Word of Life!"

God still has His faithful ones who count no sacrifice too costly to make Him known. They are willing to seal with their life's blood the testimony of their lips!

* * * *

FATHERS
(See also Parental Responsibility)

ONLY A DAD

Only a dad with a tired face,
Coming home from the daily race,
Bringing little of gold or fame,
To show how well he had played the
    game,

But glad in his heart that his own
    rejoice,
To see him come and hear his voice.

Only a dad of a brood of four,
One of ten million men or more,
Plodding along in the daily strife,

Bearing the whips and scorns of life,
With never a whimper of pain or hate,
For the sake of those who at home do
  wait.

Only a dad, neither rich nor proud,
Merely one of the surging crowd,
Toiling, striving, from day to day,
Facing whatever may come his way,
Silent whenever the harsh condemn,
Bearing it all for the love of them.

Only a dad, but he gives his all,
To smooth the way for his children
  small,
Doing with courage stern and brave,
The deeds that his father did for him;
This is the line that for him I pen:
Only a dad, but the best of men!

Edgar A. Guest,
Used by permission of
the copyright owners
Reilly & Lee, Chicago

* * * *

Tell Him Now!

A grateful son belatedly expressed his love and appreciation for his father who had been dead thirty years:

"Dear Dad, I feel that I must say something to you which I neglected to say as a boy. Only after passing through the long, hard school of life can I understand how you felt. I must have been a bitter trial to you. How foolish and undiscerning I was! I believed in my own shallow ideas; but I realize now how ridiculous they were compared to your calm, mature, character-building wisdom. I confess my failure with tears. I know now that *you did understand*. You knew me better than I knew myself. How patient and kind you were! I wish I could tell you today how much I love and appreciate you.

"Well, Dad, when we meet in the great beyond, I'll thank you that you cared enough for me to ceaselessly pray for your obstinate and headstrong boy."

* * * *

Confused

Said Warren Wiersbe in *Moody Monthly*, "If Junior hears Dad pray like a prophet on Sundays and then sees him lose his temper on weekdays, he may lose faith in Dad's Bible and the church."

Keep your temper! Nobody else wants it!

"He that ruleth his spirit [is better] than he that taketh a city."—Prov. 16:32.

* * * *

"I Want to Forget"

In a letter to her daughter, who was living with a man to whom she was not married, a distraught and brokenhearted mother wrote:

"Relatives gather together for weddings and reunions. If you ever attend them, we'll stay away. Your father says, 'I want to forget that I had a daughter!'

"You say that you and Bruce are more deeply and sincerely committed to each other than many married couples you know. I agree this is probably true, *but don't tell me that you aren't hurting anybody!*"

The commandment, "Thou shalt not commit adultery" (Exod. 20:14) has not been rescinded. It is as enduring as when first thundered from Sinai's rocky crags.

There's no sorrow like parental sorrow: "O my son Absalom, my son, my son Absalom! would God I had died for thee, O Absalom, my son, my son!" (II Sam. 18:33).

* * * *

Suppose

In *Family Life Today,* Dr. Howard Hendricks gave this hypothetical case of the reaction of a neglectful father:

"Suppose you've had a hard day at the office. You come home, have a good dinner and fall into your favorite chair with the sports page. Just as you begin to get involved, your little boy comes plowing through the middle of the paper and says, 'Hey, Dad, look what I drawed!'

"You blow your cork! 'Get outta here,' and the child runs off. But the next time he takes a little longer to come. And the next time a little longer about coming. By the time he's twelve years old, he could care less. You have provoked your child to wrath!"

* * * *

General MacArthur's Wish

At the close of a telecast showing the illustrious life of General Douglas MacArthur as a soldier, the retiring General said, "I don't want my son to remember me as a soldier, but as a father who prayed with him, 'Our Father which art in heaven, Hallowed be thy name!' "

Earthly glories are ephemeral: "All flesh is as grass, and all the glory of man as the flower of grass. The grass withereth, and the flower thereof falleth away" (I Pet. 1:24).

How aptly does the Latin proverb describe the short-lived glories of the world: *Sic transit gloria mundi*—thus passes away the glory of the world!

Heavenly glory, which awaits all God's children, is eternal: "While we look not at the things which are seen, but at the things which are not seen: for the things which are seen are temporal; but the things which are not seen are eternal" (II Cor. 4:18).

* * * *

He Gave His Life's Savings

A retired missionary told a minister of his son Henry, who had failed in several ventures and had spent all the money his father had loaned him. The minister was unimpressed until the father asked, "You know my son Henry, don't you—Henry Luce, the founder and editor of *Time, Life* and *Fortune* magazines, one of the greatest journalistic empires of the world?

"One day Henry asked me for $600. It was all I had in my life's savings. But I gave it to him. He started *Time* with it!"

How wonderful it is that our heavenly Father stands behind His children with His limitless and inexhaustible resources!

William Carey said, "Expect great

things *from* God. Undertake great things *for* God!"

Thou art coming to a King,
Large petitions with thee bring,
For His grace and pow'r are such,
None can ever ask too much.

Told by Warren Wiersbe.

* * * *

"Thou Shalt Not Steal"

"Dad and I were in a grocery store at the checkout counter," said Wesley Haystead. "Dad gave the cashier a $10 bill, but he mistakenly gave Dad change for a $20 bill. Dad called his attention to the error and returned the money. The command, 'Thou shalt not steal' means much to Dad."

Home Life.

* * * *

A Bedside Confession

The hour was late. A conscience-accused father, not being able to sleep, went to the bedside of his sleeping son and poured out his heart in a tearful confession:

"Listen, Son, I am saying this to you as you lie asleep with one little paw crumpled under your cheek and the blond curls stickily wet on your damp forehead. I have stolen in your room—alone. Just a short while ago, as I sat reading my paper in the library, a hot, stifling wave of remorse swept over me. I could not resist it. Guiltily I come to your bedside.

"These were the things I was thinking, Son: I had been cross to you. As you were dressing for school, you gave your face a dash with a towel; and I scolded you. I took you to task for not cleaning your shoes. I spoke angrily when I found that you had thrown some of your things on the floor.

"At breakfast, I found fault with you. You spilled things. You gulped down your food. You put your elbows on the table. You spread butter too thick on your bread. And, as you started off to play and I entered my car, you turned and waved your little hand and said cheerily, 'Good-bye, Daddy!' I frowned and said in reply, 'Hold your shoulders back.'

"Then it began all over again in the late afternoon. As I neared home, I spied you down on your knees playing marbles. There were holes in your stockings. I humiliated you before your boyfriends by making you march ahead of me back to the house. I said, 'Stockings are expensive and if you had to buy them, you would be more careful. Imagine that, Son, from a father! It was such a stupid thing—silly logic!'

"Do you remember, later, when I was reading in the library, how you came in softly, timidly, with a sort of hurt look in your eyes? When I glanced up over my paper, impatient at the interruption, you hesitated at the door.

'What is it you want?' I snapped. You said nothing but ran to me and in one tempestuous plunge threw your arms around my neck and kissed me again and again. Your small arms tightened with an affection that God had set blooming in your heart which even neglect could not wither. And then you were gone, pattering up the stairs.

"Well, Son, it was shortly afterwards that my paper slipped from my hand, and a terrible sickening fear came over me. Suddenly I saw myself as I really was in all my horrified selfishness, and I felt sick at heart. What had habit been doing to me—the habit of complaining, faultfinding and reprimanding? These were my rewards to you for being a boy. It was not that I did not love you. It was that I expected so terribly much of you. I was measuring you by the yardstick of my own years.

"There was so much that was good, noble and true in your character. Your little heart was as big as dawn itself. All this was shown by your spontaneous impulse to rush in and kiss me goodnight.

"Nothing matters tonight, Son! I have come to your bedside in the darkness, and I have knelt here choking with emotion and shame. It is a terrible atonement. I know you would not understand these things if I told them to you during your waking hours. Yet, I must say what I am saying. I must burn sacrificial fires alone here in your bedroom and make full confession. I have prayed to God to strengthen me in my new resolve. Tomorrow I want to be a *real* Daddy. I will chum with you, suffer when you suffer, laugh when you laugh. I will bite my tongue when impatient words come. I will keep saying, as if it were a ritual, *He is nothing but a boy, a little boy!* I am afraid I have visualized you as a man. Yet, as I see you now, Son, crumpled and weary in your bed, I see that you are still a boy. Yesterday you were in your mother's arms, your head on her shoulder!

"I have asked too much, too much of you, my dear little boy. A penitent kneels tonight at your bed as if it were a shrine. I kiss the little fingers, the damp forehead and yellow curls. If it were not for waking you, I would snatch you up and press you to my heart. I think of a greater and deeper love you displayed when you ran through the library door, embraced me and kissed me!"

Gospel Herald.

* * * *

GOD'S FORGIVENESS

The Ocean of God's Forgetfulness

As one of God's children was reading an encyclopedia, he exclaimed, "Praise the Lord!"

One asked, "What is there in an encyclopedia to elicit praise to God?"

"Sir, I just read that the ocean is five miles deep in some places!"

"But how does that call for praise to God?"

"Have you never read," asked the praiseful Christian, "of God's promise to all who seek His mercy and forgiveness: 'Thou wilt cast all their sins into the depths of the sea' (Mic. 7:19)?"

Oceanographers tell us that there are depths of the sea which have lain motionless for eons and that no surface storms, howsoever violent, can dredge up the forgiven and forgotten sins of God's children when they are submerged in the depths of God's love and forgetfulness: "Their sins and their iniquities will I remember no more" (Heb. 8:12).

Told by Ralph M. Smith.

* * * *

Blotted Out

Justification is our becoming instantly in God's sight just as if we had never sinned: "I have blotted out. . . thy transgressions" (Isa. 44:22).

* * * *

The Christian Rose

Dr. Howard A. Kelly usually wore a beautiful rose in the lapel of his coat. That was how he illustrated that the hidden source of the believer's life is in Christ.

"That's a lovely rose," friends greeting him would say.

"Actually, it's a Christian rose," the physician would reply, as he turned back the lapel of his coat and displayed a tiny bottle in which the stem of the rose was submerged in water. Then he would say, "When the Saviour pardons our sins, He unites us with Himself, thereby nourishing and strengthening us."

* * * *

Mercy's Door Still Open

At the close of World War II, the British government gave all deserters— some 18,000 men—the opportunity to report to proper authorities and receive leniency. The expiration date of the offer of mercy was March 31, 1947.

Only 1,300 accepted the offer.

God graciously offers to all who will accept it His merciful forgiveness: "Come now, and let us reason together. . .though your sins be as scarlet, they shall be as white as snow" (Isa. 1:18). However, God's Word warns, "My spirit shall not always strive with man" (Gen. 6:3).

* * * *

"Without Money"

Believing that God wanted him to put his medical billing system on a purely voluntary basis, Dr. Berry L. Moore, Jr., of El Dorado, Arkansas, felt compelled to take radical action. So he mailed letters to his patients which read: "This may be the last doctor's bill you will ever receive. Doesn't that sound good? If you desire to pay me for my services, that will be appreciated. If you are unable to pay, or even do not want to, we will not carry over bills or grudges. You will still be welcome into our office and will continue to receive the best medical care I am able to give!"

For years, Dr. Moore had been only a nominal Christian. His only motivation for attending church was the religious or moral influence it would have on his children. A young teacher's quiet Christian life eventually brought him face to face with Christ. One night, alone in his room, the proud young doctor tearfully accepted Christ as Lord of his life. He was changed drastically after that confrontation with Christ. Daily witnessing for his Saviour became an integral part of his medical practice.

Eventually Dr. Moore felt led to give God total command of the business part of his medical practice. After beginning his voluntary payment plan, collections of payments steadily declined. Several months later the reason came to light: a bookkeeper had been embezzling money, taking some $8,000! Before the bookkeeper left town, she sustained an injury. Dr. Moore treated her, forgave her, prayed for her and had the joy of leading her to Christ!

This unusual decision of the non-billing doctor is suggestive of a wonderful spiritual truth: when we come to God, He gives us His mercy and forgiveness—"without money and without price."

> Nothing in my hand I bring,
> Simply to thy cross I cling.
> Glynn Harris.

* * * *

Blotted Out

A hermit who had suffered the loss of all things in his renunciation of the world found no peace. In his lonely hut, he felt that the Lord was asking something more.

"But I have given You everything," he cried.

"All but one thing," answered the Lord.

"What is that, Lord?"

"Your sins."

The Lord has graciously promised to forgive the sins of all who penitently ask Him for it: "He will have mercy upon him. . .he will abundantly pardon" (Isa. 55:7).

> Come ye sinners, poor and needy,
> Weak and wounded, sick and sore;
> Jesus ready stands to save you,
> Full of mercy, love and pow'r.
> Joseph Hard.

* * * *

An Ugly Stain

After fishing all day in the streams of the Scottish highlands, some fishermen assembled in a small inn for tea. As the waitress sat down a cup of tea, a hand accidentally hit the teacup, knocking its contents against the whitewashed wall. An ugly brown stain appeared, marring its beauty.

One of the guests stood and said, "Never mind!"

Taking crayon from his pocket, he began to make a sketch around the stain. Presently there emerged a magnificent stag with spreading antlers!

The artist was Sir Edwin Landseer, England's foremost painter of animals.

If an artist can do that with an ugly stain, what cannot God do with lives stained by sin?

To failing, faltering and sinful mankind, God gives this gracious invitation: "Come now, and let us reason together. . .though your sins be as scarlet, they shall be as white as snow; though they be red like crimson, they shall be as wool" (Isa. 1:18).

* * * *

An Immeasurable Distance

In a chapel message at Wheaton College, then President V. Raymond

Edman said, "God's compassion and forgiveness are calculated by infinite distance: 'As far as the east is from the west, so far hath he removed our transgressions from us' (Ps. 103:12). Had He said, 'As far as the north is from the south,' it would have been far less meaningful, because we can determine that distance. As one approaches the North Pole, the distance toward the north decreases and ceases altogether when one is at the top of the earth. The reverse is true at the South Pole.

"However, there is no place where the east ends and the west begins. A Californian, for example, travels eastward to the Atlantic Ocean, but the east is still ahead of him. When he reaches Europe, he goes on to the Near East, then to the Middle East, then to the Far East. When he is there, the Pacific Ocean is still to the east of him and so is California. How true is the observation of the poet that east is east, and west is west, and never the twain shall meet."

How measureless are God's mercy and forgiveness! Long ago the question was asked, "Who is a God like unto thee, that pardoneth iniquity?" (Mic. 7:18).

* * * *

"Why Doesn't God Forgive Me?"

A woman sat across the desk from me. Weeping she said, "I have asked the Lord a thousand times to forgive me for what I did. Why doesn't He do it?"

I replied, "I don't know of one incident in the Bible that suggests that a believer has to ask God for forgiveness more than once. The Lord has forgiven you, but you have not forgiven yourself. His promise is unfailing: 'I have blotted out, as a thick cloud, thy transgressions, and . . .thy sins' (Isa. 44:22)."

Craig Massey.

* * * *

FORGIVENESS—
UNFORGIVENESS

"Forgive As We Forgive"

Jesus taught His disciples to pray: "Forgive us. . .as we forgive" (Matt. 6:12). He warned, 'If ye forgive not men their trespasses, neither will your heavenly Father forgive you.'

Some say, "I can forgive, but I can't forget."

How unlike God! When He forgives, He forgets: "Their iniquities

will I remember no more" (Heb. 8:12).

Some say, "I will forgive, but the forgiven one can go his way. I will have nothing more to do with him."

Usually the things which separate Christians are trivial, but how Spirit-grieving and self-defeating they are. Never forget: 'The little foxes. . . destroy the grapes' (Song of Sol. 2:15).

Ralph M. Smith.

* * * *

Be Kind to Yourself

How unkind we are to ourselves when we allow any root of hate or unforgiveness to rankle in our hearts! Hate and love cannot abide in the same heart at the same time: "If a man say, I love God, and hateth his brother, he is a liar: for he that loveth not his brother whom he hath seen, how can he love God whom he hath not seen?" (I John 4:20).

Said Booker T. Washington, a great black scientist, "No man is able to force me so low as to make me hate him."

Every Christian needs two bears: *Bear* and *Forebear*. "Bear ye one another's burdens" (Gal. 6:2); "Forebearing. . .and forgiving one another. . .even as Christ forgave you, so also do ye" (Col. 3:13). "Keep yourselves in the love of God" (Jude 21).

Ralph M. Smith.

* * * *

The Heel That Crushes

Forgiveness is the fragrance of the flower that clings to the heel that crushes it.

* * * *

Smoldering Embers of Anger

"Etched on the scroll of memory are my happy, carefree boyhood days in our humble home in Arkansas," said Dr. James Pleitz. "In vision, I can see my dad at bedtime on cold nights bank the fire in the huge potbelly stove and cover the embers with ashes. In the morning he would brush aside the ashes from the dormant embers, add kindling, then fan the coals into a blaze. Presently, the stove glowed cheerily in the room, which was also the kitchen-dining-living room.

"I learned a valuable lesson from Dad's night and morning chore. So many of us cover the smoldering embers of the Spirit-grieving sin of anger, which we self-excusingly call *righteous indignation.* At the slightest provocation, we brush aside restraints, and the embers of anger break forth in fiery words. Old grudges, ill will and unforgiveness burn and glow with white heat, livid intensity.

"Usually it is trivial, inconsequential things we become angry about. Remember, 'It is the little foxes that spoil the vines' (Song of Sol. 2:15). We 'fly off the handle,' give others a piece of our minds, with the resultant forfeiture of peace of mind.

"Psychologists say that it is difficult, if not impossible, for anyone to become angry if he speaks in a soft voice. Don't forget, 'A soft answer turneth away wrath: but grievous words stir up anger' (Prov. 15:1). A Chinese proverb says, 'If you have a soft voice, you don't need a big stick!'

"There is a justifiable, praiseworthy anger. If more of us were angry about the whelming evils, so alarmingly and increasingly existent, including salacious pornography, newsstands would be swept clean of this monstrous evil.

"Jesus was angry with the pretentious, hypocritical scribes and Pharisees and pronounced His severest woes against them. The sin of heart-hardness also elicited His anger: 'He . . .looked round about on them with anger, being grieved for their hardness of heart' (Mark 3:5).

"How triumphant we are when we obey the directive: 'Let all bitterness, and wrath, and anger. . .be put away from you. . .And be ye kind one to another, tenderhearted, forgiving one another, even as God for Christ's sake hath forgiven you' " (Eph. 4:31,32).

* * * *

How Unlike God

Two former college chums chanced to meet after years of separation. After exchanging greetings, one suggested that they have dinner together. During a sumptuous meal, they reminisced about cherished memories of their college days.

As they talked, the hours passed by unobserved. Chancing to look at his watch, one exclaimed, "Why, it is near midnight!"

They parted and hastened to their homes.

Later the friends met again. One spoke glowingly of the understanding of his wife about his late coming on the night of the dinner. The other man said, "I did my best to explain to my wife why I was late, but she only became *historical!*"

"You mean hysterical, don't you?"

"Oh, no, I mean *historical.* She brought up all my past sins and failures!"

How unlike God are those who can't forgive and forget past sins and failures.

When we penitently turn to God for His mercy and forgiveness, He buries our sins in the ocean of His forgetfulness, never to remember them against us: "Their sins and their iniquities will I remember no more" (Heb. 8:12).

* * * *

Needed: a New Love

George Sweeting said:

"Recently a 22-year-old lady came to me for counsel. As we talked, she poured out a story of hate and bitterness toward her parents.

"After sharing some of God's Word with her, I was able to lead her to accept Christ as her personal Saviour. Almost immediately she said, 'I want to be reconciled to my parents, but how can I love them?'

"I replied, 'By faith. Go home and believe that God will give you a new love for your mother and father. He can and He will.' "

And God did!

* * * *

For Those Who Suffer

The Presbyterian Journal gives this timely advice to those who suffer personal injury from a brother or sister in Christ: still your soul before God at the moment of impact. Apply direct pressure of understanding to the wound. Wash the wound thoroughly with kindness to remove all vindictiveness. Coat it liberally with the ointment of love, and bandage it with forgiveness. Don't pick the scab off by bringing up the subject and opening the wound. Avoid all self-pity which is painful and touchy. Take a generous dose of antibiotics from the Word of God several times daily, and stay in contact with the Great Physician at all times.

"If ye know these things, happy are ye if ye do them."—John 13:17.

* * * *

A Presidential Pardon

In granting a full, free and absolute pardon to Richard M. Nixon, President Ford said, "As President, my primary concern must always be the greatest good of all the people of the United States. As a man, my first consideration will always be to be true to my own convictions and my own conscience, which tells me clearly and certainly that I cannot prolong the bad dreams that continue to reopen a chapter that is closed.

"I do believe that right makes might, and that if I am wrong, ten angels swearing I was right would make no difference. I do believe with all my heart, mind and spirit that I, not as President but as a humble servant of God, will receive justice without mercy if I fail to show mercy. I believe that Richard Nixon and his loved ones have suffered enough, and will continue to suffer no matter what I do, no matter what we as a good and great nation can do together to make his goal of peace come true."

The Bible says, "For he shall have judgment without mercy, that hath shewed no mercy; and mercy rejoiceth against judgment" (James 2:13).

* * * *

If We Forgive Not

Lord Edward Herbert, an English journalist, said, "He who cannot forgive others breaks the bridge over which he must pass himself, for every man has need to be forgiven."

"For all have sinned, and come short of the glory of God."—Rom. 3:23.

* * * *

Unexploded Bombs

Some time ago a group of Russian bomb disposal experts removed an unexploded shell from a church bell tower at Yaroslay, northeast of Moscow. It is believed that the shell landed there during a battle of the Russian Civil War in 1918.

In the hearts of some of God's children are smoldering "bombs" of unforgiveness and bitterness. These "bombs" could erupt in fury at any moment unless they are eradicated by God's love and good will—love even for their enemies and those who may have wronged them.

"Keep yourselves in the love of God."—Jude 21.

* * * *

Locked Horns

Recently a newspaper had a picture of two buck deer whose antlers were inextricably tangled. They were found dead in a sunflower field in Douglas, Manitoba. Male deer often fight during mating season. When they cannot free their locked horns, they die of exhaustion and starvation!

Locked horns are not confined exclusively to wild creatures. Some of God's children "lock horns" and refuse to come to a peaceful settlement of their Spirit-grieving, joy-destroying enmities and unforgiving attitudes.

The Bible warns, "But if ye bite and devour one another, take heed that ye be not consumed one of another" (Gal. 5:15).

* * * *

FREEDOM
(See also Patriotism—Love for
One's Native Land)

Freedom Is Difficult—
Slavery Is Easy

Berdyalov, a Russian philosopher, said, "Men are slaves because freedom is difficult and slavery is easy."

"If the Son therefore shall make you free, ye shall be free indeed."—John 8:36.

* * * *

Our Birthright

"Freedom is the birthright of man. It belongs to him by right of his humanity, insofar as this consists with every other person's freedom," said Immanuel Kant, German philosopher.

Freedom from shackling sin is the greatest of freedoms: "For the law of the Spirit of life in Christ Jesus hath made me free from the law of sin and death" (Rom. 8:2).

Born Free

Said Rousseau, "Man is born free, and everywhere he is in chains."

There is but one answer to the anguished question asked long ago: "O wretched man that I am! who shall deliver me from the body of this death?" (Rom. 7:24). Jesus will!

Who can take away my sin?
Jesus will! Jesus will!
Make me pure without, within?
Jesus, blessed Jesus will!
Ina Dudley Ogdon.

The Saviour came "to proclaim liberty to the captives, and the opening of the prison to them that are bound" (Isa. 61:1).

* * * *

WHAT FREEDOM IS

Freedom is a breath of air,
Pine-scented, or salty like the sea;
Freedom is a field new-plowed,
Furrows of democracy.

Freedom is a country church,
A cathedral's stately spire;
Freedom is a spirit
That can set the soul on fire.

Freedom is a man's birthright,
A sacred, living rampart;
The pulsebeat of humanity,
The throb of a nation's heart.

Clara Smith Reber.

* * * *

Penalty for Preaching

Some time ago, in an eleven-day, closed-door trial, a Soviet court in Kharkov sentenced Boris M. Zdorovetz, an evangelical preacher in the Soviet Union, to three years of solitary confinement in a labor camp and seven years of exile!

"His offense?" you ask. He had led an unauthorized open-air service, attended by some 2,000 people.

How lightly and matter-of-factly do we as Americans accept our blood-bought freedoms, among the most valuable being the God-given right for each one to worship God in his own way.

* * * *

Justice Cannot Sleep Forever

Thomas Jefferson said, "Can the liberties of a nation be thought secure when we have removed their only firm basis, a conviction in the minds of the people that these liberties are the gift of God; that they are not to be violated but with His wrath? Indeed, I tremble for my country when I reflect that God is just; that His justice cannot sleep forever."

The Bible says, "He will not. . . keep his anger for ever" (Ps. 103:9).

* * * *

"Free to Die"

A man lay in a hospital bed with tubes down his throat and one feeding him through his veins. Growing weary after many days, he jerked the tubes loose and exclaimed, "I'm free!" But was he free? Yes. He was free to die!

That is what immoral permissiveness does. It gives freedom to die physically and spiritually: "For the wages of sin is death" (Rom. 6:23).

Adapted from *Decision*.

* * * *

"Heaven Forbid!"

How revealing was the comment made in *Home Life:* "In an American school, any person can say anything he wants to against God. But Heaven forbid that he say anything in God's favor! This shows to what depth our vaunted 'freedom of speech' has sunk!"

* * * *

Freedom Isn't Free

In speaking of communist oppression in Russia, Aleksandr Solzhenitsyn said, "We didn't love freedom enough. Even more, we had no awareness of the real situation. We spent ourselves in one unrestrained outburst in 1917. Then we hurried to submit. We submitted and simply deserved everything that happened later!"

Freedom isn't free! It comes at highest cost: toil, sacrifice, sweat, blood and even death.

* * * *

FRIENDS

WHO STANDS BY

When trouble comes your soul to try

You love the friend who just stands by!
Perhaps there's nothing he can do,

The thing is strictly up to you,
For there are troubles all your own,
And paths the soul must tread alone,
Times when love cannot smooth the
    road,
Nor friendship lift the heavy load,
But just to know you have a friend,
Who will "stand by" until the end,
Whose sympathy through all endures,
Whose warm handclasp is always
    yours,
It helps, someway, to pull you
    through,
Although there's nothing he can do.
And so with fervent heart you cry,
"God bless the friend who just stands
    by!"

Bertye Young Williams,
in *Christian Herald*.

* * * *

CAN NEVER REPAY

I cannot thank you as I would
    For all you've done for me;
I cannot find the words I should
    To tell you fittingly!

Your kindliness has meant so much
    That only One I know
Can e'er repay a service such
    As this one here below!

Therefore to Him I delegate
    What I cannot express;
May God repay you, early, late,
    For all your kindliness.

Author unknown.

* * * *

"I Love You"

"I love you not only for what you
are but for what I am when I'm with
you. I love you for passing over all the
foolish, weak things you can't help
seeing and drawing out in me all the
beautiful things that no one else had
looked for enough to find.

"I love you for helping me to make
of my life not a tavern but a temple,
not a reproach but a song.

"I love you because you have done
more than any mere man-made creed
could have done to make me good and
happier.

"You have done it without a word,
without a sigh. You have done it by
being yourself. Perhaps that is what
being a friend means, after all."

Author unknown.

* * * *

A Yearning Heart

When I lived in Chicago, a warm
friendship developed between an
aged Catholic and myself. This
dedicated, practicing Catholic frequently came to our home to do minor
repair jobs.

One day he bared his heart to me
and said, "At times I yearn to brush
aside all the cant, all the empty expressions of pious sentiment, all the
pomp and outward ritual and go
directly to the Saviour."

Does He not bid us to do this: "Let
us. . .come boldly unto the throne of
grace, that we may obtain mercy, and
find grace to help in time of need"
(Heb. 4:16)?

There are many today who share
that aged man's yearning. Hearts are
aching and breaking, and no mere
religious ritual can mend and comfort
them.

* * * *

OLD AND NEW FRIENDS

Old friends are good friends, so tried
and so true,
But old friends are friends you once
barely knew.
If friends you would have at the close
of the day,
Then be thou a friend to all in the
way.
Forget all the slights, watch out for
your own,
For self is not king with self on the
throne.
When thou art in youth, be friend to
the old,
When thou art in years, love youth as
pure gold.
Remember the Friend who died on
the cross,
Be thou His true friend, whatever the
loss.
His friendship is worth the pearl of
great price,
His friendship is worth thy life's
sacrifice.
And life that is lived devoid of His
love,
Has little on earth and nothing above.

Oliver W. Sumerlin Mercedes.

* * * *

THANK GOD FOR YOU

Thank God for you, good friend of
mine,

Seldom is there friendship like thine!
How very much I wish to be
As helpful as you've been to me—
Thank God for you!

When I recall from time to time
How you inspired this heart of mine,
I find myself inclined to pray:
"God bless my friend this very
day!"—
Thank God for you!

Of many prayer quests, one thou art
On whom I ask God to impart
Rich blessings from His storehouse
rare,
And grant to you His gracious care—
Thank God for you!

So often at the throne of grace
There comes a picture of your face,
And then instinctively I pray
That God may guide you all the
way—
Thank God for you!

Some day I hope with you to stand
Before the throne at God's right
hand,
And say to you at journey's end:
"Praise God, you've been to me a
friend!"—
Thank God for you!

Joseph Clard in
The Bethel Witness.

* * * *

GIVING
(See also Riches)

Holding Our Dollars in Trust for God

Years ago as a man sat meditative-
ly in his office in a building across
from the First Baptist Church, Dallas, Texas, a visitor entered. It was
during the great depression following

World War II, when there were many financial failures. As both men looked upon the great church, a searching and revealing conversation ensued.

Said the visitor, "You have a great deal of money invested in that church building, haven't you?"

"Yes," was the reply, "about $40,000."

"Well," said the visitor, "if you had that money back, you would keep it, wouldn't you?"

He replied, "When that church was being erected, you had more money than I had. I put my money in that church building; you kept yours. Now both of us are *broke*. I have something to show for my failure. What have you to show for yours? Who is the more *broke*?"

How wise we are to hold our dollars in trust for God!

* * * *

All Money Is Tainted

The deacons were ready to receive the church offering. The black pastor, challenging the congregation to give generously, humorously said, "All money is tainted. It 'taint' yours. It 'taint' mine. It's God's."

The pastor was right: "The silver is mine, and the gold is mine, saith the Lord of hosts" (Haggai 2:8).

How wise we are to hold our dollars in trust for God!

* * * *

When the Blessing Comes

A miserly churchman was asked for an offering for missions. He said,

"Oh, well, I can give $10, I guess, and not feel it."

"Make it $50 and feel it. The blessing comes when you feel it," he was told.

* * * *

"Ye Have Robbed Me"

During a revival service in Walnut Creek Church (Reno, Nevada), a man and a woman in ski masks entered carrying automatic weapons. They robbed the congregation of nearly everything but the offering plate collection.

First, the man bellowed, "I will not hesitate to kill if you do not do everything I say. Throw down your wallets and purses in the aisle!"

The people obeyed. Then the man told the children to gather them for him.

As he and his accomplice hurried from the church with their loot, he ordered the congregation of about seventy-five to remain in the church for ten minutes.

The pastor, Roy Sikes, had the people obey the robber's instruction.

In many churches, on every Lord's Day, there is another kind of robbery—the withholding of the Lord's tithes and our offerings: "Ye have robbed me, even this whole nation . . .saith the Lord of hosts" (Mal. 3:9,10).

* * * *

LITTLE IS MUCH WHEN GOD IS IN IT

God who blessed the loaves of bread
By which the multitudes were fed,

Will bless our gifts, however small,
If we but gladly give them all.
I am amazed that He can bring
A blessing from the smallest thing:
A smile, a word, a noble deed,
A hand outstretched to one in need,
A heart that shares the lingering pain
Of those who hurt, Christ serves
again.
To such as these to what extent,
Might fill us with astonishment!

Sybil Leonard Armes in
Baptist Standard.

* * * *

"Now Squirm, Old Nature!"

It was the custom of a miserly old man to sit near the pulpit in the church services with his hand cupped behind his ear to aid his hearing.

One morning in his sermon the pastor pled for a large offering for missions. The miser was impressed and soon mumbled to himself, "I'll give $10."

Immediately a fierce struggle ensued in his soul; but when the collection plate came to him, he gained the victory over greed. Tossing his well-filled billfold into the offering plate, he joyfully exclaimed, "Now squirm, old nature!"

* * * *

A Collection for Squiggles

As James ate his dinner, his father observed that he shifted to one side of his plate choice morsels of meat.

"What are you doing, James?" asked his father.

"I'm saving this for Squiggles, my dog."

Father said sternly, "You eat that meat, James. Squiggles can have the scraps."

After dinner James took a dish of scraps to Squiggles, and said dejectedly and apologetically, "Squiggles, I wanted to give you a love offering, but I can give you only a collection!"

How many of us give to God only a collection rather than gifts which represent sacrifice and express our love for Him.

David said, "Neither will I offer. . . unto the Lord my God of that which doth cost me nothing" (II Sam. 24:24).

Alice Marie Knight.

* * * *

SHARING

Not what we give, but what we share,
For the gift without the giver is bare;
Who gives himself with his alms feeds three:
Himself, his hungering neighbor, and Me.

James Russell Lowell.

Jesus said, "Inasmuch as ye have done it unto one of the least of these my brethren, ye have done it unto me" (Matt. 25:40).

* * * *

"If There Be First a Willing Mind"

A struggling church asked Dr. George W. Truett to assist it in raising $6,500 for their church building.

In telling of his efforts, Dr. Truett said, "It was the slowest and most reluctant giving I have ever encountered."

When the gifts and pledges were tabulated, they amounted to $3,000.

In exasperation, Dr. Truett said, "What do you expect of me? I don't have the other needed $3,500."

A woman sitting in the back of the church said in a quavering voice to her husband, "Charlie, would you be willing for us to give our little home? We were offered exactly $3,500 for it yesterday. Wouldn't our Saviour be pleased for us to make this sacrifice for Him?"

"Yes, Jennie! I was thinking of the same thing!"

The erstwhile illiberal ones were so deeply touched by the announcement of the sacrificial gift that within five minutes the needed goal was achieved and the noble couple didn't have to sacrifice their home after all.

* * * *

THE GRACE OF GIVING

Grant us, then, the grace of giving,
  With a spirit large and free;
That our lives and all our living,
  We may consecrate to Thee.

Andrew Murray.

* * * *

"The Lord Ain't Pressing Me."

A black minister asked one of his church members, "How are you getting along?"

"Oh, fine, fine, very fine, thank you!"

"How about your bills?"

"They, too, are fine, very fine. They are all paid up."

"How about the Lord's due? Don't you owe Him something?"

"I ain't doing so well with His due, but the Lord ain't pressing me like my other creditors," said the self-excusing, responsibility-shirking brother.

God never presses His children to give. To be acceptable to Him, our giving must be willing and from the heart: "Bring me an offering. . .every man that giveth it willingly with his heart ye shall take my offering" (Exod. 25:2).

Told by Bob Smith.

* * * *

The Gift of Self

Not what we give, but what we share,
For the gift without the giver is bare.

"And this they did. . .first [they] *gave their own selves to the Lord, and unto us by the will of God."*—II Cor. 8:5.

What can I give Him?
  As poor as I am,
If I were a shepherd
  I'd give Him a lamb;
If I were a wise man
  I'd do my part;
But what can I give Him?
  I'll give Him my heart!

Christian Rossetti.

* * * *

The Safest Repository

"I have held many things in my hands, and have lost them. But what

I have placed in God's hands, I still possess," said Martin Luther.

As an English nobleman neared death's door, he said, "What I spent, I had; what I kept, I lost; what I gave, *I have.*"

How wise we are when we hold our dollars in trust for God!

The safest repository for our riches is in Heaven. Jesus said, "But lay up for yourselves treasures in heaven, where neither moth nor rust doth corrupt" (Matt. 6:20).

* * * *

"He Goeth Before Them" (John 10:4).

He never asks me to go anywhere
  He has not gone,
To face anything He has not faced,
To love anyone He does not love,
Or to give anything He has not given.

"All things come of thee, and of thine own have we given thee."—I Chron. 29:14.

* * * *

Tax-Gatherer Versus Christ

Centuries ago Augustine said, "Our forefathers abounded in plenty because they gave God tithes and to Caesar tribute. We are unwilling to share with God by giving to Him the tenth, and now, behold, the whole is taken from us. The tax-gatherer takes from us that which Christ receives not."

* * * *

Two Pigs

A farmer asked his miserly neighbor: "If you had a million pigs, would you give me half of them?"

"I sure would," the neighbor replied.

"Well, if you had two pigs, would you give me half of them?"

"That isn't fair," said the miserly farmer. "You know I have two pigs."

Covetousness is a disease of the soul which tightens its grasp on its victims as they advance in years.

Jesus said, "Take heed, and beware of covetousness" (Luke 12:15).

That man may breathe, but never live,
Who much receives, but little gives;
Whom none can love, whom none can thank,
Creation's blot, creation's blank!

           Alice Marie Knight.

* * * *

GOSPEL

Transformed Cannibals

"I have had twenty-one years' experience as a missionary with cannibals in New Guinea and the southern seas. Wherever there had been the slightest spark of civilization among them, it has been because the Gospel had been preached to them and received by them," said James Chalmers.

We joyfully exclaim, "[We are] not ashamed of the gospel of Christ: for it is the power of God unto salvation to every one that believeth" (Rom. 1:16).

* * * *

The Gospel in a Nutshell

If all Bibles were destroyed except John 3:16, all mankind could be instantly saved by doing what the verse says! It has been called, **"The Gospel in a nutshell."**

There are four salient facts expressed in the verse:

The cause of salvation—"For God so loved the world";

The cost of salvation—"That he gave his only begotten Son";

The condition of salvation—"That whosoever believeth in him";

The consequences of salvation—"Should not perish, but have everlasting life."

In contemplation of these preciously precious truths, we exclaim:

Oh, the love that drew salvation's plan!
Oh, the grace that bro't it down to man!
Oh, the mighty gulf that God did span
**   At Calvary!**

                                Wm. R. Newell.

* * * *

Missing Link Still Missing

In 1833, Charles Darwin visited the South Sea islands looking for the elusive so-called "missing link." There he observed the cannibals and concluded that no creatures anywhere were more primitive or degraded. He believed that nothing could lift them from their low existence and abominable ways.

Thirty-four years later he returned to those islands. To his amazement he found churches, schools and Christian homes occupied by former cannibals.

Darwin learned the cause for the great change—Missionary John G. Paton had been preaching the Gospel there, and many of the cannibals had become new creatures in Christ, "transformed by grace divine!"

Darwin was so impressed by what he saw that he made a generous contribution to the London Missionary Society.

* * * *

GROWTH

Backward Walkers

On his backward-walking trek from San Francisco to Santa Monica, Plennie Fingo, age 61, claimed to be the world's champion backward walker. Mirrors were clamped to his eyeglasses as he walked in reverse.

Some of God's children are also backward walkers. They envision the future through rear-view mirrors. They incur God's displeasure: "If any man draw back, my soul shall have no pleasure in him" (Heb. 10:38).

* * * *

MAKE BETTER BEST

Good, better, best—
Never let it rest
Till the good is better
And the better is *best!*

* * * *

Wheeled Into Heaven in a Perambulator!

Years ago we often heard sermons on backsliding. Many believed that backsliding was retrograding or going backward in the Christian life.

The Prophet Hosea said of God's ancient people, "For Israel slideth back as a backsliding heifer" (Hos. 4:16).

Failure to go forward is also indicative of a backslidden state.

Sometimes a stubborn heifer stands with extended forelegs pressed firmly to the ground. No entreaty or persuasion can induce the balking heifer to go forward. The heifer's *won't power* is greater than the herdsman's *will power*.

How like a stubborn heifer are some of God's children! They fail to go forward and "grow in grace, and in the knowledge of our Lord and Saviour Jesus Christ" (II Peter 3:18). They are still in their swaddling clothes. How pleased they would be to be wheeled into Heaven in a perambulator or baby carriage!

Mr. E. Dodd said, "Conversion is only five percent of the Christian life. Ninety-five percent is going on with Christ."

"Let us go on unto perfection."— Heb. 6:1.

* * * *

Less and More

The daily plea of a growing Christian should be, "O Lord, make me *less* of what I am and *more* of what I ought to be."

Not enjoyment and not sorrow,
Is our destined end or way;
But to live that each tomorrow,
Find us further than today.
Longfellow.

* * * *

None Perfect

Dr. Leonard Reiffel, an expert on diamonds, said that lasers may discover which diamonds in milady's rings are imperfect.

"The value of diamonds," he said, "depends on their perfection. A small flaw in an otherwise beautiful stone can drop its value precipitously."

There are no perfect Christians on earth; but as we yield ourselves to the indwelling Holy Spirit, we become increasingly conformed to the image of Christ. Not until we awaken in Glory will we be completely like Him.

"Beloved, now are we the sons of God. . .we know that when he shall appear, we shall be like him; for we shall see him as he is."—I John 3:2.

* * * *

"If We Don't Go on We'll Go Off"

In his poem, *The Chambered Nautilus,* Oliver Wendell Holmes describes the life stages of a sea creature outgrowing its home, a sea shell, and emerging into larger chambers. Then Holmes exhorts us to build our lives in the same way: discarding outgrown pasts and progressing on to larger freedoms and accomplishments.

Build thee more stately mansions, O my soul,

As the swift seasons roll!
Leave thy low-vaulted past!
Let each new temple, nobler than the last,
Shut thee from Heaven with a dome more vast,
Till thou at length art free,
Leaving thine outgrown shell by Life's unresting sea!

* * * *

"Transformed By Grace Divine!"

John Newton, author of the hymn *Amazing Grace*, testified: "I am not all that I ought to be; I am not all that I am going to be; but I am surely not what I used to be: a libertine and a slave of slaves in Africa!"

* * * *

"Go on Unto Perfection"

John A. Huffman, Jr., said with concern:

"I find myself agitated by the spiritual sloth and dull-mindedness of my contemporary believers. They are caught on a merry-go-round where they keep repeating the same basic elements, never moving on to the daily relationship with God. The cardinal doctrines are important. Yet an introverted concentration on the details of basic elementary Christianity can shrivel us into legalistic individuals."

We should remain *bulldogmatic* in our adherence to "the faith which was once delivered unto the saints" as we go on unto perfection and "grow in grace, and in the knowledge of our Lord and Saviour Jesus Christ" (II Pet. 3:18).

* * * *

Fallen Arches of Midriff

"You're not an adult when you stop growing at both ends," said A. Dudley Dennison, M.D. "You're a careless prospect for a future coronary. Every pound of excess fat contains another two hundred miles of capillaries which your heart must push blood through, plus working to carry around that extra flab."

The longer the waistline, the shorter the lifeline!

"And put a knife to thy throat, if thou be a man given to appetite."—Prov. 23:2.

* * * *

Keep Moving

Dr. Paul Dudley White, renowned heart specialist, gave the following recipe for good physical and mental health: "Keep moving, and keep thinking. Don't let your brain atrophy. Too many people die from disuse of their bodies."

To maintain good spiritual health, "keep moving!"

The Christian life is like riding a bicycle: If you don't go on, you'll go off. "Let us go on unto perfection" (Heb. 6:1).

"As newborn babes, desire the sincere milk of the word, that ye may grow thereby."—I Pet. 2:2.

* * * *

Don't Vegetate

Imogene Cunningham began taking pictures in 1901. Now 90 years old, she is one of the most notable photographers in America. When a friend asked, "Which is your best and favorite picture made over the past seventy-two years?" She replied, "Hopefully the one I'll take tomorrow!"

We vegetate when we become satisfied with heights attained and laurels won. God's command to His children is: "Let us go on unto perfection" (Heb. 6:1).

* * * *

GUIDANCE

"His Way Is Perfect"

George Mueller said, "God makes no mistakes. The steps and the stops of a good man are ordered of the Lord."

We are not far advanced in the school of Christ if we cannot thank Him equally for closed doors or open doors, and say that "his way is perfect" (Ps. 18:30).

* * * *

TO A WATERFOWL

He who, from zone to zone,
    Guides through the boundless sky
    thy certain flight,
In the long way that I must tread
    alone
Will lead my steps aright.

William Cullen Bryant.

* * * *

Pingos

Pingos, found in the Arctic region, are submerged cones of ice coated with frozen mulch, about 1,000 feet wide at the base, and 100 to 200 feet high. They are formed by frost heave and geological pressures on the floor of the sea.

It is feared that one of these sub-merged arctic pingos might slice open an unsuspecting ship passing overhead. If the ship were a loaded oil tanker, the results could be disastrous.

On our voyage through life, God's imperishable Word reveals every danger for Christians.

Jesus Saviour, pilot me
Over life's tempestuous sea;
Unknown waves before me roll,
Hiding rock and treacherous shoal;
Chart and compass came from Thee:
Jesus, Saviour, pilot me.

Edward Hopper.

* * * *

"I KNOW 'TIS BEST"

I know not where my Lord may lead,
O'er barren plain or grassy mead,
Through valley or on mountain crest,
But where He leads, I know 'tis best!

Conklin.

* * * *

No Looking Back

A century ago, a missionary named Shaw and his wife went to Capetown, South Africa. They intended to press on into the interior of the continent, but the Boers discouraged them and refused to assist in any way.

Every door seemed to be closed. However Shaw had set his hand to the plow and there was no looking back. He and his wife got into an ox cart, resolved to go wherever the oxen might draw them.

For days and weeks they traveled over the pathless veldt. After they had gone some three hundred miles, they saw in the distance a company of natives. They met the band of Hottentots, who were on their way to Capetown seeking for a missionary to come to their village.

Deep in unfathomable mines
Of never-failing skill,
He treasures up His bright designs
And works His sovereign will.

Cowper.

* * * *

DOWN THE LANE OF YESTERDAY

Come with me, and walk a way
Down the Lane of Yesterday.
  Flowers beside the path are springing,
  With their perfume, mem'ries bringing,
Thoughts of all those years gone by,
When we loitered, you and I,
  In the garden fair and sweet,
  Of life's springtime, full, complete!
Days in the long ago, 'tis true,
But Memory guides our steps anew.
  So, come with me and walk a way
  Down the Lane of Yesterday.

Alice C. Sutherland.

* * * *

Greatly Needed: Spiritual Leadership

George Gallup, Jr., said:

"Never in history have the American people so craved moral and spiritual leadership as they do today. All signs point to the fact that religion is gaining a new intellectual respectability. The assumption that the educated person needs religion less, and is more ready to discard religion as a product of ignorance and superstition, is not borne out by survey findings."

How blessed are those who confess:

I need Jesus, my need I now confess;
No friend like Him in times of deep distress;
I need Jesus, the need I gladly own;
Tho' some may bear their load alone,
Yet, I need Jesus.

Geroge O. Webster.

* * * *

"O the Depth of the Knowledge of God!'

Dr. James M. Gray, a former president of the Moody Bible Institute, was convalescing from illness. His physician advised him to take an ocean voyage. As plans were being completed for the journey, he experienced an unexpected physical setback. Greatly disappointed, he began to wonder, *Why has God allowed this new affliction?*

Shortly thereafter, he read the tragic account of a vessel that had sunk after striking a reef in St. John's Harbor. There were no survivors. The ill-fated vessel was the one he had planned to sail on! Now he realized how perfectly the Lord had directed his way. His temporary sickness had delivered him from certain death.

We exclaim, "O the depth of the riches both of the wisdom and knowledge of God! how unsearchable are his judgments, and his ways past finding out!" (Rom. 11:33).

* * * *

An Unsolved Mystery

One of nature's greatest unsolved mysteries is the migration of birds to warmer climes before the coming of winter's ice and snow and their return in the springtime. Some divinely implanted power enables them to return unerringly, even across entire continents and oceans, to the place of their origin.

If God so miraculously guides His feathered creatures, will He not unerringly guide His children? He surely will! The promise is unfailing: "For this God is our God for ever and ever: He will be our guide even unto death"Ps. 48:14).

* * * *

THERE IS A GUIDE

There is a guide that never falters,
    And when He leads I cannot stray;
For step by step He goes before me,
    And marks my path—He knows the way.

Oftimes the path grows dim and dreary,
    The darkness hides the cheering ray;
Still I will trust, tho' worn and weary,
    My Saviour leads—He knows the way.

He knows the evils that surround me,
    The turnings that would lead astray;

No foes of night can ere confound me,
    For Jesus leads—He knows the way.

A. B. Ackley.

* * * *

Instruments Distrusted

Some years ago a plane, almost intact, was discovered in the Sahara Desert. Upon examination, it was learned that it was a U. S. Air Force bomber of World War II vintage. On the fuselage was the name: *Lady Be Good.*

The discovery of the craft revealed one of the mysteries of the war: "What had happened to *Lady Be Good,* the bomber that took off for a mission in North Africa and was never heard from again?"

The plane was found some four hundred miles past its destination; and when the instruments were checked, they were still operating and accurate.

Therefore, it was surmised that *Lady Be Good* had overshot its goal by four hundred miles because it got in a high-altitude air current that doubled its speed without the crew knowing it.

The crew knew how long the flight ordinarily took; and when the instruments showed that they had reached their destination in half the time, they assumed their instruments were in error and flew on. The fuel ran out, so they had to crash-land in the desert. Many miles from the plane, searchers found the skeletal remains of several members of the crew. They had perished while trying to get help!

Apparently the crew of *Lady Be Good* wouldn't believe the instruments.

How illustrative of myriads today who make shipwreck of their lives because they disbelieve and reject the trustworthy directives of God's Word.

Long ago the psalmist trustfully said, "Thou shalt guide me with thy counsel, and afterward receive me to glory" (Ps. 73:24).

Adapted from *Decision.*

* * * *

HEALING

The Healing Word: "He Sent His Word and Healed Them" (Ps. 107:20).

Dr. Stanley Blanton, a well-known psychiatrist, told about a new patient who entered his office. Seeing a Bible on his desk, the patient asked, "Do you, a psychiatrist, read the Bible?"

Dr. Blanton replied, "I not only read it, I study it. It's the greatest textbook on human behavior ever put together. If people would just absorb its message, a lot of us psychiatrists could close our offices and go fishing."

"You are talking about the Ten Commandments and the Golden Rule?" the patient asked.

"Certainly, but more, too. Dozens of other insights have profound psychiatric value. Take your own case. For the past hour you have been telling me how you have tried this, tried that, but all to no avail. Isn't it quite obvious that you are worrying yourself into a state of acute anxiety?" asked Dr. Blanton.

"That is why I am here," the patient acknowledged.

Said Dr. Blanton, "For more than three thousand years, the Bible has

been a help in time of trouble to any person wise enough to use it."

Reader's Digest;
used by permission.

* * * *

"The Great Physician Now Is Near!"

Some years ago the assistant superintendent of a large high school in Chicago, overwhelmed with discouragement, sought the solution to the enigma of life by the suicide route. He almost succeeded in his darksome effort. I visited him in the Billings Hospital. Entering sharingly and sympathetically into his pitiful situation, I imparted cheerful words of hope and encouragement. I spoke of the Mender of broken things, the Saviour, who long ago entered history's stream "to give. . .beauty for ashes, the oil of joy for mourning, the garment of praise for the spirit of heaviness" (Isa. 61:3). I didn't remotely allude to the patient's attempted self-destruction.

As I left his bedside, Dr. Acres, the hospital psychiatrist, said, "Come into my office." Then he told me, "I suppose you know you can do more for that patient than I can." He meant the One I represented, the Great Physician, could heal the distraught man spiritually and physically.

The Great Physician now is near,
The sympathizing Jesus!
He speaks the drooping heart to cheer,
Oh, hear the voice of Jesus!
                              Wm. Hunter.

* * * *

Spiritually Depleted

Through the years, writers have extolled the spiritually healing power of solitude.

Shelly wrote, "I have tranquil solitude."

Thoreau wrote, "I never found the companion that was so companionable as solitude."

Solitude often beckoned the Saviour: "And. . .rising up a great while before day, he went out, and departed into a solitary place, and there prayed" (Mark 1:35).

We become spiritually depleted when we are so enmeshed in endless activities that little or no time is left for quiet communion with God in "the secret place of the most High" (Ps. 91:1).

* * * *

Man Tends, God Mends

"There is no question that God is treating the sick today through hospitals, doctors and nurses," said Harland Cornelius Hastings, M.D., F.R.C.S. "These people may not be Christians, but they are God's instruments.

"In surgery, we don't heal anybody. We cut out a piece of tissue and sew the flesh together. If the condition would remain as we left it, it would never heal. God has to impart life as the cells grow together. We live by faith that healing will take place. If it did not, the wound would fall open as soon as we took out the sutures. Life does the healing, and God sends life."

Man may tend broken, sick bodies, but only God can mend them. The good Samaritan bound up the wounds of the stricken Jew, but only God could heal them.

* * * *

Divers Disease

To emphasize a greatly needed lesson among Christians, a black minister gave a humorous interpretation to the verse, "And he healed many that were sick of divers diseases" (Mark 1:34):

"Now the doctors can scrutinize you, analyze you, and sometimes cure your ills. But when you have *divers* disease, only the Lord can cure you. And, brethren, there is a regular epidemic of divers disease among us. Some dive for the door after Sunday school is over. Some dive for the TV set during the evening service. Some dive for the car for weekend trips, while others dive for their nickels and dimes to put in the offering, instead of tithing. Yes, it takes the Lord and love for His church to cure divers disease."

* * * *

HEAVEN

"Waiting for Me in Heaven"

Famed Canadian physician Sir William Osler was whelmed with sorrow at the death of his son in World War I. During his own terminal illness, the physician wrote, "And so the voyage is nearly over and the harbor is in view. It has been a glorious voyage, with wonderul companions on the way. But I gladly go! My boy will be waiting for me in Heaven!"

* * * *

AH! 'TIS HEAVEN AT LAST!

On the jasper threshold standing,
Like a pilgrim safely landing;
See the strange bright scenes expanding.
   Ah! 'tis Heaven at last!

What a city! what a glory!
Far beyond the fairest story,
Of the ages old and hoary.
   Ah! 'tis Heaven at last!

Christ Himself the living splendor;
Christ the sunshine mild and tender;
Praises to His name we render.
   Ah! 'tis Heaven at last!

Author unknown.

* * * *

"I Have Not Told Half of What I Saw!"

When Marco Polo, the renowned explorer who spent twenty years in ancient China, was on his deathbed, his friends pleaded with him, for the peace of his soul, to retract some of the seemingly incredible stories he had told in his book of travels. His reply to their entreaties was, "I have not told half of what I saw!"

In reference to the fadeless beauty and grandeur of Heaven, God's children can say, "The half has never been told!"

What surprises await the redeemed ones when they behold the King in His beauty! "Eye hath not seen, nor ear heard, neither have entered into the heart of man, the things which God hath prepared for them that love him" (I Cor. 2:9).

* * * *

"So Long Until Tomorrow"

On a tombstone in a cemetery in Prestwick, Scotland, occur the following words: "Ta Ta the noo," meaning, "Good-by for now."

All of God's children can joyfully sing:

In the sweet by and by,
We shall meet on that beautiful shore.
    S. F. Bennett.

* * * *

"This World Is Not My Home"

Columnist Sidney J. Harris opined that people living today have the hope of a happy state here on earth rather than in Heaven. He said:

"In the past, the western world was motivated by the hope of happiness in another world to come. For most people living today this has been replaced by the hope of a happy state in this world, for future generations if not for us. In great part, eschatological notions have been transferred to the secular field of politics, economics and society. The secularization of Heaven into a utopian goal on earth gives us both our vitality and our frictions, both our wild hopes and our bleak fears."

Christians believe in better things to come and a bright and glorious hereafter in Heaven. That belief is a mighty incentive to clean living and faithful service to God and man.

"Here have we no continuing city, but we seek one to come."—Heb. 13:14.

> This world is not my home,
> I'm just a passing thru,
> My treasures are laid up
> Somewhere beyond the blue;
> The angels beckon me
> From Heaven's open door,
> And I can't feel at home
> In this world any more.

* * * *

Indescribable!

A man visited for the first time the famed Carlsbad Caverns in New Mexico. His wife, who had gone through the caverns before, was with him. As they went forward midst scenes of dazzling beauty, he kept exclaiming, "Isn't this wonderful!"

The farther they went, the more beautiful the sights were. When they reached the King's Palace, he asked his wife, "Why haven't you told me about this?"

"I couldn't. I couldn't find words adequately sufficient to describe it!"

Heaven is a place of indescribable beauty and ineffable joy. How powerless we are to describe its glory and wonders!

The Bible says that sorrow, sickness and death are forever banished from Heaven: "And God shall wipe away all tears from their eyes; and there shall be no more death, neither sorrow, nor crying, neither shall there be any more pain" (Rev. 21:4). Hallelujah!

Told by C. E. Matthews.

* * * *

The Dawn

Victor Hugo, author of *Les Miserables,* possibly the greatest epic drama ever written, died in 1885 at the age of eighty-three. Before his demise, he wrote: "When I go down to the grave, I can say with many others that *I have finished my day's work,* but I cannot say *I have finished my life.* My day's work will begin again the next morning! The tomb is not a blind alley. It is a thoroughfare. It closes on the twilight. It opens on the dawn!"

> When I shall come to the end of my way,
> When I shall rest at the close of life's day,
> When "Welcome home" I shall hear Jesus say,
> O that will be sunrise for me!

W. C. Poole.

* * * *

Promoted to Glory

Said Eleanor Searle Whitney, lecturer, philanthropist, singer and author, "I believe in Jesus Christ and, because I do, I can look forward to meeting my loved ones some day in the life ahead of me. Someday I will be promoted to Glory, just as they have been, and I will meet Jesus face to face!"

What a time of rejoicing it will be when God's children awaken in Glory with Christ's likeness! Then we will be forever with Him and with our loved ones who died in the Lord. (Cf. Ps. 17:15; I Thess. 4:17,18.)

David looked forward with joyful anticipation to being with his child in Glory: "I shall go to him, but he shall not return to me" (II Sam. 12:23).

Oh, the dear ones in Glory, how they beckon
    me to come,
And our parting at the river I recall;
To the sweet vales of Eden they will sing
    my welcome home;
But I long to meet my Saviour first of all.
                        Fanny J. Crosby.

* * * *

No Continuing City

The city of Venice, a center of beauty and brilliance, is slowly sinking in the sea! Its 177 canals have become an open sewer, and it is in danger of losing irreplaceable and invaluable works of art, paintings, buildings and statues.

Dr. Roberto Frasetto of the National Research Council said, "There are so many polluting components in the air, the old stones can't cope with them. They survived for generations, but they can't abide the chemical and physical actions of the present atmosphere."

The eroding, gnawing tooth of time works havoc with man's most brilliant accomplishments: "For here have we no continuing city, but we seek one to come" (Heb. 13:14), "A city which hath foundations, whose builder and maker is God" (11:10).

* * * *

Covered With a Veil

Mme. de Stael said, "Divine wisdom, intending to detain us sometime on earth, has done well to cover with a veil the prospect of the life to come; for if our sight could clearly distinguish the opposite bank, who would remain on this tempestuous coast of time?"

Paul said, "For I am in a strait betwixt two, having a desire to depart, and to be with Christ; which is far better" (Phil. 1:23).

* * * *

"Only Good Night"

In imagination, television viewers can still hear the resonant voice and see the roughhewn face of Chet Huntley—a voice and a face familiar to millions—through the nightly Huntley-Brinkley newscast. Huntley died at the age of sixty-two.

In telecasting the news of Huntley's death, Brinkley concluded it by saying with a tear in his voice, "For myself, I guess I can say one more time, 'Good night, Chet!' "

When our friends and loved ones enter life eternal through faith in death's Conqueror, the Saviour, we can confidently say, "Good night!"

Only good night, beloved, not farewell;
A little while and His saints shall dwell
In hallowed union indivisible.
    Good night!
                        Sarah Dudley.

* * * *

No Traffic Jams

One has said, "There are no traffic jams on the straight and narrow way, whose terminus is Heaven and home.

Jesus said, "Because strait is the gate, and narrow is the way, which leadeth unto life, and few there be that find it" (Matt. 714).

* * * *

Answering the Roll Call

One night little Eddie had a dream about Heaven. In the dream he was standing in a great crowd of people outside Heaven. Near him stood his father, mother, two sisters and brother. The angel was calling the names written in the Lamb's Book of Life.

Presently the angel called the name *William Webster Neighbour.*

Little Eddie's father answered in a clear voice, "Here am I," and started to go through the gate into Heaven. Eddie took his hand and said, "O Father, let me go with you!"

Father answered, "No, Eddie Boy, you must wait and see if your name is written in the Book of Life. You can't go in on my name."

After a while the angel called, "*Julia Maria Neighbour.*" Little Eddie's mother answered, "Here am I." As she started toward the gate, little Eddie took her hand and said, "let me go with you, Mother."

Mother answered, "No, Eddie, you can't go in with Mother. You must wait until your name is called."

Presently the name of Eddie's sister was called. She answered and went through the gate into Heaven.

How sad and lonely little Eddie felt as he stood anxiously waiting for his name to be called!

Soon Eddie's sister Helen answered her name. Then Eddie heard his own name—*Robert Edward Neighbour!*

With a glad shout, the little boy answered, "Here am I!" He answered the name so loudly that it awakened him and also awakened his father and mother who were sleeping in a bedroom downstairs.

Little Eddie never forgot his dream. How glad he was that Jesus was his Saviour and that his name was written in the Lamb's Book of Life!

The Bible says, "And there shall in no wise enter [heaven]. . .but they which are written in the Lamb's book of life" (Rev. 21:27).

* * * *

No Continuing City

Lewis Mumford, a historian who specializes on cities, wrote, "As an agent of human interaction and cooperation, as a stage for social drama, the city is rapidly sinking out of sight."

God's Word tells what will happen someday: "And the cities of the nations fell: and great Babylon came in remembrance before God, to give unto her the cup of the wine of the fierceness of his wrath" (Rev. 16:19).

God's children need to remember that "here have we no continuing city, but we seek one to come" (Heb. 12:14). Like Abraham of old, we look "for a city which hath foundations, whose builder and maker is God" (11:10).

* * * *

The Last Turn the Best

"I shall grow old," said Henry Van Dyke, "but never lose life's zest, because the road's last turn will be the best!"

At the end of life, what joy will be ours! We will see the Saviour and hear Him say: "Well done, thou good and faithful servant. . .enter thou into the joy of thy Lord" (Matt. 25:21).

* * * *

HELL

"Hitler Is Alive!"

A Baylor University student traveling in Italy entered a watchmaker's shop to have his watch repaired. The student was incredulously amused when the watchmaker said, "Hitler is alive! Do you believe it?"

The student replied, "The preponderance of evidence affirming his death is too great to believe he is alive!"

The watchmaker opened his Bible and read the following verses: "And in hell he lift up his eyes, being in torments. . . .And he cried. . .have mercy on me. . .for I am tormented in this flame" (Luke 16:23,24).

The Bible says, "The wicked shall be turned into hell, and all the nations that forget God" (Ps. 9:17).

It would be infinite unkindness for God to force into Heaven, where there is ceaseless praise of God, an unconverted man with a "deceitful and desperately wicked" heart.

* * * *

The Reason

In speaking of the cause of England's moral slump, Sir Winston Churchill said, "The moral landslide of Great Britain is due to the fact that Heaven and Hell are no longer proclaimed throughout the land!"

Some say, "If there is no Heaven to gain and no Hell to shun, why not 'live it up'? Why not 'eat, drink and be merry'?"

* * * *

Suppose. . .

In making their last great bid to hold onto transatlantic steamship passenger traffic, the Cunard Line used this advertising slogan, "Getting there is half the fun!"

An atheist asked a Salvation Army lass, "Suppose you discover one second after death that there is no such place as Heaven; what would you say?"

Smiling, the salvationist replied, "I've had a grand and glorious time getting there!"

Then she asked, "Suppose you discover a second after death that Hell is a *reality*; what would you say?"

Silently, the unbeliever walked away.

* * * *

Only a Euphoric Place

In his book, *Beyond Death's Door,*
Dr. Maurice Rawlings, a clinical associate professor of medicine, University of Tennessee, said, "I don't
believe all the published material
about life after death as a euphoric
place called Heaven. There is a bad
place as well as a good place.

"A man 'dropped dead' while running a treadmill machine in my office. He was quickly revived and
began yelling: 'I am in Hell! I am in
Hell! Help me! Help me!' I offered an
impromptu prayer.

"The reason no one has reported
any experiences in Hell is that they
were not interviewed right after they
were revived. I believe people tend to
forget bad experiences," said Dr.
Rawlings.

* * * *

Tears in His Voice

Dr. Robert William Dale, for
thirty-six years pastor of the famed
Carr's Lane Congregational Church,
Birmingham, England, said, "Dwight
L. Moody is the only preacher I know
who has a right to preach about Hell.
I have never heard him refer to Hell
without tears in his voice!"

Does the fact that "the wicked
shall be turned into hell, and all the
nations that forget God" (Ps. 9:17)
cause us to have solicitous concern for
perishing ones? Do we "weep o'er the
erring ones," and "tell them of Jesus,
the mighty to save?"

* * * *

The Dead Are Alive!

Each individual who has died is
alive—either in Heaven or in Hell:
"Absent from the body. . .present
with the Lord" (II Cor. 5:8); "The
rich man. . .died, and was buried;
and in hell he lift up his eyes, being in
torment" (Luke 16:22,23).

* * * *

Destiny Is Fixed This Side of Grave

Eternal destiny is fixed this side of
the grave: "And beside all this,
between us and you there is a great
gulf fixed: so that they which would
pass from hence to you cannot;
neither can they pass to us, that
would come from thence" (Luke
16:26). Purgatory is a sheer invention
of the Roman Catholic Church and is
without scriptural foundation: "To
day shalt thou be with me in
paradise" (Luke 23:43); "absent from
the body. . .present with the Lord"
(II Cor. 5:8); "For I. . .[have] a desire
to depart, and to be with Christ;
which is far better" (Phil. 1:23).

* * * *

"How Shall We Escape?"

In his famous sermon, "Sinners in
the Hands of an Angry God,"
Jonathan Edwards pictured sinners
dangling helplessly above a wide, bot-
tomless pit, suspended by the fragile
strand of life which could snap at any
moment and dash them into the
"dreadful fierceness of God's fury."

Seldom if ever do we hear sermons
on the wrath of God and the sure
judgment of all who "neglect so great

salvation" (Heb. 2:3), though the Bible says, "God is angry with the wicked every day" (Ps. 7:11).

Though God "is longsuffering to us-ward, not willing that any should perish" (II Peter 3:9), "He will not. . . keep his anger for ever" (Ps. 103:9).

* * * *

HOLY SPIRIT

It's Hazardous!

Goethe said, "Take thought for thy body with steadfast fidelity. Thy soul must see through these eyes alone, and if they be dim, the whole world is clouded."

It is hazardous for a Christian to defile his body, the abode of the Holy Spirit: "If any man defile the temple of God, him shall God destroy; for the temple of God is holy, which temple ye are" (I Cor. 3:17).

"Keep thyself pure."—I Tim. 5:22.

* * * *

"Don't Go!"

Bob Hope was asked to give a graduating class a few words of advice on going out into the world. His advice was brief: "Don't go!"

God has endued His children with "power from on high," and sent them back into the world with a wondrous story to tell to the nations.

* * * *

"O Earth, Earth, Earth, Hear. . ."

An editorial in the Austin, Texas, *American-Statesman* stated: "Defective hearing is the nation's leading handicapping disability. Neither poor vision, heart disease, arthritis nor any other impairment affects as many people."

God is pleading with the spiritually deaf multitudes: "O earth, earth, earth, hear the word of the Lord" (Jer. 22:29).

The Saviour pleads with His spiritually dull children: "He that hath an ear, let him hear what the Spirit saith unto the churches" (Rev. 2:7).

* * * *

Clogged Ears

Sometime ago some dolphins got stranded on a beach near Boston. Scientists say that they may have run aground because of a hearing problem.

Dolphins use sound waves to judge depths, and it was discovered that worms had clogged the sinus cavities and inner ears of the stranded dolphins, making it difficult for them to hear.

There are some Christians who have become dull of hearing. They no longer hear the "still small voice" of the indwelling Holy Spirit.

* * * *

A Two-Headed Turtle

Strolling beside a creek one day, Caroline McDonald saw a strange creature—a two-headed turtle! The two heads had a tug of war with a morsel of meat Caroline fed them.

In commenting upon the phenomenon, Dr. Willie M. Reams, professor of biology at the University of Richmond, Virginia, said, "Two-headedness can occur in all animals, but such animals usually do not survive because of conflict of interest."

How Spirit-grieving and growth-stunting is double-headedness, or double-mindedness! James warns of the evils of double-mindedness: "For he that wavereth is like a wave of the sea driven with the wind and tossed, For let not that man think that he shall receive any thing of the Lord. A double minded man is unstable in all his ways" (Jas. 1:6-8).

* * * *

No Monopoly

After hearing Moody preach, a faultfinding critic remarked, "Moody speaks like he has a monopoly on the Holy Spirit."

"Oh, no," said his friend, who knew Moody intimately, "Moody doesn't have a monopoly on the Holy Spirit, but the Holy Spirit has a monopoly on him!"

It is God's desire that each one of His children be filled with all the fulness of God: "Be filled with the Spirit" (Eph. 5:18).

Holy Spirit, all divine,
Dwell within this heart of mine;

Cast down ev'ry idol throne,
Reign supreme, and reign alone.
Andrew Reed.

* * * *

We Can't Make Unbelievers Believe

Dwight L. Moody said, "It is not our work to make unbelievers believe. That is the work of the Holy Spirit. Our part is to give the Word of God. We can only proclaim the Word of God."

The Bible says of the Holy Spirit, "And when he is come, he will reprove [convict] the world of sin" (John 16:8).

* * * *

Noise Pollution

Dr. Leslie Doelle, an acoustician at the University of Montreal, said that rock bands and airplanes are the two most serious sources of noise pollution and that overexposure to the noise of rock bands can lead to permanent hearing damage. "In many cases the ear damage is only temporary, but it can be permanent," he said.

When anything militates against God's children hearing the still, small voice of the indwelling Holy Spirit, there is resultant disquiet and spiritual impoverishment.

* * * *

Why Pray for What Is?

Bishop Leslie Newbigin of the Church of South India said, "If we want the answer to the question,

'Where is the church?' we must ask, 'Where is the Holy Spirit recognizably present with power?' "

Christ's church does not need to pray:

Lord, send the old-time pow'r
The Pentecostal pow'r!

Why pray for that which God has already given? The Pentecostal power was sent long ago when the Holy Spirit came upon the believers. How tragic it is that so few Christians today are sufficiently emptied of self to be "filled with all the fulness of God" (Eph. 3:19).

* * * *

A Prerequisite to Conversion

"The sovereign work of the Holy Spirit must be done in a man before that man can be saved," said Charles Haddon Spurgeon.

In speaking of the convicting power of the Holy Spirit, the Saviour said, "And when he is come, he will reprove [convict] the world of sin" (John 16:8).

* * * *

Ablaze for God

Samuel Chadwick said:

"Fire is a symbol of moral passion. God is love! God is fire! The two go together. The Holy Spirit baptizes in fire. Spirit-filled souls are ablaze for God. They love with a love that glows. They believe with a faith that kindles. They serve with a devotion that consumes. They hate sin with a fierceness that burns. They rejoice with a joy that radiates. Love is perfected in the fire of God!"

The shining light of a candle is a consuming light. As the candle burns, it is consumed.

Oh, that in me the sacred fire
Might now begin to glow!
Burn up the dross of base desire,
And make the mountains flow!

* * * *

HOME

"Honorable In All"

Seven times the Lord God said of His primeval creation: "It was good."

One thing, however, God said was not good: "It is not good that man should be alone" (Gen. 2:18).

Then God became the first Matchmaker: "The Lord God. . .made he a woman, and brought her unto the man" (Gen. 2:22).

"Marriage is honourable in all" (Heb. 13:4).

Celibacy, the avoidance of marriage in accordance with religious vows, is not good. It thwarts God's changeless plan for procreating humankind in perpetuity. It attempts to change one of His basic plans, with resultant confusion.

How beautiful is the blending of two lives into one in the marital relationship: ". . .they are no more twain, but one flesh" (Mark 10:8). It is more than moonlight and roses! It is the uniting of heart and soul. It is sharing each other's joys and sorrows through life.

God's formula for the irrevocable marital tie is: "Till death do you part!"

* * * *

"Only a Piece of Paper"

Some whose lifestyle is contrary to the norms of a well-regulated society, speak lightly and self-excusingly of procuring a marriage license and a minister to consummate the sacred marital bond. "A marriage license is only a piece of paper. Why bother?"

So also is a birth certificate, a driver's license, a high school diploma, a degree in medicine and law, a passport, a divorce decree, and a ticket on a bus, train and airplane.

Nameless confusion would ensue in our society without pieces of paper. When the divinely regulated marital relationship is contemned and debased, moral and spiritual suffering are inescapable.

* * * *

RARE THINKING

My husband liked his steaks cooked rare,
And that was fine with me,
But now that beef keeps going up,
I've changed my plan, you see!

I skimp and save and cook without
A costly bill of fare,
To prove inflation can be beat,
If steaks for him are *rare*!

Pierce McBride in *Home Life.*

* * * *

PATCHWORK MARRIAGE

I got my marriage out today
To look at it again,
I hadn't looked in quite a spell—
Just do it now and then.

It's so much like a patchwork quilt,
With patches not a few!
Some patches large, some patches small,
Some patches old, some patches new.

Each patch brings back to memory
Some unkind word or deed,
By which we've learned to give and take,
And love with greater heed.

I pray the time will never come
When we patch it up no longer,
For it seems that where the patches are,
The fabric is *much stronger.*

Bill Ashworth, in *Home Life.*

* * * *

"KEEPERS AT HOME"
(Titus 2:5)

I like to spread clean sheets on beds,
I like to wield a broom,
I like to bring tranquillity
And order in a room!

I like to straighten linen shelves,
Set dresser drawers aright,
To hang crisp ruffled curtains,
And keep the silver bright!

I like to set a batch of bread,
Then watch it as it rises;
I like to plan and cook a meal
Of savory surprises!

Let other women have careers,
 None of them arouse
One twinge of envy in my heart,
 I like keeping house!

Ethel Romig Fuller.

* * * *

TV Addiction

Said Dr. Lawrence J. Friedman, author, lecturer and senior member of the faculty of Los Angeles Institute for Psychoanalysis:

"Visual communication is restrictive and addictive, much more so than sound alone.

"Children get addicted to TV much in the same way that adults get addicted to drugs.

"Television immobilizes, forces passivity. It isolates people from one another. It is one-way communication with images, not human beings. It interferes with emotional development. It forces regression. It tends to interfere with the learning of skills because it infringes on normal activity."

In Dr. Friedman's thinking, many of the problems of what he calls "our drug abuse generation"—which by graduation from high school accumulates on the average of 15,000 hours of television as opposed to 10,800 hours of school—can be linked with the influence of television. "They reject the reality of violence, yet enjoy watching it on TV, repress their own, speak of love, and become increasingly more self-destructive," said Dr. Friedman.

In using TV, adults and children should follow God's directive, ". . . know to refuse the evil, and choose the good" (Isa. 7:15).

Adapted from *Moody Monthly.*

* * * *

A WOMAN'S SPHERE

They talk about a woman's sphere
As though it had a limit;
There's not a place in Heav'n or
 earth,
There's not a task to mankind giv'n,
There's not a blessing or a woe,
There's not an answer yes or no,
There's not a life or death or birth,
That has a feather's weight of worth
But has a woman in it!

* * * *

"I Want to Live With Both of Them!"

An embittered, estranged couple and their lawyers stood before the judge and awaited his decision on the custody of the couple's six-year-old son. After much heated wrangling, the judge turned to the lad who sat forlornly near his mother and kindly asked, "My boy, which of your two parents do you wish to live with?"

After a moment's silence, the boy burst into tears and brokenly sobbed, "I - I - want - to - live with *both* of them!"

The estranged husband and wife looked penitently at each other. Tears filled their eyes. After a long embrace, they turned to the judge and said, "We have decided to become reconciled!" Taking the child by his hand, they walked happily from the court!

Divorce, like embalming, is a process which should not be begun too soon. "Till death do you part" is God's formula for the marital relationship.

* * * *

"The Highest Happiness"

William Lyon Phelps, American educator, said, "The highest happiness on earth is in marriage. Every man who is happily married is a successful man even if he has failed in everything else."

The Bible says, "Whoso findeth a wife findeth a good thing, and obtaineth favour of the Lord" (Prov. 18:22).

* * * *

When God Frowns

Southern poet Sidney Lanier said of his wife:

I marvel that God made you mine,
For when He frowns, 'tis then ye shine!

* * * *

After Verbal Combat

A married Christian couple often fussed and argued. One day after a verbal combat, the wife sullenly asked, "What would you have without me?"

The husband quipped, "Paradise!"

When mutual love, respect and understanding are lacking, the relationships between husband and wife are on a sure collision course whose smashup often ends in the divorce court!

* * * *

"Make Yourself At Home"

Spurgeon spoke eloquently of the home:

"The word home sounds like poetry to me. It does not matter if it is a cottage or mansion, home is home be it ever so homely. There is no place on earth like it. The sparrows sweetly chirrup and the swallows twitter around the chosen spot which is our joy and rest.

"Every bird loves its own nest. The owl thinks the old ruins the best spot under the moon. The fox is of the opinion that his hole in the hill is remarkably cozy. The way home is the best bit of road in the country. I like to see smoke from my own chimney better than fire on another man's hearth.

"When you go out, friends do their best; but still it is not home. 'Make yourself at home,' they say. Everybody knows to feel at home is to feel at ease. Why, at home you are at home, and what more could you want?"

* * * *

Man Incomplete Until. . .

The first thing God called not good was man's loneliness: "And the Lord God said, It is not good that the man should be alone; I will make him an help meet for him," or as rendered by Barclay, "I will make him a suitable helper, completing him" (Gen. 2:18).

"Whoso findeth a wife findeth a good thing, and obtaineth favour of the Lord."—Prov. 18:22.

* * * *

God's Mathematics

God's mathematics for the marital bond is: One plus one equals one. Long ago He said, "For this cause shall a man. . .cleave to his wife; And they twain shall be one flesh: so then they are no more twain, but one flesh" (Mark 10:7,8).

* * * *

Divorced Ministers

In addressing an annual luncheon of ministers' wives during a recent Southern Baptist Convention, marriage counselor Donald Moore spoke of the rising divorce rate among ministers.

"The minister spends an average of twenty-five hours per week with his family. That's less than one-fourth of his working hours. Those who have children spend the same amount of time at home as childless ministers or those whose children have already left home. This seems strange in light of the Christian concept of the family."

Moore also attributed the increased marital difficulties to the decline in understanding between the married partners and a loss of determination to stay married.

"The man who is indispensable to people too many hours a week may be 'playing God' more than he should," said Moore.

God hates the sundering of the marital tie: "Let none deal treacherously against the wife of his youth. For the Lord, the God of Israel, saith that he hateth putting away" (Mal. 2:15,16).

* * * *

Defusing Explosive Situations

A jovial husband said, "My wife and I have a good arrangement for getting along peaceably in the home: I rule the roost and she rules the rooster!"

Potentially explosive and divisive marital situations are often defused and overcome when a touch of humor is infused. Try it!

* * * *

The Rearward Look

A pastor was having temporary financial difficulties. He said to his wife, "Dear, please cut down on expenditures, especially for clothes, until our finances improve."

Some days later the wife came home regaled in a beautiful new dress! Eyeing it with mingled feelings, he said, "It's surely pretty, but, Honey, I asked you not to buy any clothes for a while. Remember?"

She replied, "Yes, dear, but when I was in the store I saw this lovely dress and Satan tempted me!"

"Now, Honey, you know the Bible answer to such a situation. You should have said, 'Get thee behind me, Satan!' "

Disarmingly, she replied, "I did that, dear, but when Satan got behind me, he said that it looks beautiful from the back, too!"

Happy is the household when potentially explosive situations are defused and given a humorous turn!

Told by John W. Brawand.

* * * *

One Flesh

C. S. Lewis, in illustrating how it is possible for husband and wife to be "one flesh," said, "It is like the lock and key being one mechanism, and the violin and bow being one instrument."

* * * *

A Time to Fuss

A couple came to me in a revival meeting and said, "We have been married for twelve years. We love each other devotedly. Only one thing prevents our marriage from being an ideal wedlock: *We fuss over trifles!* How childish and unseemly! It is habitual! What can we do to overcome this disruptive evil?"

This situation was different from other marital problems I had ever dealt with. I thought and then came up with a novel plan:

"Suppose you designate one day in the week, say Tuesday, and call it *fuss day* and fuss only on that day."

They agreed. It worked, They began to think: "If we can refrain from fussing six days in the week, we can refrain from fussing seven days in the week."

Often we can overcome evil habits and besetting sins by surmounting above them a day at the time. God deals with His children on a day-by-day basis: "Give us this day our daily bread" (Matt. 6:11).

A patient with a broken hip asked her doctor, "How long must I lie in this hospital bed?" The wise doctor replied, *"Just one day at a time!"*

Just for today, my Saviour,
Tomorrow is not mine;

Just for today I ask Thee
For light and health divine.
Tomorrow's care I must not bear,
The future is all Thine.

* * * *

Sullen Silence

When a disagreement occurred between a husband and wife, he sulked and became sullenly silent. She, endeavoring to placate him and restore peace in the home, tenderly asked him, "Dear, what can I fix for your breakfast?" Angrily he replied, "Nothing! Nothing at all! I will get my breakfast en route to work."

Taunt and tense, and inwardly fuming and frustrated, he drove his car onto the highway. Then it happened! He collided with an oncoming car and was instantly killed!

What havoc can result from domestic discord! Disagreements could become defused by a give-and-take attitude and lovingkindness.

"Be ye angry, and sin not: let not the sun go down on your wrath."— Eph. 4:26.

Told by Ralph M. Smith.

* * * *

Dehumanizing Family Feuds

Years ago two brothers ran a variety store at a rural crossroads. Both were mutually helpful and cooperative.

One day a customer made a $5 purchase. The bill was placed on the cash register while the brother waited on another customer. When he returned, the bill was gone!

The missing bill was the beginning

of bitter hostility between the brothers as one accused the other of stealing the money.

With the passing of time, hatred deepened. Neither spoke to the other. A partition was built, separating the store.

Then one day a man entered the store and made a startling confession: "Some years ago I stole a $5 bill which lay on the cash register. I was sick, hungry and penniless. I have come to return the money with interest. My conscience has troubled me since that day!"

What havoc is wrought by family feuds: "And Esau hated Jacob because of the blessing wherewith his father blessed him: and Esau said in his heart, The days of mourning for my father are at hand; then will I slay my brother Jacob." (Gen. 27:41).

* * * *

Divorce and Embalming

"After my first sermon in a series of meetings, a seemingly sincere man said to me, 'I love Jesus! I love Jesus! I love Jesus!'

"Throughout the series of meetings, at the close of my sermons the man would greet me and say, 'I am still loving Jesus!'

"Finally I asked the pastor, 'Tell me about this man who joyfully speaks of his love for Jesus.'

"A look of sorrow, mingled with disgust, pervaded the pastor's face as he related some revolting facts about the man.

" 'He would deceive, if it were possible, the elect; but his bare-faced hypocrisy is known to us. His wife is an honored member of our church. He cruelly divorced her for another woman. He is often in court for his failure to support his three children. His 'satanic sweetness' and avowals of love for Jesus are at variance with the cruelties which he has brought to his wife and children.' "

Great is the need to keep constantly before us what God said long ago about the enduring nature of the marital bond: "Let none deal treacherously against the wife of his youth. For the Lord. . .hateth putting away" (Mal. 2:15,16). What God hates, we, too, should hate. "Until death do you part" is God's formula His children must adhere to.

Divorce, like embalming, is a process which should not be undertaken too soon!

Told by Barry Wood.

* * * *

Character-Molding, Character-Warping—Which?

Anna Mihailovna Leuchina, the major pedagogue of early child care in the Soviet Union, said, "We believe that if you give us a child with limited potential we can make him a normal human being through providing him with a rich environment. If you have a child with a high potential and you don't put him in the best possible environment, he will stay dull forever."

We cannot overestimate the molding power of a Christian home or the character-warping power of Bibleless, prayerless homes.

A Sunday school teacher asked her class of junior boys to write a paragraph on "Religion in the home."

One boy raised his hand and said, "Teacher, we ain't got no religion in our home."

* * * *

HONESTY—DISHONESTY

"IN TIMES OF DANGER"

In times of danger, not before,
God and the doctor we adore;
When danger is past and all things righted,
God is forgotten and the doctor is slighted.

* * * *

"A Lie Can. . ."

Mark Twain said, "A lie can travel halfway around the world while truth is putting on its shoes!" Yet:

Truth crushed to earth shall rise again,
Eternal years of God are hers,
But error, wounded, writhes in pain,
And dies among her worshipers!

* * * *

Emotional Dishonesty

Dr. Stanley Lindquist, professor of psychology at California State University at Fresno, and a Christian, affirmed:

"Christians sometimes try to give the impression that God's presence keep us always on 'cloud nine,' when we know that we have times of depression. . . . A radiant front can be a form of dishonesty, and it can become psychologically damaging to the person affirming it and also for others. . . . Christian testimony of their faith tends to imply that it brings a continual state of victorious well-being, an exalted mood and no defeat. . . .One can fool himself by this sort of emotional dishonesty some of the time, and one can fool others much of the time by a vibrant testimony to what is a partial reality in his life."

At times, all Christians experience sorrow and suffering. Did not the Saviour say before His dying on the cross, "My soul is exceeding sorrowful unto death" (Mark 14:34)?

Through God's grace, however, Christians can triumph over distress and depression and become "more than conquerors through him that loved us" (Rom. 8:37).

* * * *

Equally Guilty

A woman said to her friend, "I'm going to discharge my maid."

"Why?" asked the friend.

"I caught her stealing my Holiday Inn bath towels."

How easy it is for those without conscience to judge and condemn others. How revealing are these words: "Therefore thou art inexcusable. . .that judgest: for wherein thou judgest another, thou condemnest thyself; for thou that judgest doest the same things" (Rom. 2:1).

Told by Dr. Angel Martinez.

* * * *

Ever Steal a Watermelon?

A boy was arraigned in juvenile court for stealing a watermelon.

Before passing sentence, the judge asked, "Have you anything to say?" The boy replied, "Yes, sir, Judge. Have *you* ever stolen a watermelon?" Laughter rippled through the court as the judge said, "No cross examination allowed. Case dismissed!"

* * * *

Sentenced to Wear Mittens

A professional pickpocket, Joseph Buell, was sentenced to a year in jail and five years on probation during which time he must wear mittens on his hands every time he went out in public.

Judge Richard Hayden, noting that Buell had spent nineteen of his forty-six years in prison for pickpocket offenses, said, "I want to break him of the habit."

The source of Buell's thievery was *inward,* not *outward*: "For from within, out of the heart of men, proceed. . .thefts" (Mark 7:21,22).

* * * *

Examination of Honesty

For many years Dr. Madison Sarratt taught mathematics at Vanderbilt University. Prior to giving exams, he would say, "Today I am giving *two* examinations—one in trigonometry and the other in honesty. I hope you will pass them both. If you must fail one, fail trigonometry. There are many good people in the world who can't pass trig, but there are no good

people who cannot pass the examination of honesty."

* * * *

"Where's the Bum?"

One day a communist agitator peddled into a city park on his bicycle. There he leaned the bike against a tree, mounted a soap box and began to address the crowd. "If you want something," he shouted, "raid a shop and take it! If your wife doesn't have a good coat, pick the best one you see. Ignore the law if it's against your best interests."

After finishing his harangue, he went to get his bicycle and, finding it gone, fumed, "Where's the bum who took my bicycle?"

"They that plow iniquity, and sow wickedness, reap the same."—Job 4:8.

Cecil E. Burridge.

* * * *

The Non-Debt-Paying Deacon

As a pious-looking deacon taught a class of boys, he emphasized the fact that each one of us needs to live a consistent Christian life, because God's watchful eye is upon us. He asked, "Why do you suppose that, when others see me, they think of me as a Christian?"

One boy, knowing that the deacon owed his father a debt which he refused to pay and that he had enriched himself by shady business transactions, asked, "Sir, could it be that they don't know you?"

God's children should be scrupulously honest in all their dealings with others: "Provide thing honest in the sight of all men" (Rom. 12:17).

* * * *

A CROOKED MAN

There was a crooked man
Who had a crooked smile,
Who made a crooked fortune
In a very crooked style.
He lived a crooked life,
As crooked people do,

And wondered how it turned out
His sons were crooked, too!

* * * *

Eternal Spring in My Heart

"Winter is on my head but eternal spring is in my heart," said Victor Hugo. "I breathe at this hour the lilies, the lilacs and the roses as at twenty years ago. The nearer I approach to the end, the plainer I hear around me the immortal symphonies of thy realm which invites me!"

* * * *

HOPE

Better to Hope

Martin Luther said, "All worthwhile things materialize through hope. No husbandman would sow a grain of corn if he did not hope it would spring up and bring forth the ear. How much more are we helped on by hope in the way of eternal life."

Better to hope, tho the clouds hang low,
And keep the eyes still lifted;
For the sweet, blue skies will soon peep thro
When the ominous clouds are rifted.

There was never a night without a day,
Nor an evening without a morning;
And the darkest hour, as the proverb goes,
Is the hour before the dawning.

"Why art thou cast down, O my soul? and why art thou disquieted within me? hope in God: for I shall yet praise him, who is the health of my countenance, and my God."—Ps. 43:5.

* * * *

"I Remember a Very Beautiful Person!"

A wife was a humanly hopeless alcoholic who disappointed and brought shame and great grief to her husband, but he never lost hope. One night she humiliated him in the presence of old friends. Later she wept bitterly and screamed, "Why don't you leave me?" To which the noble husband replied, "Because I remember a very beautiful person, and I believe she is still there!"

The merciless, personality-dwarfing, character-degrading evil—alcohol—reduces to horrendous caricatures myriads of God's erstwhile masterpieces who were endowed with limitless potentialities for good.

* * * *

BEYOND THE WINTER'S CHILL

My garden, in the days of spring,
Gave me heart to hope and sing.

When drowsy summer came, I felt
Its benediction while I knelt
At prayers that I had left unsaid
Because my one-time faith seemed
   dead.

My garden gave me peace and power,
I learned a lesson from each flower:
I learned to bend, but not to break,
I learned that hearts, although they
   ache,

May yet find solace in the light
Of sun by day and stars by night!

My garden, when the autumn came,
Wrote courage in the scarlet flame,
Of woodbine, growing on a wall,
Each leaf was like a trumpet call
That said, "Beyond the winter's chill
The dreams of spring are living still!"

Margaret E. Sangster
in *Christian Herald.*

* * * *

HUMILITY

Our Inadequacy

"Through many years of active public life and through observing many kinds of people," said J. Edgar Hoover, "I have found that the strongest, most competent and reliable man is the one who is first to admit his own inadequacy. Contradictory though it may seem, he is strong because he is humble, and always remembers that man is a creation of God. To trust in the Lord with all the heart is a mark of strength. It is the only path to true fulfillment."

"*Not that we are sufficient of ourselves. . .but our sufficiency is of God.*"—II Cor. 3:5.

* * * *

"Give God the Glory!"

Dr. C. Everett Koop, chief surgeon of the University of Pennsylvania Children's Hospital, and one of the world's leading pediatric surgeons, said, "My surgical skills are a gift from God. I believe He is in control of all circumstances and events. Knowing that Someone else is running the show gives me a tremendous amount of comfort. Give God the glory!"

The doctor admits he doesn't know why children suffer and die, but trustingly he says, "God never makes a mistake!"

Adapted from *Chicago Daily News.*

* * * *

The Queenliest of Christian Graces

A young Christian asked an elderly Christian, "What are the three Christian virtues which are indispensable to render acceptable service to God?"

"The first is humility; the second, humility; the third, humility," was the ready reply.

Too few of us are *big* enough to become *little* enough to be used effectively of God: "When thou wast little in thine own sight, wast thou not made the head of the tribes of Israel?" (I Sam. 15:17).

* * * *

The Top

In the book, *Man-Talk*, by Rev. James H. Doughdrill, Jr., occurs this prayer:

"God, I'm afraid of failing. I would like to rise to the top. I want to be big in the children's eyes. I want my wife to be proud of me. I guess these are okay to want, but they make pressure on me. Sometimes the pressure is so great that I try to be someone I'm not. I try to look important. I try to act important. I try to dominate.

"I want success, but, God, I don't trust it either. I have seen what success does to some people. I want real success and real humility—lots of both of them! But I know I don't get either by just wanting them.

"May I simply strive to live for You and to please You only. Amen."

"And seekest thou great things for thyself? seek them not."—Jer. 45:5.

* * * *

Only Be Willing

In the Middle Ages, as the lord of a manor lay critically ill, he asked a servant, "What do I have to do to go to Heaven?"

The servant replied, "Go to the pigsty, get on your knees in the mire and muck and pray, 'God be merciful to me a sinner!' "

The lord said, "I couldn't possibly do that."

The servant went away.

When the lord's sickness became worse, he sent for the servant again and asked, "What did you say that I would have to do to go to Heaven?"

The servant said, "Sire, you will have to go to the pigsty, get on your knees and pray, 'God be merciful to me a sinner!' "

"Well," said the lord, "if that is what I have to do, I am ready to do it!"

The old servant smiled and said, "Sire, you don't really have to go, but you have to be *willing to go!*"

Psalm 10:4 says, "The wicked, through the pride of his countenance, will not seek after God: God is not in all his thoughts."

Adapted from *Decision*.

* * * *

INFLUENCE
(See also Christian Living)

Polly Was Right

One spring, crows began to pull up a farmer's young corn. Determining to put a stop to it, he loaded his shotgun and slipped along the fence.

His very sociable parrot, discovering the crows, flew over and joined them. The farmer saw the crows but did not see the parrot. Bang! Bang! he fired away. Then he climbed over the fence to see how many crows he had hit.

How sad he was when he saw his parrot with a broken leg among the dead and maimed crows!

When the farmer took the parrot

home, his children asked, "Who hurt pretty Polly?"

In a solemn voice, the parrot answered, "Bad company! Bad company!"

The farmer said, "Yes, children, that was it. Polly was with those crows when I fired, and she received a shot intended for them."

Remember the parrot and what the bird would teach us: "Beware of bad company!"

The Bible says, "Be not deceived: evil communications [companionships] corrupt good manners" (I Cor. 15:33).

Alice Marie Knight.

* * * *

A Mother's Influence

"My mother's influence in molding my character was conspicuous. She forced me to learn long chapters of the Bible by heart. To that discipline and patient, accurate resolve I owe not only much of my general power of taking pains, but the best part of my taste for literature," said John Ruskin, English author.

* * * *

POST-MORTEM INFLUENCE

Lives of great men all remind us
We may make our lives sublime,
And departing, leave behind us
Footprints on the sands of time.

Footprints, that perhaps another,
Sailing o'er life's solemn main,
A forlorn and shipwrecked brother,
Seeing, shall take heart again.

Longfellow.

* * * *

"A Breath of Ye"

An elderly Scottish lady asked Professor Drummond to visit her terminally ill husband. She said, "He'll nae see thee, for he's blind. He'll nae hear thee, for he's deaf. But I want him to have a breath of ye about him before he dies."

Who can overestimate the value of *atmospheric religion* which emanates from Christlike Christians? Of them the Bible says, "For we are unto God a sweet savor of Christ" (II Cor. 2:15).

* * * *

Hallowed Memories

How quickly does a "Who's Who" become a "Who Was!" With the passing of time, he may fade from memory: "All flesh is as grass, and all the glory of man as the flower of grass. The grass withereth, and the flower thereof falleth away" (I Pet. 1:24).

William Cullen Bryant wrote:

**The gay will laugh when thou art gone,
The solemn brood of care plod on;
And each one will as before
Chase his favorite phantom!**

The names of some who lived long ago are excoriated. The names of others are enduringly enshrined in our hearts: "The memory of the just is blessed" (Prov. 10:7). THEIR INFLUENCE IS UNDYING: "By faith Abel offered unto God a more excellent sacrifice than Cain. . .by it he being dead yet speaketh" (Heb. 11:4).

* * * *

Persona Non Grata

Daniel Arap Moi, Vice President of Kenya, determined to keep hippies out of his country, said, "The drugs and decadent ways of foreign visitors are threatening to submerge the nation-building work habits of native Kenyans. The government of Kenya respects individual rights and will not force hippies to cut off their hair. The only alternative is to ban them from coming into our country."

The Bible says, "Evil communications [companionships] corrupt good manners" (I Cor. 15:53).

* * * *

JESUS

Mender of Broken Things

At the entrance of one of our hospitals in Austin, Texas, occur these words: "He healeth the broken in heart, and bindeth up their wounds" (Ps. 147:3).

Jesus is the Mender of broken things: broken plans, broken dreams, broken lives and broken hearts. He never fails to do this when we present to Him the broken parts. He enters healingly into our heartaches and heartbreaks: 'He is touched with the feeling of our infirmities' (Heb. 4:15).

* * * *

Don't Want to Become Involved

The question is asked, "If Christ were on earth today, would He receive the same treatment He received long ago?"

It is certain that many today are so indifferent and unconcerned about Him that they would not go to the trouble to become involved with Him.

How Spirit-grieving is the sin of indifference toward Christ and self-excusing neglect!

* * * *

God Forsaking God!

Who can fathom the depth of anguish compressed in the forlorn cry of the dying Saviour: "My God, my God, why hast thou forsaken me" (Matt. 27:46)?

Martin commented, "God forsaking God! Who can fathom that?"

* * * *

What and Who

Defeated, dispirited Christians dolefully lament, "Look what the world has come to!"

Radiant, triumphant Christians joyfully exclaim, "Look Who has come to the world: 'The Lord strong and mighty, the Lord mighty in battle' (Ps. 24:8) is 'able to do exceeding abundantly above all that we ask or think' " (Eph. 3:20).

* * * *

The Only Hope

Malcolm Muggeridge, the journalist, affirmed: "I don't believe there is any hope for the western world, from any quarter whatever, outside of Christ. In forty years of journalism I have come across no other hope. Man needs to be born again. By that I mean that he must understand what Christ stood for and follow His way of life—not only His teaching but the very way He lived, which includes, of course, the cross.

"People try to leave the cross out of the Gospel, but they can't because it's the heart of the whole thing."

How helpless are men and nations without Christ's help.

Help of the helpless, O abide with me!

* * * *

"Jesus Stood Still"

On a highway seven miles west of Green Bay, Wisconsin, a twenty-five-year-old man, David Huffstetler of Salt Lake City, killed himself after leaving a note saying his car stalled in the frigid weather and no motorist would stop to help him!

"I have been waiting eleven hours for someone to stop," said the note found next to his body. "I can't stand the cold any longer, and they just keep passing by!"

Long ago a blind beggar on the wayside called upon One who never failed to heed the plea of needy ones, saying, "Thou son of David, . . .have mercy on me" (Mark 10:48).

What occurred then abounds in comfort for all stranded, struggling mankind: "Jesus stood still. . . .and said unto him, What wilt thou that I should do unto thee? . . .Lord, that I might receive my sight. And Jesus said. . .thy faith hath made thee whole" (Mark 10:49,51,52).

* * * *

My All

A recent convert said to Billy Graham, "All my life, I'd felt that God was high and holy and unsearchable. It's hard to understand a God like that, let alone love Him. But then you showed me Jesus and quoted His words, 'He that hath seen me hath seen the Father.' And like a flash it came to me that if God is like Jesus who walked the common ways of man, loved and served the weakest of His creatures, and died on the cross to redeem us from our sins, then He can have my life, my soul, my all. I made that gift, and I've never taken it back!"

* * * *

Leader of Column of Progress

Phillips Brooks said, "Nineteen centuries have come and gone, and today Jesus Christ is the central figure of the human race and the Leader of the Column of Progress. I am far within the mark when I say that all the armies that ever marched, all the navies that ever sailed, all the parliaments that ever sat, all the kings that ever reigned, put together, have not affected the life of man on earth as has that one solitary life!"

Spiritual life in its full-orbed blessedness begins when we acclaim Him as "My Lord and my God" (John 20:28).

* * * *

He Inspired the Greatest

Henry Ward Beecher said, "Jesus painted no pictures. Yet some of the greatest paintings of Raphael, Michelangelo and Leonardo da Vinci received their inspiration from Him. Jesus wrote no poetry; but Dante, Milton and scores of the world's greatest poets were inspired by Him. Jesus composed no music; but Haydn, Handel, Beethoven, Bach and Mendelssohn reached their highest perfection in the symphonies and oratorios they composed in His praise. Every sphere of human greatness has been enriched by this humble Carpenter of Nazareth!"

* * * *

"That's Enough!"

Some years ago R. I. Williams phoned his sermon topic to the Norfolk *Ledger-Dispatch:* "The Lord Is My Shepherd."

"Is that all?" inquired the church editor.

The minister replied, "That's enough."

How amused and delighted he was when he read on the church page: "Rev. R. I. William's sermon subject for the Sunday morning service will be: 'The Lord Is My Shepherd— That's Enough!' "

* * * *

"Lord, I Have You!"

Before asking God for anything, J. Wilbur Chapman would gratefully acknowledge God's gifts to him and praise Him for them.

One day as he meditated upon God's gifts, the Lord seemed to say, "Son, what do you want?"

Chapman replied, "Lord, I have what I want now. *I have you!*"

Jesus is all this poor world needs today,

Blindly they strive, for sin darkens their way;
O to draw back the grim curtains of night,
One glimpse of Jesus and all will be bright!

All that I want is in Jesus,
He satisfies, joy He supplies;
Life would be worthless without Him,
All things in Jesus I find!

Harry Dixon Loes.

* * * *

The Enduring Foundation

In the heart of Mexico City, the foundation of the 400-year-old Catholic cathedral is slowly sinking. Government architects warn that if urgent measures are not taken, it will topple someday.

The entire city is sinking as the result of draining underground water, but the cathedral is sinking faster than most buildings.

Cathedrals and churches built of marble, stone and wood eventually succumb to the eroding, gnawing tooth of time. But Christ's church, composed of all spiritually changed men, women, boys and girls, is founded upon Christ, the enduring Rock, and it will abide forever and "the gates of hell shall not prevail against it" (Matt. 16:18).

* * * *

God's Flawless Die

As a group visited a manufacturing plant, the guide called their attention to a relatively small die that cost thousands of dollars to make. The die stamped out small metal parts— thousands of them—all alike.

For thousands of years mankind went without any earthly matrix for perfect human character. Though some great men entered the stream of history, all fell short of God's glory. None was flawless. Then it happened: "When the fulness of the time was come, God sent forth his Son, made of a woman, made under the law" (Gal. 4:4).

The sinless Son of God was God's perfect, peerless die—"without sin."

* * * *

A Divine Errand Boy

Said Irvine L. Jensen, "Don't settle for a Jesus who is just 'my buddy.' While some overemphasize Jesus' Godness, others push His humanness too far. He becomes a divine errand boy. He is the God who has been here, but *He is God.* Love and reverence Him as King of kings and Lord of lords; don't degrade Him.

The Bible says of Him, "Wherefore God also hath highly exalted him, and given him a name which is above every name" (Phil. 2:9).

* * * *

Jesus, Persona Non Grata

Before addressing a voluntary assembly at the Saguaro High School in Scottsdale, Arizona, Evangelist Freddie Gage was told by the school official that he must not mention the name of Jesus during his talk, which was to be basically about the evils of drugs. Since he was invited to the campus, Mr. Gage agreed to the request and urged the students to "live for God and to share Him."

Dr. Norman D. White, assistant superintendent of the Scottsdale School District, said that the name of Jesus is not forbidden during assemblies if He is referred to only as a historical being.

How bereft of heart-transforming power are references to Jesus only as a historical character!

"Thou shalt call his name JESUS: for he shall save his people from their sins" (Matt. 1:21); "Neither is there salvation in any other: for there is none other name under heaven given among men, whereby we must be saved" (Acts 4:12).

I know a world that is sunk in shame,
    Where hearts oft faint and tire,
But I know a Name, a precious Name,
    That can set that world on fire.
I know a Name, a precious Name,
    'Tis Jesus! 'Tis Jesus!

J. Wilbur Chapman.

* * * *

"Is Jesus Real to You?"

Years ago when Dr. George W. Truett held a revival meeting at Baylor University, God's Spirit worked mightily among the students.

Dr. Truett became greatly burdened for an atheistic student and arranged for a conference with him. Lovingly and earnestly he told him of the transforming grace of God and of the Saviour's ready willingness to reveal Himself to any honest seeker for the truth and forgiveness of sin.

After listening respectfully, the student asked, "Dr. Truett, is Jesus Christ *real* to you?"

"Real? Why He is more real to me than my hands and feet, than the skin on my body!"

How potent is our testimony when

we can experimentally say to those we are seeking to win:

I have found a friend in Jesus,
He's everything to me,
He's the fairest of ten thousand to my soul
The Lily of the Valley, in Him alone I see
All I need to cleanse and make me fully whole!
In sorrow He's my comfort, in trouble He's my stay,
He tells me ev'ry care on Him to roll:
He's the Lily of the Valley, the Bright and Morning Star,
He's the fairest of ten thousand to my soul!

Charles W. Fry.

* * * *

The Baby Jesus Must Go

A recent decision of a Court of Appeals says that either the government or the Baby Jesus must stay out of the Christmas Pageant of Peace near the White House. Apparently Jesus will be the one to go! "That's the way I see it right now," said Arthur J. Lamb, chairman of the week-long event. "A lot of people are upset, but it looks like we have no other choice."

Long ago Isaiah prophesied that the Saviour would be "despised and rejected of men" (Isa. 53:3).

Each one must answer Pilate's ancient, destiny-determining question, "What shall I do then with Jesus which is called the Christ?" (Matt. 27:22).

We cannot be neutral. Jesus said, "He that is not with me is against me" (Matt. 12:30).

Jesus is standing on trial today;
What will you do with the Saviour?
Will you accept Him, or turn Him away?
O what will you do with Him?

Cabell Foster Smith.

* * * *

"What Think Ye of Christ?"

D. L. Moody said, "It would be a great day if men would just take sides and let it be known where they stand in relationship to Jesus Christ."

Long ago this destiny-determining question was asked, "What think ye of Christ? whose Son is he?" (Matt. 22:42). What is your answer? Will you say with Peter, "Thou art the Christ, the Son of the living God" (John 6:69)?

* * * *

Magnify Him

R. A. Torrey said, "If you make a great deal of Christ, He will make a great deal of you. If you make but little of Him, He will make but little of you."

God's promise is unfailing, "Them that honour me, I will honour, and they that despise me shall be lightly esteemed" (I Sam. 2:30).

* * * *

"Thou Remainest"

The American clergyman W. C. Channing said, "The sages and heroes of the past are receding from us, and history contracts the record of their deeds into a smaller and smaller page. But time has no power over the name, deeds and words of Jesus Christ!"

Of Him we exclaim, "From everlasting to everlasting, thou art God" (Ps. 90:2). He is "the same yesterday, and to day, and for ever" (Heb. 13:8).

* * * *

Where Christ Isn't Emphasized

The Glide Memorial United Methodist Church in San Francisco recently added a distinguished Jewish rabbi, Abraham L. Feinberg, to its staff as full-time counsellor.

When reporters asked the rabbi, "Isn't it difficult for you to work in obviously Christian surroundings?" he replied, "Not at all, because in this church Christ is never emphasized!" In commenting upon the appointment, the pastor said, "It is a great step forward into the ecumenical movement!"

When any church ceases to make Christ preeminent and proclaim Him as the only way to God, it ceases to be a New Testament Christian church, and has no heart-transforming Gospel to offer to a morally corrupt and spiritually confused world.

Jesus said, "I am the way, the truth, and the life: no man cometh unto the Father but by me" (John 14:6).

Adapted from
The Presbyterian Journal.

* * * *

"Help of the Helpless"

An unbeliever said sneeringly to a trustful Christian, "You Christians depend on Jesus Christ as a crutch."

"That's right," flashed the Christian. "I am a spiritual cripple, and I greatly need the Saviour's support."

Jesus said, "For without me ye can do nothing" (John 15:5).

How helpless we are without His help. Let us daily plead:

Help of the helpless,
O abide with me!

* * * *

A Strong Tower

It is at least interesting that the name of the Lord is spelled with four letters in many languages. In Latin, it is *Deus*; in Greek, *Zeus*; in Hebrew, *Adon*; in Arabian, *Alla*; in Persian, *Syra*; in Egyptian, *Aumm*; in East Indian, *Esgi*; in Japanese, *Zain*; in Turkish, *Addi*; in Swedish, *Codd*; in Irish, *Dich*; in German, *Gott*; in French, *Dieu*; and in Spanish, *Dios*.

It isn't the spelling of the name of our Lord which is of primary significance to God's children, but what the name means to them: "The name of the Lord is a strong tower: the righteous runneth into it, and is safe" (Prov. 18:10).

* * * *

JEWS

"You Don't Have to Like Jews, But. . ."

Said Rev. Ted Hesburgh, president of the University of Notre Dame, "It's a free world. You don't have to like Jews; but if you don't, I suggest that you boycott certain Jewish products like insulin, discovered by Dr. Minkoski; the vaccine for hepatitis, discovered by Baruck Blumberg; chloral hydrate for convulsions, discovered by Dr. J. Van Leibig; the Wassermann test for syphilis; streptomycin, discovered by Dr. Selman

Abraham Waxman; the polio vaccine by Dr. Jonas Salk."

* * * *

Crowded to Christ

Said Abraham Poljak:

"I am one of the Jews who escaped from Germany. I thank God for all the strokes with which I was driven from darkness to light. It is better that we arrive beaten and bleeding at the glorious goal than that we decay happy and contented in darkness. As long as things were all right with us, we did not know anything of God, the salvation of our souls, and the world beyond. Hitler's arrows and our misery have led us to the light. We have lost our earthly home, but found the heavenly Home. We have lost our economic support, but won the friendship of the ravens of Elijah. On the bitter ways of emigration, *we have found Jesus*, the riches of all worlds!"

From *Crowded to Christ*,
by L. E. Maxwell.

* * * *

"Israel Is Annihilated!"

In a museum in Cairo, Egypt, is an ancient monolith on which occurs the inscription:

**"Israel Is Annihilated!
Israel Shall Have No Posterity!"**

The inscription was carved during the reign of Rameses II, the alleged cruel oppressor of the children of Israel, and who sought their expiration.

The arrogant monarch didn't know of God's changeless purpose for the continuous perpetuity of the people he tried to destroy: "Thus saith the Lord which giveth the sun for a light by day, and the ordinances of the moon and of the stars for a light by night. . . . The Lord of hosts is his name: If those ordinances depart from before me, saith the Lord, then the seed of Israel also shall cease from being a nation before me for ever" (Jer. 31:35,36).

The Pharaohs, the Hamans, the Hitlers, the Mussolinis are gone. Their names are excoriated. *Israel lives!*

"Pray for the peace of Jerusalem: they shall prosper that love thee" (Ps. 122:6).

* * * *

God's Barometer

In addressing Calgary's Knights of the Round Table, Rabbi Lewis Ginsburg stated, "The Jews are the barometers of civilization. How a country treats its Jews is a reflection of its moral and ethical position."

Long ago, God gave this infrangible promise to Abraham: "I will make of thee a great nation. . . And I will bless them that bless thee, and curse him that curseth thee, and in thee shall all families of the earth be blessed" (Gen. 12:2,3).

* * * *

Youthful Jews Turning to Jesus!

In the *Los Angeles Times*, Rabbi Harry Siegman, executive vice president of the Synagogue Council of America, said, "In the past, Jews who have been converted were largely on the periphery of Jewish life. A large percentage were cranks and crackpots. Now it is quite different in this very significant respect. For the first time we have predominantly young people who are interested."

* * * *

Tidal Waves of Blessings

In March 1975, in an item in the *Los Angeles Times*, it was said, "There is in Jerusalem a group of orthodox Jews known as the Watchers of the City—*Neturei Karta* in Hebrew. These deeply religious Jews maintain that the Jews long ago were sent by God into exile in punishment for sin, and until Messiah comes they are bound by divine oaths to take no forcible action to regain the Holy Land."

Believers in God's "sure word of prophecy" observe with concern Israel's impenitence and failure to accept the Messiah, Jesus Christ, who has already come. However, when He comes again, deep sorrow will be poured "upon the house of David, and upon the inhabitants of Jerusalem. . .and they shall look upon me [the Messiah] whom they have pierced, and they shall mourn for him" (Zech. 12:10).

Tidal waves of blessings will come to Israel when this happens: "And the ransomed of the Lord shall return, and come to Zion with songs and everlasting joy upon their heads: they shall obtain joy and gladness, and sorrow and sighing shall flee away" (Isa. 35:10).

May that glorious day not be distant: "Surely I come quickly. . . . Even so, come, Lord Jesus" (Rev. 22:20).

* * * *

JOY

Joy, How Found

On a murky Monday morning in Chicago, the sky was leaden. The rain descended in a dismal drizzle outside as a minister entered the Psychopathic Court to appear in the behalf of an emotionally sick patient.

The functionaries and political hangers-on in the court greeted each other gloomily and dejectedly. How different it was with the minister. He was joyous as he spoke comfortingly to a number of burdened, bothered ones whose loved ones were to be committed to a hospital for the mentally sick, and commended them to the Saviour, the Mender of broken things.

If you go out in *quest* of joy, it will elude you. If you go out to *impart* joy, you will find it.

* * * *

Smile

A smile costs nothing, but its value is priceless. It enriches the one who gives it, yet it impoverishes him not. It happens in a flash, but the memory of it lasts.

No one is so rich that he can get along without smiles. No one is so poor that he cannot afford to give them.

Smiles generate happiness in the home and good will in business, because they say, *I like you. You give me pleasure.*

If you meet an acquaintance or a friend who fails to flash a smile, give one of yours. No one needs a smile so much as the person who has none to give.

As David Livingstone looked wistfully upon a group of missionaries as they left for mission fields, a minister said to him, "My boy, would you like to be a missionary?" Later Livingstone said, "It was his smile, tender and questioning, that led me to make my final decision to serve my Saviour as a foreign missionary!"

* * * *

A Masterpiece

A group of friends were conversing with Daniel Webster about the noblest piece of literature in the English Bible. Various passages were mentioned: the Genesis account of creation; chapters 21 and 22 of the book of Revelation depicting the redeemed in Heaven; and the Sermon on the Mount.

Then from memory Webster recited Habakkuk 3:17-19:

"Although the fig tree shall not blossom, neither shall fruit be in the vines; the labour of the olive shall fail, and the fields shall yield no meat; the flock shall be cut off from the fold, and there shall be no herd in the stalls: Yet I will rejoice in the Lord, I will joy in the God of my salvation. The Lord is my strength, and he will make my feet like hinds'

feet, and he will make me to walk upon mine high places. To the chief singer on my stringed instruments."

As he finished, he commented: "I am amazed that no great artist has seen here a subject for a masterpiece! Habakkuk, sitting in the midst of dreadful desolation, still praising and rejoicing in his unseen God!"

Herschel H. Hobbs.

* * * *

Be Contagiously Joyful

Dr. Theodore Van Dellen, *Chicago Tribune* medical writer, said, "Laughter has a relaxing effect on the nervous system and improves digestion and well-being. Laughter is also good exercise. When someone laughs heartily, the diaphragm shakes up and down and air is drawn into the lungs by means of long, deep intake, and expelled in a series of bursts!"

The Bible says, "He that is of a merry heart hath a continual feast" (Prov. 15:15). *Be contagiously cheerful!*

* * * *

Lincoln's Levity

When a congressman criticized Lincoln for indulging in levity when the whole country was bowed in sorrow, Lincoln replied, "If I could not get momentary respite from the crushing burden I am constantly carrying, my heart would break."

* * * *

To Be Needed

English novelist Storm Jameson

said, "Happiness comes from the capacity to feel deeply, to enjoy simply, to think freely, to risk life, *to be needed."*

* * * *

A Dead Orthodoxy

"Much of our orthodoxy is correct and sound," said Vance Havner, "but it is like words without a tune. It does not glow and burn. It has lost its hallelujah. It is too much like a catechism and not enough like a camp meeting. One man with a glowing experience of God is worth a library full of arguments.

"When one asked Gypsy Smith his secret of keeping young and fresh through the years, he replied, 'I've never lost the wonder!' "

Is there anything more lifeless than a dead orthodoxy? The Saviour said rebukingly to a moribund church: "Thou hast a name that thou livest, and art dead" (Rev. 3:1).

* * * *

The Happiest People

George Gallup took a poll of representative groups of people to ascertain which people are the happiest. On a TV interview, he said, "Our survey showed that the happiest people are those who have a real religious experience. The most unhappy are those who frequent taverns."

How joyous are those who can say experimentally, "In thy presence is fulness of joy; at thy right hand there are pleasures for evermore" (Ps. 16:11).

* * * *

Different

A court reportedly has found that a United Pentecostal Church makes too much noise during its worship services. The congregation has appealed the court's decision, claiming that the city's anti-noise ordinance does not define how loud "loud" really is, and that the ordinance infringes on their constitutional rights.

How different are God's children in temperament! Some shout when they are happy, while others are quiet.

In this hectic world, all Christians should cherish the tranquilizing promise: "In quietness and in confidence shall be your strength" (Isa. 30:15); "Be still, and know that I am God" (Ps. 46:10).

The voice of the indwelling Holy Spirit is a "still small voice" (I Kings 19:12) and is best heard when God's children are yielded and quiescent before Him: "But the Lord is in his holy temple: let all the earth keep silence before him" (Hab. 2:20).

* * * *

CANDLE OF JOY

He who carries a candle of joy
    Will light the path for a brother,
And furnish the spark to start the
        flame
    Of hope in the heart of another.

Josephine Millard.

* * * *

JUDGMENT

Self-Discipline

"As we ate breakfast one morning," said Kiely Young, "our little two-year-old Steven became greatly interested in the top on a cereal container. Reaching forth his little hand, he tried to open it. I lightly slapped his hand. A look of bewilderment clouded his face. He didn't understand the restraining gesture. He thought he was being challenged to play the first-taught baby game: *Pattycake, Pattycake, Baker's Man.* Then he patted the back of his hand, as I had done. No thought of discipline or chastisement entered his mind."

A greatly needed spiritual lesson emerges from this breakfast-table incident: All of God's children need to practice self-judgment and self-discipline, which will obviate the necessity of God's judging and chastening us: "For if we would judge ourselves, we would not be judged. But when we are judged, we are chastened of the Lord" (I Cor. 11:31,32).

Long ago Daniel learned this lesson: "Fear not, Daniel: for. . .[when] thou didst set thine heart to understand, and to chasten thyself before thy God, thy words were heard" (Dan. 10:12).

* * * *

We're Doing It Backward!

Paul Harvey, well-known journalist and newscaster, spoke incisively of our permissive, criminal-coddling society when he said, "The guy who shot you or beat you up or robbed you, if caught and convicted, will go to prison, while you, the victim, will be further punished with additional taxes to pay for his clothing, food, housing, recreation and education. You, the victim, probably suffered physically and you surely suffered mentally. We're doing it backward—compensating criminals and penalizing their victims."

The Bible says, "Because sentence against an evil work is not executed speedily. . .the heart of the sons of men is fully set in them to do evil" (Eccles. 8:11).

* * * *

Not Medals But Scars

Vance Havner said, "A true servant of God is best measured not by how many bouquets have been pinned on him, but by how many brickbats have been hurled at him."

When God's children appear before the judgment seat of Christ, He will not look for medals but for scars.

Long ago God's intrepid servant Paul said, "I bear in my body the marks [scars] of the Lord Jesus" (Gal. 6:17).

* * * *

"Ashamed of Nothing!"

Reuel Lemmons, editor of *Firm Foundation,* said, "We have produced a generation of people who are ashamed of nothing!"

This was true of many people in

Jeremiah's day: "Were they ashamed when they had committed abominations? nay, they were not at all ashamed, neither could they blush" (Jer. 8:12).

God's judgment upon such is inevitable: "I will surely consume them, saith the Lord. . .and the things that I have given them shall pass away from them" (Jer. 8:13).

* * * *

An Appointment With God

According to *U. S. News and World Report,* before the death of China's Chairman Mao Tse-tung, he told a delegation of visiting diplomats that he was very ill and, in his words, "I have an appointment with God."

Each one of God's children has an appointment with Christ, to be judged for the *quality* of his works: "The fire shall try every man's work of what *sort* it is" (I Cor. 3:13); "For we *must* all appear before the judgment seat of Christ" (II Cor. 5:10).

Unsaved people also have an appointment with God: "It is appointed unto men once to die, but after this the judgment" (Heb. 9:27).

* * * *

Easy to Judge Others

How easy it is to judge others! The Bible warns against this evil: "Thou art inexcusable, O man, whosoever thou art that judgest: for wherein thou judgest another, thou condemnest thyself; for thou that judgest doest the same things" (Rom. 2:1).

How searching is Jesus' question: "And why beholdest thou the mote that is in thy brother's eye, but considerest not the beam that is in thine own eye?" (Matt. 7:3).

Oh, that I might understand,
And understanding cast no stone,
Knowing, too well, the sin I condemn,
But for God's grace could be my own!

Eva A. Howard.

* * * *

Twelve Billion Cells in Human Brain

There are twelve billion cells within the human brain! Each one is capable of storing memory. Dr. Wilder Penfield, noted neurosuregon of McGill University, Montreal, said, "Everything which has been in our conscious awareness is recorded in detail and stored in the brain and is capable of being 'played back' in the present! An electrode awakens—evokes—a single recollection, not a mixture of memories or generalities!"

When unsaved mankind appears before the judgment bar of God and the irrefutable life's record is "played back" as they recorded it, it cannot be disclaimed or denied. It cannot be expunged!

How sobering is the fact that God "hath appointed a day, in. . .which he will judge the world in righteousness by that man[the Saviour] whom he hath ordained" (Acts 17:31).

* ** *

Swift Judgment

Sometime ago a bomb exploded in the hand of a hold-up man as he emerged from a branch of the Canadian Imperial Bank of Commerce in

Kenora, Ontario. The thief was disintegrated, and the front of the bank was badly damaged.

Sometimes the darksome deeds of evildoers backfire and justice is meted out swiftly.

God's ultimate time of reckoning with evildoers is inescapable: "The dead were judged out of those things which were written. . .according to their works. And whosoever was not found written in the book of life was cast into the lake of fire" (Rev. 20:12,15).

* * * *

Paradoxical

Sometimes lawyers know that the surest way to win freedom for their clients who are innocent is to plead them guilty. How paradoxical!

Before the judgment bar of God, there is only one prevailing plea—guilty! Here's why: "For all have sinned and come short of the glory of God" (Rom. 3:23).

How hopeless and helpless we would be but for the grace and mercy of God: "It is of the Lord's mercies that we are not consumed, because

his compassions fail not" (Lam. 3:22).

* * * *

Only Stragglers

Dormant since 1903, St. Soufriere volcano in the Windward Islands is beginning to show signs of activity. Evacuation of the surrounding area has already begun. Some 11,000 people live in the danger zone.

Reporting on the progress of the evacuation, an AP dispatch said, "Only stragglers, the indecisive, and the eternally optimistic still remain in their homes and at jobs near St. Soufriere volcano, which threatens to erupt at any moment!"

How like those unheeding stragglers are myriads today who spurn God's offer of mercy and forgiveness. They take no steps to escape the coming day of wrath and "fearful. . .judgment and fiery indignation, which shall devour the adversaries" (Heb. 10:27).

"Behold, now is the accepted time; behold, now is the day of salvation."—II Cor. 6:2.

* * * *

KINDNESS

Good for Evil

As General Robert E. Lee rode his charger along the battlefield, a wounded Union Army soldier hurled obscenities and disparaging words at him. Calmly, General Lee dismounted, knelt beside the wounded soldier and said, "Son, I am very sorry you are hurt. I hope and pray that you will soon be on the road to recovery!"

How Christlike was the General!

Of the Saviour it is written, "Who, when he was reviled, reviled not again" (I Pet. 2:23).

* * * *

One Who Cared

Babe Ruth had hit 714 home runs during his career and this was one of his last full major league games. It was the Braves versus the Reds in Cincinnati. The great Ruth, no longer as agile as he had once been, fumbled the ball, threw badly; and in one inning alone his misplays were responsible for most of the five runs scored by Cincinnati.

As he walked off the field after the third out and headed toward the dugout, a crescendo of yelling and booing reached his ears. Just then a boy jumped over the railing onto the playing field, and with tears streaming down his face, threw his arms about the knees of his hero. Ruth picked up the boy, hugged him and set him down on his feet as he patted his head gently. The noisy fans stopped their booing, and a silence enveloped the park!

The scene of one little boy who cared for the feelings of another human being melted the hearts of the crowd.

Alfred J. Kolatch.

* * * *

A Suicide Prevented

An emotionally disturbed college student went to the dresser in his drab room and opened a drawer where he had hidden a revolver beneath his socks and underclothes. Intent on taking his life, he frantically searched for the gun. Miraculously a cartoon printed on the newspaper lining the bottom of the drawer caught his eye. Out of curiosity, the student read the caption and Bible verse on the religious cartoon, drawn by Jack Hamm, the well-known artist of Dallas, Texas.

Later the student told a friend, "The inspirational message of the drawing and the Bible verse prevented me from carrying out my fixed purpose to take my life!"

In commenting upon the incident, Hamm said, "I never found out which one of my drawings the student saw, but his friend told me it contained a Scripture that really meant something to him at that dark moment!"

How little it often takes to convert "the sinner from the error of his way [and] save a soul from death": a kind word of encouragement, a gentle hand laid on a troubled brow, a willingness to enter sharingly and understandingly into the heartaches and heartbreaks of others!

Many are waiting a kind, loving word,
Help somebody today!
Thou hast a message, O let it be heard,
Help somebody today!
Many have burdens too heavy to bear,
Help somebody today!
Grief is the portion of some ev'rywhere,
Help somebody today!"

Carrie E. Breck.

Later may be too late!

"They helped every one his neighbour; and every one said to his brother, Be of good courage."—Isa. 41:6.

* * * *

Something to Live for

Said Henry Drummond, "The man who sees a chance to do a good turn here and a little one there, and sheds a little light here and a little sunshine there, has something to live for."

Have you a had a kindness shown?
  Pass it on.
'Twas not given thee alone.
  Pass it on.

* * * *

Slumbering Potentials

While rummaging through some seemingly worthless things in his attic, an Englishman found a small blue and white porcelain vase. Reckoning it of little worth, he put it in a box in the trunk of his car.

When the vase was sold at an auction, it brought the fantastic sum of $324,000. It was a perfect specimen of the 15th century Ming dynasty of China.

Great potentials often slumber in the souls of seemingly worthless ones until

Touched by a loving heart,
Wakened by kindness,
Chords that are broken
Will vibrate once more!

* * * *

Eyelids

Woodrow Wilson liked to tell this story:

A group of professors in a certain university met regularly to consider any acts of student misconduct. In one session, when they were discussing the misdeeds of an offending student, a certain professor proposed a severe punishment for the student, saying, "After all, God has given us eyes."

"Yes," countered one of his colleagues with a kinder nature, "and eyelids, too!"

* * * *

HELP FOR THE HELPLESS

Let me be a voice for the speechless,
  Those who are small and weak;
Let me speak for all helpless
  creatures
Who have no power to speak.

I have lifted my heart to Heaven
  On behalf of the least of these:
The frightened, the homeless, the
  hungry—
  I am voicing their pleas.

If I can help any creature
  Respond to a desperate call,
I will know that my prayer is
  answered
By the God who created them all.

Helen Inwood.

* * * *

Poor and Full of Ailments

How rewarding is kindness!

"My mother, Dr. Ethel Hill Sharp, was a practicing physician," said Genevieve Sowards. "Along with her remarkable skill in diagnosing and treating disease, she had a way with people and often listened to their woes and helped them with their non-medical problems.

"Mama had one patient who was old, poor and full of ailments. Though she was a charity patient, yet Mama gave her the same kindness and patience she gave others, and listened to her troubles.

"Once, at the end of an especially

trying day, Mama came out of her office and saw the woman in her reception room. *Oh, no!* she thought. *Not today.* But she led her into her private office and gently motioned her to a chair. 'Now, my dear,' said Mama, 'What can I do for you?'

"The old woman replied, 'Doctor, you have done so much for me. This time I wanted to do something for you. I have pieced for each of your children a quilt top—double ring pattern.' Then she took them out of her shopping bag.

"Tears filled Mama's eyes. All those tiny pieces sewed by hand—three quilt tops. It must have taken her many months, maybe years. 'To think,' Mama said afterwards, 'I nearly spoke impatiently to her!'

"Many times, as I crawled beneath my beautiful comforter at night, I'd remember the old lady. Many years later I gave my quilt to my son Neil and his wife Diana along with its story."

"And be ye kind one to another, tenderhearted."—Eph. 4:32.

Adapted from *Guidepost.*

* * * *

Our Best

In the Palace of Wurzburg in West Germany is a Hall of Mirrors. As you enter it, a thousand faces greet your face, smile when you smile, and weep when you weep. When your hand is extended, many hands reach forth toward your hand.

The attitude of others toward us depends largely upon our attitude toward them. If we are kind to them, they will be kind to us. If we are helpful to them, they will be helpful to us.

For life is the mirror of king and slave,
'Tis just what you are and do;
Then give to the world the best you have,
And the best will come back to you!"

* * * *

LAWLESSNESS
(See also Crime)

Poverty and Crime

Milton S. Eisenhower said, "The correlation is not one of race with crime, but of poverty with crime."

It is true that some social evils contribute to the commission of crime, but we should never accept poverty as an excuse for the commission of crime.

Christ traced crime to its true source—the "desperately wicked" heart of man: "For from within, out of the heart of men, proceed. . .adulteries. . .murders, thefts. . .lasciviousness" (Mark 7:21,22).

* * * *

Read and Weep!

Said Senator Birch Bayh, chairman of the Senate Subcommittee on Juvenile Delinquency: "Ninety-five percent of all adult felons have juvenile records, and half the crimes in this country are committed by youngsters not old enough to vote.

These are alarming facts that point to one very sad conclusion: Whatever we are doing in the area of prevention and juvenile rehabilitation has been a dismal failure!"

What a challenge to churches is this alarming situation! Juveniles who are brought up in the church and Sunday school are not frequently brought up in court.

* * * *

A Needed Infusion

A black man was arraigned for making moonshine liquor.

The judge asked, "What's your name?"

The black man replied, "Joshua."

The judge, infusing a touch of humor into the situation, asked, "Are you the Joshua who made the sun stand still?"

The black man replied, "No, Judge, I'm the Joshua who made the moonshine still."

How helpful and fear-allaying is the infusion of a touch of humor into testing situations!

Told by Angel Martinez.

* * * *

Red Riding Hood

Once upon a time, in a faraway country, there lived a little girl named Red Riding Hood. One day her mother asked her to take a basket of fruit to her grandmother, who had been ill and lived in a cottage in the forest.

It happened that a wolf was lurking in the bushes and overheard the conversation. He decided to take a short-cut to the grandmother's house and get the fruit for himself. The wolf killed Grandma! Then he put on her nightgown and jumped into the bed to await the arrival of the little girl. When she entered the cottage, he tried to grab her! She was very frightened and ran out screaming.

A woodcutter, working nearby, heard her cries and rushed to her rescue. He killed the wolf with his axe and saved Red Riding Hood's life. All the townspeople hurried to the scene and proclaimed the woodcutter a hero.

At the inquest, however, the wolf's defenders contended that he had not been advised of his rights and that the woodcutter had made no warning swings with his axe before striking the fatal blow.

Some self-styled advocates of civil liberties stressed the point that, although the act of eating Grandma may have been in bad taste, the wolf was only "doing his thing" and didn't deserve the fate he suffered. Others contended that the killing of Grandma should be considered self-defense.

On the basis of these considerations, it was decided that there was no charge against the wolf! Moreover, the woodcutter was indicted for unprovoked assault with a deadly weapon!

Several nights later, the woodcutter's cottage was burned to the ground!

One year from the date of "The Incident at Grandma's," the cottage was made a shrine for the wolf who had bled and died there. All the village officials spoke at the dedication, but it was Red Riding Hood who gave the most touching tribute.

She said, "While I was grateful at the time for the woodcutter's intervention, I realize in retrospect that he overreacted with brutal severity."

As Red Riding Hood knelt and placed a wreath on the marker which extolled the brave wolf, there wasn't a dry eye among the townspeople who had assembled to honor the memory of the wolf!

Adapted from New Life Fellowship.

* * * *

LIGHT—DARKNESS

The Haunted House

For half a century sightseers have visited the most bizarre private residence ever built, and left wondering what it was all about. The house has 160 rooms, 10,000 windows, 40 bedrooms, 13 bathrooms, 47 fireplaces, 40 staircases and 9 kitchens. It has had only one resident, Sarah Pardee Winchester, heiress to the Winchester Arms fortune.

For thirty-eight years workmen toiled around the clock to add to the sprawling house where the mysterious recluse lived until her death in 1922, allegedly having been told by a spiritualist that she would live as long as work continued on the residence. She died there, however, at the age of eighty-five.

It is said that she spent $5.5 million of her $20 million building and furnishing the mansion.

Why did this eccentric oldster spend millions of dollars in building and furnishing this bizarre private residence? A Boston spiritualist claimed she warned Mrs. Winchester that vengeful ghosts of the thousands of men, women and children killed by her husband's guns would never leave her alone, but that she would come to no harm if she built a haunted house for friendly ghosts who would ward off the unfriendly spirits. A bell in one of the towers was tolled by one of her servants each midnight to welcome incoming flights of good spirits, and again at 2:00 a.m. as the ghosts returned to their graves.

Rejecting the eternal Word of God, unorbed, fear-craven multitudes are the easy victims of "seducing spirits, and doctrines of devils" (I Tim. 4:1).

* * * *

"WHAT IS A SAINT?"

"What is a saint?" the youngster asked,
So his parents set out to explain
By describing Saint Francis and Bernadette
They attempted to make it plain.
They told of Matthew, Mark and Luke,
And ended with John and Paul,
But the boy just couldn't relate to this,
And didn't grasp it at all.

Then the parents went to their church and showed him
The stained-glass windows there.

The faces of the elect shone out
As they preached or knelt in
prayer.
The boy was asked if he understood,
And he said, "I think I do:
From what I've seen, I'd say that a
saint
Is a person the light shines
through."

C. Frederick Stork
in *Christian Herald.*

* * * *

Gullible, Naive, Duped

Paul L. Maier said in *Christian Herald,* "As for shunning the truth and 'wandering into myths,' the human capacity to believe anything has never been stronger. If this trend continues, historians may well speak of 'The Credulous Seventies,' a time when the frightened people on this planet—perhaps in some frenzy to escape its problems—became one of the most gullible, naive, duped, superstitious and credulous generations since primitive man."

* * * *

Togetherness

A laser is a device that can generate a light beam so mighty that it can burn tiny holes in strips of steel in less than a second! In a laser beam the rays are all exactly the same and they travel "in step." Light rays in ordinary light travel in different directions. Rays in a laser beam move almost exactly in the same direction. That's why a laser beam is so powerful.

Jesus said of His followers, "Ye are the light of the world" (Matt. 5:14). When they go forward united in one direction, as did God's people long ago, victory over foes is sure: "So all the men of Israel were gathered against the city, knit together as one man" (Judg. 20:11).

* * * *

Richter Was Right

German author Jean Paul Richter said, "Without God there is for man neither purpose, nor goal, nor hope, only a wavering future, an eternal dread of every darkness."

* * * *

On Eve of Another Dark Age

Malcolm Muggeridge, former editor of *Punch,* and author of *Jesus Rediscovered,* said, "It has long seemed clear to me, beyond any shadow of doubt, that what is still called Western civilization is in an advanced stage of decomposition, and that another dark age will soon be upon us, if, indeed, it has not already begun!"

God's children need not fear the darkness. Christ's promise is unfailing: "I am the light of the world: he that followeth me shall not walk in darkness, but shall have the light of life" (John 8:12).

Said James Kelley, "I'd rather light a candle than curse the darkness!"

* * * *

Darkness May Hold Possibilities

Said Helen Keller:

"I have *felt* a bud shyly doff her green hood and blossom into a silken burst of sound, while the icy fingers of snow beat against the windowpanes. What secret power, I wonder, caused the blossoming miracle? What mysterious power guided the seedling from the dark earth up to the light, through leaf and stem and bud, to glorious fulfillment in the perfect flower? Who would have dreamed that such beauty lurked in the dark earth and was latent in the tiny seed we planted?

"Beautiful flower! You have taught me to see a little way into the hidden heart of things. Now I understand that the darkness everywhere may hold possibilities better than my hopes."

There are blossoms of gladness
 'Neath the winter's snow,
From the gloom and the darkness
 Come the springtime's glow!
Never give up the battle,
 You will win the fight,
Clouds will glow bright and sunny
 If your heart keeps right!

* * * *

LOST

"Unsaved, Though Saturated With Religion"

Ethel Steadman, a news reporter, testified:

"For fifteen years I reported crime for metropolitan dailies. I played to the hilt the traditional role of a hard-hitting reporter—cynical, pseudo-sophisticated, iconoclastic, but empty, lonely and lost.

"When 12 years of age I united with the church and grew up saturated with religion. That wasn't the answer, however. Later I dedicated my life for full-time Christian service. That didn't work either. I must have rededicated my life a half-dozen times at church, summer assemblies and youth retreats. I was seeking but never satisfied. I knew how to be saved but had never met the Saviour.

"My soul hunger persisted. So I began to feast at the world's banquet table and 'would fain [fill my] belly with the husks that the swine did eat' (Luke 15:16). My numb, awful emptiness deepened. I strayed farther and farther from God. For fourteen years I never entered a church."

"Then it happened! I met Jesus as Master, Saviour and precious Lord! He has seated me at His banqueting table where there is bread enough and to spare! With joy I exclaim, 'For the Lord is good; his mercy is everlasting; and his truth endureth to all generations.' I am eternally grateful!"

* * * *

Kittens Born in Dough Bowl

Some people ignorantly affirm, "I am a Christian because I live in America." It would be just as reasonable to say that kittens born in a dough bowl are biscuits.

How vastly different are statistical Christians from born-again ones!

* * * *

"Wrong-Way Corrigan"

Have you ever heard about *Wrong-Way Corrigan?*

Douglas Corrigan acquired this title in 1938 when he took off in his plane from Brooklyn, New York, announcing that his destination was Long Beach, California. Twenty-three hours later he landed his craft in Dublin, Ireland, and asked officials, "Is this Los Angeles?"

Not until years later did Corrigan acknowledge that he had planned to cross the Atlantic and go to Ireland after he had failed to get clearance for that flight.

How like Corrigan are many who know they are on the wrong way in life and refuse the right way: "There is a way that seemeth right unto a man, but the end thereof are the ways of death" (Prov. 16:25).

* * * *

The Supreme Tragedy

George Bernard Shaw said, "There are two tragedies in life. One is not to get your heart's desire; the other is to get it."

The supreme tragedy of life is to go out into a lost hereafter without God and without hope: "For what is a man profited, if he shall gain the whole world, and lose his own soul? (Matt. 16:26).

Have you counted the cost,
if your soul should be lost,
Tho' you gain the whole world
for your own?
Even now it may be that the
line you have crossed,

Have you counted, have you
counted the cost?
A. J. Hodge.

* * * *

Religious but Lost

H. A. Ironside sat in a railway coach reading his Bible. A woman, sitting across the aisle from him, said, "I am glad to see that there is at least one religious person on this train beside myself."

In reply, Dr. Ironside said, "That's interesting. Tell me more."

She said, "Two of my uncles are ministers and their father before them was a minister. So you see, religion runs in my family."

Dr. Ironside said, "Let's assume that your kinsmen are born-again believers through faith in Christ. You don't want to go to Heaven hanging on their coattails, do you? Salvation is a personal matter. One must individually accept Christ as one's only hope of eternal life and a home in Heaven. Isn't it interesting that the Saviour said to a devoutly *religious* man, 'Except a man be born again, he cannot see the kingdom of God' " (John 3:3)?

A puzzled look came on the face of the woman as she replied, "You don't seem to understand that religion runs in our family, and I am a very religious person."

As the woman arrived at her destination and left the train, Dr. Ironside mused, *How tragic! Religious but lost!*

* * * *

SHOULD WE GAIN

Should we to gain the world's ap-
plause,
Refuse to own the Saviour's cause,
What shame would fill us in that day
When Thou Thy glory shall display!

* * * *

Trifles

Searchers recently found the body
of a fifth victim in the group of young
men who went looking for brass casings on a western Air Force gunnery
range, and one by one fell dead in the
115-degree desert heat.

How unwise were those searchers to
hazard and forfeit their lives in quest
for brass casings!

Those who barter their souls for
mere trifles are likewise unwise:
"Esau, who for one morsel of meat
sold his birthright. . . . afterward,
when he would have inherited the
blessing, he was rejected: for he found
no place of repentance, though he
sought it carefully with tears" (Heb.
12:16,17).

* * * *

A Fatal Error

A year after medics of the U. S.
Navy told Timothy Nunley his illness
was imaginary, he died of cancer! The
Navy admitted that its doctors failed
to diagnose Nunley's true condition
and said that appropriate dis-
ciplinary and corrective action had
been taken.

People often err in their diagnosis
of a spiritually unregenerated man,
but God's Word doesn't: "The whole

head is sick, and the whole heart
faint. From the sole of the foot even
unto the head there is no soundness in
it; but wounds, and bruises, and
putrifying sores" (Isa. 1:5,6).

The daily newspaper confirms
God's diagnosis.

* * * *

Have You Counted the Cost?

The Roman statesman and philosopher Seneca said, "To lose a friend is
the greatest of all evils."

The Bible says that the greatest
and most disastrous of all losses is the
loss of one's soul: "For what is a man
profited, if he shall gain the whole
world, and lose his own soul?" (Matt.
16:25).

* * * *

Truly Lost

Dwight L. Moody said, "We will
never get men truly saved until they
realize that they are truly lost."

When a sinner sees himself as God
sees him, he will penitently confess,
"Woe is me! for I am undone; because
I am a man of unclean lips. . .for
mine eyes have seen the King, the
Lord of hosts" (Isa. 6:5).

* * * *

An Eternal Dread

German author Jean Paul Richter
said, "Without God there is for man
neither purpose, nor goal, nor hope,
only a wavering future, an eternal
dread of every darkness."

How discontented are those who
spurn God's wondrous offer of

spiritual life in Christ to those who will thirst for it and accept it: "Ho, every one that thirsteth, come ye to the waters. . .without money and without price" (Isa. 55:1). They continuously "draw water out of the wells of salvation" (Isa. 12:3).

* * * *

"I Wish I Could Vanish Into Space!"

George W. Sweeting has told of an experience he had:

"Some time ago I became engaged in conversation with a doctor and his wife. We were waiting to board a plane. After watching several jets climb into the murky darkness, the young woman said, 'I wish I could vanish into space just like that plane and start life all over again.'

"She was young and attractive, obviously a woman of wealth and position, yet her life was filled with regret.

"Why did she want to vanish? Why did she want to escape life and start all over again? Because she was burdened with the weight of sin. She had never experienced the joy of forgiveness. The future was more than she could take.

"Many people today echo the young woman's words of despair. The same desire haunts millions who do not know and live for Christ."

How disquieted we are until we rest in God. And how blessed are those who can say:

I came to Jesus as I was,
Weary and worn and sad,
I found in Him a resting place,
And He has made me glad!

* * * *

Strong Delusion

The *Journal of the American Medical Association* said, "The new occult craze—and that is just what it is—has given rise to all manner of flimflam and hocus-pocus with people's health. In this Age of Aquarius, quackery is thriving as a surprising number of people, young and old, are fleeing into superstition and unreality."

God forewarned of the direful consequences of rejecting the One who came to give spiritual life and light: "They received not the love of the truth, that they might be saved. And for this cause God shall send them strong delusion, that they should believe a lie" (II Thess. 2:10,11).

* * * *

GOD'S LOVE

How Swift!

The eyes of divine love are swifter than the feet of repentance: "But when he was yet a great way off, his father saw him, and had compassion,

and ran, and fell on his neck, and kissed him" (Luke 15:20).

Love so amazing, so divine,
Demands my soul, my life, *my all!*

* * * *

Always Green

No matter how frigid the wintry weather may be in Alberta, Canada, there is one area where the grass is always green. Why? In 1919 an underground fire broke out in the coal mine of Cadomin and the fire has never been extinguished.

In the hearts of God's children, in adversity or prosperity, the warmth and glow of God's love must never be extinguished: "And the Lord make you to increase and abound in love one toward another, and toward all men, even as we do toward you" (I Thess. 3:12).

* * * *

How the Greeks Expressed It

The ancient Greeks expressed love with three words: *Eros,* a getting or "gimme" kind of love; *philia,* a sharing love; and *agape,* a godly, selfless love.

"And above all things have [agape] *among yourselves: for* [agape] *shall cover the multitude of sins."*—I Pet. 4:8.

* * * *

MOLD ME AFTER THY WILL

Be patient—
For the Potter is not finished
With me yet.
Many blemishes
Must be smoothed away
By His skillful hands.
A useful vessel
I can become
Only when I am filled
With His love.

Be patient—
For the Potter is not finished
With me yet.
He will mold
Into me
Love and joy,
Patience and kindness,
Gentleness
And self-control.

Be patient—
For the Potter is not finished
With me yet.
Many faults and blemishes,
Many selfish motives
Destroy my usefulness.
Be patient,
For the hands of the Potter
Are full of love.

Martha Yeargin Norris.

* * * *

GOD SPEAKS IN DIVERS MANNERS

The sunflowers are dancing
so pretty and bright,
Slowly, then faster with
all of their might.
The weed patch has joined them
and waving in rhyme,
The tree branches also
are keeping the time.

Thunder and lightning add
spice to the blow,
A spectacular symphony's
opening show.
The gray of the sky adds
mystery in time,
And the rain's pitter-patter
Adds a touch sublime.

The show's almost over,
the sky's turning blue,

God has been speaking
   to me and to you.
He speaks through the
   sunflowers, the weeds and the tree,
And He tells of His love
   for you and for me.

Genevieve Melton,
in Home Life.

* * * *

"It's My Father's Voice!"

Years ago a baby girl was born in the home of a Scottish shepherd. She was the joy of her father's heart. As she grew into childhood, her father carried her on his back as he led the sheep to pasture. How impressed she was with her father's trilling, quavering voice as he called his sheep!

After growing into womanhood, the girl left her home and went to Edinburgh. There she got into sinful ways. Her father was overwhelmed with sorrow. After much anguish, he decided to go to the city and search for his daughter.

One night, as he walked along a street where brothels abounded, he trilled the call he used to call his sheep.

"Ah," said a sinful girl in an upper room, "how like my father's voice!" Listening more intently, she exclaimed, "It is my father's voice!"

Memories of her happy, innocent girlhood days awakened. Penitential tears welled in her eyes. Rushing down to the street, she ran into her father's outstretched arms and was immediately restored to his love and fellowship.

How like our heavenly Father was that Scottish shepherd! God patiently waits for the return of His straying children: "For all this his anger is not turned away, but his hand is stretched out still" (Isa. 5:25).

* * * *

Starving for Love

In his book *Love Is the Greatest,* George Sweeting said:

"Our world is literally starving for love, God's love. This is a subject about which I feel very deeply.

"A variety of personal experiences in my life awoke me to the supreme calling of God's love. The earliest occurred when I was a student right here at Moody Bible Institute. An illness led me to an operation which disclosed a serious tumor. My bed in Chicago's Swedish Covenant Hospital became my altar as I dedicated myself fully to God's service. During the course of the ensuing thirty radium treatments, I was told I possibly would not live long, and that even if I did, I would likely never be able to bear children.

"That experience, along with the reading of a pamphlet by James McConkey on God's love, prepared me to become a *living sacrifice.* That was more than thirty years ago, and I am not only still here and apparently healthy, but I have four sons!

"In weaker moments over the years I have tried to climb down from that altar. But God in His mercy has kept me there. This experience was the beginning of my search for love."

Many of God's dear children can

say with David, "Thou hast enlarged me when I was in distress" (Ps. 4:1).

* * * *

Limitless

One day Harry Rimmer took Will Snow, an Indian friend, to see the Pacific Ocean. The ocean's vastness staggered the Indian's imagination. "What's the name of this lake?" he asked. The largest lake the Indian had ever seen was Clear Lake back home.

"Will," said Dr. Rimmer, "this is not a lake. It is an ocean—the Pacific Ocean!"

In amazement, the Indian nodded and asked, "How big is it?"

Dr. Rimmer knew the answer to that question, but neither he nor anyone knows the dimensions of God's immeasurable love. Even the Apostle Paul could not define His love—its "breadth, and length, and depth, and height; And to know the love of Christ, which passeth knowledge" (Eph. 3:18,19).

Could we with ink the ocean fill,
And were the skies of parchment made,
Were ev'ry stalk on earth a quill,
And ev'ry man a scribe by trade;
To write the love of God above
Would drain the ocean dry;
Nor could the scroll contain the whole,
Tho' stretched from sky to sky.

F. M. Lehman.

* * * *

LOVE FOR OTHERS

"For God's Sake, Love Me!"

Thomas P. Malone, M.D., said, "In my practice at the Atlanta Psychiatric Clinic, people sometimes ask me what this psychiatric stuff is all about. It's increasingly clear that almost all emotional problems could be summed up in one particular kind of behavior: It's a person walking around screaming, 'For God's sake, love me! Love me! Love me! That's all!' He goes through manipulations to get somebody to love him. And that's the core of most emotional sickness."

Dr. Menninger, famed psychiatrist, said, "Love cures all, both the one who gives it and the one who receives it."

* * * *

REFLECT CHRIST'S LOVE

Lord, bless me with a listening mind,
Attune me to the smaller sounds—
The whispered plea of loneliness,
The whimper of an unloved child,
The sad, the sick, the lost—all those
Ignored, unheard by passerby.
And use me, Lord, to meet their needs
That I may, in a Christlike way,
Reflect Thy love for them each day.

Irene Sharp.

* * * *

General Lee's Example

One Sunday morning shortly after the close of the Civil War, a lone black man entered a church in Richmond, Virginia, to worship God. It was communion Sunday. The black man knelt at the altar to receive the emblems of Christ's blood and broken body.

Lingering vestiges of racial hatred vanished when a distinguished layman walked erectly down the aisle and knelt beside the black man. Who was that layman? *General Robert E. Lee.*

When we love God with all our hearts, we have unfeigned love for all mankind—people of all climes, colors and conditions: "Keep yourselves in the love of God" (Jude 21).

* * * *

OUR DAUGHTER'S IN LOVE!

Our daughter's in love, how can I tell?
She washes the dishes before I yell!
When she's asked to clean her room each day,
She does it before she goes out to play.
She smiles if she makes an unseemly remark,
Before Mom retorts with an angry bark.
She has not teased her brothers for weeks,
She answers when baby sister speaks.
She washes her blonde hair every night,
And takes a bath without a fight.
Her dress has become quite lady like,
She tries to make her behavior just right.
She flies for the phone whenever it rings.
There are these and lots more things

That lead us to know, without a doubt,
Daughter's in love, or just about.
We're hoping for reasons quite selfish, 'tis true,
That it will last at least a week or two.

Mary Alive Wertz,
in *Home Life.*

* * * *

Before and After

How great is the character-ennobling, changing power of the Gospel! In early New Testament times, its ameliorating influence was often observed.

Justin Martyr wrote, "We used to value above all else money and possessions. Now we bring together all that we have and share it with those who are in need. Formerly we hated and killed one another because of a difference in nationality or custom. Now since the coming of Christ, we all live in peace. We pray for our enemies and seek to convert those who hate us."

Tertullian wrote, "It is our care for the helpless, our practice of lovingkindness, that brands us in the eyes of many of our opponents. 'Only look,' they say, 'how they love one another!' "

Before Christianity was recognized officially in the Roman Empire by Constantine, his heartless, non-Christian predecessor Licinius decreed that no one was to show kindness to sufferers in prison by supplying them with food, and that no one was to show mercy to those who were starving in prison!

What a wonderful change in *my life* has been
wrought
Since Jesus came into my heart!

* * * *

TAKE CARE

Take care
For I care
About you!
Your hopes and dreams,
Your triumphs and failures,
Your joys and sorrows.
For loving is caring
For YOU!
Take Care!

Ruth Knight Collins.

* * * *

Why a Man Falls in Love

Senator William Proxmire, chairman of the Senate Appropriations Committee, said, "My choice for the biggest waste of the taxpayer's money is the National Science Foundation's squandering $84,000 to try to find out why people fall in love. I believe that 200 million other Americans want to leave some things in life a mystery, and right at the top of things we don't want to know is why a man falls in love with a woman and vice versa."

* * * *

Individual Forgotten

Many are so busy saving the world that they often forget the individuals near them. C. W. Vanderbergh expressed the thought in these words:

To love the whole world
For me it's no chore,

My only real problem's
My neighbor next door.

* * * *

A Piteous Plea

Sometime ago businessman Wallace Speers was accosted by an unshaved, disheveled man who said, "You look like a friendly person. Will you do something for me? There is no one in the world who cares if I live or die. Will you just think about me for a while? If I could believe someone was thinking about me as a human being, it would be worth more to me than money or anything!"

The one who pleaded for concern and understanding was an ex-convict just released from prison. After his piteous plea he melted away in the passing throng.

In speaking of the incident, Speers said, "I've been haunted by that man's loneliness ever since!"

While the souls of men are dying
For a little bit of love,
And the children, too, are crying
For a little bit of love,
Stand no longer idly by,
You may help them if you'll try;
Go then saying, "Here am I
With a little bit of love."

* * * *

Mere Tinsel

John Calvin said, "Where love is lacking, the beauty of all virtue is mere tinsel, an empty sound, not worth a straw, offensive and disgusting."

Life minus love is zero! "Love never faileth!" Try it!

* * * *

LIFE'S MIRROR

There are loyal hearts, there are
spirits brave,
There are souls that are pure and
true;
Then give to the world the best you
have,
And the best will come back to you.

Give love, and love to your life will
flow
A strength in your utmost need;
Have faith, and a score of hearts will
show
Their faith in your word and deed.

Mary Ainge De Vere.

* * * *

MISSIONS

A Cablegram From Heaven

Many years ago a secretary of the
British Missionary Society called
upon a Calcutta merchant for an offering to missions. The merchant
drew a check for $250 and gave it to
the secretary. But before the
secretary left, a cablegram was given
to the merchant. As he read it, a
troubled look clouded the face of the
merchant. He said, "This cablegram
informs me that one of my ships, with
its cargo, has gone down at sea. This
loss makes a large difference in my affairs. I shall have to write you another
check!"

The secretary said, "I understand,"
as he returned the check for $250.

The merchant, with checkbook still
open on his desk, wrote another check
and gave it to the secretary. He was
amazed when he saw it was for
$1,000!"

"Haven't you made a mistake?"
the secretary asked.

"No," replied the merchant with
tears in his eyes. "That cablegram
was a message from my heavenly
Father which read, 'Lay not up for
yourselves treasures upon earth. . .
But lay up for yourselves treasures in

heaven. . .For where your treasure is,
there will your heart be also' " (Matt.
6:19-21).

* * * *

"Do You Mean William Carey?"

As William Carey meditated upon
the verse, "Go ye into all the world,
and preach the gospel to every
creature," he asked, "Lord, do you
mean William Carey?"

The Lord seemed to say, "Yes, I
mean William Carey."

Then Carey submissively said,
"Lord, I respond. I will go and preach
the Gospel!"

Carey told his friends, "I will go
down into the well, if you will hold
the ropes."

Go-missionaries greatly need co-
missionaries at home—those who will
pray and support them: "How shall
they hear without a preacher? And
how shall they preach, except they be
sent?" (Rom. 10:14,15).

* * * *

Is It True, Madam?

A lady sat beside Wilfred Grenfell
at a dinner in London. She asked, "Is

it true, Dr. Grenfell, that you are a missionary to Labrador?"

Looking searchingly into the woman's face, Dr. Grenfell asked, "Is it true, madam, that you are *not* a missionary?"

* * * *

THE NINETY AND NINE ARE COLD!

There are ninety and nine that safely lie,
  In the shelter of the fold,
But millions are left outside to die,
  For the ninety and nine are cold!
Away in sin's delusive snare,
Hastening to death and dark despair,
Hastening to death and few to care,
For the ninety and nine are cold!

Thomas E. Stephens.

* * * *

"Why Can't God Speak Our Language?"

An Indian tribesman of Guatemala said to W. Cameron Townsend, founder of Wycliffe Bible Translators, "If your God is so great and loves us, why can't He speak our language?"

Greatly challenging the pioneer missionary, the question set him to the arduous task of translating portions of God's Word into that tribesman's language. Since then, thousands of dedicated young people—Wycliffe Bible Translators— have gone to the islands of the sea and to jungles around the world, and translated portions of the Bible into tribal languages and dialects.

These questions are pertinent and challenging: "How shall they hear without a preacher? And how shall they preach, except they be sent? . . . How beautiful are the feet of them that preach the gospel of peace, and bring glad tidings of good things!" (Rom. 10:14,15).

* * * *

FORGET THEM NOT

Forget them not, O Christ, who stand
The vanguard in the distant land,
In flood, in flame, in dark, in dread,
Sustain, we pray, each lifted head.
Exalt them over every fear,
In peril come Thyself more near.
Thine is the work they strive to do,
Their foes so many, they so few.
Be with Thine own, Thy loved, who stand,
Christ's vanguard, in the storm-swept land.

Margaret E. Sangster
in Christian Herald.

* * * *

Heart and Soul Involvement

David Livingstone was completely dedicated to his God-given work. "I am a missionary heart and soul. God had only one Son, and He was a missionary and a physician. In His service I hope to live. In it I wish to die."

There are three kinds of missionaries among Christians—*co-missionaries:* "And how shall they preach, except they be sent" (Rom. 10:15); *go-missionaries:* "The Holy Ghost said, separate me Barnabas and Saul [Paul] for the work whereunto I have called them. So they, being sent forth by the Holy Ghost, departed unto Seleucia; and from thence they sailed to Cyprus" (Acts 13:2,4); and o-missionaries: "Therefore to him that knoweth to do good, and doeth it not, to him it is sin" (Jas. 4:17); "Awake to righteousness, and sin not: for some have not the knowledge of God: I speak this to your shame" (I Cor. 15:34).

* * * *

Degenerated Into an Ambassador

William Carey hoped that his son Felix would become a missionary, but official honors which dulled his interest in spiritual things came to him in Burma. The disappointed father requested prayer for him, saying, "Pray for Felix! He has degenerated into an ambassador of the British government."

* * * *

Out-Evangelized

Declared Dr. Samuel Moffett of the Presbyterian Seminary in Seoul:
"The communists have out-evangelized us. I watched the red tide sweep across China. We evangelicals have been trying to win that country for Christ for 150 years. The communists took it in thirty years. What makes them so successful? Their armies? That is no small part of the answer, of course. But the main key to the communists's success is this: They believe in and practice evangelism for their false faith with greater intensity than we believers in Christ do for the true faith!"

"It is good to be zealously affected always in a good thing" (Gal. 4:18); "Awake to righteousness. . .for some have not the knowledge of God: I speak this to your shame" (I Cor. 15:34).

* * * *

Sleeping in Harvest

Too long I've lain me down to sleep
And prayed the Lord my soul to keep.
I should awake before I die
And realize time is passing by,
And rise and go and tell the lost,
Despite my plans, despite the cost.

Too long I've lain me down to sleep
While multitudes about me weep
And utter cries of dark despair,
For no one ever seems to care!
My life is short and soon I'll stand
With sinners' blood upon my hands,
Unless I wake before I die
And realize time is passing by!

Can we say with the Apostle Paul, "I am pure from the blood of all men. For I have not shunned to declare unto you all the counsel of God" (Acts 20:26,27)?

* * * *

"A Mile Further"

Dick Hillis, who served as a missionary in China from 1933 to 1949, reported a conversation he had with a young communist lieutenant who was leaving to join a battle in which the odds against his survival were twenty to one.

Said Hillis, "I told the nineteen-year-old boy, a farm boy now turned communist, 'Sir, the defending army is better equipped than your army. It is protected by a moat, high walls, and iron gates that are heavily sand-bagged.'

He replied, "I know that, but the enemy has no great cause to fight for and they will turn and run when the battle warms up!"

"But, sir, it won't do you any good if you get killed during your attack on the city tonight."

The youth replied, "Chairman Mao has told us we should be willing to die to change the world, and I am quite prepared to do that to carry communism a mile further!"

"Today this young misguided zealot lies beneath the soft dirt of the plains of central Honan Province. His dedication to his leader was typical of that shown by hundreds of thousands of other idealistic but deceived youths," said Hillis.

God's children should be just as zealous to obey the command of the Captain of their salvation to "go ye into all the world, and preach the gospel to every creature" (Mark 16:15).

* * * *

MOTHERS
(See also Parental Responsibility)

The Heart of a Home

If the father is the *head* of the home, the mother is the *heart* of the home. No one can take the place of the mother.

Some mothers are bereft of their husbands. The mother takes over. She becomes a "father" to her children and the breadwinner.

* * * *

Lonely

"The loss of one's mother is a sad milestone in one's life," said Clementine Churchill. "After that, one is nobody's child and it is a lonely feeling."

Long ago God gave this comforting promise to His people: "As one whom his mother comforteth, so will I comfort you" (Isa. 66:13).

* * * *

The Holes in Her Shoes

"When I was nine years old," said Pearl Hastings, "and saw my mother kneeling at an altar of prayer, I was ashamed. As she knelt, everyone could see the holes in her wet shoes. We had walked to church in the snow. I was ashamed because everyone would know how poor we were.

"Now that I am a woman and have a child of my own, I look back at that moment with much pride! The scene comes back at times when I am sick, weary and discouraged. In vision I see my mother with her gray head resting on her arms, her shoulder shaking with sobs and *holes in her shoes!*

"Now I know she wore shoes like that so seven kids could wear shoes without holes. And I'm proud, so proud!"

* * * *

The Best School

John Henry Jowett, famed minister and exegete, said, "At mother's knee, I gained my sweetest inspiration."

* * * *

"Come Before Winter"

One Sunday night Clarence Edward Macartney preached a sermon on the text, "Do thy diligence to come before winter" (II Tim. 4:21). In the message he said:

"Before winter or never! There are some things which will never be done unless they are done 'before winter!' The winter will come and the winter will pass. The flowers of the springtime will deck the breast of the earth and the graves of some of our opportunities, perhaps the grave of our dearest friend. There are golden gates wide open on this autumn day, but next October they will be forever shut!"

There was present in the service a medical student from Jefferson Medical College. When he returned to his room, the text, "Come before winter" repeated itself over and over in his mind. He thought, I had better write a letter to my mother. He sat down and wrote such a letter as a mother delights to receive from a son and went immediately and mailed it.

The next day, in the midst of his studies he received this telegram: COME AT ONCE. YOUR MOTHER IS DYING!

That evening he entrained for his country home. He found his mother still living, and she gave him a smile of recognition and satisfaction—a smile he never forgot. Under her pillow was the letter he had written her after the Sunday night service!

Before the winter of death comes to our friends and loved ones, let us speak to them words of love and encouragement. When their ears are dulled in death, such words will mean nothing!

"Do thy diligence to come before winter!"

* * * *

Ubiquitous Mothers

Charles Dickens said, "God couldn't be everywhere, so he made mothers." Wherever there is need, sorrow and suffering, there you will find mothers.

Mothers come in all sizes, shapes and colors and are found everywhere: at kitchen sinks; hunting lost school books; kissing hurt places to make them well; patching seams and dreams; settling disputes; getting meals; supervising baths and morals.

Mothers are the child's first and most important teacher. Eighty percent of what a child learns, he learns by the time he is five years old.

A mother asked a psychiatrist, "When should I start training my child?" "How hold is he?" he asked. The mother replied, "Five years old." Flashed the psychiatrist, "Woman, hurry home! You have already lost five years!"

A mother seems to have eyes in the

back of her head, ears that can hear the cookie jar lid being stealthily lifted two rooms away.

Her smiles are contagiously cheerful and light up a home, imparting hope and courage.

Theodore Roosevelt said, "America's greatest asset is home-building, God-fearing mothers."

The Bible gives her these words of praise, "In her tongue is the law of kindness. She looketh well to the ways of her household. . .Her children arise up, and call her blessed" (Prov. 31:26-28).

* * * *

The New Morality

In the column of a newspaper, a distraught mother addressed the following letter to her daughter:

"We have tried to give you a good education and help you grow straight and strong. But something went wrong! Why or how we do not know.

"Somewhere along the line you rejected our values and made your own rules. Your father and I were crushed when you and your beloved decided to live together. We expressed our strong disapproval but decided to keep our hearts and doors open, hoping and praying that your crooked thinking would straighten out in time.

"Now you have brought a child into the world. Again you tell us marriage is not important—that if two people are in love, nothing else matters.

"We have done our best to understand your point of view. It is so foreign to us, however. You are our daughter and we cannot stop loving you. But don't think because we haven't written you off that we approve of your lifestyle.

"To friends and relatives who ask us why we condone your behavior, we reply: 'It is one thing to be heartsick—and we are—and to disapprove—which we do. But to blot out twenty years of our lives as if they never happened isn't possible.'

"I know I speak not only for myself but for thousands of parents as well. Our daily prayer is, 'God help us all!' "

* * * *

Magnets

A teacher had just presented a lesson on magnets and magnetic force. Then she quizzed her pupils.

"My name starts with the letter M. I have six letters and I pick up things. What am I?"

To her amazement, the children all answered: "Mother!"

> Who ran to help me when I fell,
> And would some pretty story tell,
> Or kiss the place to make it well?
> My mother!

Told by Ruth Collins.

* * * *

Alcoholic Mothers

Long ago Aristotle observed that drunken women most often had children like themselves—morose and languid. Only recently has modern medicine confirmed this ancient fact. Alcoholic mothers often bear children with a host of birth defects: skull and facial deformities, defects in the cardiovascular system and mental and physical retardation.

Dr. David Smith of the University of Washington School of Medicine affirmed that "recent studies have underlined the warning that drink is dangerous to the unborn."

In a study of births at Boston City Hospital, researchers discovered that of nine babies born to mothers who were heavy drinkers, only one was normal.

How right was Lowell when he said, "They enslave their children's children who compromise with sin!"

* * * *

"NOW I LAY ME DOWN TO SLEEP"

"Now I lay me down to sleep,
I pray the Lord my soul to keep,"
Was my childhood's early prayer,
Taught by mother's love and care.
Many years since then have fled,
Mother slumbers with the dead.
Yet methinks I see her now,
With love-lit eyes and holy brow,
As kneeling by her side to pray,
She gently taught me how to say:
"Now I lay me down to sleep,
I pray the Lord my soul to keep!"

Oh! could the faith of childhood's
    days,
Oh! could its little hymns of praise,
Oh! could its simple, joyous trust
Be recreated from the dust
That lies around a wasted life,
The fruit of many a bitter strife!
Oh! then at night in prayer I'd bend
And call my God, my Father, Friend,
And pray with childlike faith once
    more

The prayer my mother taught of yore:
"Now I lay me down to sleep,
I pray the Lord my soul to keep!"

                        Eugene Henry Fullen.

* * * *

De Profundis

Avi was a youthful Israeli medic and the only son of proud parents. He was near the end of his compulsory military service when the Mid-East war broke out in 1973. On the day his mother Hanna received a cheerful letter from him, Avi's unit was attacked by the Egyptians in the Sinai Desert. As he was aiding the wounded, a bullet struck him in the temple and passed out the other side of his head. From that moment Avi was unconscious. The doctors said, "Only a miracle can save him!"

A news reporter wrote, "As his mother looks into his still face in the small fifth-floor room of the hospital in Tel Aviv, she laments, 'If only Avi would talk, I would take him home in any condition and be grateful. He doesn't even have to walk or see. I promise that I will be good all my life, if only Avi will live. So be it. Amen.' "

Can anyone sorrow as deeply as a true mother? How limitless are the sacrifices she cheerfully makes for those she loves more dearly than her own life!

If I were drowned in the deepest sea,
    Mother o' mine, O mother o' mine!
I know whose tears would come down to me,
    Mother o' mine, O mother o' mine!

                        Rudyard Kipling.

* * * *

NATURE

"How Great Thou Art!"

Thunderstorms, the greatest show on earth, are awesome! They occur across the country during spring and summer months, bringing delight to lovers of pyrotechnic displays, but danger to golfers, farmers and steeplejacks. They cause many forest fires.

During the thunderstorms, lightning slashes the skies with electrifying fury, embroidering fanciful designs on the dark bosom of churning clouds and edging them with silver and gold.

The National Geographic affirms that the seasonal lightning will hit from 17 to 20 thousand houses with a loss of from $7 to $100 million. Some 600 people will be killed and some 1,500 injured. Some will be unharmed victims of freak accidents, such as the steeplejack whose wristwatch was melted by a bolt of lightning, or the thunderstruck car, welding an unharmed father and his son inside the vehicle during a storm.

A single lightning stroke may have 100 million volts, enough wham to lift the ocean liner *Queen Mary* six feet into the air!

On the plus side, thunderstorms will enrich the earth by 100 million tons of nature's fertilizer—nitrogen which is literally blasted out of the sky by lightning bolts.

About 2,000 thunderstorms are raging at any one time, sending lightning down and stabbing the ground 100 times per second!

The Bible says, "He [God] maketh lightnings with rain, and bringeth forth the wind out of his treasures" (Jer. 10:13). In wonder we exclaim: "How Great Thou Art!"

* * * *

I SAW GOD WASH THE WORLD

I saw God wash the world last night
  With His sweet showers on high,
And then, when morning came, I saw
  Him hang it out to dry.

He washed each tiny blade of grass
  And every trembling tree;
He flung His showers against the hill,
  And swept the billowing sea.

The white rose is a cleaner white,
  The red rose is more red,
Since God washed every fragrant face
  And put them all to bed.

There's not a bird, there's not a bee,
  That wings along the way,
But is a cleaner bird and bee
  Than it was yesterday.

I saw God wash the world last night,
  Ah, would He had washed me
As clean of all my dust and dirt,
  As that old birch tree!

William L. Stidger.

* * * *

WHEN WINTER COMES

When winter comes, I shall remember
  The glorious day in May,
In the chill of life's coldest December,
  I shall be warmed that way.

I shall be warmed by the sunshine
  Of a world attuned to Spring;

I shall see apple trees in bloom,
  I shall hear robins sing.
No matter how the winds buffet,
  No matter how deep the snow,
Life's beauty outweighs its bitter,
  Remembering, I shall know.

Helen Lowrie Marshall.

* * * *

Insufficient Revelation

While God's grandeur is seen in nature, nature does not reveal His heart. It has no message of pardon, but says inexorably, "Whatsoever a man soweth, that shall he also reap" (Gal. 6:7). Not a whisper of forgiveness comes from the star-studded skies, though "the heavens declare the glory of God; and the firmament sheweth his handywork" (Ps. 19:1).

Nature speaks of God's power, but not of His pardon. It displays God's fingerprints; but the Bible reveals the nailprints of Jesus Christ, the Son of God who "loved us, and washed us from our sins in his own blood" (Rev. 1:5).

* * * *

Not by Accident

How thrilling are the reports given by some of the astronauts who went to the moon!

On his return to the earth, Astronaut Eugene Cernan said, "I didn't see God, but I'm convinced of God by the order out in space! I know it didn't happen by accident!"

Someone asked Astronaut James B. Irwin, "Are you going to retire from the space program and spend your time spreading the good news of Jesus Christ? Did you have some experience while on the moon that caused you to make this decision?"

Irwin replied, "I felt God's presence on the moon closer than I have ever felt it here on earth. I came back from the Apollo 15 flight to find it had changed my life! It was a real spiritual awakening! I feel myself to be one who loves all men and women, and God has given me a strong desire and compulsion to share my faith with them. The message I have, of course, is the old, old story of Jesus Christ!"

* * * *

GOD SPEAKS

God speaks with each returning
  spring,
In every joyous blossoming thing!
  God's message comes in this re-
  birth
Of all that beautifies the earth:
In lovely dawns, in sunset's glow,
In caroling birds, and streams that
  flow,
  Through field and woodland to the
  sea,
God speaks through these to you
  and me.

Rowena Cheney.

* * * *

A THING OF BEAUTY

A thing of beauty is a joy forever!
Its loveliness increases; it will never
Pass into nothingness, but will keep
A bower quiet for us, and a sleep

Full of sweet dreams, health, and
quiet breathing.

John Keats.

* * * *

"The Heavens Declare. . ."

"I can see how it might be possible
for a man to look upon the earth and
be an atheist, but I cannot conceive
how he could look up into the star-
studded sky and say there is no God,"
said Abraham Lincoln.

*"The heavens declare the glory of
God; and the firmament sheweth his
handywork."*—Ps. 19:1.

* * * *

A Wayside Sacrament

Ralph Waldo Emerson said, "Never lose an opportunity of seeing anything that is beautiful, for beauty is
God's handwriting: a wayside sacra-
ment. Welcome it in every fair face,
in every fair sky, in every flower, and
thank God for it as a cup of blessing!"

*"He [God] hath made every thing
beautiful in his time."*—Eccles. 3:11.

* * * *

Astrological Charlatans

Some 186 prominent scientists, including eighteen Nobel Prize winners,
have issued a statement challenging
"the pretentious claims of astrolog-
ical charlatans."

The statement, drafted by Bart J.
Bok, former president of the Amer-
ican Astronomical Society, declared,
"There is no such thing as influences

exerted by stars, planets and other
heavenly bodies on human affairs. It
is simply a mistake to imagine that
forces exerted by stars and planets at
the moment of one's birth can in any
way shape our fortunes."

Though the heavenly bodies—stars
and planets—declare the glory of
God, only His divine Son—the "Sun
of righteousness"—fully reveals Him
and gives the answer to questions pertaining to life present and future:
"All things that I have heard of my
Father I have made known unto you"
(John 15:15).

* * * *

A SENSE OF SPRING

Spring is in the air,
I SENSE it everywhere!
I feel it in the breeze
As it whispers among the trees
And taunts emerging leaves.
I SMELL it in the morning mist,
In the aftermath of showers,
In flowers brushed by nature's kiss.
I HEAR it in dawn's melody
As feathered arrivals trumpet:
"Listen to me."
I TOUCH it in the warmth
Of a clump of dirt
And the new blades of grass it skirts;
In a rock on which
A ray of sun did beat
And will not relinquish its heat.
I SEE it in people's vacant stares
As they long to be out there
To wander and romp without a care.
I TASTE and absorb its
Hypnotic spell,

Which I know so well,
As spring becomes part of me!

Ruth Knight Collins.

* * * *

THE YEAR'S AT THE SPRING

The year's at the spring
And day's at the morn;
Morning's at seven:
The hillside's dew-pearled;
The lark's on the wing;
The snail's on the thorn;
God's in His Heaven—
All's right with the world!

Robert Browning.

* * * *

THE ADVENTURE

"Where have you been, dear?" I don't
know;
Out in the woods where the mush-
rooms grow,
Over some logs by a chattering
stream,
Down to the pond where the minnows
dream,
Up to the meadows where grass
stands high,
Daisies were laughing as I ran by.
On through a thicket and into a tree,
Wind blew the leaves and they whis-
pered to me.
Then down the path where the star
plants flower,
Headed for home at the dinner hour,
Dirty and happy and whistling low.
"Where have you been, dear?" I don't
know.
Stones in my pockets and leaves in
my hair;
"Where have you been, dear?" Who
knows where!

Lois Duncan in *Home Life.*

* * * *

OBEDIENCE—DISOBEDIENCE

"I Knew He Would Do It!"

A black man worked among the pine trees in Florida which were tapped for turpentine. One day he left his faithful dog in charge of his lunch box and commanded the dog to watch it until he returned.

While he was away, a fire swept through the pine trees. The noble dog, obeying his master's orders, was burned to a crisp!

Weeping, the black man said, "I always had to be careful what I told that dog to do, 'cause I knew he would do it!"

Long ago the Saviour asked of disobedient ones who rendered Him only lip-service: "And why call ye me Lord, Lord, and do not the things which I say?"

Alice Marie Knight.

* * * *

"When I Have Eighty Men. . ."

A capacity audience attended a concert in the Champness Hall in Yorkshire. The orchestra was conducted by Barbirolli. A friend asked a minister who was present, "And when are you going to get the Champness

Hall filled to capacity for a Christian service?"

The minister replied, "When, like Sir John Barbirolli, I have eighty men ready to give absolute obedience to the will of Christ!"

* * * *

"Dog Yours, Ear Is Only"

In translating the Bible into a tribe's native language, a missionary in Africa had difficulty in finding a word which meant obedience.

One day as he entered a plaza of the village, his dog strayed behind. He whistled, and the dog came lickety-split to him at top speed.

An elderly native, sitting by the roadside, was deeply impressed at the instant obedience of the dog. He exclaimed, "Mui adem delegau ge!" which meant, "Dog yours, ear is only."

The missionary thought, "Your dog is all ear"—obedient. He used the native's expression to convey the meaning of obedience in his Bible translation.

May we be "all ear" to God, swift to obey and do His will.

Alice Marie Knight.

* * * *

"Not Grievous"

A wealthy man said to Mark Twain, "When I retire, I am going to take a trip to the Holy Land. There I want to stand on Mount Sinai where Moses received from God the Ten Commandments!"

Mark Twain said, "It seems to me, sir, that you could do the world a lot more good if you would stay at home and keep them!"

"His commandments are not grievous."—I John 5:3.

* * * *

ONLY LIP-SERVICE

Ye call me Master and obey Me not;
Ye call Me Light and seek Me not;
Ye call Me Way and walk Me not;
Ye call Me Life and desire Me not;
Ye call Me Wise and follow Me not;
Ye call Me Fair and love Me not;
Ye call Me Rich and ask Me not;
Ye call Me Eternal and seek Me not;
Ye call Me Gracious and trust Me not;
Ye call Me Noble and serve Me not.

"And why call ye me, Lord, Lord, and do not the things which I say."—Luke 6:46.

* * * *

Only Sick Sheep

For many years Mr. and Mrs. Emmanuel O. Jago were missionaries in Palestine. He was from the north of Ireland and when clad in a Palestinian shepherd's garb could easily pass for an Arabian shepherd.

One day while visiting the area of Beersheba, Mr. Jago encountered some shepherds sitting near the roadside while their sheep grazed on the stony hillside.

"How do you call your sheep?" he asked.

In a low voice, a shepherd gave a call to his sheep, and the missionary repeated the call quite accurately.

Then Mr. Jago borrowed the cloak

and staff of the shepherd. Walking among the grazing sheep, he called the sheep repeatedly, but not one lifted its head from the grass or flicked an ear.

Then the *true* shepherd, without cloak or staff, gave the same call as the missionary. What a difference! Immediately each sheep lifted its head and came trotting to the true shepherd.

It is said that only a sick sheep will respond to the voice of a false shepherd.

Jesus said, "And when he putteth forth his own sheep, he goeth before them. . . . And a stranger will they not follow. . .for they know not the voice of strangers" (John 10:4,5).

Told by Raymond Edman.

* * * *

"My Advice Is Brief"

A new enlistee in the army said to an old soldier, "I want to be an exemplary soldier and I will value highly any advice you may give me."

The old soldier replied, "Young man, my advice is brief: *Always obey orders.*

"But suppose orders conflict. Whose orders should I obey?"

"That will not occur, young man. But suppose you get conflicting orders. Ascertain the one highest in authority and obey him."

The highest and ultimate authority for a Christian is God.

Earthly authorities in the long ago commanded Peter and John "not to speak at all nor teach in the name of Jesus" (Acts 4:18). Courageously they replied, 'We ought to obey God rather than men'; "And daily in the temple, and in every house, they ceased not to teach and preach Jesus Christ" (5:29,42).

* * * *

Not Our Ability—Our Availability

God is more concerned about our availability than our ability: "Whom shall I send, and who will go for us? Then said I, Here am I; send me" (Isa. 6:8). Can we say:

Ready to go, ready to stay,
Ready my place to fill;
Ready for service, lowly or great,
Ready to do His will?

Charlie D. Tillman

* * * *

OLD AGE

No Substitute for Know-How

Henry Ford said, "Take all the experience and judgment of men over fifty out of the world, and there wouldn't be enough men left to run the world."

There is no substitute for experimental know-how and skill.

Long ago Laban said, "I have learned by experience" (Gen. 30:27).

* * * *

"To Drop Dead Before Eighty"

Archbishop Fulton J. Sheen said, "I have been praying for three years to drop dead before I am eighty. My big fear is that beyond eighty I will not be working at full capacity."

The Bible gives this gloom-dispelling and challenging word to God's aged children: "The righteous shall flourish like the palm tree: he shall grow like a cedar in Lebanon. They shall still bring forth fruit in old age; they shall be. . .flourishing" (Ps. 92:12,14). Long ago David said, "My times are in thy hand" (Ps. 31:15).

Could our days and years be in safer hands?

* * * *

Still Fruitful

One has given this advice for the aging: "The faculty that is continuously used will tend to remain or to be strengthened. The faculty that is not used will lessen, atrophy or disappear."

Remember: "The righteous. . . shall still bring forth fruit in old age" (Ps. 92:12,14).

* * * *

Beautiful Sunset Years

General Douglas MacArthur said on his seventy-fifth birthday:

"Youth is not entirely a time of life. It is a state of mind. It is a temper of the will, a quality of the imagination, a vigor of the emotions. Nobody grows old by living a number of years. People grow old by deserting their ideals.

"You are as young as your faith, as old as your doubts; as young as your self-confidence; as old as your fear; as young as your hope.

"In the central place of every heart there is a recording chamber. So long

as it receives messages of beauty, hope, cheer and courage, so long are you young. When the wires are all down and your heart is covered with the snow of pessimism and the ice of cynicism, then and only then, are you grown old!"

Gospel Tract Society.

* * * *

TAKE GRATEFULLY LIFE'S BEST

Age is a quality of mind;
If you have left your dreams behind,
If hope is cold,
If your ambition fires are dead,
If you no longer look ahead,
Then you are old!

But if from life you take the best,
And if in life you keep your jest,
If love you hold,
No matter how the birthdays fly,
No matter how the years go by,
You are *not* old!

* * * *

"AT EVENING TIME IT SHALL BE LIGHT" (ZECH. 14:7)

Fear not the westerning shadows,
O children of the day;
For brighter still and brighter
Shall be your homeward way;
Resplendent as the morning,
With fuller glow and power,
And clearer than the noonday
Shall be your evening hour.

* * * *

Indian Summer

Someone has well said that of all the seasons of the year in our

American climate, there is none so tender, so beautiful, so weird and unearthly, so fascinating and perfect as Indian summer.

After the buds, blossoms, heat and harvest of summer; after the autumn of fruits and frosts, when forests are mantled in crimson, fire and gold; when chill winds and vagrant snow warn of the approach of ice-mantled winter, then some invisible hand seizes the galloping steeds of the seasons and reins them up suddenly for a few days, while earth, air and sky weave around the weather-beaten brow of the year the golden crown of Indian summer. The sun pours down a soft and dreamy golden light; the sky is robed with a delicate, purplish gauze that seems to float everywhere; the air is balmy and caressing. There is a bewitching charm in the unearthly spell that has been cast upon nature.

And so God designs old age to be the Indian summer of life—the gentlest, the most beautiful of all of life's seasons. His promise is assuring and unfailing: "And even to your old age I am he; and even to hoar hairs will I carry you: I have made, and I will bear; even I will carry, and will deliver you" (Isa. 46:4).

> Grow old along with me!
> The best is yet to be,
> The last of life, for which the first was made:
> Our times are in His hand
> Who saith, "A whole I planned,
> Youth shows but half; trust God: see all, nor be afraid!"

> Robert Browning.

* * * *

"Never Too Old to Learn"

In 1974 an AP dispatch in a Jacksonville, Florida, newspaper said that when Frederick R. Noble, ninety-one years old, received his master's degree, he announced that he would go on to higher education.

Noble received a law degree from Harvard sixty-seven years ago.

"You're never too old to learn," said Noble. "The more education you have, the better. It's a great satisfaction to know. Part of my study in history was easy, because I had lived through it."

Noble said that he would go back to college to take courses in music appreciation, though he can't carry a tune. "I want to learn to appreciate music. This gives me a purpose for using my spare time in the evenings."

* * * *

Don't Take It Easy!

In addressing a meeting of the Canadian Health Food Dealers Association, Paul C. Bragg, 92 years old, said, "Death is an impostor! I've declared war on death!"

Bragg is hale and hardy. When he was 15, this tubercular patient was told that he had only three months to live. "For 92 years I have been outwitting death," he said.

The Bible calls death an enemy: "The last enemy that shall be destroyed is death" (I Cor. 15:26).

No one can declare war on death successfully: "It is appointed unto men once to die" (Heb. 9:27).

But in death's Conqueror, the Saviour, there is hope! He told God's children, "Because I live, ye shall live also" (John 14:19).

* * * *

Why Grow Old?

Did you know that thirty months is the average length of life for men after retirement? Did you know that there is a dramatic increase in physical problems right after leaving the job? These are not the result of having suddenly become 65. Most physicians feel that they are self-induced by the feeling of being put aside from the mainstream of life. Golf and gardening are not enough to take the place of a busy career.

The man may feel useless, and he thinks "OLD." Medical problems are almost sure to develop with this attitude. When you think of yourself as old, you are apt to become older than necessary.

The Austin American-Statesman.

* * * *

The Good Old Days

Warren Wiersbe asked an old gent, "What did people talk about in the good old days?"

The oldster replied with a chuckle, "Why, we were talking about the good old days!"

* * * *

How About That!

An optimist is a man who marries at age 85 and begins immediately to look for a larger house with a nursery!

* * * *

"The Devil's Leavings"

Alexander Pope said, "When men grow virtuous in their old age, they can only make a sacrifice to God of the Devil's leavings."

It must be grievous to God that so many wait until their old age to give themselves to Him. How blessed are those who obey the directive: "Remember now thy Creator in the days of thy youth" (Eccles. 12:1).

Give of your best to the Master,
  Give of the strength of your youth;
Throw your soul's fresh, glowing ardor
  Into the battle for truth.

Howard B. Grose.

* * * *

VALUES

What do I value as I grow older?
A listening ear, a comforting
  shoulder,
Friendships strong enough to last,
Souvenirs to bring back the past,
Weather mellowed by the sun,
Laughter born of carefree fun,
Health to tide me through each day,
Time to work, time to play,
Food for body, food for soul,
Belief in God to make me whole.

Wyn Hope.

* * * *

No Secret

The American Medical Association has found no "secret" to attaining long life but says most of the 100-year-olds interviewed share these traits: an easy-going disposition; a quick sense of humor, and a desire to keep as busy, physically and mentally, as possible. In addition, the AMA reports, most claim to be lifelong churchgoers.

The Austin American-Statesman.

* * * *

COUNTING

Count your garden by the flowers,
Never by the leaves that fall.
Count your day by golden hours,
Don't remember clouds at all.

Count your nights by stars, not shadows;
Count your life by smiles, not tears,
And, with joy on every birthday,
Count your age by friends—not years.

* * * *

Memories

Old age at its best is a time of wisdom and faith. The Bible says, "With the ancient is wisdom; and in length of days understanding" (Job 12:12).

Old age is a time of pleasant memories if we have lived for God and others. In the late afternoon of his life, Samuel said, "I am old and grayheaded. . .I have walked before you from my childhood. . . .whom have I defrauded? . . . And they said, "Thou hast not defrauded us" (I Sam. 12:2-4).

The wise man Solomon said, "The hoary head is a crown of glory, if it be found in the way of righteousness" (Prov. 16:31). It is a fool's cap if found in the ways of unrighteousness.

* * * *

"Grandma, You're Beautiful!"

A young woman said to an elderly lady whose face radiated charm and Christian character, "Grandma, believe me, you are truly beautiful!"

Grandma graciously replied, "Well, I ought to be! I've had 74 years to let the Lord work on me!"

* * * *

Think It over

Never resent growing old—many are denied the privilege!

* * * *

OPPORTUNITY

Devolution

Man is a physical and spiritual being: "And the Lord God formed man . . .and breathed into his nostrils the breath of life; and man became a living soul" (Gen. 2:7).

When the physical is in the ascendancy and the spiritual is neglected, man devolutes into bestian behavior. God-given potentials and opportunities for service to a needy world lie dormant and atrophy.

* * * *

"It Might Have Been"

Ivan Albright painted a picture which is now in the Chicago Art Institute. The painting shows an eight-foot door shaped like the cover of a casket. The door is nicked and scarred, and a funeral wreath of wilted flowers hangs on it.

How appropriate is the title of the picture; "That which I should have done I did not do!"

The saddest words of tongue or pen,
The saddest are these: It might have been.

"As we have. . .opportunity, let us do good unto all men, especially unto them who are of the household of faith."—Gal. 6:10.

* * * *

TOMORROW'S MORN

Purple mountain, clouds of white,
Fading gently in the night,
Tall and strong against the sky,
Another day has passed you by.

But with tomorrow's golden morn
The sun will shine, your slopes adorn,
Clothed in colorful array,
Resplendent and high as yesterday.

Author unknown.

* * * *

Man's Extremity—God's Opportunity

God sometimes uses brinkmanship and brings deliverance to His imperiled children at their rope's end, when self-effort and human help is unavailing. Our extremity is God's opportunity: "Lord, save us: we perish" (Matt. 8:25).

* * * *

Insurmountable Opportunity

Walt Kelly drew the comic strip Pogo. In one of these he represented a little possum as saying to his fellow creatures of the swamp: "The only trouble with our country is that we are surrounded with insurmountable opportunity!"

No generation of Christians ever lived in a needier world, with more opportunities to serve God and man: "Lift up your eyes, and look on the fields. . .they are white already to harvest" (John 4:35).

* * * *

THEY DO ME WRONG

They do me wrong who say I come no
    more,
    When once I knock and fail to find
    you in,
For each day I stand without your
    door,
    And bid you rise and fight and win!

Walter Malone.

* * * *

PARENTAL RESPONSIBILITY
(See also Fathers, Mothers & Children)

A Teenager's Problem

A teenager wrote, "I have this problem with my parents or myself. I don't know which:

"My parents are very easygoing. They let me get by with anything. I know a lot of kids would love it if their parents would let them do what they pleased. Well, it's not fun. It makes me feel guilty and rotten.

"One of these days I am afraid I'll do something awful. The thought of it makes me scared. Kids are lucky whose parents are strict. How I wish mine were!"

* * * *

Heavenly Wisdom Needed

Sigmund Freud said, "Being a parent is an impossible profession under even the best of circumstances."

Parents need heavenly wisdom to enter sharingly and understandingly into the problems and perplexities of our sons and daughters. A molding factor in their lives is the parental example and home influence.

A girl from a Christian home entered college. She received several letters from Mom and Dad in which they expressed great concern for her living cleanly. In writing to them she said, "You needn't have any bothersome concern about my getting into sinful ways. God has been a Guest in our home too long for me to go into forbidden paths."

* * * *

The Unkept Vineyard

B. H. Carroll, exegete and founder of the great Southwestern Baptist Theological Seminary, Ft. Worth, Texas, was seen by friends in his home wringing his hands and inconsolably lamenting, "They made me the keeper of the vineyards; but mine own vineyard have I not kept" (Song of Sol. 1:6). Dr. Carroll had a wayward and unsaved son.

Parents may merit and receive the plaudits of men, but their hearts are filled with sorrow and self-accusation if their sons and daughters are lost and bring shame to them.

Told by Ralph M. Smith.

* * * *

Dr. Spock's Mistake

Dr. Benjamin Spock's books on baby care have been sold by millions throughout the world. Now he acknowledges:

"Parents have been persuaded that the only people who know for sure how children should be managed are the psychiatrists, psychologists, teachers, social workers and pediatricians—like myself.

"This is a cruel deprivation that we professionals have imposed on mothers and fathers. Of course, we did it with the best of intentions by giving talks and writing articles on child-rearing. We didn't realize until it was too late how our know-it-all attitude was undermining the self-assurance of parents."

The ancient formula given to parents is still valid and productive of excellent results: "Train up a child in the way he should go: and when he is old, he will not depart from it" (Prov. 22:6).

Adapted from *Redbook Magazine.*

* * * *

Both Parents Lost to Alcohol

In anguish, a distressed youth said, "I have lost both my father and mother to *alcohol!* It all seems so needless, but hopefully my heartbreak may help others if I can put into words the depth of my sorrow!

"Many parents view drinking as a chance to 'celebrate.' But on the minus side, liquor can hurt feelings, create arguments, cost money, distort judgment, cause accidents, change personality, lower self-esteem, boggle minds, waste time, ruin reputations, split families, destroy health and kill people. It does a great deal more harm than good. Funny that millions of people can't see it."

Next to heart disease and cancer, alcohol is the biggest killer in our country and the number one industrial problem.

Touch not. Handle not. Taste not: "At the last it biteth like a serpent, and stingeth like an adder" (Prov. 23:32).

* * * *

PATRIOTISM—LOVE FOR ONE'S NATIVE LAND
(See also Freedom)

Intoxicated by Success

How applicable are the words to our present-day America, spoken by Lincoln long ago: "We have forgotten the gracious hand which preserved us. Intoxicated by unbroken success, we have become too self-sufficient to feel the necessity of redeeming and preserving grace, and too proud to pray to the God who made us."

Tidal waves of joy and blessings would come to our nation if even an appreciable number of God's children would penitently confess our sins, saying, "O Lord, to us belongeth confusion of face, to our kings, to our princes, and to our fathers, because we have sinned against thee" (Dan. 9:8).

* * * *

Our Country May Cease to Exist!

In *Business Week*, The Warner & Swasey Company of Cleveland, Ohio, issued from their executive offices this timely message of warning:

"Have you ever faced the possibility that your country could cease to exist? Nations richer and more powerful in their day than we are in this have been sabotaged, defeated and enslaved.

"Babylon was the largest and richest nation of its time, but its lust for luxury made it an easy mark for the Medes and Persians who overran it and divided its land and enslaved people between them.

"Rome was a great military power; but when free bread and circuses became more important to the people than hard work and patriotism, Rome was invaded and looted by the tougher vandals.

"The Incas were the most civilized, richest people in the Americas; but ruthless, better-armed invaders destroyed them as a nation and looted everything they owned and had spent generations in creating.

"In every case it was the self-indulgent weakness of the victim which made the victory of the invader easy.

"How wise is a nation which gives away so much of its substance abroad and at home that it can no longer afford to keep its own strength and protection?

"How intelligent is a nation more careful to protect the criminal than his victim?

"How weak is a nation which allows bureaucracy and a socialist philosophy to run riot and squander billions?

"Undoubtedly there were Babylonians, Romans, Incas who warned against over-indulgence and weakness, who warned that *each citizen* is responsible for his nation, and that his responsibility cannot be shrugged off onto officials. But to those who warned of impending trouble, there was then as now the smug sneer, *'It can't happen here!' But it did!'*"

* * * *

Internal Decay

"America will not be slain by the Soviets," said Bishop Fulton J. Sheen, "but America can commit suicide. Great nations rarely fall to the battering of their enemies. They wither from within from loss of soul. Sixteen out of the nineteen civilizations that have passed away from the beginning of time *decayed from within.* Very often an attack from without strengthened them. If there was an enemy invasion at the end, as there was in the Roman Empire, it was merely the visit of the vultures to the carcass!"

* * * *

SAIL ON, O SHIP OF STATE

Thou, too, sail on, O Ship of State,
Sail on, O Union, strong and great!
Humanity with all its fears,
With all its hopes of future years,
Is hanging breathless on thy fate!
Stand thou for righteousness, people
so blessed,
. . . .
Sail on, so grand, free nation of
destiny,
For as goes America, so goes the
world!

Longfellow.

* * * *

Our Sacred Honor

How thrilling are the courageous words of the signers of the Declaration of Independence. Standing tall, straight and unwavering, they pledged: "For the purpose of this Declaration, with firm reliance on the protection of Divine Providence, we mutually pledge to each other, ourselves, our fortunes, and our sacred honor!"

* * * *

Why Evil Triumphs

Edmund Burke said, "Bad officials are elected by people who don't vote. For evil to triumph, it is only necessary for good men to do nothing."

"And I was afraid, and went and hid thy talent in the earth."—Matt. 25:25.

* * * *

I Am a Reactionary!

Patricia Young, a free-lance writer, affirmed: "*I react* to philosophies and sophistries which seek to destroy those values which made this nation great. *I react* to permissiveness and those ministers who would convert my house of worship into a political forum, and to the emasculation of my faith in the name of humanistic togetherness. *I react* to being scourged with the lash of collective guilt, as if I personally poured liquor down the alcoholic's throat, peddled heroin, and robbed a bank. *I react* to those young radicals who are so enamored of their own worth that they would destroy all other worths, and who are for nothing except their 'right' to be against everything. *I react* to the portrayal of Western leaders as Fascist pigs and of communists as 'liberators' and mini Santa Clauses. *I react* to the stupefying sentimentality of amateur do-gooders who, like carved wooden monkeys, see no evil, speak no evil, and hear no evil, and who would rewrite *Little Red Riding Hood* to 'rehabilitate' the wolf while jailing the woodsman for daring to deny the wolf his civil liberties!

"You better believe it—*I am a reactionary!*"

* * * *

How America Began

"I admire and love America," said Carlos P. Momulo, Philippine statesman, general and writer. "Never forget, however, that yours is a spiritual country. Yes, I know that you are a practical people. But underlying everything else is the fact that America began as a God-loving, God-fearing, God-worshiping people. It is this respect for the dignity of the human spirit which makes America invincible. May it always endure!"

God's Word warns, "Except the Lord build the house, they labour in vain that build it: except the Lord keep the city, the watchman waketh but in vain" (Ps. 127:1).

* * * *

Rubbled Remnants

In his book *Glimpses of a Sacred Land*, Carl F. H. Henry gives this clear warning for the United States:

"Everywhere one travels in the Near East today he can find the rubbled remnants of great empires of the past. One by one they have fallen, either to extinction or second-rate powers.

"In some of these lands, the wonder of their past can be recovered only from the dust heaps disclosed by the archaeologist's shovel. The whole course of history pays its testimony to the nature and activity of God. He sends disobedient nations down to their doom!"

* * * *

The Changeless Goal—Worldwide Conquest

James R. Wilson, director of the National Security Foreign Relations Division of the American Legion, said, "Why is it that our nation finds it so difficult to understand what our enemies are saying and doing about their plans for our future? While many Americans equate detente and co-existence with peace, Soviet Party Chief Leonid Brezhnev does not hesitate to affirm:

" 'Peaceful co-existence does not mean the end of the struggle of the two world powers. The struggle between the proletariat and the bourgeoisie, between world socialism and imperialism, will be waged right up to the complete and final victory of communism on a worldwide scale!' "

* * * *

A Lifetime Dedication

Adlai Stevenson said, "True patriotism is not manifested in short, frenzied bursts of emotion. It is the tranquil, steady dedication of a lifetime."

* * * *

The Most Religious Nation

"The United States may be the most religious nation on the face of the earth," declared George Gallup, Jr., the noted pollster. He based his statement on a worldwide study of attitudes toward religion, declaring that "America is still a very religious nation, at least in terms of outward manifestations of religion. On a typical week, four out of every ten Americans go to a church or synagogue, and only six percent of American adults say they have no religious preference."

"Blessed is the nation whose God is the Lord."—Ps. 33:12.

* * * *

Author of Liberty

How wisely Thomas Jefferson spoke when he asked, "Can the liberties of a nation be thought secure when we have removed their only firm basis—a conviction in the minds of people that these liberties are the gift of God?"

* * * *

Guilty as Charged

"We have failed to respond, personally and collectively, with sacrifice and uncompromised commitment to the unmet needs of our fellowman, both at home and abroad," said Senator Mark O. Hatfield.

"As a people, we have become so absorbed with the selfish pursuits of pleasure and profit that we have blinded ourselves to God's standard of justice and righteousness for our society. It behooves us to humble ourselves before God, confess our national sins and pray for His mercy and forgiveness."

The ancient promise has not been abrogated: "If my people. . .shall humble themselves. . .and turn from their wicked ways; then will I hear from heaven, and will forgive their sin, and will heal their land" (II Chron. 7:14).

* * * *

In Mortal Peril

"Since World War II, our country has been plunging into ever-deepening moral corruption," said Billy Graham. "Honesty is taboo, virtue is vice and vice is virtue. God's displeasure is upon us: 'Woe unto them that call evil good, and good evil' (Isa. 5:20). We are enmeshed in a maelstrom of sensuous pleasure.

"The drug menace is alarmingly increasing and daily claiming new youthful victims. Though accused of punching the panic button, I am convinced that the nation is in mortal peril. The handwriting is on the wall. We need to humble ourselves and plead: 'God be merciful to me a sinner.' It is either repent or perish! Which will it be?"

* * * *

From Bondage to Spiritual Faith

All the great nations of the past, which now sleep in dusty oblivion, followed the same pattern: From bondage to spiritual faith; from spiritual faith to great courage; from courage to liberty; from liberty to abundance; from abundance to selfishness; from selfishness to complacency; from complacency to apathy; from apathy to dependency back to bondage. Where in this pattern is our beloved America today?

We must acknowledge that all the corrosive ills and sin diseases which brought the downfall of the nations of antiquity are mightily existent in America today. It is not too late, however, for a change if even an appreciable number of us would turn penitently to God and acknowledge and forsake our sins: "Turn ye again now every one from his evil way. . . and dwell in the land that the Lord

hath given unto you and to your father for ever and ever" (Jer. 25:5).

* * * *

Freedom, a Gift From God

Dr. George W. Truett said, "Freedom is the pricelessly precious gift of God: 'Stand fast. . .in the liberty wherewith Christ hath made us free' (Gal. 5:1).

"Tolerance is the gift of man—of those who arrogate to themselves the assumed right to tyrannize over the bodies and souls of men, enslave them, degrade them to the status of pack animals."

How thrilling are the shackle-sundering words, "Proclaim liberty throughout all the land unto all the inhabitants thereof" (Lev. 25:10).

* * * *

Old Glory *

I am Old Glory! For more than nine-score years I have been the banner of hope and freedom for generation after generation of Americans. Born amid the first flames of America's fight for freedom, I am the symbol of a country that has grown from a little group of thirteen colonies to a united nation of fifty sovereign states. Planted firmly on the high pinnacle of American Faith, my gently fluttering folds have proved an inspiration to untold millions. Men have followed me into battle with unwavering courage. They have looked upon me as a symbol of national unity. They have prayed that they and their fellow citizens might continue to enjoy the life, liberty and pursuit of happiness which have been granted to every American as the heritage of free men. So long as men love liberty more than life, so long as they treasure the priceless privileges bought with the blood of our forefathers, so long as the principles of truth, justice and charity for all remain deeply rooted in human hearts, I shall continue to be the enduring banner of the United States of America.

Updated. Originally written by Marine Master Sergeant Percy Webb (1879-1945). Sergeant Webb wrote this famous tribute to our flag in the original "Our Flag" booklet distributed at the Chicago World's Fair, 1922.

* * * *

How Practical!

"Put your trust in God and keep your powder dry," wisely counseled Oliver Cromwell, English general and statesman.

* * * *

Run Up the Flag, Not Down

It is a real tragedy for a person who, for his own reasons, decides publicly to withhold respect from his nation's flag. To make a point about some real or fancied wrong, he deprives himself of those generous feelings which are the privilege of one born within the borders of a free land. To reject love of one's country is to reject one of God's choice gifts. Love for homeland, whether native or adopted, is instilled by God in the heart of a man and a woman.

Breathes there the man, with soul so dead,

Who never to himself hath said:
This is my own, my native land?
Decision.

* * * *

Providential Hinge of History

Carl F. H. Henry said, "Let us guard against considering any nation, however great, as the providential hinge of history."

Of all nations, the Bible says, "Behold, the nations are as a drop of a bucket, and are counted as the small dust of the balance" (Isa. 40:15).

How blessed is "the nation whose God is the Lord; and the people whom he hath chosen for his own inheritance" (Ps. 33:12).

* * * *

He Spoke Prophetically

Thomas Macauley, English historian and statesman, spoke prophetically more than a century ago: "Your republic will be pillaged and ravaged in the twentieth century just as the Roman Empire was by the barbarians of the fifth century, with this difference: the devastators of the Roman Empire came from abroad, while your barbarians will be the people of your own country and the product of your own institutions!"

* * * *

"The Noose Is Tightening!"

In *Eternity* it was said: "The noose is tightening for Christians and other 'target' people under authoritarian governments around the world!

World reaction thus far seems to smack too much of the *silence* that accompanied Hitler's extermination of some six million Jews!

"*Amnesty International,* after a worldwide survey, states that torture and extermination of dissidents is a matter of state policy in thirty countries. Many of these are among the forty military-dominated countries of the non-communist world!"

"When the righteous are in authority, the people rejoice: but when the wicked beareth rule, the people mourn" (Prov. 29:2).

Though it may seem that "wrong [is] forever on the throne," God is still "in the shadows keeping watch over His own!"

This is my Father's world,
O let me ne'er forget
That though the wrong seems oft so strong,
God is the Ruler yet!

Maltbie D. Babcock.

* * * *

How Ephemeral Is Earthly Fame!

After Charles Lindbergh's history-making solo flight across the Atlantic to Paris, Chief Justice Charles Evans Hughes said, "We measure heroes as we do ships—by their displacement. Col. Lindbergh has displaced everything that is petty, sordid and vulgar. America is fortunate in her heroes. Her soul feeds on their deeds. Her imagination revels in their accomplishments. There are those who would rob them of their lustre, but no one can debunk Lindbergh, for there is no bunk about him!"

How ephemeral is earthly fame: "For all flesh is as grass, and all the glory of man as the flower of grass. The grass withereth, and the flower thereof falleth away" (I Pet. 1:24). But how enduring is the fadeless fame of all who do the will of God and bring perishing ones to the Saviour: "And the world passeth away. . .but he that doeth the will of God abideth for ever" (I John 2:17); "And they that be wise shall shine as the brightness of the firmament; and they that turn many to righteousness as the stars for ever and ever" (Dan. 12:3).

The boast of heraldry, the pomp of power,
    And all that beauty, all that wealth e'er gave
Await alike the inevitable hour:
    The paths of glory lead but to the grave!

Thomas Gray.

* * * *

Sound. . .Bright. . .Great

"The heart of America is sound. The conscience of America is bright. The future of America is great," said Justice William O. Douglas of the U. S. Supreme Court.

* * * *

Can It Happen Here?

Some thirty years ago Leon Jaworski, greatly disturbed by what he heard and saw as chief prosecutor of Nazi war criminals, asked himself, "Could these horrible things happen in America?"

He said, "I could not help but wonder whether my native land America is immune from encroachment of moral deterioration that might threaten its very foundation. Apathy and indifference to the wrongdoing of political leaders and acquiescence in their evil practices can prove to be as harmful as active assistance. No nation, no matter how powerful and great and whatever be its form of government, can long withstand the stranglehold of moral deterioration in its people!"

Evil trends are reversed when individuals in an appreciable number in any nation penitently turn from sin to God and seek His mercy and forgiveness: "And God saw...that they turned from their evil way; and God repented of the evil, that he had said that he would do unto them; and he did it not" (Jonah 2:10).

* * * *

Coming Up to the Colors

On the hallowed grounds of Gettysburg stands a monument to a young color-bearer. During the pivotal Civil War battle, his regiment was in full retreat before heavy enemy fire. Yet the lad and several comrades stubbornly held their ground.

A message was sent through from the major: "Bring the colors back to the regiment!"

The terse reply was, "Bring the regiment up to the colors!"

Men and nations are facing the task of coming back to where they ought to be. Americans, no less than others, must experience a recovery of morals, discipline, purpose, and goodness. Hills and valleys and rivers and plains never produce national greatness. Only persons do that!

Lanny Henninger.

* * * *

Ethical absolutes

Said Arthur Koestler, "I am not sure whether ethical absolutes exist, but I am sure that we have to act as if they exist, or civilization perishes."

Said General Dwight Eisenhower, "Without a moral regeneration throughout the world, there is no hope for us! We will suddenly disappear in the dust of a terrific atomic explosion!"

Righteousness exalteth a nation: but sin is a reproach to any people."—Prov. 14:34.

* * * *

Ceaseless Taking

This quip appeared in *The American Statesman* (Austin, Texas): "The Lord giveth and the Lord taketh, but the government taketh, and taketh, and taketh!"

* * * *

"Remember Iwo Jima?"

Billy Zeoli, along with other Wheaton College students, spent much time in witnessing to slummers in Chicago's west side. As he talked to one man, he opened his New Testament to John 3:16 and began to read it. The man stopped him and asked, "Do you know who I am?"

Zeoli replied, "No, I do not."

The man asked, "You remember Iwo Jima, don't you? I'm the man who put the flag on top of Mt. Suribachi. There were six of us, and they are building a multimillion-dollar monument to us in Washington, D.C. I don't need that verse or your Bible or your Jesus Christ!"

Three months later, Zeoli read that this self-righteous, Christ rejector had died of alcoholism, tuberculosis and exposure on an Indian reservation in Arizona. He was 32-year-old *Ira Hayes*, a Pima Indian.

* * * *

Religious Decline

Roger Babson, famed statistician, said, "Every economic depression is foreshadowed by a religious decline."

Great is the need for an authoritative voice to point the way out of our moral and spiritual confusion in America—a voice totally dedicated to God and His imperishable Word.

* * * *

Implanted

Cicero, a first-century Roman statesman and writer, said, "There is no nation so barbarous, no people so savage, that have not had implanted in them a persuasion that God exists. This common conception could be said to inhere in the mind and even the viscera of man."

* * * *

Wrapped in Flag

When the communists took over China, there was a battle near an American Christian mission being used as an orphanage. The place was so crowded with deserted babies that the missionaries had run out of clothes with which to cover them.

In the midst of barking guns, the missionaries heard a baby crying outside the door. They ran out and brought in a little naked baby, but they had nothing to wrap him in.

Just then, an American flag was shot down off the flagpole. One missionary ran out, brought back the flag, and wrapped the shivering baby in it!

That act was a demonstration of the heart of America. Side by side with our nation's flag, we must keep flying the flag of faith, the blood-stained banner of the cross of Christ. Let's run them up, not down!

Samuel A. Jeanes,
in *The Presbyterian Journal.*

* * * *

The Test of a Nation

Roger Babson, the famed statistician and writer on finance, said, "The test of a nation is the growth of its people intellectually and spiritually. Money and so-called prosperity are of very little account. Babylon, Persia, Greece, Rome and Spain all had their turns in being the richest nations in the world. Then they declined. Instead of saving them, their wealth proved to be their ruin.

"Our nation is now the richest nation, but it could easily become a second-class nation and head downward!"

How impoverished a nation is if it gains the world in space exploration or riches and loses its soul!

Not gold, but only men can make
A nation great and strong,
Men who for truth and honor's sake,
Stand fast and suffer long.

Ralph Waldo Emerson.

* * * *

Why, O Why?

A pertinent question was editorially asked in *The Presbyterian Journal:*

"Why does the World Council of Churches seem to criticize so freely the governments of the United States and other free world countries when it says so little about the discrimination and persecution of Christians in totalitarian and communist states?" We, too, wonder why.

* * * *

PEACE

The White Feather

In 1777, a little group of Quakers assembled for worship in their meetinghouse in Easton, New York.

Suddenly thirteen Indians came in noiselessly. They intended to kill the worshipers, and had their poisoned arrows ready to fly at the signal of their chief.

The chief's piercing eyes searched every corner and nook for weapons. Seeing none, he signaled for his warriors to place their arrows back in their quivers and stack their bows against the wall.

The calm blue eyes of Zebulon Hoxie, leader of the meeting, revealed only love and friendship, as the Indians quietly sat down around their chief.

The worship went on, and the atmosphere was surcharged with the very presence of God!

When the worship ended, Hoxie came and shook hands with the chief who said, "Indians came to kill white people. Indians find no guns, no arrows, no knives. White people worship Great Spirit. Great Spirit say to Indians, 'No kill them!' "

As the chief and his braves left, he placed a white feather from his arrow over the doorway of the meetinghouse, a sign of peace between the Indians and the Quakers. A New York historical marker now commemorates the incident.

How slow are rulers and nations to heed the Saviour's warning: "All they that take the sword shall perish with the sword" (Matt. 26:52).

* * * *

A GOLDEN PRAYER

Dear Lord and Redeemer of mankind,
Forgive our foolish ways!
Reclothe us in our rightful mind,
In purer lives Thy service find,
In deeper reverence, praise.

Drop Thy still dews of quietness,
Till all our strivings cease;
Take from our souls the strain and stress,
And let our ordered lives confess,
The beauty of Thy peace.

John Greenleaf Whittier.

* * * *

Christmas Eve in "No Man's Land"

'Twas Christmas Eve in "No Man's Land!" The time was World War I. A most wondrous and thrilling thing occurred. Battle-weary men in one trench began singing:

Silent night, holy night,
All is calm, all is bright!

Enemies in the opposite trench began singing:

O little town of Bethlehem,
How still we see thee lie!

Cannons ceased their booming. The Spirit of Christ, "the Prince of peace," became all-pervasive! Peace reigned 'midst scenes of carnage. For the time, foes became friends.

The incident is prophetic of the time when Jesus will return to our war-wrecked world. Then these prophecies will fruition into history: "The whole earth is at rest, and is quiet: they break forth into singing" (Isa. 14:7); "They shall beat their swords into plowshares, and their spears into pruninghooks: nation shall not lift up a sword against nation, neither shall they learn war any more" (Mic. 4:3).

Pleadingly we pray: "Even so, come, Lord Jesus."

* * * *

"I've Lived Long Enough"

George Sanders was an actor of impeccable diction and haughty manner, playing some of the wittiest roles in Hollywood films during the 1940s and 1950s.

Having grown weary of life, Sanders took his own life! He left a note:

"I commit suicide because I am boring, and because I have already lived long enough."

The passing glories of the world cannot give peace. Christ can.

O, that the world might hear Him speak
The word of comfort that men seek;
To all the lowly, and unto the meek,
Jesus whispers peace.

Della McChain Warren.

* * * *

Move Restfully

G. H. Morling said in Decision:

"Order and the beauty of peace go together. The radiance of a deep inner serenity is the product of discipline.

"It is wise to regard each day as a life in itself, a life coming as it were with the dawn, running its appointed course.

"Attend first to opening of the day. Move restfully into the day. Rush cannot live with rest. Let the first minutes of the wakening day be spent in an atmosphere of quiet and leisureliness. Immediately meet with the Lord. He is waiting for you in the inner chamber."

Long ago the psalmist said, "My voice shalt thou hear in the morning, O Lord; in the morning will I direct my prayer unto thee, and will look up" (Ps. 5:3).

I met God in the morning,
When the day was at its best,
And His presence came like sunrise,
Like a glory in my breast.

* * * *

When Moral Values Are Taboo

Dr. Charles Malik, a former president of the U. N. General Assembly, who addressed the Texas legislature and several audiences in the University of Texas, said: "The United General Assembly cannot initiate peace, cannot impose peace, cannot produce peace; but once a settlement is reached, the U. N. can be instructive. The answers, however, to world problems can never be found through government, force or the U. N. The remedy must deal with individual problems.

"The most important single malady of the world today is the total expulsion of spiritual and moral teaching from the world's universities that train the leaders. On campuses the emphasis is science, technical matters, production and learning— certainly things befitting a university. But religious and moral values have become taboo!"

* * * *

POWER

Why They Were Triumphant

When we become dewy-eyed about the past, we romanticize the Christian who lived then, and are forgetful of the fact that they were "subject to like passions as we are" (Jas. 5:17). They triumphed over sin because they were "endued with power from on high." They "overcame him [Satan] by the blood of the Lamb, and by the word of their testimony" (Rev. 12:11).

* * * *

Fatigue Failures

Sometime ago a twin-engined Beechcraft plane crashed with the loss of several lives because of "fatigue failure" in the craft's left wing. Investigation revealed that the crack in the wing had been developing for a year before the fatal crash.

God wants His children to "run with patience the race that is set before [them]." We cannot do this if

we fail to tarry daily "in the secret place of the most High" and there receive spiritual renewal and power: "He giveth power to the faint; and to them that have no might he increaseth strength" (Isa. 40:29).

* * * *

Spiritual Weaklings

Many years ago a young Italian lad in Brooklyn, New York, grew tired of being poor and a ninety-seven-pound weakling, so he set about to resolve both of these conditions and came up with an idea called "dynamic tension." We know him today as the originator and advocate of the idea which made him "Charles Atlas, the world's most perfectly developed man." He died at the age of eighty, and this indicates that the ninety-seven-pound weakling had at last found strength and longevity. He also died a multimillionaire, and there are a great many other ninety-seven-pound weaklings in the world who would gladly share that success today.

Many people are spiritually dwarfed weaklings through failure to daily wait yieldedly and unhurriedly in "the secret place of the most High," alone with God.

God's promise is unfailing: "But they that wait upon the Lord shall renew their strength; they shall mount up with wings as eagles; they shall run, and not be weary; and they shall walk, and not faint" (Isa. 40:31).

R. Norman Herbeter.

* * * *

PRAYER

Un-Asked-for Blessings

Some years ago, Kate Smith of *God Bless America* fame was in a boat on a bay when suddenly a dense fog settled on the bay. Visibility was zero. Their situation was perilous! They feared that a seaward undertow might sweep them into the ocean and death. Kate said to her friends, "There is a promise in the Bible which says, 'That if two of you shall agree on earth as touching any thing that they shall ask, it shall be done for them of my Father which is in heaven' (Matt. 18:19)."

United, they called upon Jesus to save them, as did the imperiled disciples long ago: "Lord, save us: we perish." Soon a vessel plowed through the fog and saved them.

The Saviour's promise has not been rescinded: "What things soever ye desire, when ye pray, believe that ye receive them, and ye shall have them" (Mark 11:24).

God has many un-asked-for blessings awaiting our asking. "For every one that asketh receiveth" (Matt. 7:8).

God delights to bestow the best of gifts upon His children: "No good thing will he withhold from them that walk uprightly" (Ps. 84:11).

So many of us forfeit God's blessings because we fail to ask for them: "Ye have not, because ye ask not" (Jas. 4:2).

Thou art coming to a King,
Large petitions with thee bring,
For His grace and pow'r are such,
None can ever ask too much!

Told by Ralph M. Smith.

* * * *

"Let Us Come Boldly"

As little Tad Lincoln chatted with those waiting to see President Lincoln, he was especially attracted to a sad, distressed soldier, guarded by military police, who had fallen asleep at his post of duty and had been court-martialed.

Tad said to the soldier, "Take my hand and go with me!"

Going past the guards, they went directly to the President.

Tad said, "Father, this soldier is very sad. Please, Father, have mercy on him and give him a second chance."

His intercession prevailed. The soldier was given a second chance and returned to his outfit.

Our Saviour and Intercessor is in Heaven "to appear in the presence of God for us" (Heb. 9:24). He asks us to "come boldly unto the throne of grace. . .and find. . .help in time of need" (Heb. 4:16).

In the hour of trial, Jesus plead for me,
Lest, by base denial, I depart from Thee.
When Thou see'st me waver, with a look recall,
Nor by fear or favor, suffer me to fall.

Told by Ralph M. Smith.

* * * *

If Not Nipped in the Bud

A man was cited for kneeling and praying in Westminster Abbey, where many of England's illustrious dead are interred.

At the arraignment, the prosecuting attorney said, "Your Honor, if this thing is not nipped in the bud, no telling where it will end."

But God's children may pray anywhere, for God is everywhere: "I will therefore that men pray every where, lifting up holy hands, without wrath and doubting" (I Tim. 2:8).

* * * *

"Not an Inkling of Light"

Just before a diabetic patient underwent major surgery—the amputation of a leg—a minister came to his bedside and prayed.

After the operation, the patient said of the minister's visit and prayer, "Before you stood by my bed and prayed, all was dense darkness. Not an inkling of light shone on the black clouds of discouragement. As you prayed, all was changed! Light burst

through the clouds. Hope was reborn, and I faced the impending operation without fear, knowing that God would see me through the ordeal."

The promise has not been rescinded: "And call upon me in the day of trouble: I will deliver thee, and thou shalt glorify me" (Ps. 50:15).

* * * *

Shoe Leather and Prayers

To pray prevailingly for others we must be willing to put shoe leather to our prayers, and add this postscript: "Lord, I am Your instrument. If it pleases You, I am willing that You should use me to effectuate the answer to my prayer."

* * * *

Life Is Fragile

Life is *fragile*! Handle it with *prayer*!

"For what is your life? It is even a vapour, that appeareth for a little time, and then vanisheth away."— Jas. 4:14.

* * * *

A Telephone Line to Heaven

A pastor said to an invalid who was confined to a wheelchair, "You are a great inspiration to me and to many others! Always cheerful and dynamic, though your body is often racked with pain and your limbs almost useless. How are you so contagiously cheerful?"

She replied, "I have a phone number which I constantly use!"

"A phone number?" asked the pastor, "What is it?"

The invalid replied, "It is JER-33-3."

Jeremiah 33:3 says, "Call unto me, and I will answer thee, and shew thee great and mighty things, which thou knowest not."

How different things would be with many of us if we, too, would make frequent use of this victory-bringing number!

Told by Ralph M. Smith.

* * * *

Pinpoint Your Prayers

When Billy Graham was a teenager, some businessmen of Charlotte, North Carolina, organized an evangelistic movement to bring a revival to the city.

They met daily for earnest prayer. In one of the prayer sessions, Vernon Patterson, chairman of the group, prayed, "O Lord, out of this city raise up someone to preach the Gospel to the ends of the earth!"

God answered the prayer. He reached down, touched the heart of a farm boy, Billy Graham, and has used him to proclaim the Good News of salvation to the ends of the earth.

God delights to answer the definite prayers of His children. His promise has not been rescinded: "What things soever ye desire, when ye pray, believe that ye receive them, and ye shall have them" (Mark 11:24).

Told by Bunny Graham Dienert, daughter of Billy Graham, in *Moody Monthly.*

* * * *

WHEN SATAN TREMBLES

Restraining prayer, we cease to fight, Prayer makes the Christian's armor bright, And Satan trembles when he sees, The weakest saint upon his knees.

Were half our breath oft vainly spent, To Heaven in supplication sent, Our cheerful song would oftener be: "Hear what the Lord has done for me!"

William Cowper.

* * * *

A Certainty

God sometimes denies the form of our prayers that He might fulfill the substance of our request. This is certain: "No good thing will he withhold from them that walk uprightly" (Ps. 84:11).

* * * *

A Surgeon and Prayer

Just before a skilled surgeon performed a complex operation, he bowed his head and prayed briefly that the Great Physician would guide his hands aright. After the successful operation, when an intern asked, "Why do you pray for divine help before a surgical procedure?" the surgeon replied, "After I pray, I am so aware of God's presence that I do not know where my skill ends and the hand of the Great Physician takes over!"

God's children "are labourers together with [Him]" (I Cor. 3:9), and we need His help. How helpless we would be without His help!

* * * *

Wrought Through Prayer

As John Heird, a student in Southwestern Seminary, sat at a desk in a Fort Worth motel room, a bandit entered, pressed a revolver to his head, and said, "I'm going to kill you!"

In speaking of the frightful incident later, Heird said, "Though trembling with fear, I closed my eyes and began to pray for the bandit. Then I began quoting verses from the Bible.

"Stunned and flabbergasted, the bandit asked, 'Aren't you afraid to die?' Then he pushed me into the bathroom and tied my hands to the door."

Freeing himself, the student returned to his desk. The bandit and Heird's Bible were gone. Cartridges which might have been used to take the life of the student were left!

Prayer and the quoting of God's Word had thwarted the murderous intention of the Satan-driven man.

Adapted from *Baptist Standard*.

* * * *

More things are wrought by prayer
Than the world dreams of.
Wherefore, let thy voice
Rise like a fountain for me night and day.
For what are men better than sheep or goats
That nourish a blind life within the brain,
If, knowing God, they lift not hands of prayer

Both for themselves and those who call them friend?

Alfred Tennyson.

* * * *

Prayer Is Many Things

Ruth Graham said, "Prayer has never failed me. It's something like telephoning God person-to-person. When our children are away from home and don't phone, how I miss it! Prayer is communicating with Someone we love very much. It may be a cry or a mourn or a song of praise and joy. But it is still prayer."

* * * *

Unanswered Yet?

After I shaved one morning, I removed the blade from the razor. As I did so, my little two-year-old daughter Alice stretched out her little hands and pleaded, "Give me! Give me!"

"No, no," I said, "the blade will hurt my little girl!"

She whimpered and went away.

Sometimes God, in unerring wisdom, *denies* the thing we pray for: "Ye know not what ye ask" (Matt. 20:22); "For this thing I besought the Lord thrice, that it might depart from me" (II Cor. 12:8); "For we know not what we should pray for as we ought" (Rom. 8:26).

This is certain: "No good thing will he withhold from them that walk uprightly" (Ps. 84:11).

Keep on praying when the skies are gray,
In God's presence clouds will break away;

Keep on praying till the sun shines thru,
Keep on praying, God will answer you.

Ina Pearle Whaley.

* * * *

Hazardous Praying

A fine man succumbed to a serious illness involving his brain. His wife, who loved him more than life, prayed, "O God, you must not let him die. I can't live without him!"

The prayer was answered. The man lived. But his mind was utterly blank. He continually stared vacantly into space, completely oblivious of his surroundings—a mere human vegetable.

The loved one who prayed, "O God, you must not let him die," was possibly well-intentioned; but she failed to pray submissively, as did the Saviour in Gethsemane: "O my Father, if it be possible, let this cup pass from me: nevertheless not as I will, but as thou wilt" (Matt. 26:39).

It is hazardous for us to plead for anything apart from total submission to the *perfect* will of God. This is what some did long ago: "And [God] gave them their request; but sent leanness into their soul" (Ps. 106:15).

Told by Kiely Young.

* * * *

Cut Short

Dwight L. Moody said, "Some of our prayers need to be cut short at both ends and set on fire in the middle. A man who prays much in private will usually make short prayers in public."

* * * *

HIS APPOINTMENT

Disappointment? His appointment!
No good thing will He withhold.
From denials oft we gather
Treasures of His love untold.

* * * *

"If Two of You Shall Agree"

One of the greatest challenges to earnest, united prayer occurred sometime ago: A child was hopelessly ill, and the attending physician said, "The child can't live out the night!"

Hearing about the medic's ominous words, a group of God's children united their hearts in earnest prayer, claiming the sure promise, "If two of you shall agree on earth as touching any thing that they shall ask, it shall be done for them of my Father which is in heaven" (Matt. 18:19).

In the early morning hours, a change occurred! The child recovered from the illness. God had honored the faith of His praying children.

Sometimes God answers the prayers of His children "while they are yet speaking" (Isa. 65:24). Sometimes He delays the answer, 'Lord, behold, he whom thou lovest is sick. When Jesus heard that he was sick, he abode two days still in the same place where he was' (John 11:3,6). Delays, however, are not denials. Sometimes God's answer is "No": "Ye know not what ye ask" (Matt. 20:22).

The promise has not been abrogated: "And this is the confidence that we have in him, that, if we ask any thing according to his will, he heareth us" (I John 5:14).

Told by Kiely Young.

* * * *

"They Just Prayed"

Ruth Bell Graham said, "Men of God whose prayers are recorded for us in the Bible never read a book of prayer, never went to a seminar on prayer, never heard a sermon on prayer. *They just prayed!* Satan fears prayer because God hears prayer. Satan will stop at nothing to distract a person from praying or get him to postpone prayer."

* * * *

The Soul on Its Knees

Victor Hugo said, "Certain thoughts are prayers. There are some moments when, whatever be the posture of the body, the soul is on its knees."

* * * *

"I Get Up!"

An interested student said to Dr. Harry A. Ironside, "I understand you get up very early in the morning, read your Bible and pray."

"Oh yes," said Dr. Ironside. "I've been doing that for many years."

"How do you manage to do it? Do you pray about it?" asked the student.

"No," he replied. "*I get up!*"

It is written of our Saviour, "And in the morning, rising up a great while before day, he went out, and departed into a solitary place, and there prayed" (Mark 1:35).

* * * *

No Joking Matter

During the Civil War, two Quakers were discussing the war. One said, "I think Jefferson Davis will succeed."

"Why?" asked the other.

"Because he is a praying man."

"But Lincoln is a praying man, too."

"True," said the other, "but the Lord will think Lincoln is joking."

Prayer is no joking matter. It involves *watchfulness:* "Watch and pray, that ye enter not into temptation" (Matt. 26:41); *workfulness:* "Epaphras. . .always labouring fervently for you in prayers" (Col. 4:12); *earnestness:* "And Moses returned unto the Lord, and said, Oh, this people have sinned a great sin. . . Yet now, if thou wilt forgive their sin—; and if not, blot me, I pray thee, out of thy book which thou hast written" (Exod. 32:31,32); and *submissiveness:* "O my Father, if it be possible, let this cup pass from me; nevertheless not as I will, but as thou wilt" (Matt. 26:39).

* * * *

Via God's Throne

A pastor called at the home of an invalid member of his church who was unable to attend the services. When the pastor knocked, there was no response. So he knocked again and patiently waited. Finally the invalid came to the door. Seeing her pastor, she said apologetically, "Oh, pastor, I'm so sorry I kept you waiting. I was 'visiting' two of my dear friends who are missionaries in Mexico."

The pastor thought, *She is losing her mind!*

The invalid explained: "I was having a blessed time talking to the Lord about the needs of these missionary friends, and 'visiting' with them at God's throne of grace!"

How great is the need of intercessory prayer!

Lord, help me live from day to day
In such a self-forgetful way;
That even when I kneel to pray,
My prayer may be for others.

* * * *

THE IGNORED ONES

Lord, bless me with a listening mind,
Attune me to the smaller sounds,
The whispered plea of loneliness,
The whimper of an unloved child.
The sad, the sick, the lost—all these
Ignored, unheard by passersby,
And use me, Lord, to meet their needs,
That I may, in a Christlike way,
Reflect Thy love for them each day.

Irene Sharp.

* * * *

Already Decided

"Often as we pray the thought comes to mind that the thing we pray for has already been decided one way or the other," said C. S. Lewis. "This is no good reason to cease praying, however. The event or thing certainly has been decided, even before the foundation of the world. One of the

factors, however, that really causes it to happen may be the very prayer that we are now offering."

In wonderment we exclaim, "O the depth of the riches both of the wisdom and knowledge of God! how unsearchable are his judgments, and his ways past finding out!" (Rom. 11:33).

* * * *

What Prayer Is Not

Governor Reubin Askew of Florida said, "Prayer is not an excuse for being lazy and pushing all the work off on God. It is a way of finding strength and ability to do things along with God that we could never do by ourselves."

* * * *

Prayer and a Good Toe

When Don Cockroft, punter and place kicker for the Cleveland Browns, missed a field goal in a crucial game, he did a most natural thing for him—he prayed.

One minute and fifty seconds later, with time running out, his prayer was answered and he got a second chance. This time he made good the kick to give his team a two-point victory over Pittsburgh in the last seconds of the game.

There is nothing trivial or inconsequential in the life of Christians. They may call upon God for help in any and all situations.

* * * *

"As Soon As Zion Travailed"

One time when DeWitt Talmage became deeply depressed because there were so few conversions under his ministry, he invited five Christian men to join him in prayer for souls. In telling what happened, Talmage said:

"We entered an upper room in my home. There we agonized in prayer that there would be a great turning by people from sin to God. We had agreed that we would not leave the room until we were assured in our hearts that God would send a great spiritual awakening. At the conclusion of the gathering, I requested that the meeting be kept secret.

"On the following Sunday over four hundred stood for prayer. A religious awakening took place which made that winter memorable for time and eternity!"

"For as soon as Zion travailed, she brought forth her children."—Isa. 66:8.

* * * *

METHODS RARE

I know not by what methods rare,
But this I know, God answers prayer!
I know that He has given His Word,
Which tells me prayer is always
   heard,
And will be answered soon or late,
And so I pray and calmly wait.

I know not if the blessing sought
Will come in just the way I thought,
But leave my prayer with Him alone,
Whose will is wiser than my own,
Assured that He will grant my quest,
And send some answer far more blest.

* * * *

PREACHERS

Frigid Sermons

A. J. Gordon said, "The sincere milk of the Word may be dispensed so frigidly and unfeelingly as to make it difficult to receive. In Siberia, milkmen deliver their product in chunks—it is frozen solid. This is sometimes the way we deliver God's Word—frozen into logical formulas and hardened and chilled by excessive reasonings."

How heart-warming will be our message when we can say with God's ancient prophet: "His word was in mine heart as a burning fire shut up in my bones" (Jer. 20:9).

Set us afire, Lord, still us we pray,
While the world perishes, we go our way:
Purposeless, passionless, day after day,
Set us afire, Lord, still us we pray.

* * * *

Dying Man to Dying Men

Richard Baxter said: "I preach as never sure to preach again, and as a dying man to dying men."

* * * *

Not Sent, Just Went

In speaking of misfits in the ministry—those not divinely called—

a black pastor said, "They are not *sent*. They just *went*."

Eminently qualified for the ministry are those who can say with Paul: "Woe is unto me, if I preach not the gospel" (I Cor. 9:16); or with Jeremiah, "But his word was in mine heart as a burning fire shut up in my bones. . .and I could not stay" (Jer. 20:9).

* * * *

Total Dedication

A cripple sat in a wheelchair at the rear of a church during a revival meeting. When the invitation was given by the evangelist for Christians to dedicate themselves totally to God, the cripple wheeled himself to the front of the church.

Asked he of the evangelist, "Can God use a half-man who is fully surrendered to Him?"

The evangelist replied, "God can use a half-man who is totally dedicated to Him infinitely better than a whole man who is only half-dedicated to Him!"

William Booth, founder of the Salvation Army, said, "From the first day God put the poor and the down-and-outs of London on my heart, He has had all there was of William Booth!"

God still pleads, "I beseech you. . . present your bodies a living sacrifice. . .unto God" (Rom. 12:1).

Dwight L. Moody heard a challenging statement which wrought a wondrous change in his life and ministry: "The world has yet to see what God can do with a man who is totally dedicated to Him!"

Moody responded in his heart, saying, *By the grace of God I'll be that man!*

His decision to totally dedicate himself to God led to his worldwide ministry.

Told by Ralph M. Smith.

* * * *

Sermons and Dictionaries

Some sermons are like a dictionary: a lot of information but not much inspiration.

How helpful and inspirational are sermons if it can be said of them what was said of God's servants of old: "So they read in the book in the law distinctly, and gave the sense, and caused them to understand the reading" (Neh. 8:8).

* * * *

HE HELD THE LAMP

He held the lamp each livelong day
So low that none could miss the way,
And yet so high to bring in sight
That picture fair of Christ, the Light,
That gazing up, the lamp between
The hand that held it was not seen.

He held the pitcher—stooping low,
To lips of little ones below,
Then raised it to the weary saint,
And bade him drink when sick and faint;
They drank, the pitcher thus between
The hand that held it scarce was seen.

He blew the trumpet soft and clear,
That trembling sinners need not fear,

And then with louder note and bold,
To storm the walls of Satan's fold,
The trumpet coming thus between
The hand that held it scarce was
seen.

But when the Captain says, "Well
done,
Thou good and faithful servant,
come!
Lay down the pitcher and the lamp,
Lay down the trumpet, leave the
camp!"
The weary hand will then be seen
Clasped in the pierced ones between!

Author Unknown.

* * * *

Marital Stress and Financial Difficulties

In an address before a meeting of
The Christian Life Conference, David
Mace, a marriage counsellor, said:

"Pastors and their wives are having
a rough time and, unless churches
come to their aid, there will be a rash
of divorces among clergy couples!

"Ranking fourth among causes for
marital stress are financial difficulties. We researched pastoral
salaries and found that out of 432 occupations recognized by the Bureau
of Labor Statistics, pastors ranked
325th on the hourly wage list. This
puts them in the same category as
farm labourers, cooks, waiters and
waitresses. But on the educational
level, pastors rank in the top ten.
Though these inequities obtain, the
majority of ministers and their wives
are not bitter or upset by their financial situation, because they feel that

God has called them into His service."

Adapted from Baptist Standard.

* * * *

OUR PASTOR

Who is it calls when we are ill
With cheerful words and right good
will,
And lingers gently then to pray
And soothe our care and fear away?
Our Pastor!

Who is it comes when sorrow falls,
When death of friends our heart
appalls,
And tells us of mansions fair,
And that sweet home, "just over
there"?
Our Pastor!

Who is it shares our happiest hours,
When life is crowned with wedding
flowers,
And to the scene lends added grace
By reverent voice and kindly face?
Our Pastor!

Who is it that on the Lord's Day
Points to Heaven and leads the way,
And brings a message from the Word,
Until our hearts within are stirred?
Our Pastor!

For whom then shall we daily pray
And ask for him God's grace alway,
And wish for him a glad new year,
With new-born souls his heart to
cheer?
Our Pastor!

Lean G. Browne.

* * * *

"I Never Got to First Base!"

In commenting upon the influence an aged minister exerted on his life, renowned baseball player Babe Ruth said:

"Most of the people who have really counted in my life were not famous. Few ever heard of them, except those who knew and loved them.

"I knew an old minister once whose hair was white and whose face shone. I have written my name on thousands and thousands of baseballs in my life; he wrote his name on just a few simple hearts. How I envy him! He was not trying to please himself and win the plaudits of the world. So fame never came to him. I am listed as a famous home-run hitter. Yet, beside that humble, obscure minister, who was so good and wise, I never got to first base!"

* * * *

Better for Sun to Cease Shining

It was said of Saint Christopher, a third century martyr, "It would be better for the sun to stop shining than for Christopher to stop preaching."

Who can estimate the place and power of Bible-centered, Christ-exalting preaching?

* * * *

A Sine Qua Non

Alexander Whyte said, "I am as sure as I am of anything that a minister's own soul will prosper largely in the measure that people prosper through his pastoral work. No preaching can be left to make up for the neglect of *pastoral visitation*."

Paul said, "I kept back nothing that was profitable unto you, but. . . have taught you publickly, and from house to house" (Acts 20:20).

* * * *

"Prayers for All Men"

Dr. Herschel H. Hobbs said, "Years ago when pastor of a church in Montgomery, Alabama, I had occasion to visit the mayor of the city, one of the last of the city bosses. As I terminated the visit, I asked him if I could lead in prayer." He readily agreed. After the prayer, I observed that his eyes were filled with tears.

When one of my deacons called upon the mayor after my visit, the mayor said, "During the twenty-five years I have been mayor of this city, thousands of people have entered my office. But your pastor was the first person to ask me if he could pray for me!"

When Dr. Hobbs spoke of the incident, he said, "I vowed that I would never enter a public official's office, no matter what his rank might be, without asking if I might pray for him."

The Bible says, "I exhort. . .that. . . prayers. . .be made for all men. . . for all that are in authority; that we may lead a quiet and peaceable life in all godliness and honesty" (I Tim. 2:1,2).

* * * *

Sensationmongers

Dr. Herschel Hobbs told of a budding, youthful minister who said to an older minister, "I'm going to fill my church if I have to stand on my head on the platform and work my feet!"

The veteran minister replied, "Son, you'll have better success if you will stand on your feet and work your *head.*"

* * * *

Dog's Hind Legs

Dr. Samuel Johnson, author of the English dictionary, said, "Sir, a woman's preaching is like a dog's walking on his hind legs. It is not well done, but you are surprised to find it done at all."

* * * *

Moral and Immoral Sinners

In a sermon, John Wesley spoke plainly and warningly to the elite courtiers and noblemen. At the conclusion of his sermon, one said to Wesley, "That sermon would have been quite appropriate for the down-and-outers."

"No," said Wesley, "if I had been speaking to them, my text would have been, 'Behold the Lamb of God, which taketh away the sin of the world' " (John 1:29).

Both moral and immoral sinners, the up-and-outers need to hear and heed the character-changing Gospel.

* * * *

"May the Lord of Hosts Bless Your Legs!"

In 1846 the fate of our nation depended on the legs of General Andrew Jackson's trusted messenger, Holdfast Gaines, an Indian scout.

Gaines was encamped with the American army on Mobile Bay when word was received that a large British force had set sail for New Orleans. The only hope of General Jackson was to get word as quickly as possible to General "Dandy" Carroll in Nashville, so he could rally the long rifle frontiersmen of Tennessee and Kentucky to meet him in New Orleans. But how could that be done with 600 miles of wilderness between them?

General Jackson's only hope was his trusted messenger. He gave Gaines the assignment and said, "I'll give you ten days to get there! May the Lord of Hosts bless your legs!"

At sunset on October 12, as General Carroll sat dining, Holdfast Gaines stumbled through the doorway, making the 600 miles in six days and five nights!

General Carroll rallied the long riflemen and rendezvoused with General Jackson in New Orleans. The British were defeated. New Orleans was saved because the messenger delivered his message.

The mission of the messenger is vital. It is imperative that the messenger deliver the right message. The preacher today can waste his time with frivolous issues. He can devote his message to good things and neglect the best.

What is our message? It must ever be the same as Paul stated it long ago: "For I determined not to know any thing among you, save Jesus Christ, and him crucified" (I Cor. 2:2). Our directive has not been rescinded: "Preach the word" (II Tim. 4:2).

Told by Ed Brooks Bowles.

* * * *

Converted by Own Sermon

A nineteenth century vicar of Cornwall, England, testified:

"I went into the pulpit. I gave my text and began to preach. I do not remember all I said, but I felt a wonderful light and joy coming into my soul! Whether there was something in my words or my manner or my look, I do not know. Suddenly a local visiting minister stood and exclaimed in Cornish: 'The parson is converted! The parson is converted! Hallelujah!' Others spontaneously joined in the shouts of praise. I announced the Doxology which all joyfully sang!"

Adapted from *Decision*.

* * * *

WHERE IS GOD?

The parish priest of austerity
  Climbed up the high church steeple
To be nearer to God, to bring His
  Word
Down to the people.

In sermon script he daily wrote
  What he thought was sent from
  Heaven,
And dropped it down on the people's head
Twice one day in seven.

In his age, God said, "Come down
  and die,"
And he cried out from his high
  church steeple,
"Where art Thou, Lord?" and the
  Lord replied,
"Down here among my people."

* * * *

Different Emphasis

How diverse was the emphasis given in the preaching of the spiritual giants of the years agone!

With George Whitefield it was the new or spiritual birth. His oft-repeated text was, "Ye must be born again" (John 3:7). When asked why he so frequently used the text, he replied, "Because 'ye must be born again.' "

With Jonathan Edwards the dominant note was God's sure judgment: "Because he [God] hath appointed a day, in the which he will judge the world in righteousness" (Acts 17:31).

With Billy Sunday it was sin on detective duty: "Be sure your sin will find you out" (Num. 32:23).

With Dwight L. Moody the emphasis was the love of God. "God is love. . ." (I John 4:16) was printed on each light in the old Moody Church. As Moody spoke of the love of God, tears would trickle down his face.

With Gypsy Smith the emphasis was the beauty of Jesus: "Thou art fairer than the children of men: grace is poured into thy lips. . .God hath blessed thee for ever" (Ps. 45:2).

With R. A. Torrey it was personal soul winning: "And they that be wise shall shine as the brightness of the firmament; and they that turn many to righteousness as the stars for ever and ever" (Dan. 12:3).

Of these heroes of the faith, we can affirm: They "being dead yet speaketh" (Heb. 11:4).

* * * *

Clogged Blood Vessels

In addressing the Southwestern Baptist Religious Education Association, Kenneth H. Cooper, M.D., said:

"The group with the poorest health condition of any I've found is ministers.

"Seventy-seven per cent of men over twenty-nine years old have blood vessels clogged with fat, and there is developing an alarming increase of heart attacks affecting men in the twenty-five to forty-four age bracket. Obesity, cigarette smoking and inactivity are factors contributing to heart disease. Exercise will not only help you add years to your life, but life to your years as well."

The longer the waistline, the shorter the lifeline!

"And put a knife to thy throat, if thou be a man given to appetite."— Prov. 23:2.

* * * *

Purpose of Preaching

J. Daniel Baumann, a seminary professor, described preaching as "the communication of biblical truth by man to men with the explicit purpose of eliciting behavioral change."

Paul said of preaching, "It pleased

God by the foolishness of preaching to save them that believe" (I Cor. 1:21).

* * * *

"My Wasted Years"

David Maclagan, pastor of a church in Scotland, asked a prominent minister to speak in his church.

The minister asked, "What shall I speak about?"

"Anything you like," replied Maclagan.

"How about my wasted years?" the minister suggested.

Afterward, Maclagan said:

"At the close of his sermon, he told his story: 'In 1955, as a young minister I heard Billy Graham preach in Glasgow and give an invitation to unsaved ones to receive Christ as Saviour. I stood up. An older minister next to me grabbed my jacket and said, "Sit down! You don't need to do that! You're making a fool of yourself!" So I sat down' "

"Then he informed the congregation," said Maclagan, "that he had wasted the next twelve years of his life. Sunday by Sunday he had proclaimed the Gospel of Christ but did not know Christ for himself. Then one night in a large tent in Keswick, England, he did what he should have done a dozen years earlier!"

Adapted from *Decision.*

* * * *

Can Ministers Help?"

Editorialized the prestigious *Times* (London):

"At best politicians and parliaments can mitigate the damage. They can't go to the root of the problem. What is inflation, after all? It's an economist's word for over-consumption, for living beyond your income, for taking more out of the kitty than you put in it.

"We have built into the structure of our society the deadly sins of pride, envy, avarice, gluttony and sloth. Capital, management, labor—all depend upon our continued addiction to levels of consumption which cannot possibly be sustained.

"Can the ministers of Christ help us with leadership, dogma and moral exhortation?" the *Times* asks. "If they cannot, or cannot be bothered, we are in a bad way indeed!"

* * * *

"Pitchforked"

In addressing a group of youthful ministers, Alexander Maclaren said, "I thank God that I was stuck down in a quiet little obscure place to begin my ministry. If you get pitchforked into prominent positions at once, you then fritter yourselves away in all manner of little engagements that you call duties. That is what spoils half of you young fellows. I thank God for my early years of struggle and obscurity."

The Apostle Paul said, "But when it pleased God. . .To reveal his Son in me. . .I conferred not with flesh and blood: Neither went I up to Jerusalem to them which were apostles before me; but I went into Arabia. . . .Then after three years I went up to Jerusalem" (Gal. 1:15-18).

* * * *

"Who Follows in His Train?"

A shining example of total dedication to God was David Brainerd, a missionary to the American Indians. John Wesley was deeply influenced by the example of Brainerd and recommended, "Let every preacher read carefully the life of David Brainerd. Let us be followers of him, as he was of Christ, in absolute self-devotion, in total deafness to the world and in fervent love to God and man."

We can say of these spiritual giants who wrought so nobly for God in the past, "[They] being dead yet speaketh" (Heb. 11:4).

* * * *

"Quick and Powerful"

A terrifying incident occurred on a Greyhound bus as it approached Daytona Beach, Florida. A passenger pointed a revolver at the driver and ordered, "Take me to Tampa or I'll shoot you!"

Ena Cuff, a member of the Baptist Church of the Good Shepherd in Miami, began preaching. Within minutes the would-be murderer dropped his gun, was subdued and was led off to jail.

Later, in commenting upon the incident, Cuff said, "The restraining and evil-defeating power of God's Word was enough to cause the gunman's hand to go limp."

"For the word of God is quick, and powerful, and sharper than any twoedged sword."—Heb. 4:12.

Adapted from *Christianity Today*.

* * * *

Envied by Angels

Alexander Whyte wrote to a discouraged Methodist pastor, "Never think of giving up preaching. The angels around the throne envy you your great work."

* * * *

Defused

Murdoch Campbell told of a devoted Scottish minister who married a shrewish, violent-tempered woman. As the minister sat one day before a glowing fire reading his Bible, she entered and angrily snatched the Bible from him and threw it into the fire!

Looking sorrowfully into her face, the minister said quietly as the flames consumed the Bible, "I never sat before a warmer fire!"

The soft answer wrought a change in her. She became a new and gracious wife.

The Bible says, "A soft answer turneth away wrath: but grievous words stir up strife" (Prov. 15:1).

* * * *

"Do You Want My Head or My Feet?"

When Alexander Maclaren was called to the pulpit of a great Baptist church in Manchester, England, he said to the deacons, "Gentlemen, there is one matter to be settled before I take this position."

"What's that?" they asked.

"Do you want my head or my feet?

You can have one or the other, not both. I can run around doing this and that and drinking tea if you wish me to, but then don't expect me to bring something in my messages that will shake this city!"

How ineffectual is the pulpit ministry of many who are jacks-of-all-trades, and spread their zeal thin over an amazing multiplicity of activities, leaving little or no time for quiet waiting before God and absorbing His Word!

* * * *

Weeping With Christ

A traveler visited the church in Scotland where Robert Murray McCheyne preached. When he preached, a spiritual force was unleashed, and thousands followed him into the kingdom of God.

An aged sexton conducted the visitor through McCheyne's church. When he led the way into McCheyne's study, the sexton said, "Sit in that chair."

The traveler hesitated for a moment, then sat down. On the desk before him was an open, tear-stained Bible.

"Drop your head on that Book and weep. That is the way our minister always did before he began to preach!"

Oh, that more of us were weeping with the Saviour over a distraught, despairing world: "And when he was come near, he beheld the city, and wept over it" (Luke 19:41).

* * * *

Loveless Defenders

G. Campbell Morgan wrote, "Although I stand uncompromisingly on the evangelical faith, I have no patience with those people whose fundamentalism consists in watching for heresy and indulging in self-satisfaction because they have an idea that they alone 'hold the truth'—hateful expression! In many ways I agree with their theological position, but I abominate their spirit."

What havoc loveless contenders of the faith can work! May we always stand solidly for "the faith which was once delivered unto the saints" (Jude 1:3), ever "speaking the truth in love" (Eph. 4:15).

Long ago, after blasting ungodly men for "turning the grace of God into lasciviousness, and denying the only Lord God, and our Lord Jesus Christ" (Jude 1:4), Jude pleaded with God's children, "Keep yourselves in the love of God" (vs. 21).

* * * *

The Inward Fire

Dr. W. A. Criswell said, "The Word must burn like fire within me. This is something God will do for a preacher. As I study the Holy Word, the message I want to deliver is born in my soul!"

How like God's ancient prophet is Dr. Criswell: "But his word was in mine heart as a burning fire shut up in my bones" (Jer. 20:9).

* * * *

The Pulpit

Alexander Maclaren said, "I began my ministry with the determination of concentrating all my available strength on the proper work of the Christian ministry—the pulpit. I believe that the secret of success for all in the ministry lies very largely in the simple concentrating of their intellectual force on the one work of preaching. I have been so convinced that I was best serving all the varied social, economic and political interests by preaching the Gospel of Jesus Christ that I have limited myself to that work."

* * * *

"Thy Servant Was Busy Here and There" (I Kings 20:40)

Vance Havner, an evangelist for more than sixty years, said, "Preachers are getting lost in a multitude of smaller duties. They are in danger of becoming so involved with secondary affairs that they lose the prophetic gift. The Devil doesn't care how great a success a preacher is in some other field, if he can kill the prophet in him."

Long ago, God's servants enunciated a principle which is greatly needed today: "It is not reason that we should leave the word of God, and serve tables. . . . we will give ourselves continually to prayer, and to the ministry of the word" (Acts 6:2,4).

* * * *

No Terminal Facilities

We have all listened to preachers who lack good terminal facilities. They come in for a landing three or four times before they crash land.

An Englishman was asked, "Why do you like your minster and speak so highly of him?" The Britisher replied, "When he says, 'In conclusion,' he doth conclude."

* * * *

"Not Back Far Enough"

A critic said to Billy Graham, "Your preaching has put Christianity back two hundred years."

Flashed Graham, "Thank God for that! But that's not back far enough. We must go back some 2,000 years to 'the faith which was once delivered unto the saints' " (Jude 1:3).

* * * *

It Must Be Natural

In his Yale Lectures, John A. Broadus said, "When humor is employed in preaching, it ought to be an incidental thing, and manifestly unplanned. It is so natural for some men to indulge in quaint and even odd sayings, that they as promptly and easily fall back into their prevailing seriousness."

During the darksome days of the Civil War, Lincoln said, "With the fearful strain that is on me day and night, if I did not laugh I would die."

* * * *

Spiritually Anemic

Dr. Charles E. Jefferson said, "A preacher who is spiritually anemic or intellectually impoverished or morally depleted, will wish often for a juniper tree."

Filled with fear and whelmed with discouragement because of the fearsome threats of Jezebel, God's erstwhile, intrepid prophet Elijah took to his heels, "and came and sat down under a juniper tree: and. . .requested for himself that he might die; and said, It is enough; now, O Lord, take away my life" (I Kings 19:4).

* * * *

"Recognize Reality of Sin"

In an interview with a reporter of the *Chicago Daily News*, Dr. Karl Menninger, renowned psychiatrist, said, "Mental health and moral health are identical. The only way our suffering, struggling, anxious society can hope to prevent mental ills is by recognizing the *reality of sin*."

"How can this be done?" asked the news correspondent.

Dr. Menninger replied:

"Preach! Tell it as it is. Say it from the pulpits. Cry it from the housetops. Our clergymen have become shaken reeds, smoking lamps, earthen vessels, spent arrows. They must be revived, for mental health includes all the healths: physical, social, cultural and moral health. If the concept of personal responsibility and answerableness for ourselves and for others were to return to common acceptance, and man once again would feel guilt for sins and repent and establish a conscience that would act as a deterrent for further sin, then hope would return to the world!"

God's ancient directive to His servants was: "Cry aloud, spare not, lift up thy voice like a trumpet, and shew my people their transgressions" (Isa. 58:1).

* * * *

"Stop Boring"

On the pulpit in the famed Pacific Garden Mission occur these words, unseen by the audience: "If you don't strike oil after five minutes, stop boring!"

Another has given this wise counsel to ministers, "Stand up; speak up; shut up!"

A friend asked Henry Ward Beecher: "What would you do if the man sitting next to you in church fell asleep?"

Beecher quipped, "I would send an usher to the pulpit to wake up the preacher!"

* * * *

Tearfully Concerned

As Robert Murray McCheyne preached in a church service, a woman slipped in and sat quickly in the back pew. She seemed to droop with discouragement. No one in the church recognized her, for she had never been there before. And no one could speak to her, for before the service was concluded, she slipped out as quickly as she had entered.

The next Sunday she returned. But what a difference! The peace of Heaven shone on her face. This time she stayed after the service. A lady put her arm around her and said, "Tell me, when were you converted?"

"Well," she replied, "last Sunday I came here to the kirk to hear the dominie. As I looked into his face, he looked like he would die if I were not converted. That's why I was converted!"

When we become tearfully and earnestly concerned about perishing ones, we'll experience the great joy of seeing them coming to the Saviour. Long ago He was moved with compassion when He saw the shepherdless multitude. He wept over perishing ones.

G. Allen Fleece.

* * * *

Success as a Preacher; Failure as a Pastor

When a poll of Philadelphia ministers was taken by Andrew Wallace, editor of religious news for the *Philadelphia Inquirer,* it revealed the tragic fact that most ministers don't visit their church members unless they are ill or in sorrow. The pastors of big congregations used the large numbers as an excuse for their failure to visit the homes of the people.

One pastor said, "If my associates and I were to make the attempt, we would have to ring 1,700 doorbells!" Other pastors attributed their failure to make pastoral calls to "the administrative load of church business."

A few admitted that they felt guilty for neglecting their people. One said, "A church may be a success in the

Lord's work with a pastor who is not a very good preacher. It will never be a success with a preacher, no matter how good, who is not also a pastor."

All pastors should emulate the example of Paul who wrought mightily and successfully for God in the long ago and said, "I kept back nothing that was profitable unto you, but have shewed you, and have taught you publickly, and from house to house" (Acts 20:20).

* * * *

GOD'S PRESENCE

A Very Absent Presence

H. G. Wells, author of science fiction, said, "God is a very absent help in time of trouble."

Myriads of God's children on either side of the River of Life know God to be "a very present help in trouble" (Ps. 46:1).

How comforting and sustaining is God's unfailing promise, "And call upon me in the day of trouble: I will deliver thee, and thou shalt glorify me" (Ps. 50:15).

Ralph M. Smith.

* * * *

Never Alone

When Dr. Ellis Fuller was President of the Southern Baptist Theological Seminary, Louisville, Kentucky, his little son had a tonsillectomy. During the daytime hours, Dr. Fuller sat by the hospital bed and held the hand of his son. When darkness began to filter into the hospital room at day's end, the boy said, "Daddy, this has been the best day of my life!"

Dr. Fuller asked, "How could that be when you've been in pain and not able to eat anything?"

The boy replied, "Because you've been here through the daytime hours, and are still with me!"

There is never a moment of the day or night when our sleepless heavenly Father is not with us: "He that keepeth thee will not slumber" (Ps. 121:3); "Lo, I am with you alway, even unto the end of the world" (Matt. 28:20).

* * * *

Never Unattended

Years ago one of God's saints, made in ebony, sat on the front porch of her ramshackle home, which was located far from the beaten path. As she rocked contentedly a minister rode up, dismounted from his horse, and asked, "Auntie, are you living here alone?"

"No, Sir. There's me and Jesus. Just me and Jesus!"

God's children are never unattended, no matter where they may be: "If I take the wings of the morning, and dwell in the uttermost parts of the sea; Even there shall thy hand lead me, and thy right hand shall hold me" (Ps. 139:9,10).

Told by Ralph M. Smith.

* * * *

Wealth Bequeathed to God

In Cherokee County, North Carolina, a well-to-do woman bequeathed her worldly goods to God. The court put out a summons; the sheriff couldn't figure how to serve it, so he reported back to the court: "After due and diligent search, God cannot be found in Cherokee County!"

No penitent seeker for God has failed to find Him.

* * * *

Jesus With Me in the Depth

As Jerrold Adams, a bombardier-navigator in the Vietnam War, returned from a mission to his airplane carrier in the South China Sea, his craft crashed, trapping him in the broken plane which fell in one hundred feet of water—about ten stories down into the green sea!

Afterward, Adams testified, "I knew that death was certain, not just a possibility. I was not alone, however; for I knew that no matter what happened in the next instant, Jesus was with me and *together* we would face death. In some instilled response to training, I got my lap and shoulder harness undone, pulled the CO_2 cartridges off my Mae West, and, agonizing for breath, shot up toward the surface.

"Later, as I lay in a hospital bed, I kept returning in thought to that long instant when I faced death without fear. There was no room for fear because Jesus, the Master of the sea, whom I confronted for the first time and recognized without any doubt, was there with me.

"For the past ten years that knowledge has become a complete and indispensable part of my life. I have gained the sure knowledge that God is real!"

* * * *

Felt God on Moon

Astronaut James Irwin said, "My trip to the moon was a spiritual awakening in which I was brought to a realization of my dependence upon God and my relationship to Jesus Christ. The only thing I was not prepared for on the moon was that I could feel God's presence closer than I had ever felt it before!"

Long ago the psalmist said, "Whither shall I flee from thy presence? If I ascend up into heaven, thou art there. . . .Even there shall thy hand lead me, and thy right hand shall hold me" (Ps. 139:7,8,10).

* * * *

NEVER UNATTENDED

I have heard much beautiful music,
Enjoyed the fragrance of flowers;
I have read and thrilled to much
  poetry,
Thus passing away the hours.
But sweeter than these enjoyments
Is a promise made by my Friend:
"Lo, I am with you alway,
Even unto the end!"

I have heard some inspiring sermons
Direct from the throne of God,
Of His love and His tender mercy,
Found in His unchanging Word.
But the message which brings me
  solace,

And strength to my spirit lends,
Is, "Lo, I am with you alway,
Even unto the end!"

I have passed through trials and
sorrows,
Known disappointment and grief;
I have felt alone and forsaken
Through hours void of relief.
But I've never failed to find comfort
In this promise of Jesus, my Friend:
"Lo, I am with you alway,
Even unto the end!"

Elizabeth Kieke, a blind poet.

* * * *

Not Found Through a Telescope

Said Wernher von Braun, father of
the U. S. space and rocket program,
"It is futile to look for God through a
telescope. You find God in your soul,
your faith and convictions. God is
right in us, all-embracing and all-
present. The evidence of a Creator is
overwhelming to me. I can't envision
this whole universe to come into being without a divine will. I can't envision the creation without a Creator."

The Bible says, "In him [God] we
live, and move, and have our being"
(Acts 17:28). None ever sought God
penitently and failed to find Him:
"And ye shall seek me, and find me,
when ye shall search for me with all
your heart" (Jer. 29:13).

* * * *

"Heaven of Heavens Cannot Contain Him" (II Chron. 2:6).

A scoffing unbeliever had satanic
delight in ridiculing the Bible and
speaking scornfully of those who
believed in God.

One Lord's Day morning he asked a
lad, "Where have you been, my boy?"

"I've been to Sunday school, sir, to
learn about God."

In his effort to undermine the boy's
faith, the unbeliever said, "I'll give
you an orange if you will tell me
where God is."

Thoughtfully the boy replied, "I'll
give you two oranges if you will tell
me where God isn't!"

Alice M. Knight.

* * * *

One and God

A contemporary of Luther said,
"Luther, the whole world is against
you!" The intrepid Reformer replied,
"Then it is God and Luther against
the whole world!"

One and God constitute a majority!

* * * *

Loneliness

The depressing problem of
loneliness has ever existed. Long ago
the psalmist lamented, "I am like a
pelican of the wilderness: I am like an
owl of the desert. I watch, and am as a
sparrow alone upon the house top"
(Ps. 102:6,7).

The sure remedy for loneliness is to
practice the presence of God's
sustaining presence with us in the
night of sorrow and suffering, storm
and stress: "For he [God] hath said, I
will never leave thee, nor forsake
thee. So that we may boldly say, The
Lord is my helper" (Heb. 13:5,6).

I've seen the lightning flashing,
And heard the thunder roll,
I've felt sin's breakers dashing,
Trying to conquer my soul;
I've heard the voice of Jesus,
Telling me still to fight on,
He promised never to leave me,
Never to leave me alone.

Anon.

* * * *

THE AGELONG MINUTE

Thou art the Lord who slept upon a
    pillow,
Thou art the Lord who soothed the
    furious sea;
What matter beating wind and toss-
    ing billow,
If only we are in the boat with
    Thee?

Hold us in quiet through the agelong
    minute,
While Thou art silent, and the
    wind is shrill;
Can the boat sink while Thou, dear
    Lord, art in it?
Can the heart faint that waiteth on
    Thy will?

Amy Carmichael.

* * * *

Closer Than Breathing

Tennyson said:

Speak to Him, thou, for He hears, and Spirit
    with Spirit can meet—
Closer is He than breathing, and nearer
    than hands and feet!

Long ago God gave this promise to
Moses: "My presence shall go with
thee, and I will give thee rest" (Exod.
33:14).

The Saviour gave this promise to
all the children of God: "Lo, I am
with you alway, even unto the end of
the world" (Matt. 28:20).

* * * *

GOD WAS IRONING TOO

Today I did my ironing,
    The stacks were piled real high,
Somehow it seemed no chore at all,
    For God was standing by!

I talked with Him and He with me,
    My iron just fairly flew,
Before I knew it, I looked up,
    The stacks were almost through!

And as I ironed my clothes with love,
    God's love did me enfold;
I knew that God was ironing too
    The wrinkles from my soul!

Varina C. McWhorter,
in *Home Life.*

* * * *

The Everywhereness of God

Astronaut James Irwin was asked if
he felt God was closer on the moon
than elsewhere. He replied, "No. You
can feel as close to God as you like,
whether at home, work, church or on
the moon. I did, however, reaffirm
His existence in my mind; because
when looking back at the earth, I
found it to be too beautiful, too
perfect and too logical to have happened by accident!"

"For he [God] *spake, and it was
done; he commanded, and it stood
fast."*—Ps. 33:9.

* * * *

PRIDE

(See also Humility)

Spiritual Pride

A self-deceived woman boastfully said to H. A. Ironside, "I haven't sinned in over seventeen years!"

Dr. Ironside replied, "That is a truly remarkable record, Madam. I suppose you are very proud of it!"

The woman beamingly replied, "Oh, yes, I am!"

How blinding is spiritual pride to one's true condition! Long ago some self-congratulatory ones said, "[We are] rich, and increased with goods, and have need of nothing" (Rev. 3:17).

The Bible speaks warningly of those who are "lifted up with pride [and] fall into the condemnation of the devil" (I Tim. 3:6).

* * * *

The Right People to Pluck

In addressing a student body, a proud businessman said, "I give all the credit for my financial and business success to one thing alone—pluck, pluck, pluck."

What little impression he had made was dissipated when a student unexpectedly asked, "How can we find the right people to pluck?"

It is hazardous to ascribe glory to ourselves for accomplishments: "If ye will not. . .give glory to my name. . .I will curse your blessings" (Mal. 2:2).

* * * *

Darkness

"Sometime ago I engaged an atheist in conversation," said Billy Graham.

"I asked, 'What do you have to look forward to?'

"He replied, 'Nothing. Life has been miserable for me!'

"I said, 'Why don't you give up your atheism and turn to God?'

"He said, 'My pride won't let me!' "

The Bible says, "The wicked, through the pride of his countenance, will not seek after God: God is not in all his thoughts" (Ps. 10:4).

* * * *

When We Stand Tall

Gert Behanna said, "I used to look down my nose at people. Now I look down my nose at people who look down their noses at people. I used to be proud of my sins. Now I'm proud that I am no longer proud of my sins."

The descendants of the arrogant, self-righteous Pharisee are still saying: "God, I thank thee, that I am not as other men are" (Luke 18;11).

No man ever stands so tall in God's sight as when he kneels and penitently pleads: "God be merciful to me a sinner" (Luke 18:13).

* * * *

Not Indispensable

"A man doesn't begin to attain wisdom until he recognizes that he is not indispensable," said Rear Admiral Richard E. Byrd, polar explorer.

"Be not wise in your own conceits."—Rom. 12:16.

* * * *

In Matters Controversial

Ralph McGill, longtime columnist for *The Atlanta Constitution,* wrote this of himself:

In matters controversial,
My prescription's very fine,
I always see both sides of things,
The one that's wrong and *mine*.

* * * *

Where's Your Pride?

Sunday's breakfast was over. One stood and said, "I'm going to church this morning."

"What?" exclaimed the other members of the family. "Are you going back there after the way our family has been treated? Where's your pride?"

Quietly she replied, "Today is Communion Sunday. I am going to be the Lord's guest at His Table and remember His death for me and His promise to come again. As for my pride, I say with Isaac Watts:

When I survey the wondrous cross,
On which the Prince of Glory died,
My richest gain I count but loss,
And pour contempt on all my pride."

F. G. Kee.

* * * *

Wanted: 3,000 Frogs

A want ad appeared in a newspaper which read: **Wanted: 3,000 frogs.**

A farmer, on whose land was a millpond, replied to the ad: **"Come with a truck. You'll need it. My pond is teeming with frogs!"**

How disappointed were the buyer and the farmer when, after diligent effort, they caught only three frogs!

Looking dejectedly at their catch, the farmer said, "From the noise they made, you'd have thought there were thousands of frogs in that pond."

Much bombastic boastfulness comes from the proud and arrogant ones: "Is not this great Babylon, that I have built. . .by the might of my power, and for the honour of my majesty?" (Dan. 4:30).

How different it is with truly great ones who say what John once said of Christ and of himself: "He it is, who coming after me is preferred before me, whose shoe's latchet I am not worthy to unloose" (John 1:27).

Truly big things in God's creation are silent:

With the coming of spring, life-giving sap rises noiselessly in the barren trees.

Refreshing dews fall silently on the grass.

With the coming of the new day, the sun rises noiselessly, bringing light and warmth to the awakening earth.

The voice of the indwelling Holy Spirit is "a still small voice."

"In quietness and in confidence shall be your strength."—Isa. 30:15.

* * * *

PRINTED PAGE

PRINTED PAGE

Tracked Everywhere

A Christian gave a tract to an aged black man who worked for him. Later he asked, "How did you like the tract?"

The black man replied, "It did my soul good! I never knew before why they are called tracks. Now I know. I read it and it tracked me this way and that way. When I went to the barn, it tracked me there. When I returned to the house, it tracked me there. It tracks me everywhere I go!"

Only Heaven will reveal the number of those won to the Saviour by Bible-centered, Christ-exalting tracts.

Told by Alice M. Knight.

* * * *

"The Lord Gave the Word: Great Was the Company of Those That Published it" (Ps. 68:11).

A recent AP dispatch said, "While religious periodicals generally are in a slump, the personally oriented, evangelistic magazines are thriving as never before.

"They are riding a groundswell of conservative religious feeling in this country," said Norm Rohrer, of LaCanada, California, executive secretary of the *Evangelistic Press Association.*

Dean Merrill, senior editor of *Campus Life,* said, "For too long we've pretended religion was in a separate league with no one else around, and that people would be interested whether or not we looked

good or read good. Baloney! Religion has no captive audience. Unless we've got a product that grabs interest, we're wasting our time."

"It's the conservative, evangelical publications that are going strong and whose sales are gaining," said Leslie H. Stobbe, former editor of *Moody Monthly.* "People are fed up with uncertainty," he continued. "They want publications that say, 'Thus saith the Lord,' and conservatives are saying it."

"There's real heart hunger among people for spiritual food, and we are giving them that," said Sherwood Writ, editor of *Decision Magazine,* whose circulation is 4.55 million and keeps growing. "It's a matter of supply and demand. Church publications which are losing readers are those that try to push off what they think people ought to have rather than giving them what they need. We feel that every person's heart hungers for a sense of God's power, something beyond himself, and we try to show people how that power works and what Scripture teaches is available to everyone," concluded Writ.

* * * *

Greatest Impact: Gospel Literature

Some four hundred years ago Martin Luther said, "We must throw the printers' inkpot at the Devil."

Over forty years ago Leon Trotsky said, "The most powerful means of propagating communism is the small pocket pamphlet."

Dr. Guy Playfair, director of the Sudan Interior Mission, affirmed, "I believe our gospel literature is having a greater impact for Christ in Africa than the coming of 5,000 missionaries."

A missionary in Latin America said, "In recent months I have been astonished to find that ninety percent of all converts in Latin America are either directly or indirectly the result of literature evangelism."

* * * *

A Drum of Printer's Ink

When the bombs were falling on London in World War II, an explosion hurled a drum of printer's ink upon the roof of a red-brick Queen Anne House in Gough Square. The drum of ink was a perfect missile to hit that house because, years before, its master had been Dr. Samuel Johnson, the writer, critic, and editor of the famous *Dictionary* published in 1755.

Printer's ink and the worldwide preaching of the Gospel must go hand-in-hand. Often the printed page can go where the missionary is persona non grata.

* * * *

PROPHECY
(See also Second Coming of Christ

The Rise and Fall of Hitler's Mustache

"I am not an expert in prophecy," said Vance Havner, "but I am not looking for the kingdom without the King. Some make a hobby of prophecy and are so occupied with Christ's coming they are not occupying till He comes. Some are studying the meaning of the fourth toe of the right foot of some beast in prophecy and are failing to use either foot to go and bring perishing ones to Christ. I could lecture on 'The Rise and Fall of Hitler's Mustache' and get a crowd. But if I spoke on 'Obedience,' I couldn't get some people to church with a rope and tackle.

"I do not know who the 666 in Revelation are, but *I know this world is sick, sick, sick,* and the best way to hasten the Lord's return is to win more souls for Him."

In this dispensation of grace, "God. . .[is visiting] the Gentiles, to take out of them a people for his name. And to this agree the. . . prophets; as it is written, After this I will return" (Acts 15:14-16).

* * * *

"Later Than It Has Ever Been!"

Little Johnny delighted to hear and count the chiming of the hour by the large grandfather clock. At noon one day he lay on the floor counting each gong as it sounded. This time something was wrong with the clock's mechanism. Instead of stopping at 12, it kept right on chiming. Johnny leaped to his feet and ran into the kitchen shouting, "Mommy, Mommy, it's later than it has ever been before!"

Dispensationally it is later than it has ever been before: "Little children, it is the last time" (I John 2:18); "The night is far spent, the day is at hand: let us...cast off the works of darkness, and let us put on the armour of light" (Rom. 13:12).

"The coming of the Lord draweth nigh."—Jas. 5:8.

Alice Marie Knight.

* * * *

"Nine Minutes to Midnight!"

Men of science are often more discerning of the times than those who reject "the sure word of prophecy" in the Bible. It foretells cataclysmic judgments coming upon our sin-sick, Christ-rejecting world.

Recently in Chicago a group of nuclear scientists pushed the hands of a symbolic doomsday clock three minutes closer to midnight, the hour of atomic holocaust. In advancing the hand nine minutes to midnight, the fifteen scientists warned that the international nuclear arms race is now, more than ever, beyond control. They said, "In recognition that our hopes for an awakening of sanity were misplaced and that the danger of nuclear doomsday is measurably greater today than it was in 1972, we now move the clock forward to nine minutes to midnight!"

Long ago the Saviour prophetically spoke of a significant midnight event: "And at midnight there was a cry made, Behold, the bridegroom cometh" (Matt. 25:6).

Can it be said of us what was said of some of God's children in Old Testament times: "And the children of Issachar...had understanding of the times, to know what Israel ought to do" (I Chron. 12:32)?

What God's children today ought to do is clearly revealed in His Word: "Be ye also ready: for in such an hour as ye think not the Son of man cometh" (Matt. 24:44).

Adapted from
The American-Statesman.

* * * *

"Weather Warfare"

In October, 1974, Soviet Ambassador Malik introduced a resolution in the United Nations General Assembly's main political committee which warned against "weather warfare."

The resolution said:

"Scientists have concluded that weather warriors might create 'windows' in the ozone layer of the upper atmosphere, letting deadly ultraviolet rays through to selected parts of the planet, set off a nuclear explosion inside the Arctic and Antarctic ice caps and produce an iceslide that would cause tidal waves capable of wiping whole areas from the face of the globe, and stimulate tidal waves by dumping voluminous blocks of bedrock from the continental shelf into deeper parts of the ocean!"

"Cynics may say," continued the resolution, "that these are fancies of Jules Verne, but researchers reliably prove that there is no guarantee against these possibilities becoming a reality to the detriment of man!"

Such cosmic horrors read like those depicted in the Book of Revelation. To have warned of "weather warfare" a century ago would have elicited scorn and ridicule, and be branded as vagaries of a sick mind.

* * * *

Our Problem Is Religious

In a White House Conference on Industry, Dr. Herman Kahn told 1,500 top corporation executives that the world is heading for glorious times if we can get through some "excruciatingly horrible times which lie ahead."

According to *The Washington Post*, Dr. Kahn affirmed, "The biggest single problem facing us is religious—the meaning and purpose of life. Why do we stay alive? What are we here for? My grandfather walked with God, and he knew why we are here, but we don't!"

Scripturally speaking, before the "glorious times" of the millennium come, "excruciatingly horrible" times will indeed come: "For then shall be great tribulation, such as was not since the beginning of the world to this time, no, nor ever shall be. And except those days should be shortened, there should no flesh be saved: but for the elect's sake those days shall be shortened" (Matt. 24:21,22).

How we thank God for the "sure word of prophecy"—God's blueprint for coming events! It is "a light that shineth in a dark place, until the day dawn" (II Pet. 1:19).

"Look up, and lift up your heads," children of God, "for yor redemption draweth nigh" (Luke 21:28). Hallelujah!

* * * *

Time Is Running Out

The Club of Rome is composed of influential industrialists, scientists and economists. They have been called both "prophets of doom" and the "conscience of mankind." The club takes no political sides, but simply presents situations with which mankind is grappling.

When Aurello Peccei, president of the illustrious group, was asked, "How much time has mankind to reorient itself?" he replied, "Maybe we have ten or twenty years to right ourselves. After that, it will be too late! When the collapse comes, it will be sudden!"

Long ago God averted the destruction of the sin-sodden city of Nineveh because the Ninevites repented and turned to Him. He still calls individuals and nations to repentance. He pleads, "Be zealous. . .and repent" (Rev. 3:19).

"Except ye repent, ye shall all likewise perish."—Luke 13:3.

How long may men go on in sin?
How long will God forbear?
Where does hope end, and where begins
The borderline of despair?

One answer from those skies is sent,
Ye who from God depart:
"Repent while it is called today,
And harden not your hearts!"

* * * *

RESURRECTION

(See also Death)

Identified

An editorial in the *Christian Herald* said:

"The very heart of the Christian faith rests on the belief that individuals are what count. If we were to have mere immortality, in the sense that each spirit is reunited with a general spirit, thus losing its identity like a drop of water when it flows back into the ocean, this would not represent the saving of what is most precious to us and God.

"Jesus counts each one of us as most important and of greatest value: 'For what is a man profited, if he shall gain the whole world, and lose his own soul?' " (Matt. 16:25).

* * * *

They Did Take Him Down!

Rubens' famous painting, *Descent From the Cross,* is in a cathedral at Antwerp, Belgium. One afternoon a visitor stood for a long time, looking intently at the picture. Absorbed in the scene of the Saviour's death on the cross, he was unaware of the time of day, until the caretaker said, "It's time to close the cathedral!"

"No, no, not yet! Wait until they get Him down!"

Loving hands did get Him down and place His limp, lifeless body in a tomb. There it lay for three days. Then an angelic being proclaimed the gladsome news: "He is not here: for he is risen as he said!"

Because he lives I can face tomorrow,
Because He lives all fear is gone,
Because I know He holds the future,
And life is worth the living,
Just because He lives!
                    Gloria & Wm. Gaither

* * * *

"We Shall Meet in the Morning!"

When F. B. Meyer was informed that he had but a few hours to live, he wrote: "To my surprise, I have just been told that my days and hours are numbered! It may be that before this letter reaches you, I shall have gone into the presence of the King! Don't trouble to write. We shall meet in the morning. With much love, Yours affectionately!"

"The righteous hath hope in his death."—Prov. 14:32.

* * * *

Proved

Thomas Arnold, professor of history at Oxford University, and author of a famous three-volume *History of Rome,* wrote, "I have been used for many years to study the history of other times, and examine the evidence of those who have written about them, and I know of no one fact in the history of mankind which has been proved by better evidence of every sort, to the understanding of the fair inquirer, than the great sign which God has given us that Christ died and rose again from the dead!"

The Presbyterian Journal.

* * *

The Motivating Force

Nehru, India's first prime minister, said, "In thousands of years, the religions of India have never motivated anyone to plow a field, build a house, drain a swamp, or dam a stream. But let us not deny the church its due. It has helped lift people's burdens in every part of the world. The motivating force has been the resurrection of Jesus Christ!"

* * * *

THAT DAYBREAK HOUR

O the joy of that daybreak hour,
O the raptures of the Saviour's power,
O life that broke but did not bend,
O grave that burst from end to end!

* * * *

"Your Boy Is Alive!"

At the death of his son Willie, Lincoln was convulsed in sorrow. In an effort to console him, Dr. Francis Vinton said, "Your boy is alive in Heaven!"

"Alive! Surely you mock me!"

"No," said the minister. "It is a most comforting doctrine of the church and founded upon the words of Christ Himself."

For a moment the President repeated incredulously, "Alive! Alive!" Then his sorrow abated.

Globe-girdling joy will come when the following prophecies are fulfilled and death is vanquished: "He will swallow up death in victory; and the Lord God will wipe away tears from off all faces" (Isa. 25:8). Then "sorrow and sighing shall flee away" (35:10).

* * * *

IF

If the Christ of the cross had
  stopped at the cross,
His work had been incomplete;
If the Christ of the tomb had
  stayed in the tomb,
He had only known defeat.
But the path to the cross never
  ends at the cross,
And the way to the tomb leads on,
By victorious grace to the heavenly
  place,
Where the risen Christ has gone!

Annie Johnson Flint.

* * * *

WELCOME, HAPPY MORNING!

"Welcome, happy morning!"
  age to age shall say:
"Hell today is vanquished, Heaven
  is won today!"
Lo! the dead is living, God forevermore,
Him, their true Creator, all His
  works adore!

Earth her joy confesses, clothing
  her for spring,
All fresh gifts returned with her
  returning King,
Bloom in every meadow, leaves on
  every bough,
Speak His sorrow ended, hail His
  triumph now!

Venantius Fortunatus.

* * * *

They Actually Believed

Simon Greenleaf, the famed American jurist, affirmed in *A Treatise on the Law of Evidence,* "It is impossible that the disciples could have persisted in affirming the truth of the resurrection had not Jesus actually risen from the dead."

"He shewed himself alive. . .by many infallible proofs, being seen of them [the apostles] *forty days."*— Acts 1:3.

* * * *

A Day of Victory

"If Sunday is to be a day of Christian victory, each believer must start with his own heart," said Warren W. Wiersbe in *Moody Monthly.* "The pastor must decide whether or not his ministry reflects the life of a victorious, risen Lord. Is there anything exciting about his life and his preaching? As he walks with the Lord through the highways of His Word, does he find his heart burning within him? As he goes from house to house during the week, does he share the radiance of the risen Lord?"

"Did not our heart burn within us, while he talked with us by the way, and while he opened to us the scriptures?"—Luke 24:32.

* * * *

Futility and Emptiness

Christianity Today commented that the Epicurean indifference to the afterlife is reflected in such epitaphs as: *Non fui, fui, non sum, no curo:* "I was not, I was, I am not, I do not care," and *Es, bibe, lude, veni:* "Eat, drink, play, come hither."

It was this philosophy of futility and emptiness Paul had in mind when he wrote: "If the dead rise not? let us eat and drink: for to morrow we die" (I Cor. 15:32).

* * * *

A Cloudless Morning

Peter Marshall, former Chaplain of the U. S. Senate, had a massive heart attack. As he was placed in an ambulance, he waved to his wife and said, "I'll see you in the morning!" He didn't mean the dawn of a new day, for he seemed to know he wouldn't survive his heart seizure. Friends believed he meant he would see his wife on the resurrection morning!

A glorious reunion with loved ones awaits God's children:

On that bright and cloudless morning when the dead in Christ shall rise,
And the glory of His resurrection share;
When His chosen ones shall gather to their home beyond the skies,
And the roll is called up yonder, I'll be there.
James M. Black.

* * * *

"Do You Really Know It?"

Reichel was conducting the final rehearsal before the performance of Handel's *Messiah.* The great choir and guest soloists sang through to the point where the soprano began: "I know that my Redeemer liveth!" Her technique was perfect, her breathing faultless, her note placement and enunciation accurate.

Upon the completion of the solo, all eyes turned toward Reichel to see his approval. Instead, he silenced the orchestra, approached the soloist with sorrowful eyes and asked, "My daughter, do you *really know* that your Redeemer liveth? Do you?"

Falteringly she said, "Why, yes, I think I do."

The master said, "Then sing it! Tell all who hear you that *you know* the joy and power of Christ's resurrection!" Then he motioned for the orchestra to play again.

This time the soloist sang the truth as she knew it and had *experienced* it in her soul.

With tear-dimmed eyes, the old master approached her and said, *"You do know, for you have told me!"*

* * * *

The Glorious Awakening

How enchanting and awe-inspiring is springtime! Then nature awakens from its wintry sleep, thaws its frozen assets, and regales the hills, valleys, woodlands and meadows in garments of dazzling and ineffable beauty!

Long ago an inspired Solomon joyously depicted the arrival of springtime: "For, lo, the winter is past, the rain is over and gone; The flowers appear on the earth; the time of the singing of birds is come, and the voice of the turtle is heard in our land" (Song of Sol. 2:11,12).

* * * *

Death-Defiant Words

Around the world at springtime,

God's children joyfully commemorate the Saviour's triumph over death! How thrilling are His death-defying, hope-bringing words: "I am he that liveth, and was dead; and, behold, I am alive for evermore" (Rev. 1:18). Because He lives, God's children will live eternally with Him in Glory: "I go to prepare a place for you. . . .that where I am, there ye may be also" (John 14:2,3).

How descriptive of springtime's life-awakening glory is this poetic overture:

Springtime in her royal garments
  Spread new beauty on the hills;
I can hear her softly singing
  In the valley and the rills!

I can see her fingers moving
  Through the freshly-leafing trees,
Sending forth her warm caresses
  On the flower-scented breeze!

I can see her shuttles flying
  Through the fields of golden grain,
Giving credence to the story:
  Though men die, they'll live again!

Alice Whitson Norton.

* * * *

"Strangely Warmed"

During World War I a staff officer attended an Easter service in Arabia, in a YMCA building. Afterward he testified, "I don't remember the name of the chaplain, nor what he said, but when we sang the triumphant Easter hymn, *'Christ the Lord Is Risen Today,'* the Saviour's presence became a *fact* and His forgiving love became *real* to me! I felt what John Wesley felt in the little room on Aldersgate Street in London, when his heart was 'strangely warmed!' "

"Did not our heart burn within us, while he talked with us by the way, and while he opened to us the scriptures?" (Luke 24:32).

* * * *

Only a Corpse

In refuting the falacious report of Jesus' enemies that His disciples stole His body and that He was not resurrected, Dr. Clarence Edward McCartney said:

"Suppose the disciples had been able to steal away the body. They would have had a corpse, a dead body, on their hands. Can you imagine that that dead body could have inspired them to go forth and preach their wonderful words and live their heroic lives, or that in behalf of a dead body they would willingly embrace the most cruel persecution and the most shameful death, as many of them did?"

How thrilling are the triumphant words of the risen Lord: "I am he that liveth, and was dead; and, behold, I am alive for evermore." (Rev. 1:18).

* * * *

REVIVAL

What Jesus Promised

David Haney said in *Renew My Church:* "Jesus promised those who would follow Him these three things: they would be absurdly happy, 'These things have I spoken unto you, that my joy might remain in you, and that your joy might be full' (John 15:11); entirely fearless, 'Fear not, little flock; for it is your Father's good pleasure to give you the kingdom' (Luke 12:32); and always in trouble, 'In the world ye shall have tribulation' (John 16:33)."

Wherever the Saviour's followers went, one of two things usually happened: a revival or a revolution, "And many that believed came, and confessed, and shewed their deeds. Many. . .which used curious arts brought their books. . .and burned them before all men. . . .So mightily grew the word of God and prevailed" (Acts 19:18-20); "These that have turned the world upside down are come hither also" (17:6).

* * * *

In Middle of a Circle

A pastor once asked Gypsy Smith how to start a revival. Smith replied, "Go home, lock yourself in your room, kneel down in the middle of the floor, draw a chalk circle around yourself, and ask God to start a revival inside the circle. When He has answered your prayer, the revival will be on!"

* * * *

Wasted Time

James Orr, who has studied in depth the history of revivals, said, "If half the time spent in committee meetings, organizational efforts and the like was spent in earnest prayer to God to 'revive thy work, O Lord,' God would send a true revival to our land."

L. Roy Taylor, a Presbyterian minister, also recognizes the fact that true revival must come from God when he pleaded, "Oh, that evangelical Christians would truly believe that revival does not result from Madison Avenue advertising techniques or from the mere testimony of beauty queens or the testimony of athletes with bulging muscles!"

We do not speak disparagingly of the genuine testimony of anyone who has experienced the heart-transforming grace of God if it will send us to our knees and cause us to penitently say with the psalmist of old, "For thou desirest not sacrifice; else would I give it: thou delightest not in burnt-offering. The sacrifices of God are a broken spirit; a broken and a contrite heart, O God, thou wilt not despise" (Ps. 51:16,17).

* * * *

Needed: A Bath

"I don't believe in revivals. They don't last," said a critic to Billy Graham.

Graham quipped, "Neither does a bath, but we need one frequently."

Churches would be revived if even an appreciable number of God's children would penitently plead: "Create in me a clean heart, O God; and renew a right spirit within me" (Ps. 51:10).

* * * *

Evidence of Conversion

About halfway through a nine-day Dayton, Ohio, revival meeting, conducted by Texas evangelist James Robison, a man came to the home of a local housewife and said: "Lady, you don't know me, but last summer I stole your lawn furniture. I was saved the other night at the Robison revival and I have brought it back. I want you to know I am sorry for what I did."

In speaking of the incident later, the housewife said, "I believe in revivals that do things like that to people." So do we.

A sure evidence of conversion is a ready willingness to make amends for past wrongs: "Behold, Lord. . .if I have taken any thing from any man by false accusation, I restore him fourfold" (Luke 19:8).

* * * *

"The Hope of the World"

Charles G. Finney said, "I beseech my brethren in the name of our Lord Jesus Christ to keep as far as possible from the appearance or the thought of discountenancing or looking coldly on revival efforts. They are our life. They are the salvation of the church. They are the hope of the world."

"Wilt thou not revive us again: that thy people may rejoice in thee?"—Ps. 85:6.

* * * *

Our Mission

Some time ago Wales planned to launch a large-scale evangelistic campaign called "Wales for Christ." It would have been more scripturally accurate to designate the evangelistic effort "Christ for Wales."

Christians are not commanded to win the world for Christ, but to take Christ to the world: "And this gospel of the kingdom shall be preached in all the world for a witness unto all nations" (Matt. 24:14).

* * * *

"Who Weeps Any More?"

Evangelist Ravenhill said, "The last revival mentioned in the Old Testament is recorded in the Book of Joel who said, 'Let the priests, the ministers of the Lord, weep between the porch and the altar, and let them say, Spare thy people, O Lord' (Joel 2:17).

"Well, let us face it! Who weeps anymore? We make a mistake in placing the burden for revival on the *pew*. God puts it on the *pulpit*. We need preachers eternity-conscious. I yearn to hear a voice that declares God's judgment on the godlessness so overwhelmingly existent around us. Many sermons have become religious entertainment and move no one to tears of repentance."

Wanted: Fewer sermons which cause us to stand and applaud and more sermons which will cause us to kneel and weep!

A plea: "O Lord, revive thy work in the midst of the years. . .in wrath remember mercy" (Hab. 3:2).

Adapted from *Decision.*

* * *

An Unfailing Receipt

R. A. Torrey gave this receipt for a spiritual awakening among God's children:

"First, let a few Christians get thoroughly right with God.

"Second, let them bind themselves together to pray for revival until God opens the windows of Heaven and it comes down.

"Third, let them put themselves at the disposal of God for His use, as He sees fit, in winning others to Christ. That is all.

"I have given this prescription around the world. In no instance has it failed. *It cannot fail.*"

"He that winneth souls is wise."— Prov. 11:30.

* * * *

Why There Was Failure

Said John W. Claypool, "Years ago I preached in a revival meeting in the south. I expended extraordinarily large amounts of energy proclaiming the Gospel. Yet, at the end of eight days, very little impact had been made on the community.

"I learned the cause for the failure from the frustrated pastor who told me of a split between two prominent families of the church which he was unable to heal. Both families attended church for years but refused to speak to each other."

* * * *

Why Not?

H. A. Ironside said:
"I have been surprised at the

number of people who have asked me: 'Have we any right to expect revival before the second coming of the Lord?' I cannot understand a question like that. Is there anything in the Word that intimates that there will not be a revival before the second coming of Christ, or whenever believers plead: 'Let us search and try our ways, and turn again to the Lord' (Lam. 3:40)?

"Will it ever be wrong dispensationally to pray, 'Wilt thou not revive us again: that thy people may rejoice in thee?' (Ps. 85:6). Though Habakkuk foretold the coming destruction of Jerusalem, he prayed, 'O Lord, revive thy work in the midst of the years, in the midst of the years make known; in wrath remember mercy' (Hab. 3:2).

"Some say to me, 'The days are getting so dark and apostasy is spreading over the church, we cannot expect revival and we cannot expect blessing.' We are limiting the Holy One of Israel when we say these things!"

* * * *

Purpose of Revival

"God sends revival for one of two reasons," said V. Raymond Edman, former President of Wheaton College. "The first one is that judgment might be averted: 'For if we would judge ourselves, we should not be judged' (I Cor. 11:31); 'And God saw their works, that they turned from their evil way; and God repented of the evil, that he had said that he would do unto them; and he did it not.

"The second reason is that God's people might be prepared for what they have to go through. On the eve of their being carried away into Babylonian captivity, Habakkuk pleaded, 'O Lord, revive thy work in the midst of the years. . .in wrath remember mercy' " (Hab. 3:2).

* * * *

RICHES
(See also Giving)

The Blinding Dollar Mark

A wealthy industrialist from America visited a medical missionary in Africa. From early morning he shadowed the missionary as he treated a seemingly endless number of sick ones.

The industrialist was greatly impressed as the doctor performed an intricate and serious operation, after which the American visitor asked, "What would be your fee if you had performed the same operation in America?"

Thoughtfully the missionary replied, "From $2,000 to $3,000."

"What did you receive from the operation you just performed?"

The medical missionary replied, "Not one penny. My 'pay' is to do God's will and be in the place where He wants me to be!"

The industrialist mused, *What a*

*forfeiture of the opportunity to win
fame and amass riches in America!*

* * * *

Filthy Lucre

The term "filthy lucre" has not
been used for money since ancient
times: "A bishop then must. . .not
[be] greedy of filthy lucre" (I Tim.
3:2,3); "Feed the flock of God. . .not
for filthy lucre, but of a ready mind"
(I Pet. 5:2).

The handling of filthy lucre may
jeopardize one's physical health. Drs.
Berel L. Abrams and Norton G.
Waterman of the University of
Louisville cultured a random sam-
pling of coins and paper money and
found six different kinds of potential
disease producers. They said, "A
significant number of coins and a
greater amount of paper money were
shown to be carrying potential
pathogens (disease producers)."

The Bible says that acquisition and
hoarding of "filthy lucre" is productive of great sorrow: "Which while
some coveted after. . .have erred from
the faith, and pierced themselves
through with many sorrows" (I Tim.
6:10).

Heed the warning: "If riches increase, set not your heart upon them"
(Ps. 62:10).

Hold your dollars in trust for God.

* * * *

"It's a Disgrace"

Andrew Carnegie, a multimillionaire, believed that it was a disgrace to die wealthy.

In death, all material things are left
behind: "For we brought nothing into
this world, and it is certain we can
carry nothing out" (I Tim. 6:7).

How wise we are to hold our dollars
in trust for God and use them to bring
spiritual life to others and alleviate
human hunger and need.

* * * *

"$15 Billion Up for Grabs!"

At this very moment there is more
than $15 billion lying in the vaults of
banks, insurance companies,
brokerage houses and department
stores—*unclaimed.* About $1 billion
is yearly abandoned. It is accelerating
with the velocity of the economy—
money in the form of bank accounts,
stock certificates, insurance policies,
dividends, checks, gift certificates,"
said Lynn Brenner of the Knight
News Service.

There are inestimable spiritual
riches which many of God's children
fail to claim, with resultant spiritual
impoverishment. Some are spiritual
paupers when they could have
spiritual riches untold by simply asking for them: "No good thing will he
withhold from them that walk uprightly" (Ps. 84:11).

* * * *

"The Devil Has Had It Long Enough!"

The Christian Broadcasting
Network of Virginia Beach, Virginia,
decided to keep a $15,000 gift which
was the proceeds of a winning ticket
in the New York state lottery.

The network president, M. G. Robertson, said that he opposes gambling but justified himself in keeping the gift by quoting Dwight L. Moody who said, "It doesn't matter where it (money) comes from. It used to belong to the Devil, and he has had it long enough."

The Presbyterian Journal.

* * * *

Our Rich Father

On a recent air flight I sat beside a stranger. It was evident that he was a man of affluence. Immediately we became engaged in conversation. He alluded to his material wealth and prosperous business, then said, "Tell me something about yourself."

I began, "I have a fabulously wealthy Father. Fact is, He owns this airline and all other airlines!"

"Indeed!" exclaimed the stranger amusedly and incredulously!

"What's more," I said, "the wealth of the world belongs to Him! Through his Son, the Lord Jesus Christ, I am an heir of God and a joint-heir with Him."

It began to dawn upon the stranger that I was speaking of spiritual riches which he knew little or nothing about. As I commended my Saviour to him, he said, "I have never had anyone speak so surely and convincingly to me about spiritual riches which one receives by simple faith in Christ!"

As we deplaned, I felt that he was thinking deeply about the Saviour.

How rich are God's children in imperishable riches!

Joyfully they sing:

I'm a child of the King,
A child of the King:
With Jesus my Saviour
I'm a child of the King!

Hattie E. Buell.

Ralph M. Smith.

* * * *

"Garbage Mary"

The woman was known to her neighbors as "Garbage Mary" because she dressed in rags and lived in a smelly apartment amid mounds of garbage. Much of her time was spent rummaging through garbage cans. They had no thought she was a millionaire!

Seeking information about her financial condition, the police questioned her after she was seen sifting through one garbage can in a shopping center. They were amazed to find in her apartment Mobile Oil stock certificates worth $400,000, several small stock dividend checks, documents indicating ownership of oil fields in Kansas, stock certificates from U. S. Steel, UniRoyal aand Squibb, and eight hefty bank accounts.

Her refrigerator, stove, sink, cabinets and bathtub were stuffed with garbage—worthless things.

Garbage Mary was adjudged mentally sick. Was her mental sickness progressively brought on by her insatiable desire to accumulate riches?

We know that the quest for riches and material things can so obsess us that we miss the joy of living and the finer, enduring blessing of life. How wise are those who love God and share themselves and their material possessions with others!

The Saviour said, "A man's life consisteth not in the abundance of the things which he possesseth" (Luke 12:15).

* * * *

Giving All to God

After George W. Truett preached a sermon in which he emphasized the blessedness of Christians holding all their possessions in trust for God, a wealthy ranchman said to him, "Dr. Truett, will you come with me for a while? There is a matter I must discuss with you!"

As they strolled about the vast ranch where multitudes of cattle grazed, the ranchman said, "Until I heard your sermon today, Dr. Truett, I looked upon these vast and valuable acres and these cattle as my own. As you know I haven't been a Christian long. I don't know how to pray. Will you pray with me as in my heart I give all that I have to God, to be used as He directs?"

After Dr. Truett prayed, the weeping ranchman bared the burden of his heart to God, pleading, "I have given my possessions to You, O Lord, to be used as You may direct. Now I give to You my son. O God, save him! O God, save him!"

That night during Dr. Truett's sermon, a young man suddenly stood in the back of the church and said, "Dr. Truett, I must confess my Saviour right now, and ask for His mercy and forgiveness!"

Dr. Truett didn't finish his sermon. The Holy Spirit took complete charge of the meeting. A revival broke out in the community. Many unsaved ones confessed and forsook their sins and turned to the Lord.

Oh, that more of God's children would give themselves, their children and all their possessions to God!

"Every beast of the forest is [his]; and the cattle upon a thousand hills . . . .the world is [his], and the fulness thereof" (Ps. 50:10,12); "The silver is [his], and the gold is [his], saith the Lord of hosts" (Haggai 2:8).

I knelt in tears at the feet of Christ,
  In the hush of the twilight dim;
And all that I was, or hoped, or sought,
  I surrendered unto Him!

* * * *

He Left It All

When Herman Rabbitt, a frugal farmer, recently died on his 156-acre farm, he left instructions telling where he had stashed an enormous sum of money. Six men dug down until they found the treasure. It took hours to remove it from the earth.

Commented *The Washington Post,* "Most of the money was in paper currency, but there was about $50,000 in silver dollars in three tightly closed milk cans and a small oil drum. It must have weighed a ton!"

Hoarded riches bring blight, not blessing: "Your riches are corrupted . . .Your gold and silver is cankered; and the rust of them shall. . .eat your flesh as it were fire" (Jas. 5:2,3).

Those who live for and serve mammon—riches—forfeit a life of service for God: "Ye cannot serve God and mammon" (Matt. 6:24); and accumulate manifold sorrows: "For the love of money is the root of all evil: which. . .some coveted after. . .have . . .pierced themselves through with many sorrows" (I Tim. 6:10).

> Be not selfish in thy greed,
> Pass it on!
> Look upon thy brother's need,
> Pass it on!

* * * *

"I Would Give All"

At his death, J. Paul Getty *left* a fortune estimated at between two and four billion dollars. Financially, he was a success. Maritally, he was a failure. His five marriages ended in divorce. In an interview, he had said to the interrogator, "I would give all my wealth for one successful marriage!"

* * * *

Where Jesus Put the Emphasis

"In the Gospels," said journalist Robert Sabath, "Jesus talked more about wealth and poverty than almost any other subject, including Heaven, Hell, sexual immorality or violence. In the Synoptic Gospels, an amazing one out of ten verses—288 in all—deals directly with the rich and the poor."

* * * *

PROFIT AND LOSS

I counted dollars while God counted crosses;
I counted gains while He counted losses;

I counted my worth by things gained in store;
But He sized me up by the scars that I bore.
I coveted honors and sought for degrees;
He wept as He counted the hours on my knees.
I never knew 'til one day at a grave,
How vain are these things that we spend life to save!

Author unknown.

* * * *

What Would Jesus Think?

A visitor in the home of a little girl gave her a half-dollar. After Mother tucked her in bed, turned off the light and was about to leave, she heard her daughter crying.

Mother asked, "What is my little girl crying about?"

Her reply: "O Mommy, if Jesus comes tonight, I don't want to be caught with all that money!"

Alice M. Knight.

* * * *

Living Without It

As a moving van unloaded the furniture of a new neighbor, including up-to-date appliances, posh furniture and costly paintings, a friendly, observing Quaker said to the newcomer in a small town: "Neighbor, if you find anything missing, let me know and *I'll show you how to live without it!*"

Jesus said, "For a man's life consisteth not in the abundance of the things which he possesseth" (Luke 12:15).

* * * *

A Gun At Your Back

Sir Winston Churchill said, "Socialism will work only in two places: in Heaven, where it is not needed, and in Hell where they already have it. Capitalism is the unequal distribution of wealth. Socialism is the equal distribution of poverty. Communism is nothing but socialism with a gun at your back!"

* * * *

Stashed Away

The military leaders who deposed Ethiopian Emperor Haile Selassie alleged that he had stashed away $15 billion in vaults in Swiss banks.

Whether the report is true or false, in death Selassie left all material possessions behind: "For we brought nothing into this world, and it is certain we can carry nothing out" (I Tim. 6:7).

* * * *

Not Money, but Love of Money

A man of average means, who lived simply and enjoyed the beauty of nature, said to a millionaire: "I am richer than you are."

"How's that?" asked the tycoon.
"Why, I have as much money as I need, and you don't."

* * * *

DECAYING MEN

Ill fares the land,
To hastening ills a prey,
Where wealth accumulates,
And men decay.

Oliver Goldsmith.

* * * *

Society's cement

Professor Richard Hofstader of Columbia University said, "We are living in a culture that is secular. Religion does not play the role that it used to play. This is particularly true for people under forty years of age in this country. When a strong religious bond is missing, there are few things that can hold the culture together."

* * * *

I've Lost Everything!"

A dejected businessman entered my office with face like a blown-out lamp. As he sat wearily in a chair, he gloomily said, "Pastor, I have lost my business! I have lost everything!"

After the distraught man regained his composure, I suggested, "Let's do a bit of stocktaking. You say you've lost everything. Have you in reality? Have you lost your wife?"

"No, pastor. Her heart is with me in this time of tragic loss."

"Have you lost your children?"
"No, I still have my dutiful, obedient children!"

"Have you lost your health?"
Again the answer was, "No."

"Have you lost your business acumen which would enable you to start again from 'scratch,' and recoup your business?"

"I think not," said the man. "I still have the will to win."

"Have you lost God's precious gift to you—eternal life?"

As he did some soul-searching, the man exclaimed, "I can never lose that!"

The man now realized how rich he was in the most worthwhile and greatest possessions which money can't buy!

With these same blessings, God's children can courageously face forward and carry on!

Told by Ralph M. Smith.

* * * *

"Whose Adorning Let It Not Be. . ." (I Pet. 3:3)

In a report for *The Calgary Herald,* Fred Sparks, a news correspondent, wrote, "There are one thousand women whose personal expenses exceed $200,000 annually. More than a dozen spend over $1,000,000." Then Sparks gave the following examples of compulsive spending in Paris:

Barbara Hutton once bought dress-designer Lanvin's entire collection, that is, one each of 158 dresses and coats. The average price of each was $1,100. The sum total was $173,800.

The Queen of Thailand ordered 200 dresses, including a gold lame evening gown covered with $1 million worth of diamonds from the royal collection.

* * * *

SHE'S QUICKER

Their bank account's insufficient
By one feminine flaw;
He's fast on the deposit,
But she's quicker on the draw!

* * * *

ROMANS 8:28

Spinach and Vitamins

A boy asked his teacher, "Why are there so many vitamins in spinach and so few in candy and ice cream?"

Often there are things in life which do not make sense to us, things that are distasteful. Because they do not make sense to us does not mean they do not make sense at all, or do not make sense to God. Ultimately we will know the *why* of present inexplicable happenings: "What I do thou knowest not now; but thou shalt know hereafter" (John 13:7).

Paul said in reference to his suffer-ings, "But I would ye should understand. . .that the things which happened unto me have fallen out. . . unto the furtherance of the gospel" (Phil. 1:12).

Of his cruel treatment by his brothers, Joseph said, "But as for you, ye thought evil against me; but God meant [wove] it unto good, to bring to pass, as it is this day, to save much people alive" (Gen. 50:20).

Deep in unfathomable mines
    Of never-failing skill,
He treasures up His bright designs,
    And works His sovereign will!

* * * *

No Good Thing Withheld

Years ago a young man ordered an instruction book on photography. Mistakenly a book on ventriloquism was mailed to him. He decided not to return it, but to study it.

That young man became a world-renowned ventriloquist. You ask his name? *Edgar Bergen!*

His dummy creations, Charlie McCarthy and Mortimer Snurd, have elicited gales of laughter, relieved depression and brought wholesome entertainment to young and old alike, as their manipulator ventriloquized through them.

As related to God's children, nothing of a fortuitous or accidental nature comes to them. All is by the arranging and rearranging hand of God. God often uses seemingly trivial and inconsequential happenings to bring far-reaching and wondrous blessings to His submissive children. This is certain: "The Lord will give grace and glory: no good thing will he withhold from them that walk uprightly" (Ps. 84:11).

* * * *

Seeming Disappointments

Disappointments are inescapable in life. Take the little boy who slipped under the curtained side of a mammoth tent, thinking it was a circus tent. To his surprise, he discovered that a revival meeting was in progress!

To dedicated Christians, seeming disappointments are God's appointments. Nothing of a chance or fortuitous nature can befall God's children.

* * * *

God's Arranging Hand

Said noted philosopher Dr. C. E. M. Joad, "Unless God is back of everything, you cannot find meaning in anything."

In times of storm and stress, how blessed are God's children who discern His hand arranging and rearranging things to work out His best for them: "As for God, his way is perfect" (Ps. 18:30).

Ye fearful saints, fresh courage take,
The clouds ye so much dread
Are big with mercy, and shall break
With blessings on thy head.

Willliam Cowper.

* * * *

Still on the Throne

A California businessman said, "I have never known so many uncertainties. Everything you plan turns out to be a gamble. Nothing is stable any more."

In the midst of uncertainties, it is *certain* that God is still on the throne ruling and overruling, arranging and rearranging, and causing all things to work for the good of his children. His eternal purpose is that "the living may know that the most High ruleth in the kingdom of men" (Dan. 4:17).

It is also certain that Jesus Christ is "the same yesterday, and to day, and forever" (Heb. 13:8).

O Thou who changest not,
Abide with me.

* * * *

"As for God, His Way Is Perfect"

When William Booth, founder of the Salvation Army, lost his eyesight, his son Bramwell said, "Dad, you are going to be permanently blind!"

"You mean that I am going to live the rest of my life in physical blindness?"

"I fear that you must reckon with that fact," said his son.

"Shall I never see your face again?" Booth asked.

'No," said Bramwell, "probably not in this world."

Booth's hand moved slowly across the counterpane until he grasped his son's hand, then said, "I have done what I could for God and for the people with my eyes; now I shall do what I can for God and for the people without my eyes!"

Trustingly, all of God's children can say, "As for God, his way is perfect" (Ps. 18:30).

* * * *

FRIENDLY OBSTACLES

For every hill I've had to climb,

For every stone that bruised my feet,
For all the blood and sweat and grime,
For blinding storms and burning heat,
My heart sings but a grateful song—
These were the things that made me strong!

For all the heartaches and the tears,
For all the anguish and the pain,
For gloomy days and fruitless years,
And for the hopes that lived in vain,
I do give thanks, for now I know
These were the things that helped me grow!

'Tis not the softer things of life
Which stimulate man's will to strive;
But bleak adversity and strife
Do most to keep man's will alive.
O'er rose-strewn paths the weaklings creep,
But brave hearts dare to climb the steep.

Author unknown.

* * * *

SALVATION

Obituary Column

As a man read the obituary column of his morning's newspaper, he observed that his name was listed among the decedents. Angrily he threw the paper down and phoned the editor. "This is terrible. Your error is inexcusable. It will cause me no end of embarrassment. How could you do such a thing?"

The editor apologized and expressed regret. No explanation, however, could mitigate the offended man's anger.

Finally the editor quipped, "Cheer up, fellow! I'll put your name in the birth column tomorrow and give you a fresh start!"

God gives a fresh start to the spiritually dead ones when they penitently turn from sin to the

Saviour: "Come now, and let us reason together, saith the Lord: though your sins be as scarlet, they shall be as white as snow" (Isa. 1:18).

* * * *

Sick Head and Faint Hearts

Millions of Catholics listened with reverential awe, others with mixed reactions, as Pope John II plead for social justice and the right to life of unborn children, declaring, "To destroy unborn children is an unspeakable crime!"

All lovers of mankind, irrespective of clime, color or creed, agree that the affluent nations should share with the have-not nations, the hungry, downtrodden and oppressed myriads of earth. Many welcomed his stern disapproval of extramarital sex and homosexuality. His pronouncement on the permanence of the marital bond was most timely. He said, "The covenant between a man and a woman joined in Christian marriage is as indissoluble and irrevocable as God's love for His people!"

Howsoever praiseworthy his emphasis on these objectives, people will not change appreciably until their hearts and characters are changed by Christ. How accurately does the Bible depict the unchanged heart of man: "The heart is deceitful above all things, and desperately wicked: who can know it?" (Jer. 17:9).

Our society is desperately sick—morally and spiritually. The prophet Isaiah "tells it as it is": "Ah, sinful nation, a people laden with iniquity, a seed of evildoers. . .they have forsaken the Lord. . . .the whole head is sick, and the whole heart faint" (Isa. 1:4,5). For confirmation of this indictment, read your daily newspaper.

Both the religious and the irreligious sinner, the moral and the immoral sinner need God's mercy and forgiveness: "Ye must be born again!"

* * * *

"Narrow-Minded Baptists"

A stranger approached a minister in a hotel lobby and asked, "Aren't you a minister?"

"Yes, I am."

"I hope you are not a narrow-minded Baptist who believes that only members of your flock are saved," the stranger said derisively.

"I am a Baptist minister, but I vehemently deny any insinuation that only members of my flock are saved. Fact is, there are members of my church who are not saved. I proclaim the truth that salvation inheres not in any church but in a *Person*, the Lord Jesus Christ: 'For whosoever shall call upon the name of the Lord shall be saved' " (Rom. 10:13).

How understandable is God's plan of salvation: "Look unto me, and be ye saved, all the ends of the earth: for I am God, and there is none else" (Isa. 45:22).

In describing his conversion, Spurgeon said, "I looked at Him, and He—Christ—looked at me and we became one forever!"

* * * *

"O Taste and See"

Ole Bull, the musician, and Ericsson, the inventor, were friends in their early years. Then they were separated and did not meet again until both had won renown in their respective fields.

Ole Bull invited his friend Ericsson, who had no special love for music, to one of his concerts. Ericsson said, "I have no time to waste."

"If you don't come, I'll bring my violin to your shop and play there!" said Ole Bull.

"If you do," countered Ericsson, "I'll smash your instrument!"

The great violinist kept his word. Entering the shop, he began to play. At first the inventor showed displeasure, but as Ole Bull continued, Ericsson listened in wonderment. Workmen dropped their tools and stood in silent admiration. On and on Ole Bull played.

When he ceased, the great inventor said with tears, "Don't stop! Don't stop! Go on! I never knew until now what has been lacking in my life!"

How great are the lacks in Christless lives! They lack rest: "But the wicked are like the troubled sea, when it cannot rest. . . .There is no peace, saith my God, to the wicked" (Isa. 57:20,21); they lack salvation: "Neither is there salvation in any other: for there is none other name under heaven given among men, whereby we must be saved" (Acts 4:12).

"O taste and see that the Lord is good: blessed is the man that trusteth in him" (Ps. 34:8).

* * * *

Not the Gospel

A disciple of Confucius asked him, "Is there one word which may serve as a guide rule for one's life?"

"Is not 'reciprocity' such a word?" asked Confucius. "What you do not want done to yourself, do not to others."

Epictetus, a Greek Stoic philosopher, said, "What you would avoid suffering yourself, seek not to inflict on others."

Hillieal, an ancient Jewish teacher, said, "What is hateful to yourself, do to no other. That is the whole law, and the rest is commentary."

Christ gave the precept called the Golden Rule: "Whatsoever ye would that men should do to you, do ye even so to them: for this is the law and the prophets" (Matt. 7:12).

The Golden Rule is *not* the Gospel which transforms people and gives enabling power to keep the Golden Rule. They even choose to suffer wrong or loss rather than cause another to suffer.

* * * *

"What a Racket!"

An alcoholic graduate of the University of California attended one of our meetings in San Francisco. His home had been broken up. Twice he had wended his way to the Golden Gate Bridge intent on suicide, but somehow his darksome purpose was thwarted.

At first he sneered at every phase of the service. When the offering was taken, he thought, *What a racket!*

The text for my message was, "For

what is a man profited, if he shall gain the whole world, and lose his own soul? or what shall a man give in exchange for his soul?" (Matt. 16:26).

During the meeting, he was convicted of sin and happily converted! His deliverance from enslaving alcohol was miraculous! Later he wrote, "That night I made peace with God. I never dreamed what a transformation would take place in my life. I have lost all taste for alcohol. My business is prospering. I am back with my family and we are enjoying daily devotions!"

Told by Billy Graham.

* * * *

Just Outside the Door

"**Seven Die, Eight Hurt in Crash,**" read the headline in a newspaper. It told of the frightful crash of an Air Force B52 bomber which nosedived into a residential neighborhood, one-fourth of a mile short of the runway!

In speaking of the tragic event, Lt. Gen. Russell E. Dougherty, commander of the Second Air Force, Orlando, Florida, said, "They could have bailed out, but they didn't. I conclude that they thought they had almost made it to the runway. The plane was coming out of the clouds on its final approach. The place of impact indicated it *almost made it!*"

How like that plane are myriads today who come near the entrance into eternal life. They are "just outside the door," but fail to enter!

Long ago the Saviour said to a scribe, "Thou art not far from the kingdom of God" (Mark 12:34).

O weary soul, the gate is near,
In sin why still abide?
Both peace and rest are waiting here
And you are just ouside!
Come in, be free from chains of sin,
Be glad, be satisfied,
Before the tempest breaks, come in,
And leave your past outside!

* * * *

Can Momentarily Erupt

Dr. Sherwood E. Wirt spoke factually when he said, "Providing man with more pay, better living quarters and medical care will not solve his basic problem for the simple reason that man insatiably wants more and still more. He wants his neighbor's wife as well as his own. He wants his neighbor's house. In short, he wants all he can get—power and dominion and the worship of those around him."

Resident within the unrenewed heart of man are evils which can momentarily erupt into volcanic destructiveness!

Great is man's need of the heart-changing grace of God. Without that, the ancient Greek's appraisal of man is eminently correct: "There is no good in mankind." He is "corrupt according to the deceitful lusts" (Eph. 4:22); "Dead in trespasses and sins" (2:1).

* * * *

Devastating to Human Pride

William Culbertson said, "Every religion of the earth that I know about says, 'Something in my hand I bring' as it approaches God. The New

Testament alone says, 'Nothing in my hand I bring.'

All human effort, all our man-made works, have to be passed by. It is 'not by works of righteousness which we have done,' but by grace through faith that we have been saved. How devastating this is to human pride!"

* * * *

Only Half of a Man

An Ethiopian prayed, "Half a man, Father. That's not the way You made me; it's the way I've made myself. Jesus is the other half. Now if You will just weld us together."

In the miracle of regeneration we become indissolubly welded to Christ: "We are members of his body, of his flesh, and of his bones" (Eph. 5:30).

In speaking of his spiritual transformation, Spurgeon exclaimed, "I looked at Him (Christ), and He looked at me, and we became ONE forever!"

The Bible says, "And ye are complete in him, which is the head of all principality and power" (Col. 2:10).

* * * *

Water intoxication

Knight News Service wrote of a young woman with a genius IQ who died from "water intoxication"—compulsively drinking up to four gallons a day.

Dr. Ronald Wright, a medical examiner, said, "As far as I know it's the first case of its kind. The tormented young woman, who had an IQ of 189, destroyed her body's chemical balance with her obsessive drinking of water. As a result, there was a swelling of her tissues, particularly the lungs. Death resulted when she finally couldn't breathe, an incredibly slow and painful death."

How grateful are God's children for the life-giving water which quenches their spiritual thirst. How gracious is the Saviour's all-inclusive invitation: "I will give unto him that is athirst of the fountain of the water of life freely" (Rev. 21:6).

> I heard the voice of Jesus say,
>   "Behold I freely give
> The living water, thirsty one,
>   Stoop down, and drink, and live."
>
> I came to Jesus, and I drank
>   Of that life-giving stream;
> My thirst was quenched, my soul revived,
>   And now I live in Him!
>   Horatius Bonar.

* * * *

"O Thou Blessed Epilepsy!"

In a futile effort to explain away Paul's conversion on the road to Damascus, unbelievers have said that he had an epileptic seizure which blinded him and threw him to the earth.

Showing the absurdity of this idea, Spurgeon said, "Look at him *before* the alleged epileptic seizure—a blasphemer and a murderous persecutor of Christians.

"Look at him *after* the alleged seizure—utterly submissive to God's will and willing to suffer death for Christ's sake!

"We can only exclaim, 'O thou blessed epilepsy! Great is thy transforming, character-changing power!' "

* * * *

"Fed Up With Soggy Eyeballs"

"In 1945 I was pilot at one of the largest airfields and airdrome officer," said Bill Butler. "When I reentered civilian life, my total interest was money-making and getting married. I met a beautiful girl whose father was a rich Texan. We were married. We joined the elite social and athletic clubs. We had everything one could want, *except contentment.*

"As time passed, I became 'fed up' with cocktail parties, looking at tired, soggy eyeballs, hearing risque jokes and peering into stupid faces on Saturday nights.

"A change occurred in me when I attended the funeral of a friend who had died tragically. The minister who conducted the funeral solemnities said, 'I am not going to tell you a lot of good things about the decedent, for I did not know her. If she didn't do what God wanted her to do while on earth, it is too late for her now. *How about you?'*

"The question burned its way into my soul. Later when the minister was a dinner guest in our home, he asked me, 'Are you a Christian?' I thought, *Does he think I am a cannibal?*

"In bed that night I prayed, 'Lord, I've tried everything. Nothing works. Lord, if you will come into my life, I'm ready.' Something instantly happened! I began crying like a baby. Jesus Christ changed me! I didn't give up smoking, dirty jokes, swearing. They gave me up—in a flash!"

The Bible says, "Therefore if any man be in Christ, he is a new creature: old things are passed away; behold, all things are become new" (II Cor. 5:17).

* * * *

"Try Jesus One Day"

A secretary who was not a Christian was urged by a Christian friend to try Jesus for one day.

"That seems reasonable and I'll do it," she said.

At work, when tempted to lose her temper and "fly off the handle," she prayed silently, "Jesus, help me." As she went home after work, she was fearful lest some evildoer would snatch her purse and do her bodily injury. She pleaded, "Jesus, protect me from harm."

The experiment—*Try Jesus for one day*—worked so splendidly that she resolved to try Jesus for another day, and another, and another. Her life was transformed! She became a "new creature" in Christ Jesus!

Christ does not require a blind faith of anyone, nor does He condemn us when we have honest doubts: "Thomas, Reach hither thy finger, and behold my hands. . .be not faithless, but believing" (John 20:27).

How blessed are doubtful ones who accept God's changeless challenge: "O taste and see that the Lord is good: blessed is the man that trusteth in him" (Ps. 34:8).

* * * *

Who Does the Finding?

One asked a recently converted Chinese, "How did you find Jesus?" A perplexed look came on the face of the new convert. In broken English he said, "I no find Jesus. *Jesus find me!* Jesus not lost, I the lost one!"

How hopelessly lost we are until the seeking Shepherd finds us: "I have gone astray like a lost sheep; seek thy servant" (Ps. 119:176).

I was lost, but Jesus found me,
Found the sheep that went astray,
Threw His loving arms around me,
Drew me back into His way!

F. H. Rowley.

"For the Son of man is come to seek and to save that which was lost."—Luke 19:10.

* * * *

When Moral Order Is Lost

In addressing the students at the University of Toronto, Malcolm Muggeridge, famed journalist and broadcaster, said:

"As I look back, it's amazing how much that seemed so important at the time now seems negligible—ambitions, passions and all the rest.

"You get the strange feeling that the play you were rehearsing is not the play you were actually living. This raises the question: 'What is the real drama that life is all about?' For me, the answer *now* is found in the light of the Christian message, the same truth that turned the disciples on two thousand years ago.

"We find in great wealth, poverty; in gorging, that we are still hungry; in erotic uniting of flesh, that we are still

separated from each other. We pass through the valley of abundance, through gardens of fantasy into wastelands of satiety.

"If we lose our sense of moral order, we will soon lose all other order—economic, political and social!"

* * * *

No Hopeless Ones

Of all the people of ancient Greece called "barbarians" none were more fierce or formidable than the Scythians, the hairy nomads who ranged over the steppes of Central Asia and the land north of the Black Sea, in what is now Russia. Around 3200 B. C., horses were first tamed for riding, and the Scythians were the ones to subdue them.

In the Bible, the Scythians are included in the list of those tamed and transformed by the Gospel of Christ: "Where there is neither Greek nor Jew. . .Barbarian, Scythian. . .but Christ is all, and in all" (Col. 3:11).

* * * *

The Golden Rule

One evening the chief of the Delaware Indians was sitting by a fireside with a friend. Both were silently looking into the fire. The friend broke the silence by saying, "I have been thinking of a rule, given by the Author of the Christian Religion, which is called the Golden Rule."

"Stop," said the chief; "don't praise it. Tell me what it is and let me think for myself."

The friend replied, "The rule is for

one man to do to another as he would have the other do to him."

Silence ensued for several minutes. Then the chief said, "Brother, I have been thoughtful of what you told me. If the Great Spirit who made man would give him a new heart, he could do what you say, but not else."

This is exactly what God does when we turn penitently to Him for His mercy and forgiveness: "A new heart also will I give you,: and a new spirit will I put within you: and I will take away the stony heart out of your flesh" (Ezek. 36:26).

* * * *

A Neglected Gift

We recall with a feeling of hopeless horror the time when there was no known cure for the crippling, paralyzing disease poliomyelitis! Then a new day dawned upon the darksome horizon for mankind! Bacteriologist Dr. Jonas Edward Salk discovered a *sure cure* for polio. Millions thronged to free clinics throughout the United States and took the simple remedy: a drop of vaccine on a small cube of sugar—to be followed by two booster dosages at indicated times.

What a debt of gratitude mankind owes to the discovery by Dr. Salk! And how difficult it is to believe that forty percent of the people of the United States neglected to take the immunizing remedy!

Long ago God provided an unfailing remedy for the universal spiritual malady—sin. He opened "a fountain...for sin and uncleanness" (Zech. 13:1). The vicarious death of

Christ is the unfailing remedy for sin—available to all who will appropriate it.

How tragic it is that so many spurn God's free offer of mercy and forgiveness: "Whosoever will, let him take the water of life freely" (Rev. 22:17).

"How shall we escape, if we neglect so great salvation?"—Heb. 3:3.

I know a world that is sunk in shame,
  Where hearts oft faint and tire,
But I know a Name, a precious Name,
  That can set that world on fire!
Its sound is sweet, its letters flame,
I know a Name, a precious Name,
  'Tis Jesus!

Told by Ralph M. Smith.

* * * *

God Alters Man

A communist was speaking to a group of people in Columbus Circle, New York. In extolling communism, he said, "Communism can put a new suit on a man!"

One of God's servants, standing with the group, said in a clear, calm voice, "And Christ can put a new man in the suit!"

God does not alter the robe of righteousness to fit the man. He remakes the man to fit the robe: "If any man be in Christ, he is a new creature" (II Cor. 5:17).

* * * *

A Total Person

Astronaut William R. Pogue said his eighty-four days on the Skylab III mission made him realize that man is more than just an intellectual being; he needs Christ in his heart to become a total person. "I am firmly convinced that there's more to life than the body and intellect. It's the soul. Raw intellectual capacity is just the shell. There's that kernel that most of us miss. When a person finds Christ, he becomes a total person."

The Bible says, "And ye are complete in him [Christ]" (Col. 2:10).

* * * *

"Lord, Kill Me!"

"How great is our joy when we are used of God to bring sin-enslaved ones to the Saviour! Etched on the scroll of memory is the following incident which occurred early in my ministry," said Dr. Scott Tatum.

"Late one Saturday night there was a knock on my front door. Answering the call, I beheld a tragic, pathetic sight. A man stood there heavily under the influence of liquor. Amidst sobs, he repeated over and over, like a stuck phonograph needle, 'I've done it again! I've done it again!'

"I asked him to come in. Getting on his knees with me, he prayed, 'Lord, kill me! Lord, kill me! I have disgraced Thy name and Thy church, and have brought sorrow to my pastor and shame to my family. Now, O Lord, kill me, kill me!'

"When he became silent, I prayed, 'O Lord, do kill him!'

"The astonished man asked, 'What do you mean?'

"I replied, 'I mean exactly what I prayed. I want God to kill the old man in you, the self-righteous sinner who is powerless to cease from sin. I want Him to make you a new man in

Christ and enable you to be triumphant over every shackling sin.'

"God answered my prayer that night. The drink-enslaved man, through the miracle of regeneration, became a new man in Christ Jesus!"

"If the Son therefore shall make you free, ye shall be free indeed."— John 8:36.

* * * *

Unless Defused

During a fierce gale on August 6, 1944, the American liberty ship *Richard Montgomery* broke in pieces just off the coast of England and sank in twenty-eight feet of water. The ship was laden with a cargo of 8,687 tons of unfused aerial fragmentation bombs. Nearly half of them are still there! Explosive experts say that if anything should set them off, it would produce one of the greatest nonnuclear explosions in history.

The Calgary Herald commented, "The obvious question is why the British government has allowed such a dangerous situation to exist for so long? The official answer is that it would be more dangerous to attempt to remove the bombs than to leave them where they are—undisturbed. Divers are sent down periodically to examine the wreck and its cargo. Each time their conclusion is the same: leave it alone, and pray that another ship doesn't plough into it or some amateur frogman start fooling around with it."

Latent in the unchanged and desperately wicked heart of man are smoldering evils which may erupt into volcanic fury at any moment unless they are defused and eradicated by the power of God.

* * * *

Full Heads and Empty Hearts

Decision editorialized:

"Education has filled the minds of people with facts, information and theory, but it has neglected to tell them how to live.

"Mankind needs a new heart more than new ideas. When God measures a man, He puts the tapeline around his heart, not his head. Education is good, but education can never make a man better unless it tells him the true purpose of man and gets at man's basic problem. The Bible says that Satan 'hath blinded the minds of them which believe not, lest the light of the glorious gospel of Christ . . .should shine unto them' (II Cor. 4:4). This explains why some scoff at the idea of a saving faith.

"While the battlefield of life is strewn with the wrecks of men who knew too much and believed too little, Jesus can bring a great change in the life of any person who gives himself to Him."

Jesus offers spiritual life to all who will receive it: "I am come that they might have life, and that they might have it more abundantly" (John 10:10).

* * * *

SATAN

"Where Satan's Seat Is" (Rev. 2:13).

In his famed sermon on Satan, Billy Sunday would place an empty chair on the platform and, in imagination, would seat Satan in the chair. Then he would doff his coat and roll up his sleeves. Through his fiery sermon, Sunday denounced Satan as the father of liars and the destroyer of myriads who abandon themselves to sin and Satan's clever deceptions. At the conclusion of the sermon, Sunday would fling the chair down from the rostrum.

In our encounter with Satan, we will emerge victorious by wielding "the sword of the Spirit, which is the word of God" (Eph. 6:17), and by utterly submitting ourselves to God:

"Submit yourselves. . .to God. Resist the devil, and he will flee from you" (Jas. 4:7).

Satan is powerful but not all powerful: "Greater is he that is in you, than he that is in the world" (I John 4:4).

Did we in our own strength confide,
Our striving would be losing,
Were not the right Man on our side,
The Man of God's own choosing:
Dost ask who that may be?
Christ Jesus, it is He,
Lord Sabaoth is His name,
From age to age the same,
And He must win the battle!

* * * *

Wants to Be Fooled

P. T. Barnum of the world-famed Barnum-Bailey Circus said, "The

American people want to be fooled, and I am here to fool them."

This calls to mind what the Bible says about Antichrist, the coming super-embodiment of deception: "And then shall that Wicked [lawless one] be revealed. . .whose coming is after the working of Satan with all power and signs and lying wonders, And with all deceivableness of unrighteousness in them that perish; because they received not the love of the truth" (II Thess. 2:8-10).

* * * *

Incurably Religious

Man is incurably religious. Ingrained in his being is the urge to worship *something.* Apart from God, he worships self, gold, or even Satan, the ultimate in rebellion against God.

How prone is man to change "the truth of God into a lie, and [worship] and [serve] the creature more than the Creator" (Rom. 1:25).

The first Church of Satan meets in a large, black Victorian house in San Francisco. Inside, the walls are black and the ceiling red. In the center of the room is a large coffin upended. Staring down from above is a wide-eyed owl. On the altar, during the black mass, a nude priestess reclines! How long will God allow such blatant blasphemy to continue?

One answer from those skies is sent:
    Ye who from God depart,
Repent while it is called today,
    And harden not your heart.
                    Adapted from
            The Presbyterian Journal.

* * * *

Controlled Power

"The believer needs to remember that God is motivated by His great love. His will for you is a gracious will. He may allow you to suffer loss, but only for your good. He loves you. How fear-allaying it is to know that even Satan's power is under the control of a loving God who, in Jesus Christ, has become our heavenly Father," said Gordon K. Reed.

Long ago God said to Satan concerning Job, "Behold, all that he hath is in thy power; only upon himself put not forth thine hand" (Job 1:12).

Satan is powerful, but not as powerful as God: "Greater is he that is in you, than he that is in the world" (I John 4:4).

Did we in our own strength confide,
    Our striving would be losing;
Were not the right Man on our side,
    The Man of God's own choosing!
                        Martin Luther.

* * * *

Velvet Slippers

The Devil is never more subtle or dangerous than when shod in velvet slippers, and scintillating suavity, charm and graciousness: "transformed into an angel of light" (II Cor. 11:14).

How quickly do men of *distinction*—sociable imbibers of alcoholic liquors—become men of *extinction!*

* * * *

Obsessed

A new movie entitled "Hitler: The Last Ten Days" has been produced by Shepperton Studios in London. The star of the film is Sir Alec Guinness.

In commenting upon his role, Sir Alec said to a reporter:

"I've become obsessed with this monster! I spent five months reading all the available data, seeing all the available newsreel films; and I've learned a great deal from our technical adviser, Gerhardt Boldt, who was an adjutant to General Krebs, the representative of the Chiefs of Staff of the Third Reich in the bunker. He's one of the few men still alive who saw the whole thing!

"Ever since I was offered the role, I have been obessed. My wife, my poor friends, everyone I know has had to put up with every new scrap of information."

There are myriads today who are totally obsessed with Satan: 'Taken captive by him at his will' (II Tim. 2:26). They are powerless to extricate themselves from him and sinful habits: "Having eyes full of adultery, and that cannot cease from sin. . .an heart they have exercised with covetous practices; cursed children" (II Pet. 2:14).

* * * *

SECOND COMING OF CHRIST
(See also Prophecy)

"One Taken. . .the Other Left"

In the U. S. Army, no American soldier is ever knowingly left on the battlefield, whether wounded or dead. Soldiers often risk their lives to take their fallen comrades back to their base.

One day as Pfc. Ed Bable, age 19, from Beaver Falls, Pennsylvania, and some of his comrades in Viet Nam were pushing through the jungle, they entered a trap set by the Viet Cong. A vicious crossfire caught them. Several of them fell, mortally wounded. Bable escaped and made his way back to safety, but he didn't stay long. Struggling through the muck, he returned to the scene of the ambush. Quickly he lifted two of his fallen comrades to their feet. Supporting one with each arm, he brought them back to the American zone.

At the first phase of the second coming of Christ, the redeemed ones will be raptured. The unsaved ones will be irretrievably left behind: "Then shall two be in the field; the one shall be taken, and the other left. Two women shall be grinding at the mill; the one shall be taken, and the other left. Watch. . .for ye know not what hour your Lord doth come" (Matt. 24:40-42).

If Christ came today, would you be with the saved, raptured ones or would you be left behind? What you do with Christ *now* will determine where you would be.

* * * *

"He May Come Today!"

A traveler in Switzerland came upon a beautiful villa on the shores of a lake, far from the beaten track of tourists. An aged gardener caring for the beautiful villa seemed glad to have visitors. He had lived alone here for some years.

"How often does the owner of the villa come to see you?" asked the traveler.

"He does not come often. Indeed it has been several years since his last visit," said the caretaker.

"But," exclaimed the traveler, "you have everything in such perfect order. Everything is so clean and beautiful and flourishing. It looks as if you were expecting your master to come tomorrow!"

"Oh, no," said the old man, "I am expecting him to come *today*, sir! He may come *today*, so I must have everything in order!"

"Be ye also ready: for in such an hour as ye think not the Son of man cometh."—Matt. 24:44.

Alice Marie Knight.

* * * *

"For Yet a Little While"

This is the hope that sustains us,
  This is our lamp in the night,
This is the beacon we follow,
  Waiting till faith becomes sight!

This is our pillow of nighttime,
  The promise in each golden dawn,
This is the spur for the sluggish,
  "Occupy while I am gone!"

This is our heart's choicest treasure,
  Balm for our sorrow and pain,
Words that are precious as rubies,
  "Christ Jesus is coming again!"

Martha Small Nicholson.

* * * *

"The Dawn!"

In the extreme north of Norway, the residents each year ascend a towering mountain around January 18 to get a glimpse of the sun after months of darkness. When the first rim of the sun is seen, the people joyfully shout, "The dawn! The dawn!"

As God's children cherish "the glorious appearing of the great God and [their] Saviour Jesus Christ" (Titus 2:13), and scan world horizons, they are constrained to exclaim: "The dawn! The coming of the Lord draweth nigh!"

* * * *

A Balance Staff

Said Dale Crawley, "Those who cherish the blessed hope of Christ's return do not question the verities of God's Word. When this doctrine is believed, all other doctrines are accepted with simplicity of faith. It is a balance staff which enables the believer to avoid impatience. It is a sanctifying, purifying hope: 'And every man that hath this hope in him purifieth himself, even as he is pure' (I John 3:3). To be like Christ is the goal of everyone who loves His appearing."

We do not know when Christ will return, but we are sure He will return: "For yet a little while, and he that shall come will come, and will not tarry" (Heb. 10:37).

. . . .
**Signs of His coming multiply
Morning light breaks in eastern sky,**

Watch, for the time is drawing nigh,
What if it were today?

                                    Leila N. Morris.

* * * *

"Look Up!"

In addressing a Chicago symposium, Dr. Cicely Williams, physican and nutrition expert, said, "The scientific world is shaken to its roots by today's events and developments. In spite of all the money, intricate machines, vast progress in scientific achievement, and much good will, we are terrified by violence, dishonesty, shortage of food and energy, and inflation. All these things are taken for granted when they appear in less developed countries, but they are now lapping at the feet of the scientists and of the millionaires."

The Saviour foretold the coming of global distress and disillusionment: "And there shall be. . .upon the earth distress of nations, with perplexity . . .Men's hearts failing them for fear, and for looking after those things which are coming on the earth" (Luke 21:25,26). His directive to God's children was: "And when these things begin to come to pass, then look up . . .for your redemption draweth nigh" (Luke 21:28).

* * * *

God or Devil—We'll Receive Him

Henri Spaak, one of the early planners of the European Common Market and Secretary-General of NATO, said, "We do not want another committee. We have too many already. What we want is a man of sufficient stature to hold the allegiance of all people and to lift us out of the economic morass into which we are sinking. Send us such a man and be he god or devil, we will receive him!"

In reference to the coming "super-being," the Saviour said: "I am come in my Father's name, and ye receive me not: if another shall come in his own name, him ye will receive" (John 5:43).

* * * *

Is the Stage Being Set?

The world-famed historian Arnold Toynbee said, "By forcing on mankind more and more lethal weapons, and at the same time making the world more independent economically, technology has brought mankind to such a degree of distress that we are ripe for the deifying of any new Caesar who might succeed in giving the world unity and peace!"

As God's children scan world horizons through the telescope of the "sure word of prophecy," they believe that the stage is being set for the coming of the Antichrist "through his policy. . .he shall cause craft to prosper in his hand; and he shall magnify himself in his heart, and by peace shall destroy many" (Dan. 8:25).

* * * *

"Watchman, What of the Night?"

With the coming of fall in Tromso,

Norway, the long winter night which is known as "moerketiden," or "murky time," begins. Soon it envelopes this distant corner of the earth.

"It is not much of a problem keeping up health and spirits during twenty-four hours of [summer] daylight," said Dr. Herald Reppesgard, one of the staff doctors of the Asgard Mental Hospital in Tromso, "but twenty-four hours of darkness is another matter. 'Murky time' has a sound which conveys a sense and feeling of melancholia and is a designation for this dreary, depressing and difficult season of the year. Tromso lies two hundred miles north of the Arctic Circle, and its people are 'light conscious,' in the same way that people of other cities are conscious of pollution and humidity. There is a big increase of cases involving insomnia, hypertensions, fears and psychological depression during the winter months."

Dispensationally we are now in the night. Some of God's children are asking: "Watchman, what of the night?" (Isa. 21:11), or "How far off is the night?" or "How near are we to the dawn?"

God's "sure word of prophecy" gives the answer to this insistent question: "The night is far spent, the day is at hand: let us. . .cast off the works of darkness, and let us put on the armour of light" (Rom. 13:12).

"The coming the Lord draweth nigh."—Jas. 5:8.

* * * *

"Look! There Comes Christ!"

"Some years ago a recently converted young lady gave a vesper service message in the chapel of the college where I was a student," said Ralph M. Smith. "Before she spoke, she stood silently and looked intently toward the entrance of the chapel. 'She's has stage fright,' the students thought.

"After a tense moment, she exclaimed dramatically, 'Look! There comes Christ!' Every head turned toward the door.

"From that memorable incident, I began an intensive study of God's Word, with special attention to the many references in the Bible to 'that blessed hope, and the glorious appearing of the great God and our Saviour Jesus Christ' (Titus 2:13). I cherish and proclaim the imminent return of our Saviour!"

* * * *

Becoming Unglued

A well-informed U. S. Congressman said dejectedly, "Our world is finished! I've given up! I'm just going to try to enjoy what time we have left!"

Others also gloomily affirm, "The world is coming apart"; "The global village is about to disintegrate"; "New York is a city without glue"; "The human race is ripping open at the seams!"

In the Bible we have this fear-allaying, hope-enkindling directive: "And when these things begin to come to pass, then look up, and lift up your heads; for your redemption draweth nigh" (Luke 21:28). Hallelujah!

* * * *

"Impossible No Day"

Archibishop Richard Trench said, "The second coming of Christ is possible any day, impossible no day!"

Jesus said, "Therefore be ye also ready: for in such an hour as ye think not the Son of man cometh" (Matt. 24:44). He didn't say, "Get ready." He said, "Be ready."

* * * *

All's Not Right

Poetic fancy is often regardless of stark realism. This is true of Robert Browning's beautiful poem "The Year's at the Spring":

> The years at the spring
> And day's at the morn;
> Morning's at seven:
> The hillside's dew-pearled;
> The lark's on the wing;
> The snail's on the thorn;
> God's in His heaven—
> All's right with the world!

All's not right with the world! Glaring inequalities, social injustices, and age-long evils cry pleadingly for redress, and the only response to their anguished plea is the empty echo of their wailing lament.

All will be right with the world only when Jesus, "The mighty God. . .The Prince of Peace" comes as "King of kings, and Lord of lords" (Rev. 19:16)!

Then "the earth shall be filled with the knowledge of the glory of the Lord, as the waters cover the sea" (Hab. 2:14).

Then there will be globe-girdling, all-pervasive peace: "And they shall beat their swords into plowshares, and their spears into pruninghooks: nation shall not lift up a sword against nation, neither shall they learn war any more" (Mic. 4:3).

Then tranquility will encompass the earth; "The whole earth is at rest, and is quiet: they break forth into singing" (Isa. 14:7).

When shall these glories meet our eyes? What if it were today!

* * * *

SELF-CONTROL

When to Get Angry

The only time it's not a sin to get angry is when we get angry at sin: "Abhor that which is evil" (Rom. 12:9). "Be ye angry, and sin not: let not the sun go down upon your wrath" (Eph. 4:26).

* * * *

Boys Are Like Ducks

"You must not go swimming in the mill pond," said Mother to little Johnny. "It is too dangerous!" Boys, however, take to the water as naturally as ducks.

Some days later Johnny had to pass by the mill pond. How ingenious he was in what he did! He took along his bathing suit, just in case he was tempted!

The Bible says, "But put ye on the Lord Jesus Christ, and make not provision for the flesh, to fulfill the lusts thereof" (Rom. 13:14).

Alice M. Knight.

* * * *

Rejoice! Don't Retaliate!

Angered with a private, an officer in the army struck him in the face. Restraining himself, the private said, "Sir, I'll make you sorry for that if it's the last thing I do!"

Later the officer was wounded in battle and surrounded by his enemies. The private fought his way to his side and helped him make his way back to safety. Thanking the private, the officer gripped his hand and said with deep feeling, "What a return for an insult!"

With a smile of deep satisfaction, the soldier said, "Sir, I told you that I would make you sorry for what you did if it was the last thing I did!"

The Bible says, "Overcome evil with good" (Rom. 12:21).

* * * *

"The Answer Is Simple"

A TV announcer said, "The hardest job I have is to make those easy payments."

The Bible gives this directive to God's children: "Owe no man any thing, but to love one another" (Rom. 13:8).

What can we do when we need something and have no money to procure it? The answer is simple: We can do without it."

* * * *

The Rolling Cabbage

As William Howard Taft was giving a campaign speech, a large cabbage rolled across the platform and stopped at his feet!

Taft quipped, "I see that one of my opponents has lost his head!"

How wise we are when we react humorously to intended insults and indignities! It is easy to fly off the handle, blow a fuse and give others a piece of our minds, forgetful of the fact that, when we do this, we have no peace of mind left.

"A soft answer turneth away wrath: but grievous words stir up anger."— Prov. 15:1.

* * * *

A Trivial Argument

A retired salesperson won the battle for a parking spot in downtown Miami, but lost his life in an ensuing argument. He died of a heart attack!

Police said Robert H. Mitchell, 70, turned the front of his car into a parking space. Another motorist was waiting to back into the space. The other driver jumped out of his car and began arguing angrily with Mitchell. Heated words were exchanged before a passerby, Herbert Simon, came to separate them.

Mitchell began breathing hard and perspiring profusely. "I'll be all right," he said to his competitor and pointed him to a nearby parking spot. Those were his last words. He collapsed to the ground and was pronounced dead on arrival at a nearby hospital!

As Simon walked away, he said, "It made me sick! All that tragic sorrow over a parking space!"

The Bible says, "He that is slow to anger is better than the mighty; and he that ruleth his spirit than he that taketh a city" (Prov. 16:32).

* * * *

SELFISHNESS—UNSELFISHNESS

Life Is a Boomerang!

Life is a boomerang. Each one is the inheritor of himself. We get what we give. We reap as we sow.

One has said, "You can't take a pint container to a well and bring back a gallon of water. You can't give frowns and get back smiles. You can't give a loud angry voice and get gentleness from others in return.

For life is a mirror of king or slave,
  It is just what you are and do;
Then give to the world the best you have,
  And the best will come back to you.

"By the same token, you can't plant a kind word, a thoughtful deed, a generous gift, and not reap more of the same from someone, sometime, somewhere: 'He which soweth sparingly shall reap also sparingly; and he which soweth bountifully shall reap also bountifully' (II Cor. 9:6).

That man may breathe, but never live,
Who much receives, but nothing gives,
Whom none can love, whom none can thank,
Creation's blot, creation's blank!

"Cast thy bread upon the waters: for thou shalt find it after many days."—Eccles. 11:1.

Told by Roy M. Brown.

* * * *

Service, Not Gain

In the 1940's, Peter Marshall served as chaplain of the United States Senate. He often prayed for "tall, sun-crowned men" who would neither break under the pressures of office nor capitulate to the temptations of power.

In one of his prayers for the senators, he said, "Let no personal ambition blind them to their opportunities. Help them to give battle to hypocrisy wherever they find it. Give them divine common sense and a selflessness that shall make them think of service and not of gain."

"And seekest thou great things for thyself? seek them not."—Jer. 45:5.

"But seek ye first the kingdom of God, and his righteousness; and all these things shall be added unto you."—Matt. 6:33.

* * * *

The First Law of Grace

Self-preservation may be the first law of nature, but self-denial is the first law of grace.

* * * *

SERVICE

Put Shoe Leather to Your Prayers

You cannot spell GOspel without go. You cannot spell GOd without go. You cannot spell GOod Samaritan without go.

GO is at the heart of the Great Commission: "Go ye into all the world, and preach the gospel to every creature" (Mark 16:15).

The going-out church is a delight to God, going-out where the un-anchored, unchurched and unsaved are. This is of paramount importance because the overwhelming majority never cross the threshold of any church.

To pray prevailingly, we must add this postscript to our prayers: "Lord, I am your servant, subject to your directive. If it comports with your will, use me to effectuate the answer to my prayer!"

This is certain: God uses human instruments to bring to pass His plans in the lives of men, women, boys and girls. His children are His hands and His feet.

* * * *

Gushily Effusive

A black man was gushily effusive in his effort to express his love for his best girl friend: "Honey, I wish I was an octopus. Then I would have eight arms to hug you!"

The girl quipped, "You know you ain't telling the truth, for you are not using the two arms you do have!"

How reprehensible we are before God when we piously sing:

O for a thousand tongues to sing,
My great Redeemer's praise,
and fail to use the one tongue we have to "talk of His wondrous love and care!"

* * * *

Each One Is a VIP

How important is each individual!

Aaron Burr would have become president of the United States had he not lacked one electoral vote.

One vote brought Texas into the Union.

One vote kept Andrew Johnson from being impeached.

In the sight of God, each one of His children, howsoever obscure, is a V.I.P. Each one is precious to God and is personally known to Him.

Each one of God's children, howsoever weak or obscure, has his place of service and divinely given work: "For we are his workmanship, created in Christ Jesus unto good works, which God hath before ordained that we should walk in them" (Eph. 2:10).

Told by Billy Graham.

"Well Done, Good and Faithful Servant"

When Paul Mansfield, M.D., graduated from medical school, his professors predicted that he would become a great doctor. They were right, but they didn't know how right they were.

Dr. Mansfield had commiteed himself to God at an early age, and he now resolved to serve God where he was most needed. Though lucrative partnerships were offered him by established physicians, he began his practice in a desolate village in the mining region of Appalachia, the only doctor in a 50-mile radius. His office was upstairs over the town's only dry goods store.

For forty years he ministered to the poor. He delivered babies, extracted tonsils, set broken limbs, and sutured cuts. When hospitalization of a patient was necessary, he sent the patient to the nearest hospital, fifty miles away. He helped the aged, comforted the incurables, sat beside and tended dying ones through many a long, cold night. His patients were very poor, but he never turned anyone away.

When a flu epidemic struck the mountain area, he went night and day from one distant shack to another, giving shots and antibiotics. There was little time to sleep. Often brief naps were interrupted by a knock at his door or a telephone call.

Then it happened! He succumbed to the flu and soon passed away. His last conscious act was to call for his day book in which he had recorded the accounts of his patients. With great effort, he scribbled across each account: *Paid in full!*

Great numbers of mountain folk attended his funeral to pay homage to the one who had given his life that others might live. As the multitude wended their way from the little church to the place of interment, they sang, "There's a land that is fairer than day."

After the funeral solemnities, the pastor placed on the grave a sign from the front of the dry goods store, which read: *Dr. Paul Mansfield, Office Upstairs.* The doctor had been promoted to service on high: "Absent from the body. . .present with the Lord" (II Cor. 5:8).

Servant of God, well done,
  Thy glorious warfare is past;
The battle is fought, the race is run,
  And thou art crowned at last!

* * * *

"Cumbered About Much Serving" (Luke 10:40).

In his book *Run and Not Be Weary,* Dwight L. Carlson, M.D., wrote:

"Several years ago during an extremely busy time in my life, my wife and I went away for a few days of rest. While away, I sat down and listed the activities in which I was involved. I was amazed to discover that I was involved in twenty-six specific responsibilities—committees, projects and other activities. Many were work-related, some in local hospitals. More than half were related to the church and other Christian organizations. Every one was good and worthwhile. Although I could easily justify each activity, I had to admit my life was suffering from the huge load. Obviously, I had to cut down.

"The hardest word for me to say is *no.* I would like to be able to say yes to everyone and everything, but obedience to Christ requires me at times to say *no.*"

So many of us are so occupied *for

Christ that there is little or no time left to be occupied *with* Christ.

* * * *

What He Becomes

John Ruskin, English author, said, "The highest reward for man's toil is not what he gets for it, but what he becomes by it."

* * * *

Crown-Wearers

Spurgeon said, "There are no crown-wearers in Heaven who were not cross-bearers below."

* * * *

SEND ME

Send me, Lord, to the hearts without a home,
To the lives without a love,
To the crowd without a compass,
To the ranks without a refuge.
Send me to the children whom none have blessed,
To the famished whom none have fed,
To the sick whom none have visited,
To the sinners whom none have claimed,
To the fallen whom none have lifted,
To the bereaved whom none have comforted.

George Matheson.

* * * *

Saved to Serve

John Henry Newman, the author of the hymn, "Lead, Kindly Light," said, "God has created me to do Him some definite service. He has com-mitted some work to me which He has not committed to another.

"He has not created me for naught. If I am in sickness, my sickness may serve Him. If in perplexity, my perplexity may serve Him. If in sorrow, my sorrow may serve Him. He does nothing in vain. He knows what He is about!"

David said, "Thou hast enlarged me when I was in distress" (Ps. 4:1).

* * * *

Known Only to God

In national cemeteries around the world where American soldiers are buried, the word *Unknown* occurs on many grave markers.

On the memorial of the Unknown Soldier in Arlington National Cemetery appear the words: *Known Only to God.*

Many of God's children have served Christ nobly and sacrificially in obscurity. They have worked valiantly for Him and others. Their names are not known to many, but they are known to Christ and are precious to Him. He knows the name of the Good Samaritan.

Whether we serve in obscurity or in the limelight, let us be faithful. Then, when we go to be with Christ forever, His commendation, "Well done, good and faithful servant," will be ours.

* * * *

"Stir Up the Gift of God"

"The weakest among us has a gift, howsoever seemingly trivial, which is peculiar to him and which worthily used will be a gift also to his race," said John Ruskin, English essayist.

Paul admonished the young man Timothy, "Stir up the gift of God, which is in thee" (II Tim. 1:6).

* * * *

HANDS IN SERVICE

Hands that give, hands that lend,
Hands that guide those in need,
Hands that search, hands that find,
Hands that serve all mankind,
Hands that lead, hands that do—
Are these the hands of me and you?

Author unknown.

* * * *

The Need to be Needed

To be needed, to be important and indispensable to someone is a universal yearning of human beings.

Dr. Smiley Blanton, the renowned psychiatrist, told of a case which impressed him greatly:

A young wife became seriously ill. Her doctors said that she was dying, but her husband refused to accept this verdict. His wife was only semiconscious; but he went in, knelt by her bed, took her hand and spoke to her with tremendous urgency!

"Darling," he said, "you've got to get well, I need you. The children need you. We can't get by. You must return to us!"

The results were amazing and medically inexplicable! The whole downward trend was halted. In twenty-four hours the woman was out of danger.

"There was only one explanation," said Dr. Blanton thoughtfully. "She came back to life because something in her decided that life needed her, and the will to live became stronger than the will to die."

In the service of God, each one of His children has a definite place to fill, even the weaker ones: "Those members. . .which seem to be more feeble, are necessary" (I Cor. 12:22).

Jesus said, "To every man his work" (Mark 13:34).

* * * *

"Stir What Ya Got"

A traveler entered a small-town cafe and ordered a cup of coffee. When the coffee was served, he reached for the sugar rack which contained only one packet of sugar. He asked the waitress for more.

She drawled, "We ain't got no more sugar."

"But I always put two packets of sugar in my cup of coffee," he said.

The waitress quipped, "Mister, stir what ya got!"

Each one of God's children has latent potentials which should be used for God. Let us activate them.

God's command is, "Stir up the gift of God, which is in thee" (II Tim. 1:6).

* * * *

Using What We Have

At the conclusion of Dwight L. Moody's sermon to a London audience, a self-appointed critic said to him, "You made several grammatical errors in your message today!" Moody acknowledged with regret that his grammar was faulty. Then he said to his critic, "I am using all the grammar I know for God. What are you doing with the grammar you know?"

Are *you* using what you have for God?

"God hath chosen the weak things. . .to confound the. . .mighty. That no flesh should glory in his presence."—I Cor. 1:27,29

* * * *

SEX

Fifteen-Minutes' Pleasure

A young man strode down a street in Lubbock, Texas, with his cowboy heels clinking on the pavements. A man in a wheelchair rolled out in front of a door and said, "Hey, young fellow, are you good in mathematics?"

The young man replied, "No. But what is your question?"

The occupant of the invalid's chair replied, "It is this. Fifteen-minutes' pleasure with a little Mexican girl down on the Mexican border and then twenty-two years in an invalid's chair. Now, was it worth it?"

"My God, no!" was the young man's instant reply.

The victim of crippling VD warned, "For he that soweth to his flesh shall of the flesh reap corruption" (Gal. 6:8).

John R. Rice.

* * * *

A BOOMERANG

There is a destiny that makes us brother,
None goes his way alone:
All that we send into the lives of others,

Comes back into our own.

Edwin Markham.

* * * *

Cheating or Adultery, Which?

A greatly distressed soldier, on the eve of his being sent overseas, phoned Dr. Barnell, a New York City pastor, and said, "I have the feeling that I will not return. I have lost my faith in Go. I need help. I must see you!"

Later, as the distraught soldier sat before the minister, he spoke of his doubts and of his lost faith in God and the Bible.

The minister listened sympathetically and then he asked, "Have you a picture of your wife?"

"I surely have! I wouldn't be without it," the soldier said proudly as he unfolded his wallet.

Through years of experience as counsellor, Dr. Barnell went directly to the cause of the soldier's distress and doubts.

He asked, *"Have you sinned against your wife?"*

Silently the soldier sobbed in affirmative reply.

It is not primarily our doubts in God and His Word which separate us from God. It is our sins: "But your iniquities have separated between you and your God, and your sins have hid his face from you, that he will not hear" (Isa. 59:2).

How gracious is God's offer of forgiveness to sinning ones: "Come now, and let us reason together. . . though your sins be as scarlet, they shall be as white as snow" (Isa. 1:18).

* * * *

Eating Its Own Entrails

In an editorial, the *Chicago Tribune* said, "We feel that the 'sex explosion' and the pornography are destructive to civilization! This is not the first time that this has happened. When a society gets to the point where it is eating its own entrails and its civilization is about to crumble, it immediately returns to the expression of sexuality as the only thing left to somehow titillate and excite. What we're seeing now is a kind of decay and destruction of the Judeo-Christian society with its ethics and values!

* * * *

A Society must Choose

Dr. J. D. Unwin, eminent historian of Cambridge University who has studied eighty civilizations of the past four millennia, warns nations today: "Any human society is free to choose either to display great energy or to enjoy sexual freedom. The evidence is that they cannot do both for more than one generation."

* * * *

Rampant Lesbianism and Homosexuality

The Presbyterian Journal said in an editorial: "History records three periods when the moral stench of a culture or civilization became so great that the Lord God wiped it out as the only way to cleanse the earth: the period immediately following the Flood; the period of Sodom and Gomorrah, and the period of the decline and fall of Rome. Looming large in Rome's decline and fall were sexual immorality and rampant lesbianism and homosexuality."

Today, these ancient sins against God and nature are becoming rampant in our fair land. As we observe this, we are reminded of the warning penned by God's servant Paul long ago:

"*For the wrath of God is revealed from heaven against all ungodliness and unrighteousness. . .For this cause God gave them up unto vile affections: for even the women did change the natural* [use of the woman] *into that which is against nature: And likewise also the men, leaving the natural use of the woman, burned in their lust one toward another; men with men working that which is unseemly, and receiving in themselves that recompense of their error. . . . Without understanding. . .that they which commit such things are worthy of death, not only do the same, but have pleasure in them that do them*" (Rom. 1:18,26,27,31,32).

How aptly do the words spoken against ancient evildoers describe today's lesbians and homosexuals: "Were they ashamed when they committed abomination? nay, they were not at all ashamed, neither could they blush" (Jer. 8:12).

* * * *

Can't Eat Cake and Have It

Columnist Sidney Harris said, "The trouble with man is that he wants *variety* in sex and *constancy* in love. He can't have both."

God has put His enduring sanction on the marital relationship: "Marriage is honourable in all, and the bed undefiled" (Heb. 13:4).

Inescapable judgment awaits all who indulge in illicit sexual escapades: "Whoremongers and adulterers God will judge" (Heb. 13:4).

* * * *

Sexual Promiscuity

Dr. Lofton Hudson, a veteran marital counselor, said, "Sexual promiscuity leads to a kind of superficiality in relationships. I see this in people I counsel—bachelors in their thirties who have been promiscuous through the years. They don't love anybody. They don't know what it means to love. They have loved superficially so long, they just can't form a deep attachment and can't feel deeply toward anyone."

* * * *

Blind Leaders of the Blind

A chaplain in a college in Florida said, "In respect to sexual ethics, people are free in Christ, free from the law, free from value judgments, free to deal creatively within the relationships of life, free to act responsibly in their immediate context, guided only by the controlling love of God."

How character-wrecking and home-destroying is the chaplain's pronouncement!

Long ago God gave this changeless warning to those who spurn the true and tried norms of society and advocate sexual promiscuity apart from the marital relationship: "Marriage is honourable in all, and the bed undefiled: but whoremongers and adulterers God will judge" (Heb. 13:4).

God has given a changeless directive for the lifestyle of His children: "Ye have been called unto liberty; only use not liberty for an occasion to the flesh" (Gal. 5:13).

Adapted from
The Presbyterian Journal.

* * * *

Beyond Repair

In *Family Weekly,* Harriet Van Horne, author of *Never Go Anywhere Without a Pencil,* wrote:

"Where casual (sexual) relationships ultimately lead is to a race of displaced women who are sexually exploited and deeply resentful. In abrogating the old sexual code, in deforming the basic institutions built upon that code—chiefly home and family—we are rending the whole fabric of society.

"The ways of the young will always puzzle and dismay the generation that begot them. Social conventions are in constant flux. But basic human needs remain fairly constant. This is why the young who focus on 'relationships'—shunning love, romance, commitment and all the

rest—may be damaging themselves beyond repair."

* * * *

SIN

"Abhor That Which Is Evil"

As a youth, Lowell Thomas moved with his family to Boulder, Colorado. There, crime and immorality were rampant, all of which was attributed to the status quo.

At first this situtation shocked Thomas, but as time passed he began to look upon the evils in Boulder as the people's manner of life. He thought less and less about them.

Alarmingly and increasingly existent in our nation today are all the sins and corrosive evils which brought about the decay and ultimate disintegration of the mighty nations in antiquity, such as immorality, drunkenness and murder.

Many today accept unconcernedly these character-tarnishing, nation-enfeebling sins as our manner of life and are no longer troubled about them.

There is but *one* attitude God's children can have about sin: "Abhor [detest utterly] that which is evil" (Rom. 12:9).

Edmund Burke, statesman and orator, warned, "The only thing necessary for the triumph of evil is for good men to do nothing about it!"

How urgently needed is the sounding of the rousing, conscience-stirring command, "Awake thou that

sleepest, and arise from the dead, and Christ shall give thee light" (Eph. 5:14).

* * * *

"Is There Any Hope for Me?"

One whose life had been sullied by sin's defilements asked a minister, "Is there any hope for me?"

The minister replied, "Recently as I looked skyward, I saw a fleecy white cloud—immaculately pure. As I walked along, I also saw a muddy pool of stagnant water, reeking with filth and germs. Though not seen by the eye, a miracle was occurring: The sun, shining in its resplendent glory, was lifting water from that foul water, purifying and placing it in the heaven in an immaculate, silvery cloud. If God can work that miracle of purification, can He not transform your sordid, sin-stained life?"

How hope-bringing is the wondrous promise: "Come now, and let us reason together, saith the Lord: though your sins be as scarlet, they shall be as white as snow; though they be red like crimson, they shall be as wool" (Isa. 1:18).

* * * *

Not Justice But Mercy

"This picture does not do me

justice," said an indignant lady as she viewed the proof-picture of herself. Quipped the photographer, "Madam, you do not need *justice.* You need *mercy!*"

Each one of us needs God's mercy. Here's why: "For all have sinned, and come short of the glory of God" (Rom. 3:23).

* * * *

Why We Do Bad Things

A stream ran through the pasture of a farmer. Wanting to make a place where his children and their friends could swim, he dammed up the stream. How disappointed he was when he discovered that the pool abounded with impurities!

A neighbor discovered the source of the trouble and said, "Neighbor, if you want to clean up the filth, you must remove the polluting pigs which wallow in the down-flowing stream."

Boys and girls, the Bible says that we do evil things—lie, cheat, steal—because we have an unclean heart. This is why we need to pray, "Create in me a clean heart, O God" (Ps. 51:10).

Told by B. Clayton Bell.

* * * *

Wanted: Excruciating Pain

A physician said, "If I could make one wish for the medical well-being of mankind and have it come true, it would be that cancer would begin with excruciating pain. Thus it could be detected and removed before it does its lethal work."

The beginning of sin may be plea-surable, not painful, but it ultimates in death: "Sin, when it is finished, bringeth forth death" (Jas. 1:15).

* * * *

An Inborn Tendency

How easy it is to blame others for our sins, failures and shortcomings! Adam blamed Eve for his sin: "The woman whom thou gavest to be with me, she gave me of the tree, and I did eat" (Gen. 3:12). Saul blamed the people for his willful disobedience to God's explicit command: "The people spared the best of the sheep and of the oxen, to sacrifice unto the Lord thy God" (I Sam. 15:15).

Of this inborn tendency to excuse ourselves and blame others for our sins and failures, Ann Russel wrote in *Psychiatric Folk Song:*

At three I had a feeling of
Ambivalence toward my brothers,
And so it follows naturally
I poisoned all my lovers.
But now I am happy! I have learned
The lesson this has taught:
That everything I do that's wrong
Is someone else's fault.

* * * *

Deadly Sins

The following sins have been designated as deadly by the Roman Catholic Church: avarice, sloth, pride, envy, lust, gluttony and wrath.

All sins are deadly: "For the wages of sin is death" (Rom. 6:23).

Sin separates from God: "Your iniquities have separated between you and your God" (Isa. 59:2).

Sin thwarts prayer: "Your sins

have hid his [God's] face from you, that he will not hear" (Isa. 59:2).

Sin is a malignancy for which there is but *one cure*: "The blood of Jesus Christ his Son cleanseth us from all sin" (I John 1:7).

* * * *

Presumptuous Sins

In a religious service in Jesus Christ's Church of East Lynn, West Virginia, Lonnie Richardson, age 28, handled rattlesnakes. He was bitten and later died. A few months previously his father-in-law had died in the same manner. Lonnie had successfully handled deadly snakes at the funeral of his father-in-law.

Greatly do misguided but sincere ones need to voice the prayer: "Keep back thy servant also from presumptuous sins; let them not have dominion over me" (Ps. 19:13).

* * * *

Out of the Heart

Concerning evil thoughts which beget sinful deeds, Moses taught, Don't let them out: "Thou shalt not commit adultery" (Exod. 20:14); Freud counseled, "Don't keep them in—give expression to them"; Jesus taught, Don't let them in: "Whosoever looketh on a woman to lust after her hath committed adultery with her already in his heart" (Matt. 5:28).

How wise we are to obey the command: "Keep thy heart with all diligence; for out of it are the issues of life" (Prov. 4:23).

* * * *

Keep Sharp Eye on Little Foxes

Three hundred and forty-six people were killed sometime ago in a plane crash in France. A cargo door that hadn't been shut exactly right was the reason given for the ill-fated plane to plunge to the earth. One little bolt might have made the difference.

Often it is the so-called little sins which lead to greater and character-destroying sins: "Take us the foxes, the little foxes, that spoil the vines" (Song of Sol. 2:15).

* * * *

"Come Ye Sinners"

On a Christmas Eve, Jerome, who prepared the Vulgate, the Latin version of the Bible, wanted to give a gift to the Saviour. First, he offered what was most precious to him—his translation of the Scriptures. The gift was rejected.

Then he offered what virtues he felt he possessed. They, too, were rejected.

Then the Lord seemed to say to him, "Jerome, it is your sins that I want *first*. Bring them to me that I may forgive them. Then any gift you may make will be acceptable to me."

God wants to take our sin-besmirched life and give us a new life; "If any man be in Christ, he is a new creature" (II Cor. 5:17).

Come, ye sinners, poor and needy,
  Weak and wounded, sick and sore;
Jesus ready stands to save you,
  Full of pity, love and pow'r.

Let not conscience make you linger,
  Nor of fitness fondly dream;

* * * *

Two Kinds of Sin

The Bible differentiates between two kinds of sins: sins of the *flesh* and sins of the *spirit or disposition:* "Let us cleanse ourselves from all filthiness of the flesh and spirit" (II Cor. 7:1).

Which of these sins works the greatest havoc in the home and church? Usually the latter.

Let us cease giving a clean bill of health to the Elder Brothers among us and condemning unsparingly the Prodigal Sons. How like our crop of present-day elder brothers was the Elder Brother of long ago: utterly devoid of love and compassion. With lips swollen with mulish mopings, he said to his father; "Lo, these many years do I serve thee, neither transgressed I at any time thy commandment: and yet thou never gavest me a kid, that I might make merry with my friends" (Luke 15:29).

He had no friends: "A man that hath friends must shew himself friendly" (Prov. 18:24). He needed no fatted calf to feed his friends. A pork chop would have been an abundance.

* * * *

Nothing Hidden

In *Christianity Today*, Edith Schaeffer said;

"Nation can spy upon nation, dictator upon individuals, as electronic devices 'open' telegrams and 'listen in' on phone conversations, recording them to be studied at leisure.

"Never before have there been such possibilities of discovering the secrets 'hidden' in private communications. Electronic 'arms' stick up in the desert; square pieces of what to the uneducated eye look like innocent metal shapes, protrude above buildings, directed to catch the information flying through the atmosphere. Codes can be recorded and unscrambled with amazing rapidity. Satellites circle the globe like gigantic brooms, sweeping up all the dusty bits of information. Added to this is a projection of possible future results of research: the 'reading' of brain waves. Terrifying is the thought of sinful men controlling machines that, in a sense, are being improved to control men!"

Newsweek said, "There is no hiding place!"

Long ago Jesus said, "For there is nothing covered, that shall not be revealed; and hid, that shall not be known" (Matt. 10:26).

We cannot hide *from* God: "Thou God seest me" (Gen. 16:13); "For the eyes of the Lord run to and fro throughout the whole earth" (II Chron. 16:9).

However, we can hide *in* God: "Your life is hid with Christ in God" (Col. 3:3).

* * * *

Worthless Panaceas

Dr. Richard Moran, assistant professor at Mount Holyoke College in Massachusetts, said, "Medical treatment can wipe out crime by the year 2000. We are so effective in manipulative medical techniques that criminal behavior can be controlled. Criminals found to be crime prone would be treated by implanting electronic devices in the brain which could be used to monitor their movements!"

Long ago the prophet Jeremiah said: "Can the Ethiopian change his skin, or the leopard his spots? then may ye also do good, that are accustomed to do evil" (Jer. 13:23). How worthless are manmade panaceas to change the "deceitful. . .and desperately wicked" heart of man!

God formed man; sin deformed man; Christ *alone* can transform man!

"Neither is there salvation in any other: for there is none other name under heaven given among men, whereby we must be saved."—Acts 4:12.

* * * *

An Unerring Diagnostician

Mona Carothers, a 9-year-old girl of Austin, Texas, was rushed to a hospital, suffering from nausea and severe abdominal pains. Her illness was erroneously diagnosed as viral-gastro enteritis—a stomach virus—and she was released.

Shortly thereafter the girl began vomiting and was rushed again to the hospital. She was pronounced dead upon arrival. A ruptured appendix was the cause of her death.

Man sometimes errs in diagnosing a physical illness. But the Bible never errs in diagnosing the spiritual illness of those without the Saviour: "The whole head is sick, and the whole heart faint. From the sole of the foot even unto the head there is no soundness in it; but wounds, and bruises, and putrifying sores" (Isa. 1:5,6).

* * * *

Jesus Agreed

Albert Einstein said, "The real problem is in the hearts and minds of men. It is not a problem of *physics* but of *ethics*. It is easier to denature plutonium than to denature the evil spirit of man."

Jesus agreed: "For from within, out of the heart of men, proceed. . . adulteries. . . murders. . . Thefts. . . All these evil things come from within, and defile the man" (Mark 7:21-23).

* * * *

1,000 Yards Short

The ominous headline of a newspaper recently said, "Samoa Jetliner Crash Kills 95 of 101 Aboard!" The story told of the crash of a Pan-American World Airways 707 jetliner which went down 1,000 yards short of the runway during heavy rain and burst into flames!

Aeronautically speaking, one thousand yards is an almost infinitesimal distance. Yet missing the runway by this short distance cost the lives of many and brought deep sorrow and irretrievable loss to their loved ones.

The Bible says, "For all have sinned, and come short [missed the mark] of the glory of God" (Rom. 3:23).

Imagined goodness and self-righteousness can never compensate, or make up, for shortness or failure to meet God's standard: "Be ye. . . perfect, even as your Father which is in heaven is perfect" (Matt. 5:48).

A man never stands so tall in God's sight as when he kneels and pleads, "God be merciful to me a sinner" (Luke 18:13), and confesses:

My hope is built on nothing less,
Than Jesus' blood and righteousness.

* * * *

Negative Goodness

Thomas Arnold, headmaster of Rugby School, said, "I was never sure of a boy who only loved good. Till the boy also began to hate evil, I did not feel that he was safe."

Long ago David said, "Ye that love the Lord, hate evil" (Ps. 97:10).

It is not enough for God's children to "abhor that which is evil." We must also "cleave to that which is good" (Rom. 12:9).

It is not enough to "cease to do evil." We must also "learn to do well" (Isa. 1:16,17).

How abhorrent to God and man is the loveless complaining of one long ago who had only *negative* goodness: "Lo, these many years do I serve thee, neither transgressed I at any time thy commandment" (Luke 15:29).

* * * *

Smart At Thought of Sin

"Keep thy conscience continually tender," said Richard Baxter, "and then it will check the first appearance of sinful passions and will smart at the mere thought of sin."

The Apostle Paul said, "And herein do I exercise myself, to have always a conscience void of offence toward God, and toward men" (Acts 24:16).

* * * *

"When It Is Finished"

The Texas State Department of Health affirmed, "Venereal diseases strike more people than all the other reportable diseases combined—more than fifty percent. The main target of this attack is our sexually active young people between 15 and 24!"

"In the past ten years," reported the American Medical Association, "gonorrhea alone is estimated to have struck 10 million times in this country!"

Long ago Job spoke realistically: "His bones are full of the sin of his youth, which shall lie down with him in the dust" (Job 20:11).

How rewarding and life-prolonging is clean living!

* * * *

Weights

Little Iodine, a comic strip character, was getting ready to take part in sprinting races. Her coach tied some ankle weights around her legs, explaining that they were good for sprint training. Her response was, "They're heavy!"

Little Iodine ran fifty yards wearing the ankle weights and was timed at eight seconds. Then her coach told her to walk back to the starting line, take off the weights, and run the fifty yards again. To his astonishment she again took eight seconds. What was wrong?

Explained little Iodine, "I took the weights off my feet and carried them!"

The Bible says, "Let us lay aside every weight, and the sin which doth so easily beset us, and let us run with patience the race that is set before us, Looking unto Jesus the author and finisher of our faith" (Heb. 12:1,2).

Alice Marie Knight.

* * * *

Symptoms

Dr. L. Nelson Bell said, "The basic warfare of the church is not against poverty, racism, housing, population explosion, gun control, law and order, drugs and what have you. These are *symptoms* of the disease, not the disease. The disease is sin in the human heart. This is a spiritual battle and the answer is in the outpouring of God's Spirit."

Jesus said, "For from within, out of the heart of men, proceed evil thoughts, adulteries, fornications, murders" (Mark 7:21).

* * * *

SINGING

In a Nightclub or a Church?

Sometimes I cannot tell whether I am in a nightclub listening to "blues," "torch," or "disco" music or a church while the performer is making love to the microphone. There is very little quality sacred music being taught or sung in many of our worship services.

Tad Roberts, Minister of Music, South Main Church, Houston.

* * * *

"The Spirit Is Lacking"

The members of the combined choirs of Los Angeles looked forward with keen anticipation to being conducted for the first time by Leopold Stokowski in their final rehearsal of Bach's *St. Matthew Passion.*

At the rehearsal, Stokowski went through the composition with several hundred singers and orchestra. At its conclusion, he tapped for silence and said, "Well, I guess you know the notes well enough. *But the spirit is lacking!*

"Now, I want each one of you to sit down tonight with your Bible and read St. Matthew's account of the life of Christ. Try to grasp it all! Who knows—perhaps that message is just what our listeners need in a time of doubt and despair. Then let us come back to our performance and try to convey to our audience the meaning and inspiration in these sacred words!"

How appropriate were the conductor's words in this day of doubt and despair!

We can effectively impart God's tranquilizing Word to others only when we personally are saturated with it and know its fear-allaying power.

"Wherefore comfort one another with these words."—I Thess. 4:18.

* * * *

"How Could I Keep From Singing?"

As Bob Hope and a group of entertainers entered St. Albans Hospital, they heard beautiful singing. Then they saw a badly maimed veteran of the Vietnam War pushing himself toward them in a wheelchair, using his arms, the only limbs he had left.

Hope said, "We have come to sing for you and you are singing for us."

The soldier replied, "When I stopped thinking about what I had *lost* and began looking at all I have *left,* how could I keep from singing?"

* * * *

Oneness in Song

The compilers of an Episcopal hymnal said some years ago, "When we praise God in song we become aware of the unity which underlies our differences. The carols we sing at Christmas, for example, include the Roman Catholic—'O Come, All Ye Faithful'; the Episcopal—'O Little Town of Bethlehem'; the Lutheran—

'All My Heart This Night Rejoices'; and the Congregational—'Joy to the World.' "

The hymn compilers also noted that voices are blended in oneness when we sing, "All Hail the Power of Jesus' Name," composed by a Wesleyan; "Blest Be the Tie That Binds," composed by a Baptist; and, "O Lamb of God, Still Keep Me," composed by a Plymouth Brethren.

Scriptural unity isn't an organizational unity, but a spiritual unity—oneness in Christ and the heavenly Father: "That they all may be one; as thou, Father, art in me, and I in thee, that they also may be one in us" (John 17:21).

* * * *

Atheism Is Songless

When things go wrong, 'Sing in your hearts unto the Lord' (Col. 3:16).

Song turns defeat into victory. Long ago God's children found this to be true: "And when they began to sing and to praise, the Lord set ambushments against the children of Ammon, Moab, and mount Seir. . . and they were smitten" (II Chron. 20:22).

Christianity is a singing religion. Atheism and agnosticism are songless. They produce nothing to sing about.

* * * *

SORROW—SUFFERING

The Best Part of the Pig

In our workaday world, with its sorrow and suffering, its problems and perplexities, one of God's greatest gifts to His children is a sense of humor. Let me illustrate:

A few years ago I visited a terminal patient in one of our Austin, Texas, hospitals. She referred humorously to her name—HOGG. Her touch of humor opened wide the door for me to enter and I stepped right in and told a story:

Some years ago a minister, Dr. John W. Ham, sat in a railway coach. In came a bumpkin and plopped down beside the minister. Wanting to be sociable, he asked, "What might be your name?"

Dr. Ham replied, "My name is the best part of the pig!"

The backwoodsman grabbed his hand and exclaimed, "O, Mr. Chitterlings, I am so glad to meet you!"

The patient laughed heartily and said, "That story does me more good than the doctor's pill!"

Who is so undiscerning to say that it didn't?"

* * * *

"Take My Hand, Precious Lord"

"In 1932, my wife Hettie and I were living in Chicago," said Thomas A. Dorsey, a black man and a well-known writer of Gospel songs. "We were expecting our first child. En route to St. Louis for a revival meeting, I discovered that I didn't have my briefcase; and I returned

home. Nettie was asleep. So I slipped the briefcase from under the bed and resumed my trip.

"Two nights later, I received a telegram from Chicago saying my wife had died in childbirth! Some friends drove me home and I learned that the baby boy had died also. We buried mother and son in the same casket.

"That was double trouble and I couldn't take it. I said, 'God, You aren't worth a dime to me right now.' "

A few days later, however, the fog lifted from Dorsey's sorrow-riven soul. As his fingers moved along the keyboard of his piano, the words of the hymn *Precious Lord, Take My Hand* came to him.

Born in the matrix of overwhelming sorrow, the hymn imparts its sorrow-assuaging message to millions of broken hearts:

Precious Lord, take my hand, Lead me on,
  help me stand;
I am tired, I am weak, I am worn;
Thru the storm, thru the night,
Lead me on to the light,
Take my hand, precious Lord, lead me home.

When my way grows drear,
  Precious Lord, linger near;
When my life is almost gone,
Hear my cry, hear my call,
Hold my hand lest I fall;
Take my hand, precious Lord, lead me home.

"Thou hast enlarged me when I was in distress."—Ps. 4:1.

* * * *

SHUT-IN

Shut-in, I never liked the word,
It held a plaintive note,
Until a different view I got
From what one shut-in wrote:

"Shut-in?" she said, "Oh, yes indeed,
Shut in from noise and strife,
But shut out are so many things
That cluttered up my life.

"Shut-in are peace, and faith, and
hope,
Shut out are fear and doubt;
Shut-in are words and deeds of cheer,
No heart can do without.

"Shut-in my mind are memories
Of gayer, brighter years;
I smile, sometimes remembering,
Sometimes I yield to tears.

"Shut-ins are friends I cannot lose,
I hold them in my heart,
And though the miles stretch
between,
We are never apart.

"Shut-in! Why it's a blessed word!
My soul will one day trod
On happy feet to Heaven's door,
And be forever shut-in with God!"

Ruth Adams Belcher,
in *Open Window*.

* * * *

Mender of Broken Things

God will accept broken hearts if we
will bring to Him all the broken parts:
"He healeth the broken in heart, and
bindeth up their wounds" (Ps. 147:3).

The Great Physician is the Mender
of broken things. He came into our
distraught, distressed world for this
purpose: "He hath sent me to heal
the brokenhearted" (Luke 4:18).

There is a Balm in Gilead,
To make the wounded whole;
There is a Balm in Gilead,
To heal the sin-sick soul!

* * * *

Glibly Charismatic Leaders

Said R. Norman Herbert, "One of
the tragedies of the church today is
the always smiling, glibly char-
ismatic leaders who convey to the
people in the pew that they never
have a down moment or a dismal day.
Not so! At times I am just as despon-
dent as anyone. God help me if I
claim it is not so!"

Our Saviour, the "man of sorrows,"
was not always joyous. He said at
Gethsemane, "My soul is exceeding
sorrowful, even unto death" (Matt.
26:38).

"Man is born unto trouble, as the
sparks fly upward" (Job 5:7), but,
through God's enabling grace, he may
rise above his trouble and live
radiantly and triumphantly: "More
than conquerors through him that
loved us" (Rom. 8:37).

* * * *

How Like a Pig!

A pig never looks up unless it is flat
on its back. How like a pig are many
people in this regard. They look up to
God only when some tragedy overtakes them, or some sickness puts
them flat on their backs.

It is *good* to call upon God in times
of trouble: 'And call upon me in the
day of trouble" (Ps. 50:15).

It is *better* to continuously call upon God: "Men ought always to pray, and not to faint" (Luke 18:1); "Pray without ceasing" (I Thess. 5:17).

* * * *

Comfort and Discomfort

"One of my teachers at Southwestern Seminary," said Kiely Young, "often said to the youthful ministerial students, 'Comfort the afflicted and afflict the comforted.'"

As "grief is the portion of some every where," the ministry of comforting the disconsolate ones is greatly needed: "Comfort ye, comfort ye my people, saith your God" (Isa. 40:1).

As many of God's children have succumbed to lethargy and deadly unconcern, they greatly need to be discomforted and awakened from their wintry sleep: "Awake thou that sleepest. . .and Christ shall give thee light" (Eph. 5:14).

God's displeasure is upon *take-it-easy* ones in His service: "Woe to them that are at ease in Zion" (Amos 6:1).

* * * *

Inexplicable, Heaven-Sent Gifts

Often Satan is the deliveryman to convey to God's children some testing, inexplicable and Heaven-sent *gift*: "There was given to me a thorn in the flesh, the messenger of Satan to buffet me" (II Cor. 12:7).

By unquestioning submission to God, His children prove the sufficiency of His grace and emerge

refined and purified: "When he hath tried me, I shall come forth as gold" (Job 23:10).

Judge not the Lord by feeble sense,
But trust Him for His grace;
Behind a frowning providence,
He hides a smiling face!

William Cowper.

* * * *

When Heart Is Broken

Upon the completion of a young singer's solo, beautifully rendered, there was thunderous applause!

Two voice teachers who had come to hear her sat together. One exclaimed, "How beautiful! What a voice!"

The other more elderly teacher said, "Some day she will be a truly great singer—*when her heart is broken!*"

He meant that the depth of feeling and pathos is attained only when we have sorrowed and suffered.

I walked a mile with Pleasure,
She chattered all the way,
But left me none the wiser
For all she had to say.

I walked a mile with Sorrow,
And not a word said she;
But, oh, the things I learned from her
When Sorrow walked with me!

Robert B. Hamilton.

* * * *

A DARKENED ROOM

Many a rapturous minstrel
Among the suns of light,
Will say of his sweetest music,
"I learned it in the night."

And many a rolling anthem

That fills the Father's throne,
Sobbed at its first rehearsal,
In the shroud of a darkened room.

Tennyson.

* * * *

AGAINST A THORN

Once I heard a song of sweetness
  As it cleft the morning air,
Sounding in its blest completeness,
  Like a tender pleading prayer.
And I sought to find the singer
  Whence the wondrous song was
    born,
And I found a bird, sorely wounded,
  Pinioned by a cruel thorn.

I have seen a soul in sadness,
  While its wings with pain were
    furled,
Giving hope and cheer and gladness,
  That would bless a weeping world.
And I knew that life of sweetness
  Was of pain and sorrow borne,
And a stricken soul was singing
  With its heart against a thorn.

We are told of One who loves us,
  Of a Saviour crucified;
We are told of nails that pinioned,
  And a spear that pierced His side.
We are told of cruel scourging,
  Of a Saviour bearing scorn,
And He died for our salvation,
  With his brow against a thorn.

Ye are not above the Master,
  Will you breathe a sweet refrain?
And His grace will be sufficient,
  When your heart is pierced with
    pain.
Will you live to bless His loved ones,
  Tho' your life be bruised and torn,

Like a bird that sang so sweetly,
  With its heart against a thorn?

Author unknown.

* * * *

God Understands

God knows about and understands
the heartaches and heartbreaks of His
children: "I know their sorrows" (Exod. 3:7).

God understands your sorrow,
  He sees the falling tear,
And whispers, "I am with thee,"
  Then falter not, nor fear!

God understands your heartache,
  He knows the bitter pain;
O trust Him in the darkness,
  You cannot trust in vain!

Oswald J. Smith.

* * * *

The Gospel of Broken Hearts

John Henry Jowett said, "The
gospel of a broken heart demands the
ministry of a bleeding heart. We can
never heal the hurts that we do not
feel."

How Christlike we are when we
enter sharingly and feelingly into the
heartaches and heartbreaks of others:
"Touched with the feeling of [their]
infirmities" (Heb. 4:15).

* * * *

Challenged

As Michelangelo viewed the
painting of a young artist, he in-
scribed thereon one word: **Amplius**—
larger!

In the School of Sorrow and Suffering, God enlarges His submissive children spiritually: "Thou hast enlarged me when I was in distress" (Isa. 4:1).

In wonderment we exclaim, "O the depth. . .of the wisdom. . .of God! how unsearchable are his judgments, and his ways past finding out!" (Rom. 11:33).

* * * *

None Escape

A young mother, overwhelmed with sorrow because of the loss of her son, sought help from a Chinese sage. He told her, "I will be able to help you if you will bring me some mustard seed obtained from a home that has never had any sorrow."

Eagerly the sorrowing mother began her search. In every home she visited, however, there had been sorrow, and in some homes there had been loss of loved ones.

Returning to the sage, she exclaimed, "How selfish I have been! Sorrow is common to all."

"Ah, you have learned a valuable lesson, and now you are prepared to sympathize with others."

Grief is the portion of some everywhere, Help somebody today.

* * * *

Where Deeply Felt

Faber said, "There is no place where earth's sorrows are more deeply felt than in Heaven." The Bible says of our heavenly Father, "In all their affliction he was afflicted" (Isa. 63:9).

* * * *

"Follow Me"

Eugenia Price said, "The only direct statement of Jesus which is simple enough for me to comprehend when my heart is breaking or when I'm discouraged and scared is, 'Follow me.' I cannot understand life, because life is not understandable. I can, however, understand the directive, 'Follow me.' "

* * * *

How Christlike

How like Christ we are when we enter sharingly and understandingly into the sorrows and sufferings of others, making them our very own. Of Him it is written, "Himself took our infirmities, and bare our sicknesses" (Matt. 8:17).

* * * *

"I Will Carry"

An aged servant of God dreamed she walked along a beach with her Saviour. She noticed footprints in the sand. At times there was only one set of footprints—her own. In her dream she asked the Lord, "When I needed You most, why were You not there, walking beside me?"

The Lord replied, "The times you have seen only one set of footprints is when I carried you!"

In sorrow and suffering and in the winter of encroaching old age, with its attendant enfeeblement, how sustaining is God's unfailing promise: "And even to your old age. . .I will bear; even I will carry, and will deliver you" (Isa. 46:4).

* * * *

Shattered Ruins of a Broken Body

In his book, *The Divine Yes*, Dr. E. Stanley Jones testifies:

"At the age of 88, I am sitting in a rehabilitation hospital. My eyesight is cut in half, my speech barely intelligible, my locomotive powers almost nil. I am having to learn to walk again like a baby. The muscles that I smile with have been destroyed. I can't smile any more because I don't have the apparatus.

"But am I unhappy? If so, I haven't discovered it. I belong to an unshakable kingdom and an unchanging Person—Christ. My feet are on the Way. Jesus is the divine Yes, when there isn't much yes in my surroundings to rejoice in, except in Him!"

Through grace, God's children can triumph over the shattered ruins of a broken body, claiming the *sure* and sustaining promise: "And even to your old age I am he; and even to hoar hairs will I carry you: I have made, and I will bear; even I will carry, and will deliver you" (Isa. 46:4).

* * * *

BEAUTY FOR ASHES

Beauty for ashes, gold for my dross,
Joy for my sorrow, a crown for my cross,
Peace for my heartache, balm for my pain,
Sunshine for shadows, a rainbow after rain.

Widmeyer.

* * * *

Sorrow Wrought Wondrously

Sometime ago the front page of a great city newspaper had the picture of Ethel Kennedy, the widow of the slain Senator Robert F. Kennedy, and Governor George Wallace who was sitting in an invalid's chair, convalescing from a would-be assassin's bullets.

A look of sympathetic sorrow pervaded both faces as Ethel Kennedy gripped the governor's hand. Heretofore political, sectional and motivational differences had separated them. At the moment, all misunderstanding and misgivings vanished. Mutual sorrow had wrought wondrously!

Shakespeare said, "Sweet are the uses of adversity!"

* * * *

Triumphant!

In the operating room of a hospital, a young nurse had her first day of full responsibility in helping a surgeon.

After an operation, she said, "You've removed eleven sponges, Doctor, but we used twelve."

The doctor replied, "I've removed them all. We'll now close the incision."

"No," the nurse protested, "we used twelve."

Dogmatically the surgeon replied, "I'll take the responsibility. Suture!"

"Doctor, don't do that," exclaimed the concerned nurse.

Smiling, the surgeon lifted his foot and showed the nurse the twelfth sponge on the floor. "I was testing you for your integrity and efficiency.

You'll make a splendid nurse," he said.

God often submits His children to severe testings to prove them. Job is an excellent example. He emerged triumphant from the severest ordeals and said, "But he [God] knoweth the way that I take: when he hath tried me, I shall come forth as gold" (Job 23:10).

* * * *

"Joy Cometh in the Morning!"

How inspiring it is in the dark night to watch the full moon rise and throw a lane of silver across the inky waters!

For His children, God sheds golden light across the ominous clouds of their grief with His sorrow-assuaging promise: "Weeping may endure for a night, but joy cometh in the morning" (Ps. 30:5).

* * * *

IF WE COULD SEE

If we could see beyond today, as God can see;
If all the clouds should roll away, the shadows flee;
O'er present griefs we would not fret,
Each sorrow we would soon forget;
For many joys are waiting yet for you and me.

"If we could see, if we could know," we often say,
But God in love, a veil doth throw across our way;
We cannot see what lies before,
And so we cling to Him the more;
He leads us till this life is o'er,
Trust and obey.

Moody Monthly.

* * * *

LORD, THIS IS A THORN

I stood a mendicant of God,
Before His royal throne,
And asked Him for one priceless gift
For me to call my own.

I took the gift from out His hand,
But as I would depart,
I cried, "But Lord, this is a thorn,
And it has pierced my heart!

"It's a strange and hurtful gift
Which Thou hast given me":
He said, "I love to give good gifts,
I gave my best to thee."

I took it home, and thought at first
The cruel thorn hurt sore,
As long years passed I grew at last
To love it more and more.

I learned God never gives a thorn
Without this added grace:
He takes the thorn to pin aside
The veil which hides His face!

Author unknown.

* * * *

SOUL WINNING

Concern for Others

A zealous, concerned lady invited a young man to visit her church. He responded. Hearing an earnest message by the pastor, he was deeply moved. He asked Christ to come into his life and use him in His service. God answered his prayer. Who was that young man? *Dr. Russell H. Conwell* who became pastor of the Temple Baptist Church, Philadelphia, Pennsylvania, founded an orphanage, Temple University, and Temple Hospital.

His outstanding achievements for God and man qualify him for this biblical appraisal: "He being dead yet speaketh" (Heb. 11:4).

Should less be said of the lady, who is known only to God, whom God used to redirect a life onto a high and enduring plain of service for God and man?

* * * *

Pots and Pans

One of the charges against John Bunyan, author of *Pilgrim's Progress,* was, "The tinker tries to mend souls as well as pots and pans!"

* * * *

Appealing or Appalling?

A barber, brimming with soul-winning zeal, said as he stropped his razor after lathering the face of a customer, "Are you prepared to die?"

The frightened customer bolted from the chair and ran from the shop! The barber lost not only a potential convert, but a customer as well.

Enthusiasm can be appealing! It can also be appalling!

God's Word says, "It is good to be zealously affected always in a good thing" (Gal. 4;18). Our zeal, however, must be tempered with knowledge.

Of Israel, Paul said, "They have a zeal of God, but not according to knowledge" (Rom. 10:2).

* * * *

Mayor Daley Was Right

Speaking of his years as mayor of Chicago, Richard Daley said, "I have had dedicated people who go from door to door and talk to other people. I have found that the most successful politics is on a door-to-door basis."

The door-to-door method is the best way to reach and win people to Christ. Long ago Paul said, "I have taught you publickly, and from house to house" (Acts 20:20).

If we would reach the unchurched, unsaved multitudes, we must deem it more necessary to ring doorbells than churchbells.

* * * *

Unhappy Because Loved Ones Are Unsaved

Dr. G. Campbell Morgan received a letter from a boy which began: "Dear Dr. Morgan, last night I received the Lord Jesus Christ in your meeting. I have been unhappy ever since. . . ."

Sadly Dr. Morgan looked up from the letter. Then, resuming the reading, he observed with joy that the sentence concluded, ". . .because my father is not a Christian!"

Oh, that more of us were unhappy because loved ones and friends are unsaved! How few today can say with God's ancient prophet; "Oh that my head were waters, and mine eyes a fountain of tears, that I might weep day and night for. . .my people" (Jer. 9:1).

* * * *

A Two-Pronged Resolution

I was converted as a teenage boy. 'Twas then I made a two-pronged resolution that I would memorize every day at least two verses from the Bible, and every day speak to an unsaved person about Christ. What dividends of joy this resolution has brought to me!

* * * *

"Then Go to Hell!"

Dr. Len G. Broughton told of an incident which occurred during an invitation he gave at the close of a sermon for the unsaved ones to come and confess Christ, the Saviour.

A half-witted fellow, filled with zeal for his Lord, asked a self-righteous man near him, "Do you want to go to Heaven?"

The man angrily replied, "No!"

The half-wit said, "Then go to Hell!"

As the Christ-rejector left the church, his slumbering conscience began to awaken. He thought, *I don't want to go into a lost hereafter.*

Shortly thereafter he sorrowed for sin and publicly confessed Christ as his only hope of eternal life.

* * * *

JUST ONE SOUL

Perhaps in heaven one day to me,
  Some blessed soul will come and say,

"All hail, dear one! but for thee,
  My soul to death had been a prey!"
Ah, then, what sweetness in the thought,
One soul to Glory to have brought!

"For what is our hope, or joy, or crown of rejoicing? Are not even ye in the presence of our Lord Jesus Christ at his coming. For ye are our glory and joy."—I Thess. 2:19,20.

* * * *

Where Perishing Ones Are

While in Europe, Dr. Robert William Dale wrote to his wife in Birmingham, England:

"Lake Lucerne is before me—the noblest scenery, as some think, in all Europe. But I declare that there is nothing in this magnificent view which makes me feel half the thrill I have sometimes felt when I have looked down on the smoky streets of Birmingham from the railway, as I returned to my work there after a holiday. The thought that you and I together may, with God's help, save multitudes in our smoky city sends the blood through my veins with an exultation and glow which the most magnificent views of earth cannot create!"

In this day when our great cities desperately need a steady evangelical witness, this kind of excitement is greatly needed.

Told by Warren W. Wiersbe.

* * * *

LOST IN SIN

Lead me to some soul today,

O teach me, Lord, just what to say,
Friends of mine are lost in sin
And cannot find the way.
Few there are who seem to care,
And few there are who pray;

Melt my heart and fill my life,
Give me one soul today!

Will H. Houghton.

* * * *

THANKSGIVING

"Fearfully and Wonderfully Made"

"Man's best efforts to duplicate your brain fall far short of what many believe is God's most fantastic creation," said Dr. Albert J. Smith, chairman of the biology department at Wheaton (Illinois) College. "As computers have been developed, intricate and astounding as they are, they merely point up similarities that prove that the brain, as God's computer, is matchless.

"The brain has perhaps thirty million neurons, but each has connections with other brain cells. Each of these connections has the capacity of varying communication with neighboring cells. Thus information passed by a neuron is almost limitless. The storage capacity of the brain is vastly superior to the computer. To provide a computer with such capacity is far beyond the technology of our day. Impressed as we are with what is known about the human brain, there is even more that is not known. Whatever the reason for our shortcomings to fully understand the brain, *what we do know creates an awe of God!*" said Dr. Smith.

In wonderment we exclaim, "I will praise thee; for I am fearfully and wonderfully made: marvellous are thy works; and that my soul knoweth right well." (Ps. 139:14).

* * * *

Triumphant and Grateful

Some thieves took the pocketbook of Matthew Henry, the famed exegete. Later he wrote in his diary: "I am thankful because I was never robbed before. Although they took my purse, they did not take my life. Although they took all I had, it was not much. I am thankful, too, because it was I who was robbed, and not I who robbed."

"In every thing give thanks: for this is the will of God in Christ Jesus concerning you."—I Thess. 5:18.

* * * *

THE PRIVILEGE OF LIVING

Thank God for the privilege of living,
     The privilege of breathing His air,
The privilege of being alive in the
     midst
     Of such beauty everywhere!

Thank the good Lord for His mercy,
     Of giving me eyes to see,
A mind to learn, and a voice to speak
     Of a faith in eternity!

Thank Him for the privilege of living,
     For sharing His earth and His sky,

That a gift so rare as the gift of life
Was given to such as I!

Helen Lowrie Marshall.

* * * *

One of God's Best Gifts

A dejected and defeated young man had some perplexing problems with which he grappled unsuccessfully. He confided in a trusted friend and asked, "Why is it that I can't seem to cope with these problems?"

Thoughtfully and wisely the friend replied, "Maybe it's because you aren't grateful enough."

"Grateful? What are you talking about?" he asked in astonishment.

The friend replied, "I am talking about a law of living that you will discover someday. Focus upon adversities, as you are doing, and you'll attract more of them. Be grateful for the privilege of living, and your life will grow increasingly bright. Be less of a complainer and more of a thanksgiver!"

One of God's greatest gifts to His children is a glowing, grateful heart—thankful for anything, thankful for everything: "In every thing give thanks: for this is the will of God in Christ Jesus concerning you" (I Thess. 5:18).

* * * *

"WHERE ARE THE NINE?"

I had started back, yea, Luke, I had
started to find
The Healer so mighty, so tender
and kind;
But work pressed upon me: my business, you know,
For all of those years I was forced to
let go;
I had tools to collect, I had orders to
get,
I found my poor family burdened
with debt;
My time was all taken with labour
and care,
The days went more swiftly than I
was aware,
With the practical problems I had to
attack,
But I meant to go back, oh, I meant to
go back!
I never supposed He would wait my
return,
Just one of the ten, and would linger
and yearn,
As you tell me He did; why, Luke,
had I thought
There is no one on earth I would
sooner have sought,
I would have shown Him my body,
perfect and strong,
I would have thanked Him and
praised Him before the throng,
I would have followed Him gladly
forever and aye,
Had I thought that He minded my
staying away,
He so great, I so little and paltry!
Alack—
Had I only gone back! Had I only
gone back!

Amos R. Wells.

* * * *

TIME

Time Marches On

In the airport in St. Louis, Missouri, is a mammoth watch with hands that run backward. Beneath it are the words, "Make Time Run Backward!"

If it were possible to do this, and you could relive the years agone, what would you do differently?

The past is returnless. The future is unsure. The present *now* is here!

> Trust no future, howe'er pleasant!
> Let the dead Past bury its dead!
> Act, act in the living present!
> Heart within, and God o'erhead!
> **Longfellow.**

"So teach us to number our days, that we may apply our hearts unto wisdom."—Ps. 90:12.

* * * *

Inestimable Importance

Each new day God gives to us is of inestimable importance, for it is a day of our life. When tomorrow comes, this day will be gone forever!

At the threshold of each new day, God gives this changeless, sustaining promise to His children: "As thy days, so shall thy strength be" (Deut. 33:25).

* * * *

A GIFT FROM GOD

A gift was delivered at seven,
Just as I woke where I lay,
The gift was marked, "From Heaven"—
My gift was this beautiful day.

One wonderful shining good morning,
Entrusted by God to my care,
It came bearing only this warning:
"Fragile! Handle with prayer!"

Anon.

* * * *

HE THAT BELIEVETH

He that believeth shall not make haste,
In useless hurry his strength to waste;
Who walks with God can afford to wait,
For He can never arrive too late.

He that believeth shall not delay,
Who carries the word of the King on its way;
Keeps pace with the Saviour's marching tune,
And He can never arrive too soon.

He that believeth shall walk serene,
With ordered steps and leisured mien;
He dwells in the midst of eternities,
And the timeless ages of God are his.

Annie J. Flint.

* * * *

"OH TO LEARN THIS LESSON WELL!"

Day by day the manna fell,
Oh, to learn this lesson well;
Still by constant mercy fed,
Give us, Lord, our daily bread.

Day by day the promise reads,
Daily strength for daily needs;
Cast foreboding fears away,
Take the manna for today.

Thou my daily task shall give,
As for Thee I daily live;
Thus shall added years fulfill,
Not mine own, but thine own will.

Author unknown.

* * * *

The Hurrier, the Behinder

An Amish man said, "The hurrier I
go, the behinder I get!"

"Make haste slowly" is good advice. How difficult it is to do this in
our hurry, worry, bury day! We are
getting nowhere fast.

The Bible says, "He that believeth
shall not make haste" (Isa. 28:16).

* * * *

So Teach Us

Today is the first day of the rest of
your earthly life! Life is fragile. Handle it with prayer!

*"For what is your life? It is even a
vapour, that appeareth for a little
time, and then vanisheth away."—*
Jas. 4:14.

*"So teach us to number our days,
that we may apply our hearts unto
wisdom."—*Ps. 90:12.

* * * *

Hope, Despair

In describing the time of the
French Revolution, the English
novelist Charles Dickens said, "It was
the *best* of times, it was the *worst* of
times. It was the spring of hope, it
was the winter of despair."

This is true of any time. Good and
evil are ever present.

Long ago the Apostle Paul said,
"When I would do good, evil is present with me" (Rom. 7:21).

*"Be not overcome of evil, but over-
come evil with good."—*Rom. 12:21.

* * * *

One Day At a Time

One of God's aged saints fell and
broke her hip. As she lay discouraged
in a hospital bed, she asked the doctor, "How long will I have to stay
here?"

The wise doctor replied, "Just one
day at a time!"

God deals with His children on a
day-by-day basis: "As thy days, so
shall thy strength be" (Deut. 33:25);
"Give us this day our daily bread"
(Matt. 6:11).

> Just for today, my Saviour,
>   Tomorrow is not mine;
> Just for today, I ask Thee
>   For light and health divine;
> Tomorrow's care I must not bear,
>   The future is all Thine.

* * * *

Time Stays! We Go!

In *The Paradox of Time,* Henry
Dobson said, " 'Time goes,' you say.
Ah, no! Alas, time stays! We go!"

Long ago the psalmist said, "We
spend our years as a tale that is told"
(Ps. 90:9).

Let us pray, "So teach us to number our days, that we may apply our
hearts unto wisdom" (Ps. 90:12).

Art is long, and time is fleeting,
   And our hearts, though stout and brave,

Still like muffled drums are beating
Funeral marches to the grave!

Longfellow.

* * * *

"Just for Today, Lord"

"We have each day to be faithful—just one short day. Then the long years of a long life will take care of themselves without the sense of their length or their weight ever being a burden," said Andrew Murray.

Jesus said, "Sufficient unto the day is the evil thereof" (Matt. 6:34). The promise is unfailing: "As thy days, so shall thy strength be" (Deut. 33:25).

* * * *

TONGUE

Carping Critics

As a minister waited to be served breakfast in a railway dining car, a husband and wife were seated by the waiter. When the meal was being served, the wife began to complain: "This omelet is cold and tasteless, and this grapefruit is not chilled." On and on she complained, ad nauseum.

To clear the atmosphere of complaint, the minister asked the gentleman, "What business are you in?"

He replied, "I am a manufacturer."

Continuing, he said, "My wife, too, is a manufacturer."

"How interesting," said Dr. Peale. "What does she manufacture?"

He replied, "She manufactures misery for herself and others!"

Some people are happy only when they are miserable and when making others miserable.

* * * *

90% Lye

"Pleasant words are as an honeycomb, sweet to the soul, and health to the bones" (Prov. 16:24).

Sincere, encouraging words dispel gloom and bring hope: "They helped every one his neighbour; and every one said to his brother, Be of good courage" (Isa. 41:6).

Softsoap or flattering words may be a snare: "A man that flattereth his neighbour spreadeth a net for his feet" (Prov. 29:5).

Beware! Softsoap is ninety percent lye (lie).

* * * *

Soft Answer and No Answer

The Bible says that a "soft answer turneth away wrath" (Prov. 15:1.) Only God knows what no answer at all may turn away! No answer is often the right answer: "And when he was accused of the chief priests and elders, he answered nothing" (Matt. 27:12).

* * * *

"Every Idle Word"

Some years ago Chaplain Wyatt Willard, author of *The Leathernecks Come Through*, was asked to give the principal address at an installation of newly appointed officers of the Aaron Post of the American Legion, Chicago. After the long ritualistic program, at a late hour the post commander announced, "Now Chaplain Willard will give his address."

Chaplain Willard stood and said, "My address is—Wesley Avenue, Wheaton, Illinois. Come to see me!" Bravo! Then he sat down.

Church groups, which squander precious time in talking about trivial or worthless things, could profit greatly by the courageous "address" of Chaplain Willard.

How searching are the Saviour's words: "Every idle word that men shall speak, they shall give account thereof in the day of judgment" (Matt. 12:36).

One said of an aged minister, "The older he grew, the *less* he spoke and the *more* he said."

* * * *

Mouth Wide Open

Years ago I visited the mansion of the aged John D. Rockefeller in Ormond Beach, Florida. How impressed I was with a mounted large fish with its mouth wide open. Beneath it were the words: "If you had kept your mouth shut you would not be here."

Is anything opened by mistake more often than the mouth?

* * * *

Rumors Are Never Idle

NBC-TV's Barbara Walters asked Mrs. Mamie Eisenhower if the rumor about her being a dipsomaniac were true.

The gracious lady replied, "My problem is not the bottle, but a sinus condition which causes me to lose my balance and bump into things. I have what is called carotid sinus where a vein presses on the inner ear. I'm black and blue from walking around in my own house."

"Have the rumors upset you?" she was asked.

Smiling, the gracious lady replied, "I live with myself. I knew they were not true."

Newsweek, Nov. 12, '73.

* * * *

SAY IT NOW

Say it now!
If you have a friend who's true,
Always loyal, kind to you,
And you love him dearly too,
Say it now!

Say it now!
If one has helped along the way,
Ask no favors you repay,
Now your gratitude display
Say it now!

Say it now!
If some joy should come his way,
Then rejoice with him each day,
And your happiness convey,
Say it now!

Say it now!
If an honor he should win,
Show real interest, not chagrin,
Let your pride be genuine,
Say it now!

Say it now!
If some sorrow he must bear,
Walk with him in his despair,
Let him know how much you care,
Say it now!

Say it now!
You cannot afford to delay
Love increases day by day,
If you give it all away,
Say it now!

Etta Hart Smithey Borger,
in *Baptist Standard*.

* * * *

"Even a Fool"

Lincoln said, "Better to remain silent and be thought a fool than to speak out and remove all doubt."

The Bible says, "Even a fool, when he holdeth his peace, is counted wise" (Prov. 17:28).

* * * *

Wags Tail Good

A mangy, mongrel dog followed Ned home.

"Look, Dad," exclaimed little Ned, "what I have—a dog! I want to keep him."

"You can't," said Dad with finality. "The dog is thin, mangy and dirty. Nothing is good about him."

"But, Dad, there is something good in him," protested Ned. "He wags his tail good!"

Look for some good in others, and never speak ill of them: "Speak evil of no man" (Tit. 3:2).

One has said, "There is so much bad in the best of us, and so much good in the worst of us, that it doesn't behoove any of us to talk about the rest of us."

Alice Marie Knight.

* * * *

Just Listening Terms

A social worker asked an oldster who was having family difficulties, "Are you on speaking terms with your wife?"

He replied, "No, miss. Just listening terms!"

Often it is best to be on listening terms with others: "In the multitude of words there wanteth not sin: but he that refraineth his lips is wise" (Prov. 10:19).

* * * *

Not Always Golden

"Silence is golden," it is often said. But this is not always true. Sometimes silence is *yellow*: 'Among the chief rulers. . .they believed on him; but because of the Pharisees they did not confess him. . .for they loved the praise of men more than the praise of God' (John 12:42,43).

* * * *

Death and Life
Sullen Silence

What havoc a glib, faultfinding tongue can work: "Death and life are in the power of the tongue" (Prov. 18:21).

Suppressed, smoldering, sullen silence, too, can be disruptive and disastrous psychologically: "Now his elder son. . .was angry, and would not go in" (Luke 15:25,28).

What blessings a kind tongue can impart: "The Lord God hath given me the tongue of the learned, that I should know how to speak a word in season to him that is weary" (Isa. 50:4).

* * * *

If Two Are Dead

"Three persons can keep a secret if two of them are *dead!*" said Benjamin Franklin.

The Bible says, "A talebearer revealeth secrets: but he that is of a faithful spirit concealeth the matter" (Prov. 11:13).

Nothing is opened by mistake more often than the mouth.

Long ago the psalmist prayed, "Set a watch, O Lord, before my mouth; keep the door of my lips" (Ps. 141:3).

* * * *

Will Ever Regret

Loose your tongue when angry and you will make the greatest speech you will ever regret.

Boys flying kites may haul in their white-winged birds,
You can't do that when you are flying words;
Words unspoken fall back dead,
But God can't kill them when they're said!

"And the tongue is a fire, a world of iniquity."—Jas. 3:6.

* * * *

TRUST
(See also Faith)

"I TRUST IN THEE"

I will not doubt, though all my ships at sea
  Come drifting home with broken masts or sails;
I shall believe the Hand which never fails,
  From seeming evil worketh good to me;
  And, though I weep because those sails are battered,
  Still will I cry, while my best hopes lie shattered,
      "I trust in Thee!"

I will not doubt, though all my prayers return
  Unanswered from the still, white realm above;
  I shall believe it is an all-wise Love

Which has refused those things for which I yearn;
  And though, at times, I cannot keep
  from grieving,
  Yet the pure ardor of my fixed believing
      Undimmed shall burn.

I will not doubt, though sorrows fall like rain,
  And troubles swarm like bees about a hive;
I shall believe the heights for which I strive,
  Are only reached by anguish and by pain;
  And, though I groan and tremble with my crosses,
  I yet shall see, through my severest losses,
      The greater gain.

I will not doubt; well anchored in
the faith,
Like some stanch ship, my soul
braves every gale,
So strong its courage that it will
not fail
To breast the mighty, unknown sea of
death.
Oh, may I cry when body parts
with spirit,
"I do not doubt," so listening
worlds may hear it
With my last breath.

Ella Wheeler Wilcox.

* * * *

"Forgive Us Our Ulcers!"

In one of his prayers in the U. S.
Senate, Peter Marshall prayed, "O
Lord, forgive us our ulcers, the badges
of our anxieties and insecurities!"

To allay anxious fears and corroding cares, many resort to tranquilizers, which are now the largest
selling prescription drugs in the
United States.

Quiet trust in the provident care of
God is the best remedy for corroding
care and anxious, disquieting fears:
"Trust in the Lord with all thine
heart. . . .and depart from evil"
(Prov. 3:5,7).

* * * *

"Has It Come to That?"

An elderly lady was greatly distressed by her many troubles, both
real and imaginary. Members of her
family lovingly said, "Grandma,
we've done all we can for you. You'll
have to trust God for the rest."

A look of hopelessness pervaded
Grandma's face as she forlornly
asked, "Oh, dear, has it come to
that?"

Hearing of the incident, Vance
Havner said, "It always comes to
that! God's Word tells us to bring
every concern once and for all to the
Lord. Since He offers to handle our
problems, why not let Him do it?"

* * * *

"I STILL BELIEVE"

Although I've asked God every day
These many anxious years,
And yet the blessing has not come,
I still believe He hears.

I know that He does answer prayer,
Sometimes unseen to man,
Then I shall trust and wait 'till I
Can see God's deeper plan.

Perhaps the things for which I prayed
Were not the best for me,
But 'till I know, I'll importune,
And trust God patiently.

F. M. Bates.

* * * *

"The Central Neurosis"

Carl Jung, the famed Swiss psychiatrist, said, "The central neurosis
of our time is *emptiness.*"

Nothing temporal can assuage the
aching void in our hearts. Only God
can do that: "In returning and rest
shall ye be saved; in quietness and in
confidence shall be your strength"
(Isa. 30:15). "I will trust, and not be
afraid" (Isa. 12:2).

* * * *

Clear-Air Turbulence

On January 8, 1972, a National Airlines jumbo jet, bound for Los Angeles with 351 passengers aboard, ran into clear-air turbulence at an altitude of 31,000 feet over Texas. In describing the frightful happening, a passenger said, "All of a sudden the tail went up and it seemed like we were on a roller coaster!"

A newspaper commented, "Meteorologists know little about the air turbulence that slammed off the plane's tail. Such turbulence occurs in generally clear weather between 20,000 and 35,000 feet. It cannot be detected, even by radar."

At times, Christians encounter clear-air turbulence in their lives. They may be going along serenely when suddenly they collide with some overwhelming sorrow or difficulty whose impact is like a bolt of lightning out of the blue!

When clear-air disturbance comes, it is good to know experimentally the One who long ago spoke peace to His terrified disciples: "Be of good cheer; it is I; be not afraid" (Matt. 14:27). *"I will trust, and not be afraid."*— Isa. 12:2.

* * * *

Leave Results With God

General Dwight D. Eisenhower said, "This is what I found out about religion: It gives you courage to make the decision you must make in a crisis and the confidence to leave the results with a higher Power. Only by trust in God can a man carrying responsibility find repose."

With unshakable trust in the provident care of God, His children can say, "I will trust, and not be afraid" (Isa. 12:2).

* * * *

VICTORY

"AND HE DID IT!"

Somebody said that it couldn't be done,
But he with a chuckle replied,
That maybe it couldn't, but he would be one
Who wouldn't say so, till he had tried.

So he buckled in with a trace of a grin,
And if he worried he hid it;
He started to sing as he tackled the thing
That couldn't be done and he did it!

There are thousands to tell you it can't be done,
There are thousands to prophesy failure,
There are thousands to point out to you, one by one,
The dangers which wait to assail you.

But just buckle in with a will to win,
Without any doubt of quit it.
Just start in to sing as you tackle the thing
That "can't be done" and you'll do it!

Author Unknown

* * * *

"No Victory at Bargain Prices"

On the eve of D-Day, June 6, 1944, when the Allies invaded France in World War II, General Dwight Eisenhower briefed his soldiers thus: "There is no victory at bargain prices!" He knew that the sandy beaches of Normandy would be crimsoned with the blood and strewn with the mangled bodies of heroic men!

The Christian life is a warfare. Each one of God's children is a soldier: "Therefore endure hardness, as a good soldier of Jesus Christ" (II Tim. 2:3).

> Must I be carried to the skies
> On flow'ry beds of ease,
> While others fought to win the prize
> And sailed thro' bloody seas?
>
> Isaac Watts.

* * * *

"What Are You Doing Under There?"

Tom Malone asked an elderly Christian, "How are you getting along?"

He replied, "Pretty good, under the circumstances."

Dr. Malone quipped, "What are you doing *under* them?"

Triumphant Christians live radiantly *above* the vicissitudes of life. they "mount up with wings as eagles" (Isa. 40:31); "[They] are more than conquerors through him that [loves them]" (Rom. 8:37).

* * * *

"THE ONE I FEED"

Two natures struggle in my breast,

The one is foul, the other blest;
The "new" I love—the "old" I hate,
The one I feed will dominate.

* * * *

PROVEN LONG AGO

You cannot keep a good man down,
Is an old, time-honored tale,
'Twas proven many years ago
By Jonah and the whale.

* * * *

"With Wings of Eagles"

One day a man discovered an eagle's nest among the rocky crags, high up on a mountain. He took one of the eggs home and placed it under a setting hen. In time an eaglet and a number of chicks emerged from the eggs in the nest. All responded to the clucks of the mother hen as she scratched for worms.

The eaglet grew rapidly and became much larger than the chicks. Then one day it lifted its beak toward the sky, flapped its enormous wings and flew upward.

Like the eagle, man is endowed with certain inherent possibilities. Through God's enabling power, he can rise above the miasmic quagmires of earth and scale heights of grandeur in noble service for God and man.

God's promise is unfailing: "But they that wait upon the Lord. . .shall mount up with wings as eagles; they shall run, and not be weary; and they shall walk, and not faint" (Isa. 40:31).

* * * *

"Life Is a Jail Sentence"

In a college newspaper, students gave these definitions of life: "Life is a joke that isn't funny"; "Life is a jail sentence for the crime of being born"; "Life is a disease that afflicted the earth in its old age, for which the only cure is death."

The dedicated Christian triumphantly says of life: "For me to live is Christ" (Phil. 1:21).

* * * *

Glory-Crowned Revelations

I stood on the balcony of my hotel room in Switzerland and watched an indescribably glorious and dazzlingly beautiful scene—sunrise over the Bernese Alps. Standing there in hushed silence and reverential awe, I saw three shining snow-capped peaks—Eiger, Monch and Jungfrau.

I thought of three glory-crowned peaks in the book of Romans: *no condemnation:* "There is. . .now no condemnation to them which are in Christ Jesus" (8:1); *no accusation:* "Who shall lay anything to the charge of God's elect? It is God that justifieth" (vs. 33); and *no separa-*

tion: "For I am persuaded, that neither death, nor life. . .shall. . . separate us from the love of God, which is in Christ Jesus our Lord" (vss. 38,39).

If we live, Christ will be with us: "Lo, I am with you alway" (Matt. 28:20). If we die, we will be instantly in His presence: "Absent from the body. . .present with the Lord" (II Cor. 5:8).

* * * *

OUR FINEST THRILL

On the gridiron, on the diamond,
  On the link, or on the court,
It is when the game is hardest
  That you get your finest sport!

There's no joy in easy battles,
  And no victory in a game,
That is not won without a struggle,
  And in life, it's just the same.

It is when the going is heavy,
  And the pull is all uphill,
And you have to work to conquer,
  That you get your finest thrill!

Author unknown.

* * * *

VISION

Viewing the Future Through Rear View Mirror

One day as I sat in my office 'neath my juniper tree, down in the mouth and overwhelmed with discouragement, a radiant Christian entered. Observing my dejection and wanting to lift my spirit onto a plane of

jubilant praise, the friend said, "Ralph, get your eyes off the tail lights and put your gaze on the headlights!"

How ill prepared we are to daily grapple with the relentless realities of our stressful times if we view the future through the rear-view mirror.

The backward look could be disastrous: "But his wife looked back from behind him, and she became a pillar of salt" (Gen. 19:26);

The inward look could bring despair: "O wretched man that I am! who shall deliver me from the body of this death?" (Rom. 7:24);

The upward look brings radiance: "They looked unto him and were lightened [sparkled]" (Ps. 34:5).

The natives of Burma called Adoniram Judson "Mr. Gloryface" because his face glowed with the glory of God!

Turn your eyes upon Jesus,
   Look full in His wonderful face;
And the things of earth will grow strangely dim
   In the light of His glory and grace.

Helen H. Lemmel.

* * * *

Why Perish?

Some years ago a shoe salesman went to a tribe in Africa. To his amazement, he discovered that all members of the tribe went barefooted. He sent a cablegram to his company which read:

CANCEL ORDER FOR SHOES. THERE IS NO MARKET FOR SHOES IN THIS TRIBE.

Later another shoe salesman went to the same tribe. He immediately sent a cablegram to his company which read:

DOUBLE ORDER FOR SHOES! THERE IS A LIMITLESS MARKET FOR SHOES IN THIS TRIBE!

One salesman was destitute of vision; the other envisioned each member of the tribe shod with shoes—wearing footgear.

The Bible warns, "Where there is no vision, the people perish" (Prov. 29:18)

When Lord Tennyson was close to death, a friend asked, "Is there anything you need?" Tennyson feebly replied, "Yes, a new vision of God!"

Is that not the need of each one of us?

* * * *

Look and Live!

On Sunday, January 6, 1850, a 16-year-old boy walked through a town some fifty miles north of London on a bitterly cold day, and the snow was falling fast. Seeking warmth, he entered a little Methodist chapel. He sat near the back, beneath the gallery.

The minister for the morning service had been delayed by the weather, so a layman entered the pulpit and began to conduct the service. He announced his text: "Look unto me, and be ye saved, all the ends of the earth: for I am God, and there is none else" (Isa. 45:22). His sermon was short—he spoke for ten minutes.

Observing the young man in the back of the church, he said, "You need to look to Jesus right now and be saved." From the depth of his innermost being the youth beheld "the Lamb of God, which taketh away the sin of the world" (John 1:29). Instantly he passed from spiritual death into spiritual life in Christ!

His name? Charles Haddon Spurgeon who for forty-two years proclaimed the heart-transforming grace of God by tongue and pen.

In after years, in speaking of his instantaneous conversion, he said, "I looked upon Him—Christ—and He looked upon me, and we became one forever!"

* * * *

More Business Than God Intended

Dwight L. Moody said, "We ought to see the face of God every morning before we see the face of man. If we have so much business to attend to that we have not time to pray, depend upon it, we have more business than God ever intended we should have."

* * * *

Different Visions

H. G. Wells envisioned humanity "scattered over the world, dispersed, conflicting and unawakened." He said, "I see life as an unavoidable waste and confused, the spectacle of futility. All these people reflect and are part of the waste and discontent of my life."

The Saviour envisioned humanity as sheep without a shepherd and was "moved with compassion on them" (Matt. 9:36).

* * * *

"The Brightness of His Glory"

As we look into the sky we say, "I see the sun." Actually we do not see that celestial body. We see only rays, the effulgence and outshining of the sun's brightness.

When we look upon "the sun of righteousness"—Jesus Christ—we see the brightness of God's glory.

As we daily behold "as in a glass the glory of the Lord, [we] are changed into the same image from glory to glory. . .as by the Spirit of the Lord" (II Cor. 3:18).

* * * *

Kneeling Ones

Moody said, "A Christian sees more on his knees than a philosopher sees on his tiptoes."

We never stand so tall spiritually as when we kneel and plead, "Open thou mine eyes, that I may behold wondrous things out of thy law" (Ps. 119:18).

* * * *

"I Saw Jesus!"

Captain James E. Ray was a POW in North Vietnam. He was a senior officer and one of the longest held prisoners. After deliverance, he testified at Clark Air Base in the Philippines, "I saw Jesus Christ as I was taken to a prison camp. As I trudged up and down those muddy hills, I would look up and see Christ and He'd say, 'Jim, you'll make it!' "

The promise is unfailing: "Lo, I am with you alway" (Matt. 28:20).

* * * *

WAR

More Than $1 Billion a Minute

According to the Stockholm International Peace Research Institute, the world spent $500 billion, or more than $1 billion a minute, in 1980 on armaments and other military spending. The largest spenders were the United States and Russia.

* * * *

IN FLANDERS FIELDS

In Flanders fields, the poppies blow,
Between the crosses, row on row,
That mark our place; and in the sky
The larks, still bravely singing, fly,
Scarce heard amid the guns below.

We are the Dead. Short days ago
We lived, felt dawn, saw sunset glow,
Loved and were loved, and now we lie
In Flanders fields.

Take up our quarrel with the foe:
To you from falling hands we throw
The torch; be yours to hold it high!
If ye break faith with us who die
We shall not sleep, though poppies grow
In Flanders fields.

John McCrae.

* * * *

So-Called Religious Wars

So-called religious wars are the cruelest wars. The Koran specifically sanctions them. It says, "When ye encounter the infidels, strike off their heads until ye have made a great slaughter of them."

How slow are nations to heed the command of the Saviour: "Put up again thy sword into his place: for all they that take the sword shall perish with the sword" (Matt. 26:52).

* * * *

The World's Leading Arms Salesman!

"The United States is the world's leading arms salesman. From 1966 to 1975 we sold $34.9 billion worth of weaponry to foreign nations, more than all the other major arms suppliers in the world."

The Austin-American Statesman.

* * * *

"From Whence Come Wars?" (Jas. 4:1).

Air Chief Marshall Sir Arthur Harris of Great Britain said, "If you couple the atomic bomb with the projected missile, you have something with possibilities that hardly bear contemplation! The whole world is now in the range of this weapon. War will go on until there is a change in the human heart, and I can see no signs of that!"

* * * *

It Couldn't Have Happened

In commenting upon the report of a U. S. military research team, studying ways and means of avoiding the outbreak of another major war, *The Calgary Herald* said:

"In the course of its research, the team fed a computer with all the data pertaining to the First World War. The computer responded with the assertion that World War I was an impossibility, that it never really happened, that blunders and casualties of such magnitude could only be conjecture, not hard reality.

"But World War I did happen! It cost an estimated $105 billion, and killed an estimated 10 million human beings. And it's recalled today with an unmistakable sense of outrage that the war and the folly and carnage which it represented really did take place."

How near are we to the righteous reign of Christ, "The Prince of Peace," when the longed-for era of globe-girdling tranquility will come to our war-weary world? Maybe nearer than we think: "For yet a little while, and he that shall come will come, and will not tarry" (Heb. 10:37); "He maketh wars to cease unto the end of the earth" (Ps. 46:9).

* * * *

Our Brother Rat

Dr. Konrad Lorenz, an Australian naturalist, said, "There are only two creatures which have no inhibitions about attacking their own kind—*men and rats!*"

* * * *

Attributes of Beasts

In his book, *The Book of Daniel*, W.

C. Stevens answers the question, "Why Beasts for Symbols of the Empires?"

"What are the attributes of beasts? To keep their own at any cost within their might; to quarrel over what they do not have, but what they want; to fly easily into blood-thirsty rage at any affront, at any aggression, for any coveted object. Under passion, to take utmost satisfaction in the blood, the agonies, the loss, the death of the object of their rage. In a word, to be supreme in rule, in possession, in indulgence, insofar as their power can avail."

The peace most nations seek is spelled PIECE, not peace.

* * * *

War in Heart

Herbert Hoover said, "Peace is not made at the council table, or by treaties, but in the hearts of men."

Long ago the psalmist said, "The words of his mouth were smoother than butter, but war was in his heart: his words were softer than oil, yet were they drawn swords" (Ps. 55:21).

* * * *

Deus Vult—God Wills It

Out of the shadows of earliest history strode Cain with a crimson mark on his forehead and a bloody bludgeon in his hand. Behind him have marched all the murderous and destroying armies of the centuries in whose blood-drenched wake have lain 15 thousand millions of the slain! What a pyramid of skulls their fleshless heads would make!

Since the dawn of time, war has been the rule on earth, and peace the exception. Many warring nations have sought justification for their militant onslaughts by saying, "God wills it." *Deus vult*—"God wills it"— was the battle cry of the Crusaders as they went forth to free the Holy Land from the Turks.

American soldiers in World War II sang, "Praise the Lord and pass the ammunition."

In the late wars in the Middle East, Mohammedan soldiers who died in battle were assured of an entrance into Heaven.

A German proverb says, "War leaves a country with three armies: an army of cripples, an army of mourners, and an army of thieves."

In the Bible, James indicates the source of wars: "From whence come wars and fightings among you? come they not hence, even of your lusts that war in your members?" (Jas. 4:1).

In an address to the House of Commons, Clement Attlee said, "The problem of the world is not the bomb. The problem of the world is man."

Today myriads yearn and pray for the coming of "the Prince of Peace" and His righteous, globe-girdling reign of tranquility. Then this prophecy will fruition into history: "The whole earth is at rest, and is quiet: they break forth into singing" (Isa. 14:7).

"Surely I come quickly. Amen. Even so, come, Lord Jesus."—Rev. 22:20.

* * * *

Shells Above Men

Field Marshal Horatio Herbert Kitchener, in discussing the battle of Neuve Chapelle in 1915 with David Lloyd George and Arthur James Balfour, complained that Field Marshal Sir John French had been wasteful with his ammunition.

Asked Balfour, "What were the casualties?"

Kitchener replied, "They numbered around 8,700 men!" Then he added, "But it isn't the men I mind! I can replace them at once. But I can't replace the shells so easily!"

How dehumanizing and depraving is war!

* * * *

What War Isn't

Said Benedict Spinoza, Dutch philosopher, "Peace is not the absence of war. It is a virtue, a state of mind, a disposition for benevolence, confidence and justice."

The psalmist said, "Great peace have they which love thy law: and nothing shall offend them" (Ps. 119:165).

* * * *

Goat Sense

Martin Luther told of two mountain goats which met head-on on a narrow mountain ledge. Neither could turn around. What did these wise goats do? One lay down and the other walked over him. *Both goats lived!*

How slow are nations to heed the changeless dictum: "For all they that take the sword shall perish with the sword" (Matt. 26:52).

* * * *

The Other Cheek

Walter Robert Matthews said, "Any extreme form of pacificism which renounces all use of force in every circumstance is incompatible with the status of a citizen in a national state which is menaced by other armed states. To think that the Sermon on the Mount can be directed to international relations is misleading. It is not possible for a nation, as such, to turn the other cheek."

Only when Jesus comes and reigns in righteousness will there be globe-girdling peace. Long ago the Prophet Micah envisioned that longed-for era of tranquility; "And he shall judge among many people, and rebuke strong nations afar off; and they shall beat their swords into plowshares, and their spears into pruninghooks: nation shall not lift up a sword against nation, neither shall they learn war any more" (Mic. 4:3).

Until that time, "nation shall rise against nation, and kingdom against kingdom" (Matt. 24:7).

* * * *

WILL OF GOD
(See also Guidance)

"In Full-Time Ministry"

John Yoman, owner and president of Service Master Steel Corporation, Chicago, was urged by a pastor to go into full-time ministry for the Lord. Yoman replied, "I'm in full time ministry right here at Service Master Steel!" This dedicated Christian was eminently right. Whatever any Christian does *in the will of God* is full-time service for that Christian.

The Bible says, "And whatsoever ye do in word or deed, do all in the name of the Lord Jesus, giving thanks to God and the Father by him" (Col. 3:17).

* * * *

I ORDERED THE LORD

I ordered the Lord:

"Get right with me,
My will be done,
And instantly!"

And I don't know why,
But prayers fell numb,
Till I learned to pray
In Jesus' way:
"Thy kingdom come,
Thy will be done."

Henry Hubert Hutto.

* * * *

The Greatest Experience

Dr. George W. Truett said, "To know the will of God is the greatest knowledge. To do the will of God is the greatest experience."

* * * *

You'll Find the Way

When Emanuel Sanden was seeking God's will for his life, R. A. Torrey gave him this sage advice: "Follow God's leading step by step, and you will find the way."

One step thou seest, then go forward boldly,
One step is far enough for faith to see;
Take that, and the next duty shall be told thee.
For step by step the Lord is leading thee.

* * * *

Light for Next Step

When I was a boy in a small town in Georgia, people carried lanterns as they wended their way along the dark streets at night. When they took one step forward, there was sufficient light for the next step.

As God's submissive children go forward step by step along life's pathway, the way becomes increasingly luminous: "But the path of the just is as the shining light, that shineth more and more unto the perfect day" (Prov. 4:18).

* * * *

WITNESSING
(See also Soul Winning)

Miss America of 1975

Shirley Cothran, Miss America of 1975, said:

"I *thought* I became a Christian when I was nine. But I found He (Christ) was not really in my life like He should be. So when I was about 16, I really accepted Christ as my Saviour, and since then He has played an extremely important role in my life!

"I have found that when I try to take over my own problems and try to take hold of what I think the answer is, I'm quite often wrong. But when I let Jesus take over, I find out the problems aren't really as big as I thought they were.

"My church has always been a vital dimension in my life. I have been attending the First Baptist Church of Denton, Texas, since I was three weeks old, when my mother enrolled me in the cradle department."

Questioned about drug addiction, Shirley said, "I've never tried marijuana. I don't see any need for it, nor for alcoholic beverages. I don't believe in stimulants in my body. I have a natural 'high,' which is the Lord Jesus Christ!"

Baptist Standard.

* * * *

Playing Fair With God

Bill Glass, famed athlete, said, "I have found that I must play fair with myself, with others, and with God. This is the only way to win in life. I chose to play fair with God when I got on the team of His Son, Jesus Christ."

* * * *

A Split Second From Death

How thrilling is the testimony of Captain Hiram Cassedy Sumrall!

"On December 2, 1961, I was captain of a DC-7 on a regularly scheduled flight, executing what I thought was a routine instrument approach to a major airport. We were told by the central tower that we were two miles from the end of the runway and should have it in sight. The copilot continued to fly by instruments according to standard operating procedure. To my surprise, instead of seeing the runway, all I could see were large trees coming up at us through the smoky fog. We were really one mile to the left and several miles short of our intended destination!

"I applied full power to all four engines and pulled way back on the flight controls. It was a reflex action. In the next few seconds, an eternity passed. I was startled to realize that we were still flying and gaining altitude. In spite of the fact that it could have been a fatal accident, no one was injured. We alerted the control tower and had the crews stand by with crash equipment for an emergency landing. We then made a safe landing, though one engine and a propeller were severely damaged.

"This experience had a tremendous effect on me. We were just a split second from death! I knew that God had performed a miracle in delivering us. He was trying to get my attention, and He did. I spent sleepless nights during the next two years reviewing my life and diligently searching for God.

"When Jesus said, 'I will come in . . .if you will open the door,' it meant surrendering our will to His. During forty-seven years of church attendance I had missed this truth. All these years I had been spiritually blind.

"Returning home one night, I quietly knelt before God and surrendered my will to Christ's will. I asked Him to come into my life, forgive my sins and make me the kind of person He wanted me to be. I turned over every area of my life absolutely to Him. I told Him to take the mess I had made of my life and do something with it. That was truly the beginning of a new life.

"As a Christian pilot, I now have an additional responsibility. Not only am I a representative of my company, but also a representative of Jesus Christ."

Adapted from *Decision*.

* * * *

Singing a Lie

Second-century philosopher Celsus said of the early Christians, "Fullers and weavers and teachers are constantly talking about Jesus!"

The Bible says of them, "They were all scattered. . .except the apostles . . .they that were scattered abroad went every where preaching the word" (Acts 8:1,4).

Are we guilty of lying when we lustily sing, "I love to tell the story," when we are as silent as a sphinx about the Saviour and His mightiness to transform lives?

* * * *

"Keep Not Silence"

Dr. George Sweeting said, "Some Christians try to be secret believers, but this is a mistake. Just imagine Dr. Jonas Salk keeping the Salk vaccine a secret! That would have been criminal. So, too, a knowledge of salvation places us in debt to the whole world. Silence really is sinful because we owe the world a witness."

Jesus told of a lost soul in the abode of anguish and remorse who believed in the destiny-determining power of witnessing to unsaved ones. The lost one pleaded, "I pray thee therefore, father [Abraham], that thou wouldest send him [Lazarus] to my father's house: For I have five brethren; that he may testify unto them, lest they also come into this place of torment" (Luke 16:27,28).

"Ye that make mention of the Lord, keep not silence."—Isa. 62:6.

* * * *

Wooden Christians

Years ago there lived in New York City a scrubwoman, widely known in Christian circles as "Sophie the Scrubwoman." She truly loved her Lord and never missed an opportunity to speak for Him.

One day she was seen witnessing to a wooden Indian standing in front of a store which sold cigars. A nominal Christian standing nearby joshed her and said, "Sophie, don't you know you are taking to a wooden Indian?"

She replied, "No, I didn't know I was talking to a wooden Indian about Christ. My eyesight is very bad. But talking to a wooden Indian about

Christ is not as bad as being a wooden Christian and never talking to anybody about the Lord Jesus!" She was right!

You talk about the weather,
    And crops of corn and wheat;
You speak with friends and neighbors,
    That pass along the street;
You call yourself a Christian,
    And like the gospel plan;
Then why not speak for Jesus,
    And witness where you can?

Told by Alice M. Knight.

* * * *

Miss America 1973

Terry Anne Neeuwsen, Miss America of 1973, testified:

"I was born and reared in a very small town in Wisconsin. I knew who Christ was, who God was and was raised on Bible stories, though I had never read the Bible myself. But along the way the message that there was a living Christ available to me was totally lost, and I was just not aware of it.

"One night a friend asked, 'Terry, are you a Christian?' Here I was 22 years old, had been raised in a church, had been baptized and confirmed, had been taught to pray before I went to bed and when I got up in the morning, but no one in twenty-two years had ever asked me if I was a Christian.

"I replied, 'Well, I think I believe in God.'

"The friend replied, 'No, you don't understand. Half the word *Christ*ian is Christ. God wants to love you just as you are, and if there is anything in your life which needs to be changed, don't worry about it. He will take care of the changes Himself. If you want love and peace which come from knowing Christ personally, you may have it now.' "

Later Terry said, "Jesus Christ came into my heart and life and changed me! We worry about things which are going to happen tomorrow, and we miss the fact that Christ is here today. If we take His hand and walk down that road, there is nothing to worry about."

* * * *

My Lord Buddha

U. Thant was a former secretary-general of the United Nations. Upon his retirement from this position, a dinner was given in his honor. Many influential leaders were present. He was toasted and praised.

In responding to the lavish encomiums, he said: "If any of the things said about me are true, I would like to give the honor to my lord— Buddha! I was raised in a Buddhist home. Every day I read the sayings of Buddha. I believe Buddha was the greatest religious teacher. Every day I examine my life to see if I have been worthy to be called a disciple of Buddha!"

Undoubtedly some Christians were present. We wonder how many of them would have stood in similar circumstances and said: "For all that I am or have I give full honor to my Lord and Saviour Jesus Christ! He is not only a great Teacher, but the Saviour of all who will look to Him for mercy and forgiveness!"

* * * *

"It Is No Secret"

Immediately after his conversion, Stuart Hamblen began to obey the command of the Saviour: "Go home to thy friends, and tell them how great things the Lord hath done for thee, and hath had compassion on thee" (Mark 5:19). He also began to change his life in conformity to the life of a Christian. Some of his adjustments entailed financial loss.

Among the first ones Hamblen encountered was his friend John Wayne. "A wonderful thing has happend to me," he said. "I have found the Saviour and I want to share my experience of His saving grace with you and others!"

For a moment Wayne listened respectfully, then said, "I don't have time now to listen. I have an appointment."

A twinge of discouragement came to Hamblen. He thought he might have offended his friend. Going to his room, Hamblen sat down and wrote a song which has brought hope and cheer to thousands of defeated, disconsolate ones:

The chimes of time ring out the news,
  Another day is through,
Someone slipped and fell,
  Was that someone you?
You may have longed for added strength,
  Your courage to renew,
Do not be disheartened,
  For I bring hope to you.

It is no secret what God can do,
What He's done for others, He'll do
  for you.
With arms wide open, He'll pardon you,
It is no secret what God can do.

* * * *

WORK

(See also Service)

FOR AN AUTOGRAPH

Life is a leaf of paper white
Whereon each of us may write
His word or two, and then comes
  night.
Greatly begin! though thou have time
But for a line, be that sublime,—
Not failure, but low aim, is crime.

James Russell Lowell.

* * * *

Saved But Singed

Some of God's children will be saved but *singed:* "Saved; yet so as by fire" (I Cor. 3:15). Their "wood, hay, stubble" works will be incinerated!

Not the *quantity* of our work will be God's standard of judgment, but the *quality* of our work: "The fire shall try every man's work of what *sort* it is" (I Cor. 3:13).

* * * *

Born Lazy and Had a Relapse

After a thorough physical examination by a medic, the patient said, "Now, Doc, tell me in plain language: What's the real trouble with me?"

"Do you really want it straight?" asked the doctor.

"Yes," replied the patient.

"Well, there isn't a thing in the world wrong with you, except that *you are just plain lazy!*"

The patient drawled, "Okay, Doc. Now give me the *medical term* for it so I can tell my wife!"

Some people were born lazy and had a relapse. Such could be helped by observing one of God's working creatures, the ant: "Go to the ant, thou sluggard; consider her ways, and be wise" (Prov. 6:6).

* * * *

"I Must Hurry!"

Peter Ilich Tchaikovsky, the great Russian composer, wrote his music during the last half of the nineteenth century. His nature was susceptible to the most divergent currents of thought and feeling. His melancholic spirit often mounted to violence and passionate rebellion, which greatly accentuated his ever-present sense of the transience of time. He expressed it often and vehemently: "I must hurry, hurry, hurry! I am afraid I shall die with all this music in me!"

God's children should always reckon with the transitoriness of life and "give every passing moment something to keep in store." Job said, "My days are swifter than a weaver's shuttle" (7:6).

A sense of urgency characterized the earth-life of the Saviour: "Wist ye not that I must be about my Father's business?" (Luke 2:49); "I must works the works of him that sent me, while it is day: the night cometh, when no man can work" (John 9:4).

Work, for the night is coming,
  Under the sunset skies;
While their bright tints are glowing,
  Work, for daylight flies.
Work till the last beam fadeth,

Fadeth to shine no more;
Work, while the night is dark'ning,
When man's work is o'er.

Annie L. Coghill.

* * * *

Thank God for Work

Charles Kingsley admonished: "Thank God every morning that you have something to do which must be done whether you like it or not. Being required to work and doing so to the best of your ability will breed in you self-control, diligence, contentment and many other virtues which the idle never know."

* * * *

Keep Busy

Benjamin Disraeli said, "Action may not always bring happiness, but there is no happiness without action."

"Not slothful in business; fervent in spirit; serving the Lord."—Rom. 12:11.

* * * *

Our Hands Needed

George Eliot said, " 'Tis God's skill, but it needs our hands."

The Bible says, "We then [are] workers together with him [God]" (II Cor. 6:1).

* * * *

"To Every Man His Work"

James Russell Lowell said, "No man is born into the world whose work is not born with him. There is always work, and tools to work with, for those who will [work]. Blessed be the horny hands of toil."

* * * *

OUR UTMOST

Better to strive and climb,
And never reach the goal,
Than to drift along with time,
An aimless, worthless soul.

Aye, better to climb and fall,
Or sow, though the yield be small,
Than to throw away day after day,
And never strive at all.

Author unknown.

* * * *

Unless You Work

Said John D. Rockefeller, Sr., "Do the common work in an uncommonly good way. No plan will work unless you work."

* * * *

No Pessimistic Hens

Hard work means nothing to a hen. She just keeps on digging worms and laying eggs regardless of what the business prognosticators say about the outlook for this or any other year. If the ground is hard, she scratches harder. If it is dry, she digs deeper. If it's wet, she digs where it is dry. If she strikes a rock, she works around it. If she gets a few more hours of daylight, she gives us a few more eggs. But she always digs up worms, and turns them into hard-shelled profits as well as tender, profitable broilers.

Did you ever see a pessimistic hen?

Did you ever hear of one starving to death waiting for worms to dig themselves up? Did you ever hear one cackle because the work was hard? Not on your life! Hens save their breath for digging, and their cackles for eggs. Success means digging. Are *you* digging?

From Moody Monthly.

* * * *

Put Everything You've Got Into It

Said Edward Bok, American philanthropist, "Find your place and hold it. Find your work and do it, and put everything you've got into it!"

To those who are at ease in God's spiritual Zion comes the awaking, alerting challenge: "Press toward the mark for the prize of the high calling of God in Christ Jesus" (Phil. 3:14).

> Not enjoyment and not sorrow
> Is our destined end or way,
> But to live that each tomorrow
> Find us further than today.
>
> Longfellow.

* * * *

Pocketed Hands

It has been said that success is a ladder which cannot be climbed with our hands in our pockets.

The Bible says, "Whatsoever thy hand findeth to do, do it with thy might" (Eccles. 9:10).

* * * *

A Silent Teacher

Benjamin Franklin said, "None teaches better than the ant, and she says nothing."

The Bible says, "Go to the ant, thou sluggard; consider her ways, and be wise" (Prov. 6:6).

* * * *

"It Might Have been"

Gian-Carlo Menotti, an American composer, said, "Hell begins when God grants us a clear vision of all that we might have achieved, of all the gifts which we have wasted, of all that we might have done which we did not do!"

> The saddest words of tongue or pen,
> The saddest are these: "It might have been!"

Let us ever be wakeful, watchful and workful: "Whatsoever thy hand findeth to do, do it with thy might" (Eccles. 9:10.).

* * * *

"SPARE THESE HANDS, I PRAY"

Dear Lord, when age has made my step unsure,
Perhaps some loss of hearing I'll endure,
Or forced by failing sight I'll grope and seek,
But Lord, please never let my hands grow weak.

The strength and knowledge of my hands retain,
Then give them younger lives to shape and train;
Such skills as they possess let them unfold,
But spare these hands from ever growing old.

Preserve in them the grip of friendship's clasp,
Grant them the playful tug of children's grasp;
Find work for them to do that you have blessed,
Until these hands of mine repose in rest.

Jesse V. Ragan,
in *Christian Herald.*

* * * *

Don't Take It Easy

For many cardiac patients, the frustration, incident to the slower pace of retirement, can be more lethal than the strain of a highly active life.

Vice Admiral George G. Burkley, the late President Lyndon Johnson's physician, affirmed, "He did better when he was under pressure. I think it was better for him when he was in harness than when he wasn't. I think his retirement increased the stress. High demands seemed to keep his body at a good metabolic rate."

After Johnson's death, Dr. Howard Burchell, one of the specialists called in as a consultant during his 1955 heart attack, affirmed that many people who retire no longer enjoy as good health as when they were active. Of the pressures Johnson experienced in the Senate and White House, Burchell said, "Such stresses, when compensated by rewards and satisfaction, may be no worse than sitting in a rocking chair and fretting."

Long ago the Apostle Paul said, "We were pressed out of measure, above strength" (II Cor. 1:8). Did he retire and "take it easy?" The op-

posite is true. His unchanging, undeviating purpose was indicated in his words, "I press toward the mark for the prize of the high calling of God in Christ Jesus" (Phil. 3:14).

Rest and relaxation are good at times, but challenging work with ensuant tenseness is necessary for mental and physical health.

When we cease to be tense we become past tense!

* * * *

Fish

An ancient proverb says, "Give a man a fish and you feed him for a day. Teach him how to fish and you feed him for the rest of his life."

"For even when we were with you, this we commanded you, that if any would not work, neither should he eat."—II Thess. 3:10.

* * * *

A Thoughtless Act

Sir Winston Churchill said, "To build may have to be the slow and laborious task of years. To destroy can be the thoughtless act of a single day."

* * * *

Worry, Not Work, Kills

Dr. Charles H. Mayo, co-founder of the Mayo Clinic, said, "Worry affects the circulation, the heart, the glands, the whole nervous system and profoundly affects the health. I have never known a man who died from overwork, but many who died from worry."

* * * *

Stronger Backs

Roger Babson, famed statistician, said, "Let us not pray for lighter burdens but for stronger backs."

"He giveth power to the faint: and to them that have no might he increaseth strength."—Isa. 40:29.

* * * *

Lessons From the Honeybee

Valuable lessons may be learned from God's tiny creatures, including the honeybee.

The average worker bee is able to carry a burden equal to half its own weight. It flies as far as three miles in search of raw materials for honey, and it has been estimated that a pound of honey represents nearly 300,000 miles of bee flight.

A worker bee seldom dies of old age, but literally works itself to death! To be "busy as a bee" means there are no idle moments.

The Bible says, "Whatsoever thy hand findeth to do, do it with thy might" (Eccles. 9:10).

As many as 50,000 bees labor together harmoniously in one hive for the common good of the colony.

All of God's children are members of the body of Christ, and they should work agreeably together for the good of all.

How precious is the relationship which Christlike Christians have with one another: "And whether one member suffer, all the members suffer with it. . . .Now ye are the body of Christ, and members in particular" (I Cor. 12:26,27).

* * * *

To Be Needed

Joe Alex Morris said in *The Los Angeles Times:*

"Violence against people, things or institutions is one manifestation of the fury caused by being unneeded, insignificant and left out.

"Man's primary psychological need is to be needed. For most people, that means being economically needed.

"Alienation, though worldwide, is most rampant in the United States not because Americans are especially predisposed to violence, but because their economy is the most technologically advanced. Technology's very function is to make people, as workers, unneeded in production."

Until God's children awaken with the likeness of Christ in glory, there will be work for each one of them to do: "Occupy till I come" (Luke 19:13); "Whatsoever thy hand findeth to do, do it with thy might" (Eccles. 9:10).

We'll work till Jesus comes,
And we'll be gathered home!

* * * *

TRUE REST

Rest is not quitting
The busy career,
Rest is the fitting
Of self to one's sphere.

'Tis loving and serving,

The highest and best;
'Tis onward, unswerving,
And this is true rest.

Goethe.

* * * *

The Highest Reward

John Ruskin said, "The highest reward for a man's toil is not what he gets out of it but what he becomes by it."

* * * *

A Pot-Sniffer

Bob Buesing has a problem because a dog he has trained is too efficient and too dedicated to work. *The Wall Street Journal* told the story:

"Buesing can't take Ginger, his German shepherd dog, for a walk in Los Angeles without frequent embarrassment. She continuously sniffs at the pockets of long-haired passersby and scratches at the fenders of psychedelic Volkswagens!"

" 'That's the penalty of training Ginger as a pot-sniffer. She doesn't know when to quit work. I just "good doggy" her and reward her and keep on walking!' "

Pastors would like to have church members like Ginger—faithful and totally dedicated to their work for God.

Adapted from *Baptist Standard.*

* * * *

Finished!

Jesus' first recorded words were, "Wist ye not that I must be about my Father's business?" (Luke 2:49). As he died on the cross, He exclaimed victoriously, "It is finished!"

He was so dedicated to doing His heavenly Father's work that He was able to say, "I have finished the work which thou gavest me to do" (John 17:4).

May we be so dedicated to God's will that at journey's end we can say what Jesus said, "I have finished the work which thou gavest me to do!"

* * * *

How Wise!

Moody said, "I had rather put ten men to work than to do the work of ten men."

* * * *

How to Measure Success

Robert Louis Stevenson said, "That man is a success who has lived well, laughed often and loved much; who has gained the respect of intelligent men and the *love of children*; who has filled his niche and accomplished his task; who leaves the world better than he found it whether by a perfect poem or a rescued soul; who never lacked appreciation of earth's beauty or failed to express it; who looked for the best in others and gave the best he had."

* * * *

Each One Is Essential

"In my childhood days," said Synesio Lyra, Jr., "I loved to hear a story which vividly illustrates the need of togetherness among God's children:

"The carpenter's tools had a conference. Brother Hammer was in the chair. The meeting had informed him that he must leave, because he was too noisy. But he said, 'If I am to leave this carpenter's shop, Brother Gimlet must go, too. He is so insignificant that he makes very little impression.'

"Brother Gimlet arose and said, 'All right, but Brother Screw must go also. You have to turn him around and around again and again to get him anywhere.'

"Brother Screw then said, 'If you wish, I will go, but Brother Plane must leave also. All his work is on the surface. There is no depth to it.'

"To this Brother Plane replied, 'Well, Brother Rule will have to withdraw if I do, for he is always measuring other folks as though he were the only one right.'

"Brother Rule then complained against Brother Sandpaper and said, 'He is rougher than he ought to be and he is always rubbing people the wrong way.'

"In the midst of the discussion, the Carpenter of Nazareth walked in. He had come to perform His day's work. He put on his apron and went to the bench to make a pulpit. He employed the screw, the gimlet, the sandpaper, the saw, the hammer and the plane and all the other tools.

"After the day's work was over and the pulpit was finished, Brother Saw arose and said, 'Brethren, I perceive that all of us are labourers together with God!'"

* * * *

WORLDLINESS

All Things in Jesus

"When I was a boy," said Dr. Grady Cothen, "a dollar was given to me to take in the sights and sounds of the fair. How thrilled I was! The merry-go-round, Ferris wheel, and freak exhibits dribbled away my dollar until I had only fifteen cents left. How could I spend it?

"As I looked at the tempting, headsize, pink cotton candy, I decided that was what I wanted with my last fifteen cents.

"When I took a bite of the cotton candy, it instantly vanished in my mouth. Then I wrapped my hands around it, pressed it and it shrank to practically nothing in my sticky hands.

"In after years I thought, *How like that cotton candy are the ephemeral and enticing things of the world without Christ. Though colorful and dazzingly beautiful, they are totally devoid of worth and enduring pleasure.*"

Friends all around us are trying to find
What the heart yearns for, by sin undermined;
I have the secret, I know where 'tis found:
Only true pleasures in Jesus abound.

All that I want is in Jesus,
He satisfies. . .joy He supplies,
Life would be worthless without Him,
All things in Jesus I find!

Harry D. Loes.

* * * *

Not Repellent Smugness

A businessman was a member of a club whose members gambled, drank and indulged in obscenities and vulgarities. One Sunday night he was genuinely converted. Being only a beginning Christian, he knew little of what the Bible teaches about amalgamating with Christ-dishonoring social groups.

When he went to the club as usual that week, a member said, "What are you doing here? We heard about your becoming a Christian. This is no place for you to be now!"

God's children can't avoid going where there are non-Christians, "for then must [they] go out of the world" (I Cor. 5:10). They are never, however, to be "partakers of [their] sins" (Rev. 18:4).

Scriptural separation isn't pharisaic aloofness from our sin-sodden and spiritually confused world, nor is it I-am-holier-than-thou-ism or repellent smugness. Christ ate and mingled with publicans and sinners, but inwardly He was "separate from sinners" (Heb. 7:26) and never partook of their sins.

* * * *

A Lost Life

At the bedside of a terminally ill mother, I explained simply the way of salvation through faith in the Saviour. She received Christ as her only hope of eternal life and testified to the fact. Then a look of ineffable sadness clouded her face. She said regretfully, "I have wasted my life living for the vain, empty things of this world. What a pity that I can give to Christ only the closing hours of my life!"

Oh, the tragedy of having a saved soul but a lost life!

* * * *

"That's What It Cost Me"

Said a worldly young lady to a dedicated Christian, "I would give the world to have 'your peace of mind!"

"That's exactly what it cost me— the world—with its ephemeral, sinful pleasures."

How wise Moses was in his choice in the long ago, choosing "rather to suffer affliction with the people of God, than to enjoy the pleasures of sin for a season" (Heb. 11:25).

The Christian life, in its full-orbed blessedness, begins when we sincerely say, in the words of Fanny J. Crosby,

> Take the world, but give me Jesus,
> All its joys are but a name;
> But His love abideth ever,
> Thro' eternal years the same!

* * * *

WORRY

Worry Warts

A chronic worrier, or worry wart, went to a psychiatrist for consultation. It didn't take the medic long to diagnose her trouble.

"Worry is the source of your

frustration and failure to grapple with the inescapable problems and perplexities of life. Be honest with me and pinpoint one instance where worry has helped you."

How ingenious and yet factual was her reply: "Well, ninety percent of the things I worry about never happen."

* * * *

Sit Loose

A 90-year-old black was asked the secret of her longevity. She replied, "When I works, I works hard, When I sit, I sit loose. When I worry, I go to sleep!"

Absolute trust in the provident care of God is the sure panacea for worry: "I will trust, and not be afraid" (Isa. 12:2).

* * * *

Why Anxious?

Dr. Howard A. Kelly asked a distressed Christian who was seeking help from Dr. Henry Phipps, a psychiatrist at Johns Hopkins Hospital, "What brings you to Dr. Phipps?"

The man replied, "My anxiety, tension and obsessive concern about my heart and my feelings of insecurity."

Dr. Kelly exclaimed, "What on earth are you, a child of God, anxious about? You could not possibly be more secure than you are! You feel insecure because you are looking *inward* rather than *outward* toward our Lord and Saviour!"

Fewer psychiatrists would be needed if *more* of God's distressed children were obeying His fear-allaying directive: "Be careful for nothing" (Phil. 4:6.) "Do not worry about anything" is the Philipps translation.

* * * *

A Sure Killer

Henry Ward Beecher said, "It is not work that kills people. It is worry. Work is healthy. You can hardly put more work on a man than he can bear. Worry is rust upon the blade. It is not the revolution that destroys the machinery, but friction. Worry secretes acids, but love and trust are sweet juices."

* * * *

Hurry, Worry, Bury

Said Bertrand Russell, "A happy life must be to a great extent a quiet life, for it is only in an atmosphere of quiet that true joy can live."

Our hurry, worry, bury age greatly needs to enter into the tranquilizing blessedness of the sure promise: "In returning and rest shall ye be saved; in quietness and in confidence shall be your strength" (Isa. 30:15).

* * * *

Interest Paid

George Lyons said, "Worry is the interest paid by those who borrow trouble."

* * * *

A Divided Mind

The word "worry" comes from the

Greek word *merimnao,* a combination of two words—*merizo,* which means to divide, and *nous,* which means mind. Worry therefore means "to divide the mind."

James told the result of worrying: "A double minded man is unstable in all his ways" (Jas. 1:8).

In the spring of 1871, a young man read twenty-one words that completely changed his life. This medical student at the Montreal General Hospital was worried about final examinations. He was also troubled about where and how he should establish his medical practice.

The words that changed this man's life were written by Thomas Carlyle. The man who was challenged was William Osler, a founder of Johns Hopkins School of Medicine. These are the twenty-one words: *Our main business is not to see what lies dimly at a distance, but to do what lies clearly at hand.*

George Sweeting.

* * * *

YOUTHS

Hallowed Memories

A daughter, becoming restive of the restraints of home, left her home and went to a distant city where she got into sinful ways.

One night on her way back to her boarding house, she chanced to see an open Bible in the window of a rescue mission. Beneath the Bible was a sizable picture. As she glanced at the picture, she thought, *That picture looks so much like my mother!* Returning to the mission next day, she definitely saw that the picture was indeed the picture of her mother! Beneath the picture were the tender, beseeching words, "Come home!"

A train of hallowed memories of her happy, carefree girlhood days in her Christian home raced through her mind, bringing penitential tears.

Sometimes memory results in our reversing our downward way: "And when he came to himself, he said,

How many hired servants of my father's have bread enough and to spare, and I perish with hunger: I will arise and go to my father" (Luke 15:17,18).

Sometimes memory awakens too late: "Son, remember that thou in thy lifetime received thy good things, and likewise Lazarus evil things: but now he is comforted, and thou art tormented" (Luke 16:25).

Told by Ralph M. Smith.

* * * *

When Our Work Is Over

George Macdonald said, "When we are out of sympathy with the young, our work in the world is over."

How wise we are when we enter understandingly and sympathetically into the problems and perplexities of the youths!

* * * *

Futility

A teenager asked a minister, "Why should I study and work and be moral? The world is falling apart anyway. So what's the use? Why not blow it all now? Tomorrow is a bummer!"

Life is empty and futile apart from the Saviour who gives radiant, joyous life to all who will receive it: "I am come that they might have life, and that they might have it more abundantly" (John 10:10).

* * * *

Believe in Them

In an editorial, *The Presbyterian Journal* said, "If you want to keep your children from rebelling and running off to join an anti-establishment cult, try rejoicing with them where they are. Believe in them as people. Give them your confidence and loyalty. They will respond as true children can. But try to keep them tied to your apron strings, and they'll rebel and go dashing off into all sorts of anti-Mom activities."

Youths need not so much advice as they need parental example. Usually they won't abandon self-respect and condemn the true and tried standard of morals when moms and dads bring them up in the right way and go that way themselves.

* * * *

Corruption of Timeless Values

Said Harry Reasoner, a newscaster, "Our young people have pride in what they achieve. I respect that, the same way I expect them to respect what we accomplish. Nor would I fault them for lack of values. As I see their protests, they are not mocking the traditions of love, charity and concern for one's neighbor. They are mocking the corruption of those timeless values. The young are often practicing the Christianity that too many adults just preach."

* * * *

Bravo!

"If I hadn't gotten help, I probably would not have made it," said Mrs. James Evans, a nurse.

Her eight-year-old son Jimmy ran three miles through a heavy mountain snow to get help when his mother developed pregnancy complications. Too weak to stand, she scribbled a note and told Jimmy to seek help. Several nearby homes had telephones but there was no service due to the storm.

When George Sibley offered to drive Jimmy to a distant phone, Jimmy said that he wasn't supposed to ride with strangers, ran back home to ask permission to ride with him and returned to the Sibley home. When phone service had been restored, Jimmy called his dad at work eight miles away in Boulder, Colorado.

"I'm awfully proud of Jimmy," his mother said. "He always did what we told him to do and never let us down!"

"It was one of the most remarkable things I've ever seen a boy do," said the neighbor, George Sibley.

Misdemeanors and waywardness of

youths are publicized far and near. The sterling character and nobility of the overwhelming majority of youths are seldom mentioned. How wrong!

* * * *

A Teenager Confessed:

"We drink for happiness and become unhappy. We drink for relaxation and get the shakes. We drink for joy and become miserable. We drink for sociability and become argumentative.

"We drink for sophistication and become obnoxious. We drink for friendship and make enemies. We drink for sleep and awaken without rest. We drink for strength and become weak. We drink for bravery and become afraid. We drink for confidence and become doubtful.

"We drink to make conversation and slur our speech. We drink to feel heavenly and end up feeling wretched and dejected. We drink to forget and are forever haunted. We drink for freedom and become slaves. We drink to erase problems and see them multiply. We drink to cope with life and invite death."

"Wine is a mocker, strong drink is raging: and whosoever is deceived thereby is not wise."—Prov. 20:1.

* * * *

Fouled-Up Misfits

A sorrowing mother wrote a letter to Ann Landers asking, "What has happened between parents and children in the last fifteen years? The Bible says, 'Train up a child in the way he should go: and when he is old, he will not depart from it' (Prov. 22:6).

"I don't believe it. Our own children are living proof. We have four. We always went to church together. They had plenty of love and responsibility. Everything was fine until they started to high school, or went away to college.

"Now our sons and daughters look like bums. They have no interest in decent clothes. Three are college graduates, yet they don't find jobs they like. Don't they realize that life isn't all fun and pleasure? Parents are fed up with scraggly appearance, foul language, and total disrespect for authority.

"My husband is in his early 50's, and he is a broken man. We cry for each other, and for thousands of other parents who feel they have failed. We did our best and can't figure out what went wrong!"

How wise was the columnist's reply: "Don't despair. The jury is still out. Many children come home again if the door is open and a light is in the window. Plenty of far-out children do a complete reversal, become conservative, even square. It could occur with your children. I pray it will."

How great is parental sorrow! Long ago David lamented, "O my son Absalom, my son, my son Absalom! would God I had died for thee, O Absalom, my son, my son!" (II Sam. 18:33).

* * * *

An Empty Void

Dr. Basil Jackson, chairman of Department of Psychiatry, Lutheran Hospital and director of Jackson Psychiatric Clinic, Milwaukee, Wisconsin, said:

"Young people are asking what life is all about. They are complaining of lack of purpose. They are being swallowed up in meaninglessness and lack of hope. As they reach out for the future, they clutch an empty void. Anxiety is the inevitable result and drugs are a favorite self-prescribed tranquilizer.

"But such will always fail to supply the answer and provide a sense of relief. These young people need to be introduced to Jesus Christ and to hear the life-giving message of the Gospel. In Him, they can have the experience of purpose and meaning and the ultimate in tranquilization, namely, 'the peace of God, which passeth all understanding' " (Phil. 4:7).

* * * *

Inner Void and Frustration

The famed psychiatrist and neurologist, Dr. Victor Frankel, said:

"Pornography, crimes and violence, drug addiction, alcoholism, and the growing suicide rate are symptoms of a much deeper sickness in the modern soul. The sense of inner void and frustration is spreading. Modern educationalists [are] reinforcing the meaninglessness felt by youth, which reduces them to the level of nothing but an animal.

"As a survivor of Auschwitz and three other Nazi death camps, I want to bear witness to the incredible and unexpected extent to which a man can brave the worst conditions man could ever face and still triumph over them! Those prisoners most oriented toward the future, those who clung to some shred of meaning, were the most likely to pull through."

How meaningless is life for those who have no hope in God: "For we are saved by hope: but hope that is seen is not hope: for what a man seeth, why doth he yet hope for?" (Rom. 8:24).

"Why art thou cast down, O my soul?. . .hope thou in God."—Ps. 42:5.

* * * *

From Dope to Alcohol

"Those who drink and those who encourage children to drink by setting the example, ought to be acutely aware of the potential dangers inherent in this worldwide problem," affirmed Christian Science Monitor News Service. "The need of awareness is, perhaps, greater than ever before because so many young people seek external physical stimulants as a substitute for pure, hygienic mental activity.

"Sociologists tell us that nonprescription drugs are not in such wide use today by teenagers as they were previously. But that good news is quickly followed by the bad news that alcoholism is on the rise, and that those who once 'turned on' with dope are now 'cooling it' with drink!

"Some youngsters are switching because the penalties for using dope are so much harsher than those for drinking.

"New York State has extremely harsh punishments for youths found using, sharing or selling even the mildest forms of nonprescription drugs.

"Yet those who use, share and sell liquor are protected by a number of laws, one which sets an early age when it is 'legal' to sell liquor to minors. There is, of course, no law to protect those in the United States who sell drugs to youngsters.

"Those who would teach young people not to need or want dope *must* teach them also not to need or want alcohol."

Adapted from
Austin American-Statesman.

* * * *